T3-BHB-130

The Romantic Tradition in American Literature

The Romantic Tradition in American Literature

Advisory Editor

HAROLD BLOOM
Professor of English, Yale University

The Complete Poetical Works

OF

Joaquin Miller

[CINCINNATUS HINER MILLER]

ARNO PRESS
A NEW YORK TIMES COMPANY
New York • 1972

Reprint Edition 1972 by Arno Press Inc.

Reprinted from a copy in The Princeton
University Library

The Romantic Tradition in American Literature
ISBN for complete set: 0-405-04620-0
See last pages of this volume for titles.

Manufactured in the United States of America

Library of Congress Cataloging in Publication Data

Miller, Joaquin, 1841?-1913.
The complete poetical works of Joaquin Miller.

(The Romantic tradition in American literature)
I. Series.
PS2395.A2 1972 811'.4 72-4967
ISBN 0-405-04638-3

The Complete Poetical Works

OF

Joaquin Miller

1—Oregon, 1868.
2—London, 1870.
3—Cuba, 1876.
4–San Francisco, 1887.
5—Louisville, Ky., 1897.
6–In the Sierras, 1882.

The Complete Poetical Works

OF

Joaquin Miller.

THE HIGHTS.

SAN FRANCISCO:

THE WHITAKER & RAY CO.

(INCORPORATED)

1897

To

COLLIS P. HUNTINGTON,

Who was first to lead the steel shod cavalry of conquest through the Sierras to the Sea of Seas, and who has done the greater West and South more enduring good than any other living man, I dedicate this final revision of my complete poems.

JOAQUIN MILLER.

THE HIGHTS, CAL.,
1897.

PREFACE.

I HAVE BEEN so busy and bothered all my life till late years that I have had to hastily feed my corn out, weed or flower or ripe corn from the four quarters of the world, with a pitchfork, as I ran. Hence the need of this revision. And yet, even now, after all my cutting and care, I am far from satisfied, and can commend to my lovers only the few last poems in the book. True, the earlier ones have color and clime and perfume of wood or waste, and I am not ungrateful for the friends they brought me, but I fear they fall short of the large eternal lesson which the seer is born to teach—the vision of worlds beyond. I have tried to mend this fault in my later work; to give my new poems not only body but soul.

The purpose here, outside of revising entirely and gathering into this book such poems as are to be preserved, is to blaze some trees along the trail; a note of warning here, a campfire there, the experience of a pioneer; so that those who come after may not falter or go astray in the wilderness that darkens along the foothills of Olympus. George Sand said all Americans are poets. Certainly all American writers are poets, or, as a rule, begin as such. True, many of our great lawyers began by writing poetry, like Blackstone. Perhaps our greatest poets at heart never took the world into confidence at all in the maturity of power, but kept a cold and severe visage for all men, and went to their graves as practical merchants, lawyers, doctors, and so on, with only one little corner of the heart for flowers and a bird all their own. And what pleasure to write for such readers!

There are others — not in business or disposed to be — those who would or could be poets, and yet will not. Let me address myself to these, for they have foolish notions as to what a poet is and what it costs to be a poet, or rather what it costs to not be a poet.

A great land without a great literature, were such a thing possible, must be to the end worse than spouseless. Jerusalem was ever but a small place. You can cover her on the map of the world with a pin's head, yet is she more than all the Babylons that have been. She loved, and devoutly loved, the sublime and the beautiful. From this love was born her poets. The cedars of Lebanon, the lilies of the valley, these were the first letters of their alphabet. And as there cannot be a great land on the page of history without first a great literature, so there cannot be a great literature without first a deep, broad, devout and loving religion.

The great poet of this great land of ours, these westmost mountains and the ultimate sea bank, so like the olive-set Syrian hills, will come when we, too, have learned to love, and religiously love, the sublime and beautiful.

Why not permit the coming poet to take up his work in the morning of life where it is now laid down in the twilight of one who is going away?

To this end let us divest the prophets of all that mystery and special evil and special good with which ignorance and superstition have garmented them. They were ever plain men. They were ever human; and the more human the broader, richer, deeper their divine voices of the land.

Is there such a thing as genius, inspiration? I think there is no such thing. Rather let us call it a devout and all-pervading love for the sublime, the beautiful and good, the never-questioning conviction that there is nothing in this world that is not beautiful or trying to be beautiful; that there is no man with the breath of God in his nostrils who is not good or trying in his poor, blind way as best he may to be good. "And He looked upon all He had made and behold it was very good."

Genius is love that is born of this truth, leading ever by plain and simple ways, and true toil and care, as all nature toils and cares, as God toils and cares; that is all. I write this down for those who may come atter. We will have higher results from the plain sweet truth.

And when your great poet comes, as he surely will and soon, do not mock because he goes apart from folly or trade to meditate. Ever from the first the prophets went up into the mountains to pray. A poet need not be "eccentric" to turn apart from getting and getting. In truth he would be no real poet if he did not. A good poet need not be a bad man. He may not be a better man than yourself, but he is not necessarily worse for being a poet. I repeat, he is merely a plain, sincere human being in love with the beautiful world "and all that is His."

Byron, in a letter to Moore, says, "The night to me has been everything." In another he says, "I read Spenser half the time, as I write Childe Harold, in order to keep the measure and melody in my brain." Burns says, "I keep as many as half a dozen poems maturing in my mind at the same time, and write them down when matured and I find time." These and like little side lights from other great poets have done me so much good that I have decided to tell by way of foot-notes as we go forward so much of my own methods of work as may possibly light the path of some discouraged Keats of coming days. For the greater the poet the greater his sensibility, and the greater the sensibility the greater his sufferings in the somber foothill forests of Parnassus.

Also for the help and good of the poets who may take up my work where I lay it down, divested of all folly and falsehood with which it has been so cruelly garmented from the first, I shall write the story, source, purpose of my poems, so far as may be of use and interest. The photographs are put in to show that, whatever there may be in eccentricity of dress and manner, I dressed and bore myself as others and kept quietly and plainly along about my work like other men mainly.

The first thing of mine in print was the valedictory class poem, Columbia College, Eugene, Oregon, 1859. Oregon, settled by missionaries, was a great place for schools from the first. At this date, Columbia College, the germ of the University, had many students from California, and was famous as an educational center. Divest the mind at once of the idea that the schools of Oregon were in the least inferior to the best in the world. I have never since found such determined students and omniverous readers. We had all the books and none of the follies of great centers.

I had been writing, or trying to write, since a lad. My two brothers and my sister were at my side, our home with our parents, and we lived entirely to ourselves, and really often made ourselves ill from too much study. We were all school teachers when not at college. In 1861 my elder brother and I were admitted to practice law, under George H. Williams, afterwards Attorney-General under President Grant. Brother went at once to the war, I to the gold mines.

My first act there came near costing my life, and cost me, through snow-blindness, the best use of my eyes from that time forth. The agony of snow-blindness is unutterable; the hurt irreparable. In those days men never murmured or admitted themselves put at disadvantage. I gave up the law for the time and laid hand to other things; but here is a paragraph from the February (1897) *Oregon Teacher*, telling how this calamity came about:

"The first man I met among the fevered crowd was Oregon s poet, my old schoolmate, Joaquin Miller. His blue eyes sparkled with kindly greeting, and, as I took his hand, I knew by its quickening pulse and tightened clasp that he, too, was sharing in the excitement of the gold hunter. He was then in the first flush of manhood, with buoyant spirits, untiring energy, and among a race of hardy pioneers, the bravest of the brave. He possessed more than ordinary talent and looked forward with hope to the battle of life, expecting to reap his share of its honors and rewards. For years he was foremost in every desperate enterprise—crossing snow-capped mountains, swollen rivers, and facing hostile Indians. When snow fell fifteen feet on Florence mountain, and hundreds were penned in camp without a word from wives, children and loved ones at home, he said, 'Boys, I will bring your letters from Lewiston.' Afoot and alone, without a trail, he crossed the mountain tops, the dangerous streams, the wintry desert of Camas Prairie, fighting back the hungry mountain wolves, and returned bending beneath his load of loving messages from home. One day he was found, in defense of the weak, facing the pistol or bowie knife of the desperado; and the next day he was washing the clothes and smoothing the pillow of a sick comrade. We all loved him, but we were not men who wrote for the newspaper or magazine, and his acts of heroism and kindness were unchronicled save in the hearts of those who knew him in those times and under those trying circumstances."

Right into the heart of the then unknown and unnamed Idaho (I*dah*-ho) and Montana; gold dust was as wheat in harvest time. I, and another, born to the saddle, formed an express line and carried letters in from the Oregon river and gold dust out, gold dust by the horse load after horse load, till we earned all the gold we wanted. Such rides! and each alone. Indians holding the plunging horses ready for us at relays. I had lived with and knew, trusted the red men and was never betrayed. Those matchless night rides under the stars, dashing into the Orient doors of dawn before me as the sun burst through the shining mountain pass—this brought my love of song to the surface. And now I traveled, Mexico, South America, I had resolved as I rode to set these unwritten lands with the banner of song.

I wrote much as I traveled but never kept my verses, once published. I thought, and still hold that under right conditions and among a right people—and these mighty American people are perhaps more nearly right than any other that have yet been—anything in literature that is worth preserving will preserve itself. As none of my verses with this following exception have come down on the river of Time it is safe to say nothing of all I wrote could serve any purpose except to feed foolish curiosity. I give the following place, written years after the college valedictory, not only because it is right in spirit but because it shows how old, how very old I was as a boy, and sad at heart over the cruelties of man to man. This was my first poem printed, after the valedictory, about 1866, and has been drifting around ever since:

IS IT WORTH WHILE?

Is it worth while that we jostle a brother
 Bearing his load on the rough road of life?
Is it worth while that we jeer at each other
 In blackness of heart ?—that we war to the knife?
 God pity us all in our pitiful strife.

God pity us all as we jostle each other;
 God pardon us all for the triumphs we feel
When a fellow goes down; poor heart-broken brother,
 Pierced to the heart; words are keener than steel,
 And mightier far for woe or for weal.

Were it not well in this brief little journey
 On over the isthmus down into the tide,
We give him a fish instead of a serpent,
 Ere folding the hands to be and abide
 For ever and aye in dust at his side?

Look at the roses saluting each other;
 Look at the herds all at peace on the plain—
Man, and man only, makes war on his brother,
 And dotes in his heart on his peril and pain—
 Shamed by the brutes that go down on the plain.

* * * * * * * *

Why should you envy a moment of pleasure
 Some poor fellow-mortal has wrung from it all?
Oh! could you look into his life's broken measure—
 Look at the dregs—at the wormwood and gall—
 Look at his heart hung with crape like a pall—

Look at the skeletons down by his hearthstone—
 Look at his cares in their merciless sway,
I know you would go and say tenderly, lowly,
 Brother—my brother, for aye and a day,
 Lo! Lethe is washing the blackness away.

Home again in Oregon I had a little newspaper in the interest of Peace, my Quaker father's creed, and opposing the "March to the Sea" and the invasion of States, the paper was suppressed for alleged treason. Poor once more, broken in heart and health, the gold mines again; then a campaign against an insurrection of savages; then elected Judge; and once more my face to books, night and day, as at school.

Had I melted into my surroundings, instead of reading and writing continually, life had not been so dismal; but I lived among the stars, an abstemious ghost. Then "Specimens," a thin book of verse, and some lawyers laughed, and political and personal foes all up and down the land derided. This made me more determined, and the next year "Joaquin *et al.*," a book of 124 pages, resulted. Bret Harte, of the *Overland*, behaved bravely; but, as a rule: "Can any good thing come out of Nazareth?"

The first little book has not preserved itself to me, but from a London pirated copy of the second one I find that it makes up about half of my first book in London; the songs my heart had sung as I galloped alone under the stars of Idaho years before.

But my health and eyes had failed again; besides, everything was at sixes and sevens, and, being a "cold water man," and a sort of preacher and teacher on all political occasions, I was so unpopular that when I asked a place on the Supreme Bench at the convention, I was derisively told: "Better stick to poetry." Three months later, September 1, 1870, I was kneeling at the grave of Burns. I really expected to die there in the land of my fathers; I was so broken and ill.

May I proudly admit that I had sought a place on the Supreme Bench in order that I might the more closely stick to poetry? I have a serious purpose in saying this. Was Lowell a bad diplomat because he was a good poet? Is Gladstone less great because of his three hundred books and pamphlets? The truth is there never was, never will be, a great general, judge, lawyer, anything, without being, at heart at least, a great poet. Then let not our conventions, presidents, governors, despise the young poet who does seek expression. We have plenty of lawyers, judges, silent great men of all sorts; yet the land is songless. Had my laudable ambition not been despised, how much better I might have sang; who shall say?

Let us quote a few lines from the last pages of my little book, published before setting out. They will show, not poetry perhaps, but resignation, a belief in immortality, a hope to be read in Europe, and a singularly early desire to not be formally buried, but to pass in clouds and ashes. The little book, "Joaquin *et al.*," from which the following lines were taken, was first published in Portland (Oregon) in 1868:

ULTIME.

* * * * * * * * *

Had I been content to live on the leafy borders of the scene
Communing with the neglected dwellers of the fern-grown glen,
And glorious storm-stained peaks, with cloud-knit sheen,
And sullen iron brows, and belts of boundless green,
A peaceful, flowery path, content, I might have trod,
And carolled melodies that perchance might have been
Read with love and a sweet delight. But I kiss the rod.
I have done as best I knew. The rest is with my God.

Come forward here to me, ye who have a fear of death,
Come down, far down, even to the dark waves' rim,
And take my hand, and feel my calm, low breath;
How peaceful all! How still and sweet! The sight is dim,
And dreamy as a distant sea. And melodies do swim

Around us here as a far-off vesper's holy hymn.
  This is death. With folded hands I wait and welcome him;
And yet a few, some few, were kind, I would live and so be known,
That their sweet deeds might be as bread on the waters thrown.

I go, I know not where, but know I will not die,
  And know I will be gainer going to that somewhere;
For in that hereafter, afar beyond the bended sky,
  Bread and butter will not figure in the bill of fare,
  Nor will the soul be judged by what the flesh may wear.
But with all my time my own, once in the dapple skies,
  I will collect my fancies now floating in the air
And arrange them, a jewel set, that in a show-case lies
And when you come will show you them in a sweet surprise.

It was my boy-ambition to be read beyond the brine,
  But this you know was when life looked fair and tall,
Erewhile this occidental rim was my dream's confine,
  And now at last I make no claim to be read at all,
  And write with this wild hope, and even that is small,
That when the last pick-ax lies rusting in the ravine,
  And its green bent hill-sides echo the shepherd's call,
Some curious wight will thumb this through, saying, "Well, I ween
He was not a poet, but yet, and yet, he might have been."

* * * * * * * * *

But to conclude. Do not stick me down in the cold wet mud,
  As if I wished to hide, or was ashamed of what I had done,
Or my friends believed me born of slime, with torpid blood.
  No, when this the first short quarter of my life is run,
  Let me ascend in clouds of smoke up to the sun.
And as for these lines, they are a rough, wild-wood bouquet,
  Plucked from my mountains in the dusk of life, as one
Without taste or time to select, or put in good array,
Grasps at once rose, leaf, briar, on the brink, and hastes away.

Fault may be found, as with Hawthorne when he gathered up his Tales, that all I have written is not here. Let me answer with him that all I wish to answer for is here. The author must be the sole judge as to what belongs to the public and what to the flames. Much that I have written has been on trial for many years. The honest, wise old world of to-day is a fairly safe jury. While it is true the poet must lead rather than be led, yet must he lead pleasantly, patiently, or he may not lead at all. So that which the world let drop out of sight as the years surged by I have, as a rule, not cared to introduce a second time.

For example take the lines written on the dead millionaire of New York. There were perhaps a dozen verses at first, but the world found use for and kept before it only the two following:

The gold that with the sunlight lies
  In bursting heaps at dawn,
The silver spilling from the skies
  At night to walk upon,
The diamonds gleaming in the dew
He never saw, he never knew.

He got some gold, dug from the mud,
  Some silver, crushed from stones;
But the gold was red with dead men's blood,
  The silver black with groans;
And when he died he moaned aloud
"They'll make no pocket in my shroud."

The antithesis of this ugly truth in poetry, the lines to Peter Cooper's memory also shared the same fate. The world did not want all I had to say of this gentle old man and kept only the three little verses:

Honor and glory forever more
  To this great man gone to rest;
Peace on the dim Plutonian shore;
  Rest in the land of the blest.

I reckon him greater than any man
  That ever drew sword in war;
Nobler, better than king or khan,
  Better, wiser by far.

Aye, wisest he in this whole wide land,
  Of hoarding till bent and gray;
For all you can hold in your cold, dead hand
  Is what you have given away.

May I, an old teacher, in conclusion, lay down a lesson or two for the young in letters? After the grave of Burns, then a month at Byron's tomb, then Schiller, Goethe; before battle fields. Heed this. The poet must be loyal, loyal not only to his God and his country, but loyal, loving, to the great masters who have nourished him.

This devotion to the masters led me to first set foot in London near White Chapel, where Bayard Taylor had lived; although I went at once to the Abbey. Then I lived at Camberwell, because Browning was born there; then at Hemmingford Road, because Tom Hood died there.

A thin little book now, called "Pacific Poems," and my watch was in pawn before it was out, for I could not find a publisher. One hundred were printed, bearing the name of the printer as publisher. What fortune! With the press notices in hand, I now went boldly to the most aristocratic publisher in London.

As to the disposal of our dead, except so far as it tends to the good of the living, most especially the poor, who waste so much which they can ill spare in burials, the young poet may say or do as he elects. But in the matters of resignation to the Infinite and belief in immortality, he shall have no choice. There never was a poet and there never will be a poet who disputed God, or so degraded himself as to doubt his eternal existence.

One word as to the choice of theme. First, let it be new. The world has no use for two Homers, or even a second Shakespeare, were he possible.

And now think it not intrusion if one no longer young should ask the coming poet to not waste his forces in discovering this truth: The sweetest flowers grow closest to the ground. We are all too ready to choose some lurid battle theme or exalted subject. Exalt your theme rather than ask your theme to exalt you. Braver and better to celebrate the lowly and forgiving grasses under foot than the stately cedars and sequoias overhead. They can speak for themselves. It has been scornfully said that all my subjects are of the low or savage. It might have been as truly said that some of my heroes and heroines, as Reil and Sophia Petrowska, died on the scaffold. But believe me, the people of heart are the unfortunate. How unfortunate that man who never knew misfortune! And thank God, the heart of the world is with the unfortunate! There never has yet been a great poem written of a rich man or gross. And I glory in the fact that I never celebrated war or warriors. Thrilling as are war themes, you will not find one, purposely, in all my books. If you would have the heart of the world with you, put heart in your work, taking care that you do not try to pass brass for gold. They are much alike to look upon, but only the ignorant can be deceived. And what is poetry without heart! In truth, were I asked to define poetry, I would answer in a single word, *Heart*.

A true seer will see that which is before him, and about him, in and of his own land and life. "The eyes of the fool are in the ends of the earth." The real and reasonable should best inspire us. I do not care to explore impossible hells with either dolorous Dante or majestic Milton. I do not believe there are any such places, save as we make them in our own minds. Indeed, life would be fearful could I be made to believe that the heart of this beautiful globe is filled with human beings writhing in eternal torments under my feet. Such books can do no good; and the only excuse for any book is the pleasure it can give and the good it can do.

Let me again invoke you, be loyal to your craft, not only to your craft, but to your fellow scribes. To let envy lure you to leer at even the humblest of them is to admit yourself beaten; to admit yourself to be one of the thousand failures betraying the one success. Braver it were to knife in the back a holy man at prayer. I plead for something more than the individual here. I plead for the entire Republic. To not have a glorious literature of our own is to be another Nineveh, Babylon, Turkey. Nothing ever has paid, nothing ever will pay a nation like poetry. How many millions have we paid, are still paying, bleak and rocky little Scotland to behold the land of Burns? Byron led the world to scatter its gold through the ruins of Italy, where he had mused and sang, and Italy was rebuilt. Greece survived a thousand years on the deathless melodies of her mighty dead, and now once again is the heart of the globe.

Finally, use the briefest little bits of baby Saxon words at hand. The world is waiting for ideas, not for words. Remember Shakespeare's scorn of "words, words, words." Remember always that it was the short Roman sword that went to the heart and conquered the world, not the long tasseled and bannered lance of the barbarian. Write this down in red and remember.

Will we ever have an American literature? Yes, when we leave sound and words to the winds. American science has swept time and space aside. American science dashes along at fifty, sixty miles an hour; but American literature still lumbers along in the old-fashioned English stage-coach at ten miles an hour; and sometimes with a red-coated outrider blowing a horn. We must leave all this behind us. We have not time for words. A man who uses a great big sounding word when a short one will do is to that extent a robber of time. A jewel that depends greatly on its setting is not a great jewel. When the Messiah of American literature comes he will come singing, so far as may be, in words of a single syllable.

TABLE OF CONTENTS.

SONGS OF THE SIERRAS.

THE ARIZONIAN.

Come to my sunland! Come with me
To the land I love; where the sun and sea
Are wed for ever; where the palm and pine
Are fill'd with singers; where tree and vine
Are voiced with prophets! O come, and you
Shall sing a song with the seas that swirl
And kiss their hands to that cold white girl,
To the maiden moon in her mantle of blue.

"And I have said, and I say it ever,
As the years go on and the world goes over,
'Twere better to be content and clever,
In the tending of cattle and the tossing of clover,
In the grazing of cattle and growing of grain,
Than a strong man striving for fame or gain;
Be even as kine in the red-tipped clover:
For they lie down and their rests are rests,
And the days are theirs, come sun, come rain,
To rest, rise up, and repose again;
While we wish and yearn, and do pray in vain,
And hope to ride on the billows of bosoms,
And hope to rest in the haven of breasts,
Till the heart is sicken'd and the fair hope dead—
Be even as clover with its crown of blossoms,
Even as blossoms ere the bloom is shed,
Kiss'd by the kine and the brown sweet bee—
For these have the sun, and moon, and air,
And never a bit of the burthen of care:
Yet with all of our caring what more have we?

"I would court content like a lover lonely,
I would woo her, win her, and wear her only.
And would never go over the white sea wall
For gold or glory or for aught at all."

He said these things as he stood with the Squire
By the river's rim in the field of clover,
While the stream flow'd on and the clouds flew over,
With the sun tangled in and the fringes afire.

So the Squire lean'd with a kindly glory
To humor his guest, and to hear his story;
For his guest had gold, and he yet was clever,
And mild of manner; and, what was more, he,
In the morning's ramble had praised the kine.

The clover's reach and the meadows fine,
And so made the Squire his friend forever.

His brow was brown'd by the sun and weather,
And touch'd by the terrible hand of time;
His rich black beard had a fringe of rime,
As silk and silver inwove together.
There were hoops of gold all over his hands,
And across his breast in chains and bonds,
Broad and massive as belts of leather.

And the belts of gold were bright in the sun,
But brighter than gold his black eyes shone
From their sad face-setting so swarth and dun—
Brighter than beautiful Santan stone,
Brighter even than balls of fire,
As he said, hot-faced, in the face of the Squire:—

"The pines bow'd over, the stream bent under,
The cabin was cover'd with thatches of palm
Down in a cañon so deep, the wonder
Was what it could know in its clime but calm;
Down in a cañon so cleft asunder
By sabre-stroke in the young world's prime,
It look'd as if broken by bolts of thunder,
And burst asunder and rent and riven
By earthquakes driven that turbulent time
The red cross lifted red hands to heaven.

"And this in that land where the sun goes down,
And gold is gather'd by tide and by stream,
And the maidens are brown as the cocoa brown,
And life is a love and a love is a dream;
Where the winds come in from the far Cathay
With odor of spices and balm and bay,
And summer abideth with man alway,
Nor comes in a tour with the stately June,
And comes too late and returns too soon.

"She stood in the shadows as the sun went down,
Fretting her hair with her fingers brown,
As tall as the silk-tipp'd tassel'd corn—
Stood watching, dark brow'd, as I weighed the gold
We had wash'd that day where the river roll'd;
And her proud lip curl'd with a sun-clime scorn,
As she ask'd, 'Is she better, or fairer than I?—
She, that blonde in the land beyond,
Where the sun is hid and the seas are high—
That you gather in gold as the years go by,
And hoard and hide it away for her
As the squirrel burrows the black pine-burr?

"Now the gold weigh'd well, but was lighter of weight
Than we two had taken for days of late,
So I was fretted, and brow a-frown,
I said, half-angered, with head held down—
'Well, yes, she is fairer; and I loved her first:
And shall love her last, come worst to the worst.'

"Her lips grew livid, and her eyes afire
As I said this thing; and higher and higher
The hot words ran, when the booming thunder

Peal'd in the crags and the pine-tops under,
While up by the cliff in the murky skies
It look'd as the clouds had caught the fire—
The flash and fire of her wonderful eyes!

"She turn'd from the door and down to the river,
And mirror'd her face in the whimsical tide,
Then threw back her hair as one throwing a quiver,
As an Indian throws it back far from his side
And free from his hands, swinging fast to the shoulder
When rushing to battle; and, turning, she sigh'd
And shook, and shiver'd as aspens shiver.
Then a great green snake slid into the river,
Glistening green, and with eyes of fire;
Quick, double-handed she seized a boulder,
And cast it with all the fury of passion,
As with lifted head it went curving across,
Swift darting its tongue like a fierce desire,
Curving and curving, lifting higher and higher,
Bent and beautiful as a river moss;
Then, smitten, it turn'd, bent, broken and doubled
And lick'd, red-tongued, like a forked fire,
Then sank and the troubled waters bubbled
And so swept on in the old swift fashion.

"I lay in my hammock: the air was heavy
And hot and threat'ning; the very heaven
Was holding its breath; and bees in a bevy
Hid under my thatch; and birds were driven
In clouds to the rocks in a hurried whirr
As I peer'd down by the path for her.

"She stood like a bronze bent over the river,
The proud eyes fix'd, the passion unspoken.
Then the heavens broke like a great dyke broken;
And ere I fairly had time to give her
A shout of warning, a rushing of wind
And the rolling of clouds and a deafening din
And a darkness that had been black to the blind
Came down, as I shouted 'Come in! Come in!
Come under the roof, come up from the river,
As up from a grave—come now, or come never!'
The tassel'd tops of the pines were as weeds,
The red-woods rock'd like to lake-side reeds,
And the world seemed darken'd and drown'd forever,
While I crouched low; as a beast that bleeds.

"One time in the night as the black wind shifted,
And a flash of lightning stretch'd over the stream,
I seemed to see her with her brown hands lifted—
Only seem'd to see as one sees in a dream—
With her eyes wide wild and her pale lips press'd,
And the blood from her brow, and the flood to her breast;
When the flood caught her hair as flax in a wheel,
And wheeling and whirling her round like a reel;
Laugh'd loud her despair, then leapt like a steed,
Holding tight to her hair, folding fast to her heel,
Laughing fierce, leaping far as if spurr'd to its speed!

"Now mind, I tell you all this did but seem—
Was seen as you see fearful scenes in a dream;
For what the devil could the lighting show
In a night like that, I should like to know?

"And then I slept, and sleeping I dream'd
Of great green serpents with tongues of fire,
And of death by drowning, and of after death—
Of the day of judgment, wherein it seem'd
That she, the heathen, was bidden higher,
Higher than I; that I clung to her side,
And clinging struggled, and struggling cried,
And crying, wakened all weak of my breath.

"Long leaves of the sun lay over the floor,
And a chipmunk chirp'd in the open door,
While above on his crag the eagle scream'd,
Scream'd as he never had scream'd before.
I rush'd to the river: the flood had gone
Like a thief, with only his tracks upon
The weeds and grasses and warm wet sand,
And I ran after with reaching hand,
And call'd as I reach'd, and reach'd as I ran,
And ran till I came to the cañon's van,
Where the waters lay in a bent lagoon,
Hook'd and crook'd like the horned moon.

"And there in the surge where the waters met,
And the warm wave lifted, and the winds did fret
The wave till it foam'd with rage on the land,
She lay with the wave on the warm white sand;
Her rich hair trailed with the trailing weeds,
While her small brown hands lay prone or lifted
As the waves sang strophes in the broken reeds,
Or paused in pity, and in silence sifted
Sands of gold, as upon her grave.

"And as sure as you see yon browsing kine,
And breathe the breath of your meadows fine,
When I went to my waist in the warm white wave
And stood all pale in the wave to my breast,
And reach'd my hands in her rest and unrest,
Her hands were lifted and reach'd to mine.

"Now mind, I tell you, I cried, 'Come in!
Come into the house, come out from the hollow,
Come out of the storm, come up from the river!'
Aye, cried, and call'd in that desolate din,
Though I did not rush out, and in plain words give her
A wordy warning of the flood to follow,
Word by word, and letter by letter;
But she knew it as well as I, and better;
For once in the desert of New Mexico
When we two sought frantically far and wide
For the famous spot where Apaches shot
With bullets of gold their buffalo,
And she stood faithful to death at my side,
I threw me down in the hard hot sand
Utterly famish'd, and ready to die;
Then a speck arose in the red-hot sky—
A speck no larger than a lady's hand—
While she at my side bent tenderly over,
Shielding my face from the sun as a cover,
And wetting my face, as she watch'd by my side,
From a skin she had borne till the high noontide,

(I had emptied mine in the heat of the morning)
When the thunder mutter'd far over the plain
Like a monster bound or a beast in pain:
She sprang the instant, and gave the warning,
With her brown hand pointed to the burning skies,
For I was too weak unto death to rise.
But she knew the peril, and her iron will,
With a heart as true as the great North Star,
Did bear me up to the palm-tipp'd hill,
Where the fiercest beasts in a brotherhood,
Beasts that had fled from the plain and far,
In perfectest peace expectant stood,
With their heads held high, and their limbs a-quiver.
Then ere she barely had time to breathe
The boiling waters began to seethe
From hill to hill in a booming river,
Beating and breaking from hill to hill—
Even while yet the sun shot fire,
Without the shield of a cloud above—
Filling the cañon as you would fill
A wine-cup, drinking in swift desire,
With the brim new-kiss'd by the lips you love!

"So you see she knew—knew perfectly well,
As well as I could shout and tell,
That the mountain would send a flood to the plain,
Sweeping the gorge like a hurricane,
When the fire flash'd and the thunder fell.

"Therefore it is wrong, and I say therefore
Unfair, that a mystical, brown-wing'd moth
Or midnight bat should forevermore
Fan past my face with its wings of air,
And follow me up, down, everywhere,
Flit past, pursue me, or fly before,
Dimly limning in each fair place
The full fixed eyes and the sad, brown face,
So forty times worse than if it were wroth!

"I gather'd the gold I had hid in the earth,
Hid over the door and hid under the hearth:
Hoarded and hid, as the world went over,
For the love of a blonde by a sun-brown'd lover,
And I said to myself, as I set my face
To the East and afar from the desolate place,
'She has braided her tresses, and through her tears
Look'd away to the West for years, the years
That I have wrought where the sun tans brown;
She has waked by night, she has watch'd by day,
She has wept and wonder'd at my delay,
Alone and in tears, with her head held down,
Where the ships sail out and the seas swirl in,
Forgetting to knit and refusing to spin.

"She shall lift her head, she shall see her lover,
She shall hear his voice like a sea that rushes,
She shall hold his gold in her hands of snow,
And down on his breast she shall hide her blushes,
And never a care shall her true heart know,
While the clods are below, or the clouds are above her.

"On the fringe of the night she stood with her pitcher
At the old town fountain: and oh! passing fair.
'I am riper now,' I said, 'but am richer,'
And I lifted my hand to my beard and hair;

'I am burnt by the sun, I am brown'd by the sea;
I am white of my beard, and am bald, may be;
Yet for all such things what can her heart care?'
Then she moved; and I said, 'How marvelous fair!'
She look'd to the West, with her arm arch'd over;
'Looking for me, her sun-brown'd lover,'
I said to myself, and my heart grew bold,
And I stepp'd me nearer to her presence there,
As approaching a friend; for 'twas here of old
Our troths were plighted and the tale was told.

"How young she was and how fair she was!
How tall as a palm, and how pearly fair,
As the night came down on her glorious hair!
Then the night grew deep and my eyes grew dim,
And a sad-faced figure began to swim
And float by my face, flit past, then pause,
With her hands held up and her head held down,
Yet face to my face; and that face was brown!

"Now why did she come and confront me there,
With the flood to her face and the moist in her hair,
And a mystical stare in her marvelous eyes?
I had call'd to her twice, 'Come in! come in!
Come out of the storm to the calm within!'
Now, that is the reason I do make complain
That for ever and ever her face should rise,
Facing face to face with her great sad eyes.

"I said then to myself, and I say it again,
Gainsay it you, gainsay it who will,
I shall say it over and over still,
And will say it ever; for I know it true,
That I did all that a man could do
(Some men's good doings are done in vain)
To save that passionate child of the sun,
With her love as deep as the doubled main,
And as strong and fierce as a troubled sea—
That beautiful bronze with its soul of fire,
Its tropical love and its kingly ire—
That child as fix'd as a pyramid,
As tall as a tule and pure as a nun—
And all there is of it, the all I did,
As often happens was done in vain.
So there is no bit of her blood on me.

'She is marvelous young and is wonderful fair,'
I said again, and my heart grew bold,
And beat and beat a charge for my feet.
'Time that defaces us, places, and replaces us,
And trenches our faces in furrows for tears.
Has traced here nothing in all these years.
'Tis the hair of gold that I vex'd of old,
The marvelous flowing, gold-flower of hair,
And the peaceful eyes in their sweet surprise
That I have kiss'd till the head swam round.
And the delicate curve of the dimpled chin,
And the pouting lips and the pearls within
Are the same, the same, but so young, so fair!'
My heart leapt out and back at a bound,
As a child that starts, then stops, then lingers.
'How wonderful young!' I lifted my fingers
And fell to counting the round years down
That I had dwelt where the sun tans brown.

"Four full hands, and a finger over!
'She does not know me, her truant lover,'
I said to myself, for her brow was a-frown
As I stepp'd still nearer, with my head held down,
All abash'd and in blushes my brown face over;
'She does not know me, her long lost lover,
For my beard's so long and my skin's so brown
That I well might pass myself for another.'
So I lifted my voice and I spake aloud:
'Annette, my darling! Annette Macleod!'
She started, she stopped, she turn'd, amazed,
She stood all wonder, her eyes wild-wide,
Then turn'd in terror down the dusk way-side,
And cried as she fled, 'The man he is crazed,
And he calls the maiden name of my mother!'

"Let the world turn over, and over. and over,
And toss and tumble like beasts in pain,
Crack, quake, and tremble, and turn full over
And die, and never rise up again;
Let her dash her peaks through the purple cover,
Let her plash her seas in the face of the sun—
I have no one to love me now, not one,
In a world as full as a world can hold;
So I will get gold as I erst have done,
I will gather a coffin top-full of gold,
To take to the door of Death, to buy—
Buy what, when I double my hands and die?

"Go down, go down to your fields of clover,
Go down with your kine to the pastures fine,
And give no thought, or care, or labor
For maid or man, good name or neighbor;
For I gave all as the years went over—
Gave all my youth, my years and labor,
And a heart as warm as the world is cold,
For a beautiful, bright, and delusive lie:
Gave youth, gave years, gave love for gold;
Giving and getting, yet what have I?

"The red ripe stars hang low overhead,
Let the good and the light of soul reach up,
Pluck gold as plucking a butter-cup:
But I am as lead, and my hands are red.

"So the sun climbs up, and on, and over,
And the days go out and the tides come in,
And the pale moon rubs on her purple cover
Till worn as thin and as bright as tin;
But the ways are dark and the days are dreary,
And the dreams of youth are but dust in age,
And the heart grows harden'd and the hands grow weary,
Holding them up for their heritage.

"For we promise so great and we gain so little;
For we promise so great of glory and gold,
And we gain so little that the hands grow cold,
And the strained heart-strings wear bare and brittle,
And for gold and glory we but gain instead
A fond heart sicken'd and a fair hope dead.

"So I have said, and I say it over,
And can prove it over and over again,
That the four-footed beasts in the red crown'd clover,
The piéd and hornéd beasts on the plain
That lie down, rise up, and repose again,
And do never take care or toil or spin,
Nor buy, nor build, nor gather in gold,
As the days go out and the tides come in,
Are better than we by a thousand-fold;
For what is it all, in the words of fire,
But a vexing of soul and a vain desire?"

I had left school in Oregon in the early fifties; ran away, it is told. The truth is new gold mines had been found a few hundred miles to the south, near the California line, and, as we were always poor, my elder brother and I thought it a good thing that I should rush in and locate a mining claim. We could not get heart to tell our parents and I left at night, taking my school books. As was so often the case, the rich mines were "a little farther on," and I could not turn back; for an Indian war was impending between where I was and home, so I kept on. Once in sight of Mount Shasta I must see more, and finally found an old mountaineer who had often camped by us in Oregon with his pack animals and companioned with Papa. He had been with Fremont, was a graduate of Heidelberg, and gladly helped me along with my Latin. His trade was the buying of wild horses by the herd from the Mexicans far south and driving them up to his Soda Spring ranch and rich grasses at the base of Mount Shasta, then on to Oregon till tamed, then returning to California with a pack train of Oregon produce. By attaching myself to him the way seemed clear to get back home, in the course of time.

He finally gave me a share in his wild ranch and ventures, and I made two of these long, glorious trips of mountains, deserts, snow, color; gorgeousness and gorgeousness. My position was rather that of cook and servant than companion and partner, for he had some rough men with him and left things to them. But I could live on horseback by day and read by our camp-fire at night, and that was enough.

Mountain Jo was a good man at heart, but a sad drunkard and a hopelessly helpless business man. Besides, the Indians were continually provoked to war by his rough men as well as by heartless gold hunters, and we could do little but fight. He lost an eye and when I got back home after years, I had little to show on my return except some ugly and still painful wounds. But I had not been idle, and with help from Papa and some indulgence soon took my place in my class and wrote a part of this poem crudely, about that time.

The sudden storm, cloud-burst and flood here described is as I saw it in Arizona; the comely Indian girl I saw perish as described, near Mount Shasta. I located the final scene and the hero in Scotland because I first set foot there in Europe, and because our family was of Scotland. Mountain Jo used to carry in his pocket a rough gold bullet which he said he cut from the neck of his horse after a battle with Apaches. The whole story was not written down till in London. I liked it best, and so put it first in "The Songs of the Sierras." I tell all this to the young writer for a purpose.

In Rome I once watched a great sculptor fashion a noble statue, and I noticed that he had many models. From one he shaped the arms, from another the legs, from another the pose of the head.

So, my coming poet of the Sierras and great sea, you may gather your bouquet of song from many hillsides but do not entirely imagine all your flowers. For however beautiful they may seem to you, they will not seem quite real to others.

This book, in the following lines, was dedicated To Maud:

Because the skies were blue, because
The sun in fringes of the sea
Was tangled, and delightfully
Kept dancing on as in a waltz,
And tropic trees bowed to the seas
And bloomed and bore years through and through,
And birds in blended gold and blue
Were thick and sweet as swarming bees,
And sang as if in Paradise
And all that Paradise was spring—
Did I too sing with lifted eyes,
Because I could not choose but sing.

With garments full of sea winds blown
From isles beyond of spice and balm
Beside the sea, beneath her palm,
She waits, as true as chiseled stone.
My childhood's child, my June in May,
So wiser than thy father is,
These lines, these leaves, and all of this
Are thine—a loose, uncouth bouquet—
So, wait and watch for sail or sign,
A ship shall mount the hollow seas
Blown to thy place of blossomed trees,
And birds, and song, and summer-shine.

I throw a kiss across the sea,
I drink the winds as drinking wine,
And dream they all are blown from thee—
I catch the whispered kiss of thine.
Shall I return with lifted face,
Or head held down as in disgrace
To hold thy two brown hands in mine?

England, 1871.

WITH WALKER IN NICARAGUA.

That man who lives for self alone
Lives for the meanest mortal known.

I.

He was a brick: let this be said
Above my brave dishonor'd dead.
I ask no more, this is not much,
Yet I disdain a colder touch
To memory as dear as his;
For he was true as God's north star,
And brave as Yuba's grizzlies are,
Yet gentle as a panther is,
Mouthing her young in her first fierce kiss.

A dash of sadness in his air,
Born, may be, of his over care,
And may be, born of a despair
In early love—I never knew;
I question'd not, as many do,
Of things as sacred as this is;
I only knew that he to me
Was all a father, friend, could be;
I sought to know no more than this
Of history of him or his.

A piercing eye, a princely air,
A presence like a chevalier,
Half angel and half Lucifer;
Sombrero black, with plume of snow
That swept his long silk locks below;
A red serape with bars of gold,
All heedless falling, fold on fold;
A sash of silk, where flashing swung
A sword as swift as serpent's tongue,
In sheath of silver chased in gold;
And Spanish spurs with bells of steel
That dash'd and dangled at the heel;
A face of blended pride and pain,
Of mingled pleading and disdain,
With shades of glory and of grief—
The famous filibuster chief
Stood front his men amid the trees
That top the fierce Cordilleras,
With bent arm arch'd above his brow;—
Stood still—he stands, a picture, now—
Long gazing down the sunset seas.

II.

What strange, strong, bearded men were these
He led above the tropic seas!
Men sometimes of uncommon birth,
Men rich in histories untold,
Who boasted not, though more than bold,
Blown from the four parts of the earth.

Men mighty-thew'd as Samson was,
That had been kings in any cause,
A remnant of the races past;
Dark-brow'd as if in iron cast,
Broad-breasted as twin gates of brass,—
Men strangely brave and fiercely true,
Who dared the West when giants were,
Who err'd, yet bravely dared to err,
A remnant of that early few
Who held no crime or curse or vice
As dark as that of cowardice;
With blendings of the worst and best
Of faults and virtues that have blest
Or cursed or thrill'd the human breast.

They rode, a troop of bearded men,
Rode two and two out from the town,
And some were blonde and some were brown,
And all as brave as Sioux; but when
From San Bennetto south the line
That bound them in the laws of man
Was pass'd, and peace stood mute behind
And stream'd a banner to the wind
The world knew not, there was a sign
Of awe, of silence, rear and van.

Men thought who never thought before;
I heard the clang and clash of steel
From sword at hand or spur at heel
And iron feet, but nothing more.
Some thought of Texas, some of Maine,
But one of rugged Tennessee,—

And one of Avon thought, and one
Thought of an isle beneath the sun,
And one of Wabash, one of Spain,
And one turned sadly to the Spree.

Defeat meant something more than death;
The world was ready, keen to smite,
As stern and still beneath its ban
With iron will and bated breath,
Their hands against their fellow-man,
They rode—each man an Ishmaelite.
But when we topped the hills of pine,
These men dismounted, doff'd their cares,
Talk'd loud and laugh'd old love affairs,
And on the grass took meat and wine,
And never gave a thought again
To land or life that lay behind,
Or love, or care of any kind
Beyond the present cross or pain.

And I, a waif of stormy seas,
A child among such men as these,
Was blown along this savage surf
And rested with them on the turf,
And took delight below the trees.
I did not question, did not care
To know the right or wrong. I saw
That savage freedom had a spell,
And loved it more than I can tell,
And snapp'd my fingers at the law.
I bear my burden of the shame,—
I shun it not, and naught forget,
However much I may regret:
I claim some candor to my name,
And courage cannot change or die,—
Did they deserve to die? they died!
Let justice then be satisfied,
And as for me, why, what am I?

The standing side by side till death,
The dying for some wounded friend,
The faith that failed not to the end,
The strong endurance till the breath
And body took their ways apart,
I only know. I keep my trust.
Their vices! earth has them by heart.
Their virtues! they are with their dust.

How we descended troop on troop,
As wide-winged eagles downward swoop!
How wound we through the fragrant wood,
With all its broad boughs hung in green,
With sweeping mosses trail'd between!
How waked the spotted beasts of prey,
Deep sleeping from the face of day,
And dashed them like a troubled flood
Down some defile and denser wood!

And snakes, long, lithe and beautiful
As green and graceful bough'd bamboo,
Did twist and twine them through and through
The boughs that hung red-fruited full.
One, monster-sized, above me hung,
Close eyed me with his bright pink eyes,
Then raised his folds, and sway'd and swung,
And lick'd like lightning his red tongue,
Then oped his wide mouth with surprise;
He writhed and curved and raised and lower'd
His folds like liftings of the tide,
Then sank so low I touch'd his side,
As I rode by, with my bright sword.

The trees shook hands high overhead,
And bow'd and intertwined across
The narrow way, while leaves and moss
And luscious fruit, gold-hued and red,
Through all the canopy of green,
Let not one shaft shoot between.

Birds hung and swung, green-robed and red,
Or droop'd in curved lines dreamily,
Rainbows reversed, from tree to tree,
Or sang low hanging overhead—
Sang low, as if they sang and slept,
Sang faint like some far waterfall,
And took no note of us at all,
Though nuts that in the way were spread
Did crush and crackle where we stept.

Wild lilies, tall as maidens are,
As sweet of breath, as pearly fair
As fair as faith, as pure as truth,

Fell thick before our every tread,
In fragrant sacrifice of ruth.
The ripen'd fruit a fragrance shed
And hung in hand-reach overhead,
In nest of blossoms on the shoot,
The very shoot that bore the fruit.

How ran lithe monkeys through the leaves!
How rush'd they through, brown clad and blue,
Like shuttles hurried through and through
The threads a hasty weaver weaves!

How quick they cast us fruits of gold,
Then loosen'd hand and all foothold,
And hung limp, limber, as if dead,
Hung low and listless overhead;
And all the time with half-oped eyes
Bent full on us in mute surprise—
Look'd wisely, too, as wise hens do
That watch you with the head askew.

The long day through from blossom'd trees
There came the sweet song of sweet bees,
With chorus-tones of cockatoo
That slid his beak along the bough,
And walk'd and talk'd and hung and swung,
In crown of gold and coat of blue,
The wisest fool that ever sung,
Or wore a crown, or held a tongue.

Oh! when we broke the somber wood
And pierced at last the sunny plain,
How wild and still with wonder stood
The proud mustangs with banner'd mane,
And necks that never knew a rein,
And nostrils lifted high, and blown,
Fierce breathing as a hurricane:
Yet by their leader held the while
In solid column, square and file
And ranks more martial than our own!

Some one above the common kind,
Some one to look to, lean upon,
I think is much a woman's mind;
But it was mine, and I had drawn
A rein beside the chief while we
Rode through the forest leisurely;
When he grew kind and question'd me
Of kindred, home, and home affair,
Of how I came to wander there,
And had my father herds and land
And men in hundreds at command?
At which I silent shook my head,
Then, timid, met his eyes and said:
"Not so. Where sunny foothills run
Down to the North Pacific sea,
And Willamette meets the sun
In many angles, patiently
My father tends his flocks of snow,
And turns alone the mellow sod
And sows some fields not over broad,
And mourns my long delay in vain,
Nor bids one serve-man come or go;
While mother from her wheel or churn,
And may be from the milking shed,
Oft lifts an humble, weary head
To watch and wish her boy's return
Across the camas' blossom'd plain."

He held his bent head very low,
A sudden sadness in his air;
Then turn'd and touch'd my yellow hair
And tossed the long locks in his hand,
Toy'd with them, smiled, and let them go,
Then thrumm'd about his saddle bow
As thought ran swift across his face;
Then turning sudden from his place,
He gave some short and quick command.
They brought the best steed of the band,
They swung a rifle at my side,
He bade me mount and by him ride,
And from that hour to the end
I never felt the need of friend.

Far in the wildest quinine wood
We found a city old—so old,
Its very walls were turned to mould,
And stately trees upon them stood.
No history has mention'd it,
No map has given it a place;
The last dim trace of tribe and race—
The world's forgetfulness is fit.

It held one structure grand and moss'd,
Mighty as any castle sung,
And old when oldest Ind was young,
With threshold Christian never cross'd;
A temple builded to the sun,
Along whose somber altar-stone
Brown, bleeding virgins had been strown
Like leaves, when leaves are crisp and dun,
In ages ere the Sphinx was born,
Or Babylon had birth or morn.
My chief led up the marble step—
He ever led, through that wild land—
When down the stones, with double hand
To his machete, a Sun priest leapt,
Hot bent to barter life for life.
The chieftain drave his bowie knife,
Full through his thick and broad breast-bone,
And broke the point against the stone,
The dark stone of the temple wall.
I saw him loose his hold and fall
Full length with head hung down the step;
I saw run down a ruddy flood
Of smoking, pulsing human blood.
Then from the wall a woman crept
And kiss'd the gory hands and face,
And smote herself. Then one by one
Some dark priests crept and did the same,
Then bore the dead man from the place.
Down darken'd aisles the brown priests came,
So picture-like, with sandal'd feet
And long, gray, dismal, grass-wove gowns,
So like the pictures of old time,
And stood all still and dark of frowns,
At blood upon the stone and street.
So we laid ready hand to sword
And boldly spoke some bitter word;
But they were stubborn still, and stood
Fierce frowning as a winter wood,
And mutt'ring something of the crime
Of blood upon a temple stone,
As if the first that it had known.

We strode on through each massive door
With clash of steel at heel, and with
Some swords all red and ready drawn.
I traced the sharp edge of my sword
Along both marble wall and floor
For crack or crevice; there was none.
From one vast mount of marble stone
The mighty temple had been cored
By nut-brown children of the sun,
When stars were newly bright and blithe
Of song along the rim of dawn,
A mighty marble monolith!

* * * * * * * *

III.

* * * * * * * *

Through marches through the mazy wood
And may be through too much of blood,
At last we came down to the seas.
A city stood, white wall'd, and brown
With age, in nest of orange trees;
And this we won and many a town
And rancho reaching up and down,
Then rested in the red-hot days
Beneath the blossom'd orange trees,
Made drowsy with the drum of bees,
And drank in peace the south-sea breeze,
Made sweet with sweeping boughs of bays.

Well! there were maidens, shy at first,
And then, ere long, not over shy,
Yet pure of soul and proudly chare.
No love on earth has such an eye!
No land there is, is bless'd or curs'd
With such a limb or grace of face,
Or gracious form, or genial air!
In all the bleak North-land not one
Hath been so warm of soul to me
As coldest soul by that warm sea,
Beneath the bright hot centred sun.

No lands where northern ices are
Approach, or ever dare compare
With warm loves born beneath the sun—
The one the cold white steady star,
The lifted shifting sun the one.
I grant you fond, I grant you fair,
I grant you honor trust and truth,
And years as beautiful as youth,
And many years beneath the sun,

And faith as fix'd as any star;
But all the North-land hath not one
So warm of soul as sun-maids are.

I was but in my boyhood then,—
I count my fingers over, so,
And find it years and years ago,
And I am scarcely yet of men.
But I was tall and lithe and fair,
With rippled tide of yellow hair,
And prone to mellowness of heart,
While she was tawny-red like wine,
With black hair boundless as the night.
As for the rest I knew my part,
At least was apt, and willing quite
To learn, to listen, and incline
To teacher warm and wise as mine.

O bright, bronzed maidens of the Sun!
So fairer far to look upon
Than curtains of the Solomon,
Or Kedar's tents, or any one,
Or any thing beneath the Sun!
What follow'd then? What has been done?
And said, and writ, and read, and sung?
What will be writ and read again,
While love is life, and life remain?—
While maids will heed, and men have tongue?

What follow'd then? But let that pass.
I hold one picture in my heart,
Hung curtain'd, and not any part
Of all its dark tint ever has
Been look'd upon by any one
Beneath the broad all-seeing sun.

Love well who will, love wise who can,
But love, be loved, for God is love;
Love pure, as cherubim above;
Love maids, and hate not any man.
Sit as sat we by orange tree,
Beneath the broad bough and grape-vine
Top-tangled in the tropic shine,
Close face to face, close to the sea,
And full of the red-centred sun,
With grand sea-songs upon the soul,
Roll'd melody on melody,
As echoes of deep organ's roll,
And love, nor question any one.

If God is love, is love not God?
As high priests say, let prophets sing,
Without reproach or reckoning;
This much I say, knees knit to sod,
And low voice lifted, questioning.

Let hearts be pure and strong and true,
Let lips be luscious and blood-red,
Let earth in gold be garmented
And tented in her tent of blue.
Let goodly rivers glide between
Their leaning willow walls of green,
Let all things be fill'd of the sun,
And full of warm winds of the sea,
And I beneath my vine and tree
Take rest, nor war with any one;
Then I will thank God with full cause,
Say this is well, is as it was.

Let lips be red, for God has said
Love is as one gold-garmented,
And made them so for such a time.
Therefore let lips be red, therefore
Let love be ripe in ruddy prime,
Let hope beat high, let hearts be true,
And you be wise thereat, and you
Drink deep and ask not any more.

Let red lips lift, proud curl'd to kiss,
And round limbs lean and raise and reach
In love too passionate for speech,
Too full of blessedness and bliss
For anything but this and this;
Let luscious lips lean hot to kiss
And swoon in love, while all the air
Is redolent with balm of trees,
And mellow with the song of bees,
While birds sit singing everywhere—
And you will have not any more
Than I in boyhood, by that shore
Of olives, had in years of yore.

Let the unclean think things unclean;
I swear tip-toed, with lifted hands,

That we were pure as sea-wash'd sands,
That not one coarse thought came between;
Believe or disbelieve who will,
Unto the pure all things are pure;
As for the rest, I can endure
Alike your good will or their ill.

Aye! she was rich in blood and gold—
More rich in love, grown over-bold
From its own consciousness of strength.
How warm! Oh, not for any cause
Could I declare how warm she was,
In her brown beauty and hair's length.
We loved in the sufficient sun,
We lived in elements of fire,
For love is fire in fierce desire;
Yet lived as pure as priest and nun.

We lay slow rocking by the bay
In slim canoe beneath the crags
Thick-topp'd with palm, like sweeping flags
Between us and the burning day.
The alligator's head lay low
Or lifted from his rich rank fern,
And watch'd us and the tide by turn,
As we slow cradled to and fro.

And slow we cradled on till night,
And told the old tale, overtold,
As misers in recounting gold
Each time to take a new delight.
With her pure passion-given grace
She drew her warm self close to me;
And her two brown hands on my knee,
And her two black eyes in my face,
She then grew sad and guess'd at ill,
And in the future seem'd to see
With woman's ken of prophecy;
Yet proffer'd her devotion still.
And plaintive so she gave a sign,
A token cut of virgin gold,
That all her tribe should ever hold
Its wearer as some one divine,
Nor touch him with a hostile hand.
And I in turn gave her a blade,
A dagger, worn as well by maid
As man, in that half lawless land.
It had a massive silver hilt,
It had a keen and cunning blade,
A gift by chief and comrades made
For reckless blood at Rivas spilt.
"Show this," said I, "too well 'tis known,
And worth a hundred lifted spears,
Should ill beset your sunny years;
There is not one in Walker's band,
But at the sight of this alone,
Will reach a brave and ready hand,
And make your right, or wrong, his own."

IV.

Love while 'tis day; night cometh soon,
Wherein no man or maiden may;
Love in the strong young prime of day;
Drink drunk with love in ripe red noon,
Red noon of love and life and sun;
Walk in love's light as in sunshine,
Drink in that sun as drinking wine,
Drink swift, nor question any one;
For fortunes change, as man or moon,
And wane like warm full days of June.

Oh Love, so fair of promises,
Bend here thy brow, blow here thy kiss,
Bend here thy bow above the storm
But once, if only this once more.
Comes there no patient Christ to save,
Touch and re-animate thy form
Long three days dead and in the grave:
Spread here thy silken net of jet;
Since fortunes change, turn and forget,
Since man must fall for some sharp sin,
Be thou the pit that I fall in;
I seek no safer fall than this.
Since man must die for some dark sin,
Blind leading blind, let come to this,
And my death crime be one deep kiss.

V.

Ill comes disguised in many forms:
Fair winds are but a prophecy
Of foulest winds full soon to be—
The brighter these, the blacker they;
The clearest night has darkest day,

And brightest days bring blackest storms.
There came reverses to our arms;
I saw the signal-light's alarms
All night red-crescenting the bay.
The foe poured down a flood next day
As strong as tides when tides are high,
And drove us bleeding to the sea,
In such wild haste of flight that we
Had hardly time to arm and fly.

Blown from the shore, borne far at sea,
I lifted my two hands on high
With wild soul plashing to the sky,
And cried, "O more than crowns to me,
Farewell at last to love and thee!"
I walked the deck, I kiss'd my hand
Back to the far and fading shore,
And bent a knee as to implore,
Until the last dark head of land
Slid down behind the dimpled sea.

At last I sank in troubled sleep,
A very child, rock'd by the deep,
Sad questioning the fate of her
Before the savage conqueror.

The loss of comrades, power, place,
A city wall'd, cool shaded ways,
Cost me no care at all; somehow
I only saw her sad brown face,
And—I was younger then than now.

Red flashed the sun across the deck,
Slow flapped the idle sails, and slow
The black ship cradled to and fro.
Afar my city lay, a speck
Of white against a line of blue;
Around, half lounging on the deck,
Some comrades chatted two by two.
I held a new-fill'd glass of wine,
And with the Mate talk'd as in play
Of fierce events of yesterday,
To coax his light life into mine.

He jerked the wheel, as slow he said,
Low laughing with averted head,
And so, half sad: "You bet they'll fight;
They follow'd in canim, canoe,
A perfect fleet, that on the blue
Lay dancing till the mid of night.
Would you believe! one little cuss"—
(He turned his stout head slow sidewise,
And 'neath his hat-rim took the skies)—
"In petticoats did follow us
The livelong night, and at the dawn
Her boat lay rocking in the lee,
Scarce one short pistol-shot from me."
This said the mate, half mournfully,
Then peck'd at us; for he had drawn,
By bright light heart and homely wit,
A knot of men around the wheel,
Which he stood whirling like a reel,
For the still ship reck'd not of it.

"And where's she now?" one careless said,
With eyes slow lifting to the brine,
Swift swept the instant far by mine;
The bronzed mate listed, shook his head,
Spirted a stream of ambier wide
Across and over the ship side,
Jerk'd at the wheel, and slow replied:

"She had a dagger in her hand,
She rose, she raised it, tried to stand,
But fell, and so upset herself;
Yet still the poor brown savage elf,
Each time the long light wave would toss
And lift her form from out the sea,
Would shake a sharp bright blade at me,
With rich hilt chased a cunning cross.
At last she sank, but still the same
She shook her dagger in the air,
As if to still defy and dare,
And sinking seem'd to call your name."

I let my wine glass crashing fall,
I rush'd across the deck, and all
The sea I swept and swept again,
With lifted hand, with eye and glass,
But all was idle and in vain.
I saw a red-bill'd sea-gull pass,
A petrel sweeping round and round,
I heard the far white sea-surf sound,
But no sign could I hear or see
Of one so more than seas to me.

I cursed the ship, the shore, the sea,
The brave brown mate, the bearded men;
I had a fever then, and then
Ship, shore and sea were one to me;
And weeks we on the dead waves lay,
And I more truly dead than they.
At last some rested on an isle;
The few strong-breasted, with a smile,
Returning to the hostile shore,
Scarce counting of the pain or cost,
Scarce recking if they won or lost;
They sought but action, ask'd no more;
They counted life but as a game,
With full per cent. against them, and
Staked all upon a single hand,
And lost or won, content the same.

I never saw my chief again,
I never sought again the shore,
Or saw my white-walled city more.
I could not bear the more than pain
At sight of blossom'd orange trees,
Or blended song of birds and bees,
The sweeping shadows of the palm
Or spicy breath of bay and balm.
And, striving to forget the while,
I wandered through a dreary isle,
Here black with juniper, and there
Made white with goats in shaggy coats,
The only things that anywhere
We found with life in all the land,
Save birds that ran long-bill'd and brown,
Long legg'd and still as shadows are,
Like dancing shadows up and down
The sea-rim on the swelt'ring sand.

The warm sea laid his dimpled face,
With all his white locks smoothed in place,
As if asleep against the land;
Great turtles slept upon his breast,
As thick as eggs in any nest;
I could have touch'd them with my hand.

VI.

I would some things were dead and hid,
Well dead and buried deep as hell,
With recollection dead as well,
And resurrection God forbid.
They irk me with their weary spell
Of fascination, eye to eye.
And hot mesmeric serpent hiss,
Through all the dull eternal days.
Let them turn by, go on their ways,
Let them depart or let me die;
For life is but a beggar's lie,
And as for death, I grin at it;
I do not care one whiff or whit
Whether it be or that or this.

I give my hand; the world is wide;
Then farewell memories of yore,
Between us let strife be no more;
Turn as you choose to either side;
Say, Fare-you-well, shake hands and say—
Speak fair, and say with stately grace,
Hand clutching hand, face bent to face—
Farewell forever and a day.

O passion-toss'd and piteous past,
Part now, part well, part wide apart,
As ever ships on ocean slid
Down, down the sea, hull, sail, and mast;
And in the album of my heart
Let hide the pictures of your face,
With other pictures in their place,
Slid over like a coffin's lid.

VII.

The days and grass grow long together;
They now fell short and crisp again,
And all the fair face of the main
Grew dark and wrinkled as the weather.
Through all the summer sun's decline
Fell news of triumphs and defeats,
Of hard advances, hot retreats—
Then days and days and not a line.

At last one night they came. I knew
Ere yet the boat had touched the land
That all was lost; they were so few
I near could count them on one hand;
But he, the leader, led no more.
The proud chief still disdain'd to fly,
But like one wreck'd, clung to the shore,
And struggled on, and struggling fell

From power to a prison-cell,
And only left that cell to die.

My recollection, like a ghost,
Goes from this sea to that sea-side,
Goes and returns as turns the tide,
Then turns again unto the coast.
I know not which I mourn the most,
My chief or my unwedded wife.
The one was as the lordly sun,
To joy in, bask in, and admire;
The peaceful moon was as the one,
To love, to look to, and desire;
And both a part of my young life.

VIII.

Years after, shelter'd from the sun
Beneath a Sacramento bay,
A black Muchacho by me lay
Along the long grass crisp and dun,
His brown mule browsing by his side,
And told with all a Peon's pride
How he once fought; how long and well,
Broad breast to breast, red hand to hand,
Against a foe for his fair land,
And how the fierce invader fell;
And, artless, told me how he died:

How walked he from the prison-wall
Dress'd like some prince for a parade,
And made no note of man or maid,
But gazed out calmly over all.
He look'd far off, half paused, and then
Above the mottled sea of men
He kiss'd his thin hand to the sun;
Then smiled so proudly none had known
But he was stepping to a throne,
Yet took no note of any one.

A nude brown beggar Peon child,
Encouraged as the captive smiled,
Look'd up, half scared, half pitying;
He stopp'd, he caught it from the sands,
Put bright coins in its two brown hands,
Then strode on like another king.

Two deep, a musket's length, they stood
A-front, in sandals, nude, and dun
As death and darkness wove in one,
Their thick lips thirsting for his blood.
He took each black hand one by one,
And, smiling with a patient grace,
Forgave them all and took his place.

He bared his broad brow to the sun,
Gave one long, last look to the sky,
The white wing'd clouds that hurried by,
The olive hills in orange hue;
A last list to the cockatoo
That hung by beak from mango-bough
Hard by, and hung and sung as though
He never was to sing again,
Hung all red-crown'd and robed in green,
With belts of gold and blue between.—

A bow, a touch of heart, a pall
Of purple smoke, a crash, a thud,
A warrior's raiment rolled in blood,
A face in dust and—that was all.

Success had made him more than king;
Defeat made him the vilest thing
In name, contempt or hate can bring;
So much the leaded dice of war
Do make or mar of character.

Speak ill who will of him, he died
In all disgrace; say of the dead
His heart was black, his hands were red—
Say this much, and be satisfied;
Gloat over it all undenied.
I simply say he was my friend
When strong of hand and fair of fame:
Dead and disgraced, I stand the same
To him, and so shall to the end.

I lay this crude wreath on his dust,
Inwove with sad, sweet memories
Recall'd here by these colder seas.
I leave the wild bird with his trust,
To sing and say him nothing wrong;
I wake no rivalry of song.

He lies low in the levell'd sand,
Unshelter'd from the tropic sun,
And now of all he knew not one

Will speak him fair in that far land.
Perhaps 'twas this that made me seek,
Disguised, his grave one winter-tide;
A weakness for the weaker side,
A siding with the helpless weak.

A palm not far held out a hand,
Hard by a long green bamboo swung,
And bent like some great bow unstrung,
And quiver'd like a willow wand;
Perch'd on its fruits that crooked hang,
Beneath a broad banana's leaf,
A bird in rainbow splendor sang
A low, sad song of temper'd grief.

No sod, no sign, no cross nor stone
But at his side a cactus green
Upheld its lances long and keen;
It stood in sacred sands alone,
Flat-palm'd and fierce with lifted spears;
One bloom of crimson crown'd its head,
A drop of blood, so bright, so red,
Yet redolent as roses' tears.

In my left hand I held a shell,
All rosy lipp'd and pearly red;
I laid it by his lowly bed,
For he did love so passing well
The grand songs of the solemn sea.
O shell! sing well, wild, with a will,
When storms blow loud and birds be still,
The wildest sea-song known to thee!

I said some things with folded hands,
Soft whisper'd in the dim sea-sound,
And eyes held humbly to the ground,
And frail knees sunken in the sands.
He had done more than this for me,
And yet I could not well do more:
I turn'd me down the olive shore,
And set a sad face to the sea.

LONDON, 1871.

I first wrote this poem for John Brown. You can see John Brown of Harper's Ferry in his bearing, for Walker was not of imposing presence; also in his tenderness to the colored child on his way to death. But when about to publish I saw a cruel account of Gen. Walker and his grave at Truxillo, Honduras, in a London newspaper. It stated, among other mean things, that a board stood at the head of his grave with this inscription:

"Here lies buried W. W.,
Who never more will trouble you, trouble you."

I by good fortune had ready for my new book an account of a ride through a Central American forest. Putting this and the John Brown poem together in haste and anger, and working them over, I called the new poem "With Walker in Nicaragua."

I had known Walker in California, as a brave and gentle man of books. After I had been hurt a second time in the Indian wars, Gen. Crook, with whom I had been as guide and interpreter, sent me to San Francisco to be treated, where an officer asked me to go East with him to finish school, and I gladly set out with him, as there was a possibility of West Point ahead of me. We found trouble between the transit ship line and Gen. Walker, and we could not pass through Nicaragua. I should like, were it possible, to say how much I owe to these army officers of the remote border. They were, many of them, years after, the heroes of the Civil war. Yet were they ever, even there in the most savage wilderness the gentlest of gentle men. With such men on the one hand and the wild red men on the other I touched and took in at once the very extremes of existence, and the stream of life, even this early, flowed swift and strong and deep and wide. See here again how fortunate were my misfortunes! For had it not been for my many cruel wounds in Indian wars these men, busy with graver things, would not have been drawn to their "Boy veteran" and helped him along with his books and their sympathy and their better sense in so many ways. And how true they were, and still are, the very few survivors, as witness, more than a quarter of a century after the old Modoc days, in their loyalty and love they made me a comrade in the Army of the Potomac. Truly, as Bayard Taylor says:

"The bravest are the tenderest;
The loving are the daring."

The officer returned but I stayed with Walker a little time till a ship from Chile going to the Columbia for lumber took me away. And so, knowing how good and dauntless he was, I determined to defend the grave of my dead, even though it should wreck my book and fortunes. For it was the English who, indirectly, put him to death, and now to heap disgrace upon his lowly grave, it was to me intolerable, and made me reckless of results. However, the British showed their greatness by treating me all the better for hitting back hard as I could for my helpless dead. I was teaching school in Washington Territory when the story of John Brown's raid and death reached me and then and there I began this poem.

THE TALE OF THE TALL ALCALDE.

Shadows that shroud the to-morrow,
Glists from the life that's within,
Traces of pain and of sorrow,
And maybe a trace of sin,
Reachings for God in the darkness,
And for—what should have been.

Stains from the gall and the wormwood,
Memories bitter like myrrh,
A sad brown face in a fir wood,
Blotches of heart's blood here,
But never the sound of a wailing,
Never the sign of a tear.

Where mountains repose in their blueness,
Where the sun first lands in his newness,
And marshals his beams and his lances,
Ere down to the vale he advances
With visor erect, and rides swiftly
On the terrible night in his way,
And slays him, and, dauntless and deftly,
Hews out the beautiful day
With his flashing sword of silver,—
Lay nestled the town of Renalda,
Far famed for its stately Alcalde,
The iron judge of the mountain mine,
With heart like the heart of woman,
Humanity more than human;—
Far famed for its gold and silver,
Fair maids and its mountain wine.

* * * * * * * *

The feast was full, and the guests afire,
The shaven priest and the portly squire,
The solemn judge and the smiling dandy,
The duke and the don and the commandante,
All, save one, shouted or sang divine,
Sailing in one great sea of wine;
Till roused, red-crested knight Chanticleer
Answer'd and echo'd their song and cheer,
Some boasted of broil, encounter, in battle,
Some boasted of maidens most cleverly won,
Boasted of duels most valiantly done,
Of leagues of land and of herds of cattle,
These men at the feast up in fair Renalda.
All boasted but one, the calm Alcalde:
Though hard they press'd from first of the feast,
Press'd commandanté, press'd poet and priest,
And steadily still an attorney press'd,
With lifted glass and his face aglow,
Heedless of host and careless of guest—
"A tale! the tale of your life, so ho!
For not one man in all Mexico
Can trace your history two decade."
A hand on the rude one's lip was laid:
"Sacred, my son," the priest went on,
"Sacred the secrets of every one,
Inviolate as an altar-stone.
Yet what in the life of one who must
Have lived a life that is half divine—
Have been so pure to be so just,
What can there be, O advocate,
In the life of one so desolate

Of luck with matron, or love with maid,
Midnight revel or escapade,
To stir the wonder of men at wine?
But should the Alcalde choose, you
know,"—
(And here his voice fell soft and low,
As he set his wine-horn in its place,
And look'd in the judge's careworn face)—
"To weave us a tale that points a moral.
Out of his vivid imagination,
Of lass or of love, or lover's quarrel,
Naught of his fame or name or station
Shall lose in luster by its relation."

Softly the judge set down his horn,
Kindly look'd on the priest all shorn,
And gazed in the eyes of the advocate
With a touch of pity, but none of hate;
Then look'd he down in the brimming
horn,
Half defiant and half forlorn.

Was it a tear? Was it a sigh?
Was it a glance of the priest's black eye?
Or was it the drunken revel-cry
That smote the rock of his frozen heart
And forced his pallid lips apart?
Or was it the weakness like to woman
Yearning for sympathy
Through the dark years,
Spurning the secrecy,
Burning for tears,
Proving him human,—
As he said to the men of the silver mine,
With their eyes held up as to one divine,
With his eyes held down to his untouch'd
wine:

"It might have been where moonbeams
kneel
At night beside some rugged steep;
It might have been where breakers reel,
Or mild waves cradle one to sleep;
It might have been in peaceful life,
Or mad tumult and storm and strife,
I drew my breath; it matters not.
A silver'd head, a sweetest cot,
A sea of tamarack and pine,
A peaceful stream, a balmy clime,
A cloudless sky, a sister's smile,
A mother's love that sturdy Time
Has strengthen'd as he strengthens wine,
Are mine, are with me all the while,
Are hung in memory's sounding halls,
Are graven on her glowing walls.
But rage, nor rack, nor wrath of man,
Nor prayer of priest, nor price, nor ban
Can wring from me their place or name,
Or why, or when, or whence I came;
Or why I left that childhood home,
A child of form yet old of soul,
And sought the wilds where tempests roll
O'er snow peaks white as driven foam.

"Mistaken and misunderstood,
I sought a deeper wild and wood.
A girlish form, a childish face,
A wild waif drifting from place to place.

"Oh for the skies of rolling blue,
The balmy hours when lovers woo,
When the moon is doubled as in desire,
And the lone bird cries in his crest of fire,
Like vespers calling the soul to bliss
In the blessed love of the life above,
Ere it has taken the stains of this!

"The world afar, yet at my feet,
Went steadily and sternly on;
I almost fancied I could meet
The crush and bustle of the street,
When from my mountain I look'd down.
And deep down in the cañon's mouth
The long-tom ran and pick-ax rang,
And pack-trains coming from the south
Went stringing round the mountain high
In long gray lines, as wild geese fly,
While mul'teers shouted hoarse and high,
And dusty, dusky mul'teers sang—
'Senora with the liquid eye!
No floods can ever quench the flame,
Or frozen snows my passion tame,
O Juanna with the coal-black eye!
O senorita, bide a bye!'

"Environed by a mountain wall,
That caped in snowy turrets stood;
So fierce, so terrible, so tall,
It never yet had been defiled
By track or trail, save by the wild
Free children of the wildest wood;
An unkiss'd virgin at my feet,
Lay my pure, hallow'd, dreamy vale,
Where breathed the essence of my tale;
Lone dimple in the mountain's face,
Lone Eden in a boundless waste
It lay so beautiful! so sweet!

"There in the sun's decline I stood
By God's form wrought in pink and pearl,
My peerless, dark-eyed Indian girl;
And gazed out from a fringe of wood,
With full-fed soul and feasting eyes,
Upon an earthly paradise.
Inclining to the south it lay,
And long league's southward roll'd away,
Until the sable-feather'd pines
And tangled boughs and amorous vines
Closed like besiegers on the scene,
The while the stream that intertwined
Had barely room to flow between.
It was unlike all other streams,
Save those seen in sweet summer dreams;
For sleeping in its bed of snow,
Nor rock nor stone was ever known,
But only shining, shifting sands,
Forever sifted by unseen hands.
It curved, it bent like Indian bow,
And like an arrow darted through,
Yet uttered not a sound nor breath,
Nor broke a ripple from the start;
It was as swift, as still as death,
Yet was so clear, so pure, so sweet,
It wound its way into your heart
As through the grasses at your feet.

"Once, through the tall untangled grass,
I saw two black bears careless pass,
And in the twilight turn to play;
I caught my rifle to my face,
She raised her hand with quiet grace
And said: 'Not so, for us the day,
The night belongs to such as they.'

"And then from out the shadow'd wood
The antler'd deer came stalking down
In half a shot of where I stood;
Then stopp'd and stamp'd impatiently,
Then shook his head and antlers high,
And then his keen horns backward threw
Upon his shoulders broad and brown,
And thrust his muzzle in the air,
Snuff'd proudly; then a blast he blew
As if to say: "No danger there."
And then from out the sable wood
His mate and two sweet dappled fawns
Stole forth, and by the monarch stood,
Such bronzes, as on kingly lawns;
Or seen in picture, read in tale.
Then he, as if to reassure
The timid, trembling and demure,
Again his antlers backward threw,
Again a blast defiant blew,
Then led them proudly down the vale.

"I watch'd the forms of darkness come
Slow stealing from their sylvan home,
And pierce the sunlight drooping low
And weary, as if loth to go.
Night stain'd the lances as he bled,
And, bleeding and pursued, he fled
Across the vale into the wood.
I saw the tall grass bend its head
Beneath the stately martial tread
Of Shades, pursuer and pursued.

"'Behold the clouds,' Winnema said,
'All purple with the blood of day;
The night has conquer'd in the fray,
The shadows live, and light is dead.'

"She turn'd to Shasta gracefully,
Around whose hoar and mighty head
Still roll'd a sunset sea of red,
While troops of clouds a space below
Were drifting wearily and slow,
As seeking shelter for the night

Like weary sea-birds in their flight;
Then curved her right arm gracefully
Above her brow, and bow'd her knee,
And chanted in an unknown tongue
Words sweeter than were ever sung.

"'And what means this?' I gently said.
'I prayed to God, the Yopitone,
Who dwells on yonder snowy throne,'
She softly said with drooping head;
'I bow'd to God. He heard my prayer,
I felt his warm breath in my hair,
He heard me all my wishes tell,
For God is good, and all is well.'

"The dappled and the dimpled skies,
The timid stars, the spotted moon,
All smiled as sweet as sun at noon.
Her eyes were like the rabbit's eyes,
Her mien, her manner, just as mild,
And though a savage war-chief's child,
She would not harm the lowliest worm.
And, though her beaded foot was firm,
And though her airy step was true,
She would not crush a drop of dew.

"Her love was deeper than the sea,
And stronger than the tidal rise,
And clung in all its strength to me.
A face like hers is never seen
This side the gates of paradise,
Save in some Indian Summer scene,
And then none ever sees it twice—
Is seen but once, and seen no more,
Seen but to tempt the skeptic soul,
And show a sample of the whole
That Heaven has in store.

"You might have plucked beams from the moon,
Or torn the shadow from the pine
When on its dial track at noon,
But not have parted us one hour,
She was so wholly, truly mine.
And life was one unbroken dream
Of purest bliss and calm delight,
A flow'ry-shored, untroubled stream
Of sun and song, of shade and bower,
A full-moon'd serenading night.

"Sweet melodies were in the air,
And tame birds caroll'd everywhere.
I listened to the lisping grove
And cooing pink-eyed turtle dove,
I loved her with the holiest love;
Believing with a brave belief
That everything beneath the skies
Was beautiful and born to love,
That man had but to love, believe,
And earth would be a paradise
As beautiful as that above.
My goddess, Beauty, I adored,
Devoutly, fervid, her alone;
My Priestess, Love, unceasing pour'd
Pure incense on her altar-stone.

"I carved my name in coarse design
Once on a birch down by the way,
At which she gazed, as she would say,
'What does this say? What is this sign?'
And when I gaily said, 'Some day
Some one will come and read my name,
And I will live in song and fame,
Entwined with many a mountain tale,
As he who first found this sweet vale,
And they will give the place my name,'
She was most sad, and troubled much,
And looked in silence far away;
Then started trembling from my touch,
And when she turn'd her face again,
I read unutterable pain.

"At last she answered through her tears,
'Ah! yes; this, too, foretells my fears:
Yes, they will come—my race must go
As fades a vernal fall of snow;
And you be known, and I forgot
Like these brown leaves that rust and rot
Beneath my feet; and it is well:
I do not seek to thrust my name
On those who here, hereafter, dwell,
Because I have before them dwelt;

They too will have their tales to tell,
They too will have their time and fame.

"'Yes, they will come, come even now;
The dim ghosts on yon mountain's brow,
Gray Fathers of my tribe and race,
Do beckon to us from their place,
And hurl red arrows through the air
At night, to bid our braves beware.
A footprint by the clear McCloud,
Unlike aught ever seen before,
Is seen. The crash of rifles loud
Is heard along its farther shore.'

* * * * * * * *

"What tall and tawny men were these,
As somber, silent, as the trees
They moved among! and sad some way
With temper'd sadness, ever they,—
Yet not with sorrow born of fear.
The shadow of their destinies
They saw approaching year by year,
And murmur'd not. They saw the sun
Go down; they saw the peaceful moon
Move on in silence to her rest,
Saw white streams winding to the west;
And thus they knew that oversoon,
Somehow, somewhere, for every one
Was rest beyond the setting sun.
They knew not, never dream'd of doubt,
But turn'd to death as to a sleep,
And died with eager hands held out
To reaching hands beyond the deep,—
And died with choicest bow at hand,
And quiver full, and arrow drawn
For use, when sweet to-morrow's dawn
Should waken in the Spirit Land.

"What wonder that I linger'd there
With Nature's children! Could I part
With those that met me heart to heart,
And made me welcome, spoke me fair,
Were first of all that understood
My waywardness from others' ways,
My worship of the true and good,
And earnest love of Nature's God?
Go court the mountains in the clouds,
And clashing thunder, and the shrouds
Of tempests, and eternal shocks,
And fast and pray as one of old
In earnestness, and ye shall hold
The mysteries; shall hold the rod
That passes seas, that smites the rocks
Where streams of melody and song
Shall run as white streams rush and flow
Down from the mountains' crests of snow,
Forever, to a thirsting throng.

* * * * * * *

"Between the white man and the red
There lies no neutral, halfway ground.
I heard afar the thunder sound
That soon should burst above my head,
And made my choice; I laid my plan,
And childlike chose the weaker side;
And ever have, and ever will,
While might is wrong and wrongs remain,
As careless of the world as I
Am careless of a cloudless sky.
With wayward and romantic joy
I gave my pledge like any boy,
But kept my promise like a man,
And lost; yet with the lesson still
Would gladly do the same again.

"'They come! they come! the pale-face come!'
The chieftain shouted where he stood,
Sharp watching at the margin wood,
And gave the war-whoop's treble yell,
That like a knell on fond hearts fell
Far watching from my rocky home.

"No nodding plumes or banners fair
Unfurl'd or fretted through the air;
No screaming fife or rolling drum
Did challenge brave of soul to come:
But, silent, sinew-bows were strung,
And, sudden, heavy quivers hung
And, swiftly, to the battle sprung
Tall painted braves with tufted hair,
Like death-black banners in the air.

"And long they fought, and firm and well
And silent fought, and silent fell,

Save when they gave the fearful yell
Of death, defiance, or of hate.
But what were feathered flints to fate?
And what were yells to seething lead?
And what the few and untrained feet
To troops that came with martial tread,
And moved by wood and hill and stream
As thick as people in a street,
As strange as spirits in a dream?

"From pine and poplar, here and there,
A cloud, a flash, a crash, a thud,
A warrior's garments roll'd in blood,
A yell that rent the mountain air
Of fierce defiance and despair,
Told all who fell, and when and where.
Then tighter drew the coils around,
And closer grew the battle-ground,
And fewer feather'd arrows fell,
And fainter grew the battle yell,
Until upon that hill was heard
The short, sharp whistle of the bird:
Until that blood-soaked battle hill
Was still as death, so more than still.

"The calm, that cometh after all,
Look'd sweetly down at shut of day,
Where friend and foe commingled lay
Like leaves of forest as they fall.
Afar the somber mountains frown'd,
Here tall pines wheel'd their shadows round,
Like long, slim fingers of a hand
That sadly pointed out the dead.
Like some broad shield high overhead
The great white moon led on and on,
As leading to the better land.
All night I heard the cricket's trill,
That night-bird calling from the hill—
The place was so profoundly still.

"The mighty chief at last was down,
A broken gate of brass and pride!
His hair all dust, and this his crown!
His firm lips were compress'd in hate
To foes, yet all content with fate;
While, circled round him thick, the foe
Had folded hands in dust, and died.
His tomahawk lay at his side,
All blood, beside his broken bow.
One arm stretch'd out, still over-bold,
One hand half doubled hid in dust,
And clutch'd the earth, as if to hold
His hunting grounds still in his trust.

"Here tall grass bow'd its tassel'd head
In dewy tears above the dead,
And there they lay in crook'd fern,
That waved and wept above by turn:
And further on, by somber trees,
They lay, wild heroes of wild deeds,
In shrouds alone of weeping weeds,
Bound in a never-to-be-broken peace.

"No trust that day had been betrayed;
Not one had falter'd, not one brave
Survived the fearful struggle, save
One—save I the renegade,
The red man's friend, and—they held me so
For this alone—the white man's foe.

"They bore me bound for many a day
Through fen and wild, by foamy flood,
From my dear mountains far away,
Where an adobé prison stood
Beside a sultry, sullen, town,
With iron eyes and stony frown;
And in a dark and narrow cell,
So hot it almost took my breath,
And seem'd but some outpost of hell,
They thrust me—as if I had been
A monster, in a monster's den.
I cried aloud, I courted death,
I call'd unto a strip of sky,
The only thing beyond my cell
That I could see, but no reply
Came but the echo of my breath.
I paced—how long I cannot tell—
My reason fail'd, I knew no more,
And swooning, fell upon the floor.
Then months went on, till deep one night,
When long thin bars of cool moonlight

Lay shimmering along the floor,
My senses came to me once more.

"My eyes look'd full into her eyes—
Into her soul so true and tried,
I thought myself in paradise,
And wonder'd when she too had died.
And then I saw the stripéd light
That struggled past the prison bar,
And in an instant, at the sight,
My sinking soul fell just as far
As could a star loosed by a jar
From out the setting in a ring,
The purpled semi-circled ring
That seems to circle us at night.

"She saw my senses had return'd,
Then swift to press my pallid face—
Then, as if spurn'd, she sudden turn'd
Her sweet face to the prison wall;
Her bosom rose, her hot tears fell
Fast as drip moss-stones in a well,
And then, as if subduing all
In one strong struggle of the soul
Be what they were of vows or fears,
With kisses and hot tender tears,
There in the deadly, loathsome place,
She bathed my pale and piteous face.

"I was so weak I could not speak
Or press my pale lips to her cheek;
I only looked my wish to share
The secret of her presence there.
Then looking through her falling hair,
She press'd her finger to her lips,
More sweet than sweets the brown bee sips.
More sad than any grief untold,
More silent than the milk-white moon,
She turned away. I heard unfold
An iron door, and she was gone.

"At last, one midnight, I was free;
Again I felt the liquid air
Around my hot brow like a sea,
Sweet as my dear Madonna's prayer,
Or benedictions on the soul;
Pure air, which God gives free to all,
Again I breathed without control—
Pure air that man would fain enthrall;
God's air, which man hath seized and sold
Unto his fellow-man for gold.

"I bow'd down to the bended sky,
I toss'd my two thin hands on high,
I call'd unto the crooked moon,
I shouted to the shining stars,
With breath and rapture uncontroll'd,
Like some wild school-boy loosed at noon,
Or comrade coming from the wars,
Hailing his companiers of old.

"Short time for shouting or delay,—
The cock is shrill, the east is gray,
Pursuit is made, I must away.
They cast me on a sinewy steed,
And bid me look to girth and guide—
A caution of but little need.
I dash the iron in his side,
Swift as the shooting stars I ride;
I turn, I see, to my dismay,
A silent rider red as they;
I glance again—it is my bride,
My love, my life, rides at my side.

"By gulch and gorge and brake and all,
Swift as the shining meteors fall,
We fly, and never sound nor word
But ringing mustang hoof is heard,
And limbs of steel and lungs of steam
Could not be stronger than theirs seem.
Grandly as in some joyous dream,
League on league, and hour on hour,
Far from keen pursuit, or power
Of sheriff or bailiff, high or low,
Into the bristling hills we go.

"Into the tumbled, clear McCloud,
White as the foldings of a shroud;
We dash into the dashing stream,
We breast the tide, we drop the rein,
We clutch the streaming, tangled mane—
And yet the rider at my side
Has never look nor word replied.

"Out in its foam, its rush, its roar,
Breasting away to the farther shore;
Steadily, bravely, gain'd at last,
Gain'd, where never a dastard foe
Has dared to come, or friend to go.
Pursuit is baffled and danger pass'd.

"Under an oak whose wide arms were
Lifting aloft, as if in prayer,
Under an oak, where the shining moon
Like feather'd snow in a winter noon
Quiver'd, sifted, and drifted down
In spars and bars on her shoulders brown:
And yet she was as silent still
As block stones toppled from the hill—
Great basalt blocks that near us lay,
Deep nestled in the grass untrod
By aught save wild beasts of the wood—
Great, massive, squared, and chisel'd
stone,
Like columns that had toppled down
From temple dome or tower crown,
Along some drifted, silent way
Of desolate and desert town
Built by the children of the sun.
And I in silence sat on one,
And she stood gazing far away
To where her childhood forests lay,
Still as the stone I sat upon.

"I sought to catch her to my breast
And charm her from her silent mood;
She shrank as if a beam, a breath,
Then silently before me stood,
Still, coldly, as the kiss of death.
Her face was darker than a pall,
Her presence was so proudly tall,
I would have started from the stone
Where I sat gazing up at her,
As from a form to earth unknown,
Had I possess'd the power to stir.

"'O touch me not, no more, no more;
'Tis past, and my sweet dream is o'er.
Impure! Impure! Impure!' she cried,
In words as sweetly, wierdly wild
As mingling of a rippled tide,
And music on the waters spill'd. . . .
'But you are free. Fly! Fly alone.
Yes, you will win another bride
In some far clime where nought is known
Of all that you have won or lost,
Or what your liberty has cost;
Will win you name, and place, and power,
And ne'er recall this face, this hour,
Save in some secret, deep regret,
Which I forgive and you'll forget.
Your destiny will lead you on
Where, open'd wide to welcome you,
Rich, ardent hearts and bosoms are,
And snowy arms, more purely fair,
And breasts—who dare say breasts more
true?

"'They said you had deserted me,
Had rued you of your wood and wild.
I knew, I knew it could not be,
I trusted as a trusting child.
I cross'd yon mountains bleak and high
That curve their rough backs to the sky,
I rode the white-maned mountain flood,
And track'd for weeks the trackless wood.
The good God led me, as before,
And brought me to your prison-door.

"'That madden'd call! that fever'd
moan!
I heard you in the midnight call
My own name through the massive wall,
In my sweet mountain-tongue and tone—
And yet you call'd so feebly wild,
I near mistook you for a child.

The keeper with his clinking keys
I sought, implored upon my knees
That I might see you, feel your breath,
Your brow, or breathe you low replies
Of comfort in your lonely death.
His red face shone, his redder eyes
Were like a fiend's that feeds on lies.
Again I heard your feeble moan,
I cried—unto a heart of stone.
Ah! why the hateful horrors tell?
Enough! I crept into your cell.

" 'I nursed you, lured you back to life,
And when you knew, and called me wife
And love, with pale lips rife
With love and feeble loveliness,
I turn'd away, I hid my face,
In mad reproach and such distress,
In dust down in that loathsome place.

" 'And then I vow'd a solemn vow
That you should live, live and be free.
And you have lived—are free; and now
Too slow yon red sun comes to see
My life or death, or me again.
Oh, death! the peril and the pain
I have endured! the dark, dark stain
That I did take on my fair soul,
All, all to save you, make you free,
Are more than mortal can endure;
But flame can make the foulest pure.

" 'Behold this finished funeral pyre,
All ready for the form and fire,
Which these, my own hands, did prepare
For this last night; then lay me there.
I would not hide me from my God
Beneath the cold and sullen sod,
But, wrapp'd in fiery shining shroud,
Ascend to Him, a wreathing cloud.'

"She paused, she turn'd, she lean'd apace
Her glance and half-regretting face,
As if to yield herself to me;
And then she cried, 'It cannot be,
For I have vow'd a solemn vow,
And, God help me to keep it now!'

"I stood with arms extended wide
To catch her to my burning breast;
She caught a dagger from her side
And, ere I knew to stir or start,
She plunged it in her bursting heart,
And fell into my arms and died—
Died as my soul to hers was press'd,
Died as I held her to my breast,
Died without one word or moan,
And left me with my dead—alone.

"I laid her warm upon the pile,
And underneath the lisping oak
I watch'd the columns of dark smoke
Embrace her red lips, with a smile
Of frenzied fierceness, while there came
A gleaming column of red flame,
That grew a grander monument
Above her nameless noble mould
Than ever bronze or marble lent
To king or conqueror of old.

"It seized her in its hot embrace,
And leapt as if to reach the stars.
Then looking up I saw a face
So saintly and so sweetly fair,
So sad, so pitying, and so pure,
I nigh forgot the prison bars,
And for one instant, one alone,
I felt I could forgive, endure.

"I laid a circlet of white stone,
And left her ashes there alone. . . . . .
Years after, years of storm and pain,
I sought that sacred ground again.
I saw the circle of white stone
With tall, wild grasses overgrown.
I did expect, I know not why,
From out her sacred dust to find
Wild pinks and daisies blooming fair;
And when I did not find them there
I almost deem'd her God unkind,
Less careful of her dust than I.

"But why the dreary tale prolong?
And deem you I confess'd me wrong,
That I did bend a patient knee
To all the deep wrongs done to me?
That I, because the prison mould
Was on my brow, and all its chill
Was in my heart as chill as night,
Till soul and body both were cold,
Did curb my free-born mountain will
And sacrifice my sense of right?

"No! no! and had they come that day
While I with hands and garments red
Stood by her pleading, patient clay,
The one lone watcher by my dead,

With cross-hilt dagger in my hand,
And offer'd me my life and all
Of titles, power, or of place,
I should have spat them in the face,
And spurn'd them every one.
I live as God gave me to live,
I see as God gave me to see.
'Tis not my nature to forgive,
Or cringe and plead and bend the knee
To God or man in woe or weal,
In penitence I cannot feel.

"I do not question school nor creed
Of Christian, Protestant, or Priest;
I only know that creeds to me
Are but new names for mystery,
That good is good from east to east,
And more I do not know nor need
To know, to love my neighbor well.
I take their dogmas, as they tell,
Their pictures of their Godly good,
In garments thick with heathen blood;
Their heaven with his harp of gold,
Their horrid pictures of their hell—
Take hell and heaven undenied,
Yet were the two placed side by side,
Placed full before me for my choice,
As they are pictured, best and worst,
As they are peopled, tame and bold,
The canonized, and the accursed
Who dared to think, and thinking speak,
And speaking act, bold cheek to cheek,
I would in transports choose the first,
And enter hell with lifted voice.

* * * * *

"Go read the annals of the North
And records there of many a wail,
Of marshalling and going forth
For missing sheriffs, and for men
Who fell and none knew how nor when,—
Who disappear'd on mountain trail,
Or in some dense and narrow vale.
Go, traverse Trinity and Scott,
That curve their dark backs to the sun:
Go, prowl them all. Lo! have they not
The chronicles of my wild life?
My secrets on their lips of stone,
My archives built of human bone?
Go, range their wilds as I have done,
From snowy crest to sleeping vales,
And you will find on every one
Enough to swell a thousand tales.

* * * * *

"The soul cannot survive alone,
And hate will die, like other things;
I felt an ebbing in my rage;
I hunger'd for the sound of one,
Just one familiar word,—
Yearn'd but to hear my fellow speak,
Or sound of woman's mellow tone,
As beats the wild, imprison'd bird,
That long nor kind nor mate has heard,
With bleeding wings and panting beak
Against its iron cage.

"I saw a low-roof'd rancho lie,
Far, far below, at set of sun,
Along the foot-hills crisp and dun—
A lone sweet star in lower sky;
Saw children passing to and fro,
The busy housewife come and go,
And white cows come at her command,
And none look'd larger than my hand.
Then worn and torn, and tann'd and brown,
And heedless all, I hasten'd down;
A wanderer, wandering lorn and late,
I stood before the rustic gate.

"Two little girls, with brown feet bare,
And tangled, tossing, yellow hair,
Play'd on the green, fantastic dress'd,
Around a great Newfoundland brute
That lay half-resting on his breast,
And with his red mouth open'd wide
Would make believe that he would bite,
As they assail'd him left and right,
And then sprang to the other side,
And fill'd with shouts the willing air.
Oh, sweeter far than lyre or lute
To my then hot and thirsty heart,
And better self so wholly mute,
Were those sweet voices calling there.

"Though some sweet scenes my eyes have seen,
Some melody my soul has heard,
No song of any maid, or bird,
Or splendid wealth of tropic scene,
Or scene or song of anywhere,
Has my impulsive soul so stirr'd,
As those young angels sporting there.

"The dog at sight of me arose,
And nobly stood with lifted nose,
Afront the children, now so still,
And staring at me with a will.
'Come in, come in,' the rancher cried,
As here and there the housewife hied;
'Sit down, sit down, you travel late.
What news of politics or war?
And are you tired? Go you far?
And where you from? Be quick, my Kate,
This boy is sure in need of food.'
The little children close by stood,
And watch'd and gazed inquiringly,
Then came and climbed upon my knee.

"'That there's my Ma,' the eldest said,
And laugh'd and toss'd her pretty head;
And then, half bating of her joy,
'Have you a Ma, you stranger boy?-
And there hangs Carlo on the wall
As large as life; that mother drew
With berry stains upon a shred
Of tattered tent; but hardly you
Would know the picture his at all,
For Carlo's black, and this is red.'
Again she laugh'd, and shook her head,
And shower'd curls all out of place;
Then sudden sad, she raised her face
To mine, and tenderly she said,
'Have you, like us, a pretty home?
Have you, like me, a dog and toy?
Where do you live, and whither roam?
And where's your Pa, poor stranger boy?'

"It seem'd so sweetly out of place
Again to meet my fellow-man.
I gazed and gazed upon his face
As something I had never seen.
The melody of woman's voice
Fell on my ear as falls the rain
Upon the weary, waiting plain.
I heard, and drank and drank again,
As earth with crack'd lips drinks the rain,
In green to revel and rejoice.
I ate with thanks my frugal food,
The first return'd for many a day.
I had met kindness by the way!
I had at last encounter'd good!

"I sought my couch, but not to sleep;
New thoughts were coursing strong and deep
My wild, impulsive passion-heart;
I could not rest, my heart was moved,
My iron will forgot its part,
And I wept like a child reproved.

"I lay and pictured me a life
Afar from peril, hate, or pain;
Enough of battle, blood, and strife,
I would take up life's load again;
And ere the breaking of the morn
I swung my rifle from the horn,
And turned to other scenes and lands
With lighten'd heart and whiten'd hands.

"Where orange blossoms never die,
Where red fruits ripen all the year
Beneath a sweet and balmy sky,
Far from my language or my land,
Reproach, regret, or shame or fear,
I came in hope, I wander'd here—
Yes, here; and this red, bony hand
That holds this glass of ruddy cheer—"

"'Tis he!" hiss'd the crafty advocate.
He sprang to his feet, and hot with hate
He reach'd his hands, and he call'd aloud,
"'Tis the renegade of the red McCloud!"

Slowly the Alcalde rose from his chair;
"Hand me, touch me, him who dare!"
And his heavy glass on the board of oak
He smote with such savage and mighty stroke,
It ground to dust in his bony hand,

And heavy bottles did clink and tip
As if an earthquake were in the land.
He tower'd up, and in his ire
Seem'd taller than a church's spire.
He gazed a moment—and then, the while
An icy cold and defiant smile
Did curve his thin and his livid lip,
He turn'd on his heel, he strode through the hall
Grand as a god, so grandly tall,
Yet white and cold as a chisel'd stone;
He passed him out the adobé door
Into the night, and he pass'd alone,
And never was known or heard of more.

The lesson of this poem is that of persistent toil and endeavor. It certainly is not "a little thing dashed off before breakfast," for it was twice revised and published before its first appearance in London, and has been cut and revised at least half a dozen times since; and is still incomplete and very unsatisfying to the writer, except as to the descriptions. It was my first attempt at telling a story in verse, that was thought worth preserving. It was begun when but a lad, camped with our horses for a month's rest in an old adobe ruin on the Reading Ranch, with the gleaming snows of Mount Shasta standing out above the clouds against the cold, blue north. The story is not new, having been written, or at least lived in every mountain land of intermixed races that has been: a young outlaw in love with a wild mountain beauty, his battles for her people against his own, the capture, prison, brave release, flight, return, and revenge—a sort of modified Mazeppa. But it has been a fat source of feeding for grimly humorous and sensational writers, who long ago claimed to have found in it the story of my early life; and strangely enough I was glad when they did so, and read their stories with wild delight. I don't know why I always encouraged this idea of having been an outlaw, but I recall that when Trelawny told me that Byron was more ambitious to be thought the hero of his wildest poems than even to be king of Greece I could not help saying to myself, as Napoleon said to the thunders preceding Waterloo, "We are of accord."

The only serious trouble about the claim that I made the fight of life up the ugly steeps from a hole in an adobe prison-wall to the foothills of Olympus instead of over the pleasant campus of a college, is the fact that "our friends the enemy" fixed the date at about the same time in which I am on record as reading my class poem in another land. Besides, I was chosen to the bench on the very ticket when the very sheriff who should have kept me in his adobe prison was elected senator, and by some of the very men of my Mount Shasta with whom I had served in war against these same Indians for whom it is said I sold my birthright. Or did I have a double, and was it the other self who was at college? And is it not possible that I am even now the original and only real Joaquin Murietta? For more than once in the old days I was told (and how pleased I was to hear it said) that no other than Joaquin Murietta could ever ride as I rode. But here again is confusion, even more than the confusion of dates and deeds and names. For his hair was as black as a whole midnight, while mine was the hue of hammered gold. And, after all, was it not my vanity and willingness to be thought Joaquin, rather than pity for the brave boy outlaw, driven to desperation by wrongs too brutal to be told, that made me write of him and usurp his bloody name? Anyhow, I'd rather to-day be Joaquin Murietta, dead or living, than the wretch who got the reward for his alleged taking off. And was Joaquin Murietta really killed when that party of Texans surprised and butchered a band of unarmed Mexicans? Nine men in ten will say not.

Mrs. Gale Page, daughter of an early governor of Oregon, told me at Walla Walla, July 5th, 1896, in her own house, that her father, who knew and liked Joaquin, when a miner, had had two letters from him, dated and postmarked Mexico, years after his alleged death. So he certainly was not killed as told. But pity, pity, that men should so foolishly waste time with either me or mine when I have led them into the mighty heart of majestic Shasta. Why yonder, lone as God and white as the great white throne, there looms against the sapphire upper seas a mountain peak that props the very porch of heaven; and yet they bother with and want to torment a poor mote of dust that sinks in the grasses at their feet! Why, I know a single cañon there so deep, so bottomless, and broad and somber that a whole night once housed there and let a gold and silver day glide on and on and over it all the vast day long, and all day long night lay there undiscovered. Yet in this presence there be those who will stoop to look at a mere mote at their feet, or on their shoes, and bother to know whether it be a black speck or a white; preferring, however, to find it black.

THE LAST TASCHASTAS.

The hills were brown, the heavens were blue,
A woodpecker pounded a pine-top shell,
While a partridge whistled the whole day through
For a rabbit to dance in the chapparal,
And a grey grouse drumm'd, "All's well, all's well."

I.

Wrinkled and brown as a bag of leather,
A squaw sits moaning long and low.
Yesterday she was a wife and mother,
To-day she is rocking her to and fro,
A childless widow, in weeds and woe.

An Indian sits in a rocky cavern
Chipping a flint in an arrow head;
His children are moving as still as shadows,
His squaw is moulding some balls of lead,
With round face painted a battle-red.

An Indian sits in a black-jack jungle,
Where a grizzly bear has rear'd her young,
Whetting a flint on a granite boulder.
His quiver is over his brown back hung—
His face is streak'd and his bow is strung.

An Indian hangs from a cliff of granite,
Like an eagle's nest built in the air,
Looking away to the east. and watching
The smoke of the cabins curling there,
And eagle's feathers are in his hair.

In belt of wampum, in battle fashion
An Indian watches with wild desire.
He is red with paint, he is black with passion;
And grand as a god in his savage ire,
He leans and listens till stars are a-fire.

All somber and sullen and sad, a chieftain
Now looks from the mountain far into the sea.
Just before him beat in the white billows,
Just behind him the toppled tall tree
And woodmen chopping, knee buckled to knee.

II.

All together, all in council,
In a cañon wall'd so high
That no thing could ever reach them
Save some stars dropp'd from the sky.
And the brown bats sweeping by:

Tawny chieftains thin and wiry,
Wise as brief, and brief as bold;
Chieftains young and fierce and fiery
Chieftains stately, stern and old,
Bronzed and battered—battered gold.

Flamed the council-fire brighter,
Flash'd black eyes like diamond beads,
When a woman told her sorrows,
While a warrior told his deeds,
And a widow tore her weeds.

Then was lit the pipe of council
That their fathers smoked of old,
With its stem of manzanita,
And its bowl of quartz and gold,
And traditions manifold.

How from lip to lip in silence
Burn'd it round the circle red,
Like an evil star slow passing
(Sign of battles and bloodshed)
Round the heavens overhead.

Then the silence deep was broken
By the thunder rolling far,
As gods muttering in anger,
Or the bloody battle-car
Of some Christian king at war.

' 'Tis the spirits of my Fathers
Mutt'ring vengeance in the skies;

And the flashing of the lightning
Is the anger of their eyes,
Bidding us in battle rise,"

Cried the war-chief, now uprising,
Naked all above the waist,
While a belt of shells and silver
Held his tamoos to its place,
And the war-paint streaked his face.

Women melted from the council,
Boys crept backward out of sight,
Till alone a wall of warriors
In their paint and battle-plight
Sat reflecting back the light.

"O my Fathers in the storm-cloud!"
(Red arms tossing to the skies,
While the massive walls of granite
Seem'd to shrink to half their size,
And to mutter strange replies)—

"Soon we come, O angry Fathers,
Down the darkness you have cross'd:
Speak for hunting-grounds there for us;
Those you left us we have lost—
Gone like blossoms in a frost.

"Warriors!" (and his arms fell folded
On his tawny swelling breast,
While his voice, now low and plaintive
As the waves in their unrest,
Touching tenderness confess'd),

"Where is Wrotto, wise of counsel,
Yesterday here in his place?
A brave lies dead down in the valley,
Last brave of his line and race,
And a Ghost sits on his face.

"Where his boy the tender-hearted,
With his mother yestermorn?
Lo! a wigwam door is darken'd,
And a mother mourns forlorn,
With her long locks toss'd and torn.

"Lo! our daughters have been gather'd
From among us by the foe,
Like the lilies they once gather'd
In the spring-time all aglow
From the banks of living snow.

"Through the land where we for ages
Laid the bravest, dearest dead,
Grinds the savage white man's plow-
share
Grinding sires' bones for bread—
We shall give them blood instead.

"I saw white skulls in a furrow,
And around the cursed plowshare
Clung the flesh of my own children,
And my mother's tangled hair
Trailed along the furrow there.

"Warriors! braves! I cry for vengeance!
And the dim ghosts of the dead
Unavenged do wail and shiver
In the storm cloud overhead,
And shoot arrows battle-red."

Then he ceased, and sat among them,
With his long locks backward strown;
They as mute as men of marble,
He a king upon the throne,
And as still as any stone.

Then uprose the war chief's daughter,
Taller than the tassell'd corn,
Sweeter than the kiss of morning,
Sad as some sweet star of morn,
Half defiant, half forlorn.

Robed in skins of stripéd panther
Lifting loosely to the air
With a face a shade of sorrow
And black eyes that said, Beware!
Nestled in a storm or hair;

With her stripéd robes around her,
Fasten'd by an eagle's beak,
Stood she by the stately chieftain,
Proud and pure as Shasta's peak,
As she ventured thus to speak:

"Must the tomahawk of battle
Be unburied where it lies,
O, last war chief of Taschastas?

Must the smoke of battle rise
Like a storm cloud in the skies?

"True, some wretch has laid a brother
With his swift feet to the sun,
But because one bough is broken,
Must the broad oak be undone?
All the fir trees fell'd as one?

"True, the braves have faded, wasted
Like ripe blossoms in the rain,
But when we have spent the arrows,
Do we twang the string in vain,
And then snap the bow in twain?"

Like a vessel in a tempest
Shook the warrior, wild and grim,
As he gazed out in the midnight,
As to things that beckon'd him,
And his eyes were moist and dim.

Then he turn'd, and to his bosom
Battle-scarr'd, and strong as brass,
Tenderly the warrior press'd her
As if she were made of glass,
Murmuring, "Alas! alas!

"Loua Ellah! Spotted Lily!
Streaks of blood shall be the sign,
On their cursed and mystic pages,
Representing me and mine!
By Tonatiu's fiery shrine!

"When the grass shall grow untrodden
In my war path, and the plow
Shall be grinding through this cañon
Where my braves are gather'd now,
Still shall they record this vow:

"War and vengeance! rise, my warrior,
Rise and shout the battle sign,
Ye who love revenge and glory!
Ye for peace, in silence pine,
And no more be braves of mine."

Then the war yell roll'd and echoed
As they started from the ground,
Till an eagle from his cedar
Starting, answer'd back the sound,
And flew circling round and round.

"Enough, enough, my kingly father,"
And the glory of her eyes
Flash'd the valor and the passion
That may sleep but never dies,
As she proudly thus replies:

"Can the cedar be a willow,
Pliant and as little worth?
It shall stand the king of forests,
Or its fall shall shake the earth,
Desolating heart and hearth!"

* * * * * *

III.

* * * * * *

From cold east shore to warm west sea
The red men followed the red sun,
And faint and failing fast as he,
They knew too well their race was run.
This ancient tribe, press'd to the wave,
There fain had slept a patient slave,
And died out as red embers die
From flames that once leapt hot and high;
But, roused to anger, half arose
Around that chief, a sudden flood,
A hot and hungry cry for blood;
Half drowsy shook a feeble hand,
Then sank back in a tame repose,
And left him to his fate and foes,
A stately wreck upon the strand.

* * * * * *

His eye was like the lightning's wing,
His voice was like a rushing flood;
And when a captive bound he stood
His presence look'd the perfect king.

'Twas held at first that he should die:
I never knew the reason why
A milder council did prevail,
Save that we shrank from blood, and save
That brave men do respect the brave.
Down sea sometimes there was a sail,
And far at sea, they said, an isle,
And he was sentenced to exile;
In open boat upon the sea

To go the instant on the main,
And never under penalty
Of death to touch the shore again.
A troop of bearded buckskinn'd men
Bore him hard-hurried to the wave,
Placed him swift in the boat; and then
Swift pushing to the bristling sea,
His daughter rush'd down suddenly,
Threw him his bow, leapt from the shore
Into the boat beside the brave,
And sat her down and seized the oar,
And never question'd, made replies,
Or moved her lips, or raised her eyes.

His breast was like a gate of brass,
His brow was like a gather'd storm;
There is no chisell'd stone that has
So stately and complete a form,
In sinew, arm, and every part,
In all the galleries of art.

Gray, bronzed, and naked to the waist,
He stood half halting in the prow,
With quiver bare and idle bow.
The warm sea fondled with the shore,
And laid his white face to the sands.
His daughter sat with her sad face
Bent on the wave, with her two hands
Held tightly to the dripping oar;
And as she sat, her dimpled knee
Bent lithe as wand or willow tree,
So round and full, so rich and free,
That no one would have ever known
That it had either joint or bone.

Her eyes were black, her face was brown,
Her breasts were bare and there fell down
Such wealth of hair, it almost hid
The two, in its rich jetty fold—
Which I had sometime fain forbid,
They were so richer, fuller far
Than any polish'd bronzes are,
And richer hued than any gold.
On her brown arms and her brown hands
Were bars of gold and golden bands,
Rough hammer'd from the virgin ore,
So heavy, they could hold no more.

I wonder now, I wonder'd then,
That men who fear'd not gods nor men
Laid no rude hands at all on her,—
I think she had a dagger slid
Down in her silver'd wampum belt;
It might have been, instead of hilt,
A flashing diamond hurry-hid
That I beheld—I could not know
For certain, we did hasten so;
And I know now less sure than then:
Deeds strangle memories of deeds,
Red blossoms wither, choked with weeds,
And years drown memories of men.
Some things have happened since—and then
This happen'd years and years ago.

"Go, go!" the captain cried, and smote
With sword and boot the swaying boat,
Until it quiver'd as at sea
And brought the old chief to his knee.
He turn'd his face, and turning rose
With hand raised fiercely to his foes:
"Yes, I will go, last of my race,
Push'd by you robbers ruthlessly
Into the hollows of the sea,
From this my last, last resting-place.
Traditions of my fathers say
A feeble few reach'd for this land,
And we reach'd them a welcome hand
Of old, upon another shore;
Now they are strong, we weak as they,
And they have driven us before
Their faces, from that sea to this:
Then marvel not if we have sped
Sometime an arrow as we fled,
So keener than a serpent's kiss."

He turn'd a time unto the sun
That lay half hidden in the sea,
As in his hollows rock'd asleep,
All trembled and breathed heavily;
Then arch'd his arm, as you have done,
For sharp masts piercing through the deep.
No shore or kind ship met his eye,
Or isle, or sail, or anything,

Save white sea gulls on dipping wing,
And mobile sea and molten sky.

"Farewell!—push seaward, child!" he cried,
And quick the paddle-strokes replied.
Like lightning from the panther-skin,
That bound his loins round about
He snatch'd a poison'd arrow out,
That like a snake lay hid within,
And twang'd his bow. The captain fell
Prone on his face, and such a yell
Of triumph from that savage rose
As man may never hear again.
He stood as standing on the main,
The topmast main, in proud repose,
And shook his clench'd fist at his foes,
And call'd, and cursed them every one.
He heeded not the shouts and shot
That follow'd him, but grand and grim
Stood up against the level sun;
And, standing so, seem'd in his ire
So grander than some ship on fire.

And when the sun had left the sea,
That laves Abrup, and Blanco laves,
And left the land to death and me,
The only thing that I could see
Was, ever as the light boat lay
High lifted on the white-back'd waves,
A head as gray and toss'd as they.

We raised the dead, and from his hands
Pick'd out some shells, clutched as he lay
And two by two bore him away,
And wiped his lips of blood and sands.

We bent and scooped a shallow home,
And laid him warm-wet in his blood,
Just as the lifted tide a-flood
Came charging in with mouth a-foam:
And as we turn'd, the sensate thing
Reached up, lick'd out its foamy tongue,
Lick'd out its tongue and tasted blood;
The white lips to the red earth clung
An instant, and then loosening
All hold just like a living thing,
Drew back sad-voiced and shuddering,
All stained with blood, a stripéd flood.

Tc'hastas; a name given to King John by the French, a corruption of chaste; for he was a pure, just man and a great warrior. He was king of the Rouge (Red) River Indians of Oregon, and his story is glorious with great deeds in defense of his people. When finally overpowered he and his son Moses were put on a ship at Port Orford and sent to Fort Alcatraz in the Golden Gate. In mid-ocean, these two Indians, in irons, rose up, and, after a bloody fight, took the ship. But one had lost a leg, the other an arm, and so they finally had to let loose the crew and soldiers tumbled into the hold and surrender themselves again; for the ship was driving helpless in a storm toward the rocks. The king died a prisoner, but his son escaped and never again surrendered. He lives alone near Yreka and is known as "Prince Peg-leg Moses." A daughter of the late Senator Nesmith sends me a picture, taken in 1896, of the king's devoted daughter, Princess Mary, who followed his fortunes in all his battles. She must be nearly one hundred years old. I remember her as an old woman full forty years ago, tall as a soldier, and most terrible in council. I have tried to picture her and her people as I once saw them in a midnight camp before the breaking out of the war; also their actions and utterances, so like some of the old Israelite councils and prophecies. This was the leading piece in my very first book, "Specimens," published in Oregon in 1867-8, if I remember rightly.

JOAQUIN MURIETTA.

Glintings of day in the darkness,
Flashings of flint and of steel,
Blended in gossamer texture
The ideal and the real,
Limn'd like the phantom ship shadow,
Crowding up under the keel.

I stand beside the mobile sea,
And sails are spread, and sails are furl'd;
From farthest corners of the world,
And fold like white wings wearily.
Some ships go up, and some go down
In haste, like traders in a town.

Afar at sea some white ships flee,
With arms stretch'd like a ghost's to me,
And cloud-like sails are blown and curl'd,
Then glide down to the under world.
As if blown bare in winter blasts
Of leaf and limb, tall naked masts
Are rising from the restless sea.
I seem to see them gleam and shine
With clinging drops of dripping brine.
Broad still brown wings flit here and there,
Thin sea-blue wings wheel everywhere,
And white wings whistle through the air;
I hear a thousand sea gulls call.
And San Francisco Bay is white
And blue with sail and sea and light.

* * * * * * * *

Behold the ocean on the beach
Kneel lowly down as if in prayer,
I hear a moan as of despair,
While far at sea do toss and reach
Some things so like white pleading hands.
The ocean's thin and hoary hair
Is trail'd along the silver'd sands,
At every sigh and sounding moan.
The very birds shriek in distress
And sound the ocean's monotone.
'Tis not a place for mirthfulness,
But meditation deep, and prayer,
And kneelings on the salted sod,
Where man must own his littleness,
And know the mightiness of God.

Dared I but say a prophecy,
As sang the holy men of old,
Of rock-built cities yet to be
Along these shining shores of gold,
Crowding athirst into the sea,
What wondrous marvels might be told!
Enough, to know that empire here
Shall burn her loftiest, brightest star;
Here art and eloquence shall reign,
As o'er the wolf-rear'd realm of old;
Here learn'd and famous from afar,
To pay their noble court, shall come,
And shall not seek or see in vain,
But look and look with wonder dumb.

Afar the bright Sierras lie
A swaying line of snowy white,
A fringe of heaven hung in sight
Against the blue base of the sky.

I look along each gaping gorge,
I hear a thousand sounding strokes
Like giants rending giant oaks,
Or brawny Vulcan at his forge;
I see pickaxes flash and shine;
Hear great wheels whirling in a mine.
Here winds a thick and yellow thread,
A moss'd and silver stream instead;
And trout that leap'd its rippled tide
Have turn'd upon their sides and died.

Lo! when the last pick in the mine
Lies rusting red with idleness,

And rot yon cabins in the mold,
And wheels no more croak in distress,
And tall pines reassert command,
Sweet bards along this sunset shore
Their mellow melodies will pour;
Will charm as charmers very wise,
Will strike the harp with master hand,
Will sound unto the vaulted skies,
The valor of these men of old—
These mighty men of 'Forty-nine;
Will sweetly sing and proudly say,
Long, long agone there was a day
When there were giants in the land.

* * * * *

Now who rides rushing on the sight
Hard down yon rocky long defile,
Swift as an eagle in his flight,
Fierce as a winter's storm at night
Blown from the bleak Sierra's height!
Such reckless rider!—I do ween
No mortal man his like has seen.
And yet, but for his long serape
All flowing loose, and black as crape,
And long silk locks of blackest hair
All streaming wildly in the breeze,
You might believe him in a chair,
Or chatting at some country fair
He rides so grandly at his ease.

But now he grasps a tighter rein,
A red rein wrought in golden chain,
And in his tapidaros stands,
Turns, shouts defiance at his foe.
And now he calmly bares his brow
As if to challenge fate, and now
His hand drops to his saddle-bow
And clutches something gleaming there
As if to something more than dare.

The stray winds lift the raven curls,
Soft as a fair Castilian girl's,
And bare a brow so manly, high,
Its every feature does belie
The thought he is compell'd to fly;
A brow as open as the sky
On which you gaze and gaze again
As on a picture you have seen
And often sought to see in vain,
A brow of blended pride and pain,
That seems to hold a tale of woe
Or wonder, that you fain would know
A boy's brow, cut as with a knife,
With many a dubious deed in life.

Again he grasps his glitt'ring rein,
And, wheeling like a hurricane,
Defying wood, or stone, or flood,
Is dashing down the gorge again.
Oh, never yet has prouder steed
Borne master nobler in his need!
There is a glory in his eye
That seems to dare and to defy
Pursuit, or time, or space, or race.
His body is the type of speed,
While from his nostril to his heel
Are muscles as if made of steel.

What crimes have made that red hand red?
What wrongs have written that young face
With lines of thought so out of place?
Where flies he? And from whence has fled?
And what his lineage and race?
What glitters in his heavy belt,
And from his furr'd cantenas gleam?
What on his bosom that doth seem
A diamond bright or dagger's hilt?
The iron hoofs that still resound
Like thunder from the yielding ground
Alone reply; and now the plain,
Quick as you breathe and gaze again,
Is won, and all pursuit is vain.

* * * * *

I stand upon a mountain rim,
Stone-paved and pattern'd as a street;
A rock-lipp'd cañon plunging south,
As if it were earth's open'd mouth,
Yawns deep and darkling at my feet;
So deep, so distant, and so dim
Its waters wind, a yellow thread,
And call so faintly and so far,
I turn aside my swooning head.

I feel a fierce impulse to leap
Adown the beetling precipice,
Like some lone, lost, uncertain star;
To plunge into a place unknown,
And win a world, all, all my own;
Or if I might not meet that bliss,
At least escape the curse of this.

I gaze again. A gleaming star
Shines back as from some mossy well
Reflected from blue fields afar.
Brown hawks are wheeling here and there,
And up and down the broken wall
Clings clumps of dark green chapparal,
While from the rent rocks, grey and
bare;
Blue junipers hang in the air.

Here, cedars sweep the stream and here,
Among the boulders moss'd and brown
That time and storms have toppled down
From towers undefiled by man,
Low cabins nestle as in fear,
And look no taller than a span.
From low and shapeless chimneys rise
Some tall straight columns of blue smoke,
And weld them to the bluer skies;
While sounding down the somber gorge
I hear the steady pickax stroke,
As if upon a flashing forge.

* * * * *

Another scene, another sound!—
Sharp shots are fretting through the air,
Red knives are flashing everywhere,
And here and there the yellow flood
Is purpled with warm smoking blood.
The brown hawk swoops low to the
ground,
And nimble chipmunks, small and still,
Dart striped lines across the sill
That manly feet shall press no more.
The flume lies warping in the sun,
The pan sits empty by the door,
The pickax on its bedrock floor,
Lies rusting in the silent mine.
There comes no single sound nor sign
Of life, beside yon monks in brown
That dart their dim shapes up and down
The rocks that swelter in the sun;
But dashing down yon rocky spur,
Where scarce a hawk would dare to
whirr,
A horseman holds his reckless flight.
He wears a flowing black capote,
While over all do flow and float
Long locks of hair as dark as night,
And hands are red that erst were white.

All up and down the land to-day
Black desolation and despair
It seems have set and settled there,
With none to frighten them away.
Like sentries watching by the way
Black chimneys topple in the air,
And seem to say, Go back, beware!
While up around the mountain's rim
Are clouds of smoke, so still and grim
They look as they are fasten'd there.

A lonely stillness, so like death,
So touches, terrifies all things,
That even rooks that fly o'erhead
Are hush'd, and seem to hold their
breath,
To fly with muffled wings,
And heavy as if made of lead.
Some skulls that crumble to the touch,
Some joints of thin and chalk-like bone,
A tall black chimney, all alone,
That leans as if upon a crutch.
Alone are left to mark or tell,
Instead of cross or cryptic stone,
Where Joaquin stood and brave men
fell.

* * * * * * * *

The sun is red and flush'd and dry,
And fretted from his weary beat
Across the hot and desert sky,
And swollen as from overheat,
And failing too; for see, he sinks
Swift as a ball of burnish'd ore:
It may be fancy, but methinks
He never fell so fast before.

I hear the neighing of hot steeds,
I see the marshaling of men
That silent move among the trees
As busily as swarming bees
With step and stealthiness profound,
On carpetings of spindled weeds,
Without a syllable or sound
Save clashing of their burnish'd arms,
Clinking dull, deathlike alarms—
Grim bearded men and brawny men
That grope among the ghostly trees.
Were ever silent men as these?
Was ever somber forest deep
And dark as this? Here one might sleep
While all the weary years went round,
Nor wake nor weep for sun or sound.

A stone's throw to the right, a rock
Has rear'd his head among the stars—
An island in the upper deep—
And on his front a thousand scars
Of thunder's crash and earthquake's shock
Are seam'd as if by sabre's sweep
Of gods, enraged that he should rear
His front amid their realms of air.

What moves along his beetling brow,
So small, so indistinct and far,
This side yon blazing evening star,
Seen through that redwood's shifting bough?
A lookout on the world below?
A watcher for the friend—or foe?
This still troops sentry it must be,
Yet seems no taller than my knee.

But for the grandeur of this gloom,
And for the chafing steeds' alarms,
And brown men's sullen clash of arms,
This were but as a living tomb.
These weeds are spindled, pale and white,
As if nor sunshine, life, nor light
Had ever reach'd this forest's heart.
Above, the redwood boughs entwine
As dense as copse of tangled vine—
Above, so fearfully afar,
It seems as 'twere a lesser sky,
A sky without a moon or star,
The moss'd boughs are so thick and high.
At every lisp of leaf I start!
Would I could hear a cricket trill,
Or hear yon sentry from his hill,
The place does seem so deathly still.
But see a sudden lifted hand
From one who still and sullen stands,
With black serape and bloody hands,
And coldly gives his brief command.

They mount—away! Quick on his heel
He turns and grasps his gleaming steel—
Then sadly smiles, and stoops to kiss
An upturn'd face so sweetly fair,
So sadly, saintly, purely rare,
So rich of blessedness and bliss!
I know she is not flesh and blood,
But some sweet spirit of this wood;
I know it by her wealth of hair,
And step on the unyielding air;
Her seamless robe of shining white,
Her soul-deep eyes of darkest night;
But over all and more than all
That can be said or can befall,
That tongue can tell or pen can trace,
That wonderous witchery of face.

Between the trees I see him stride
To where a red steed fretting stands
Impatient for his lord's commands:
And she glides noiseless at his side.

One hand toys with her waving hair,
Soft lifting from her shoulders bare;
The other holds the loosen'd rein,
And rests upon the swelling mane
That curls the curved neck o'er and o'er,
Like waves that swirl along the shore
He hears the last retreating sound
Of iron on volcanic stone,
That echoes far from peak to plain,
And 'neath the dense wood's sable zone,
He peers the dark Sierras down.

His hand forsakes her raven hair,
His eyes have an unearthly glare;

She shrinks and shudders at his side
Then lifts to his her moisten'd eyes,
And only looks her sad replies.
A sullenness his soul enthralls,
A silence born of hate and pride;
His fierce volcanic heart so deep
Is stirr'd, his teeth, despite his will,
Do chatter as if in a chill;
His very dagger at his side
Does shake and rattle in its sheath,
As blades of brown grass in a gale
Do rustle on the frosted heath:
And yet he does not bend or weep,
But sudden mounts, then leans him o'er
To breathe her hot breath but once more.
I do not mark the prison'd sighs,
I do not meet the moisten'd eyes,
The while he leans him from his place
Down to her sweet uplifted face.

A low sweet melody is heard
Like cooing of some Balize bird,
So fine it does not touch the air,
So faint it stirs not anywhere;
Faint as the falling of the dew,
Low as a pure unutter'd prayer,
The meeting, mingling, as it were,
In that one long, last, silent kiss
Of souls in paradisal bliss.

"You must not, shall not, shall not go!
To die and leave me here to die!
Enough of vengeance, Love and I?
I die for home and—Mexico."

He leans, he plucks her to his breast,
As plucking Mariposa's flower,
And now she crouches in her rest
As resting in some rosy bower.

Erect, again he grasps the rein!
I see his black steed plunge and poise
And beat the air with iron feet,
And curve his noble glossy neck,
And toss on high his swelling mane,
And leap—away! he spurns the rein!
He flies so fearfully and fleet,
But for the hot hoofs' ringing noise
'Twould seem as if he were on wings.

And they are gone! Gone like breath,
Gone like a white sail seen at night
A moment, and then lost to sight;
Gone like a star you look upon,
That glimmers to a bead, a speck,
Then softly melts into the dawn,
And all is still and dark as death,
And who shall sing, for who may know
That mad, glad ride to Mexico?

The third poem in my first London book, if I remember—you see I never kept my books about me, nor indeed any books now, and have for present use only a copy that has been many times revised and cut down—was called "California," but it was called "Joaquin" in the Oregon book. And it was from this that I was, in derision, called "Joaquin." I kept the name and the poem too, till both were at least respected. But my brother, who had better judgment and finer taste than I, thought it too wild and bloody; and so by degrees it has been allowed to almost entirely disappear, except this fragment, although a small book of itself, to begin with.

INA.

Sad song of the wind in the mountains
And the sea wave of grass on the plain,
That breaks in bloom foam by the fountains,
And forests, that breaketh again
On the mountains, as breaketh a main.

Bold thoughts that were strong as the grizzlies,
Now weak in their prison of words;
Bright fancies that flash'd like the glaciers,
Now dimm'd like the luster of birds,
And butterflies huddled as herds.

Sad symphony, wild, and unmeasured,
Weed warp, and woof woven in strouds
Strange truths that a stray soul had treasured,
Truths seen as through folding of shrouds
Or as stars through the rolling of clouds.

Scene I.

A Hacienda near Tezcuco, Mexico. Young Don Carlos *alone, looking out on the moonlit mountain.*

Don Carlos.

Popocatapetl looms lone like an island,
Above white-cloud waves that break up against him;
Around him white buttes in the moonlight are flashing
Like silver tents pitch'd in the fair fields of heaven
While standing in line, in their snows everlasting,
Flash peaks, as my eyes into heaven are lifted,
Like mile-stones that lead to the city Eternal.

Ofttime when the sun and the sea lay together,
Red-welded as one, in their red bed of lovers,
Embracing and blushing like loves newly wedded,
I have trod on the trailing crape fringes of twilight,
And stood there and listen'd, and lean'd with lips parted,
Till lordly peaks wrapp'd them, as chill night blew over,
In great cloaks of sable, like proud somber Spaniards,
And stalk'd from my presence down night's corridors.

When the red-curtained West has bent red as with weeping
Low over the couch where the prone day lay dying,
I have stood with brow lifted, confronting the mountains
That held their white faces of snow in the heavens,
And said, "It is theirs to array them so purely,

Because of their nearness to the temple eternal;"
And childlike have said, "They are fair resting places
For the dear weary dead on their way up to heaven."

But my soul is not with you to-night, mighty mountains:
It is held to the levels of earth by an angel
Far more than a star, earth fallen or unfall'n,
Yet fierce in her follies and headstrong and stronger
Than streams of the sea running in with the billows.

Very well. Let him woo, let him thrust his white whiskers
And lips pale and purple with death, in between us;
Let her wed, as she wills, for the gold of the graybeard.
I will set my face for you, O mountains, my brothers,
For I yet have my honor, my conscience and freedom,
My fleet-footed mustang, and pistols rich silver'd;
I will turn as the earth turns her back on the sun,
But return to the light of her eyes never more,
While noons have a night and white seas have a shore.

INA, *approaching*.

INA.

"I have come, dear Don Carlos, to say you farewell,
I shall wed with Don Castro at dawn of to-morrow,
And be all his own—firm, honest and faithful.
I have promised this thing; that I will keep my promise
You who do know me care never to question.
I have mastered myself to say this thing to you;
Hear me: be strong, then, and say adieu bravely;
The world is his own who will brave its bleak hours.
Dare, then, to confront the cold days in their column;
As they march down upon you, stand, hew them to pieces,
One after another, as you would a fierce foeman,
Till not one abideth between two true bosoms."

[DON CARLOS, *with a laugh of scorn, flies from the veranda, mounts horse, and disappears.*]

INA *(looking out into the night, after a long silence).*

How doleful the night hawk screams in the heavens,
How dismally gibbers the gray coyote!
Afar to the south now the turbulent thunder,
Mine equal, my brother, my soul's one companion,
Talks low in his sleep, like a giant deep troubled;
Talks fierce in accord with my own stormy spirit.

SCENE II.

Sunset on a spur of Mount Hood. LAMONTE *contemplates the scene.*

LAMONTE.

A flushed and weary messenger a-west
Is standing at the half-closed door of day,
As he would say, Good night; and now his bright
Red cap he tips to me and turns his face.
Were it an unholy thing to say, an angel now
Beside the door stood with uplifted seal?

Behold the door seal'd with that blood red seal
Now burning, spreading o'er the mighty West.
Never again shall that dead day arise
Therefrom, but must be born and come anew.

The tawny, solemn Night, child of the East,
Her mournful robe trails o'er the distant woods,
And comes this way with firm and stately step.
Afront, and very high, she wears a shield,
A plate of silver, and upon her brow
The radiant Venus burns, a pretty lamp.
Behold! how in her gorgeous flow of hair
Do gleam a million mellow yellow gems,
That spill their molten gold upon the dewy grass.
Now throned on boundless plains, and gazing down
So calmly on the red-seal'd tomb of day,
She rests her form against the Rocky Mountains,
And rules with silent power a peaceful world.

'Tis midnight now. The bent and broken moon,
All batter'd, black, as from a thousand battles,
Hangs silent on the purple walls of heaven.
The angel warrior, guard of the gates eternal,
In battle-harness girt, sleeps on the field:
But when to-morrow comes, when wicked men
That fret the patient earth are all astir,
He will resume his shield, and, facing earthward,
The gates of heaven guard from sins of earth.

'Tis morn. Behold the kingly day now leaps
The eastern wall of earth, bright sword in hand,
And clad in flowing robe of mellow light,
Like to a king that has regain'd his throne,
He warms his drooping subjects into joy,
That rise renewed to do him fealty,
And rules with pomp the universal world.

DON CARLOS *ascends the mountain, gesticulating and talking to himself.*

DON CARLOS.

Oh, for a name that black-eyed maids would sigh
And lean with parted lips at mention of;
That I should seem so tall in minds of men
That I might walk beneath the arch of heaven,
And pluck the ripe red stars as I pass'd on,
As favor'd guests do pluck the purple grapes
That hang above the humble entrance way
Of palm-thatch'd mountain inn of Mexico.

Oh, I would give the green leaves of my life
For something grand, for real and undream'd deeds!
To wear a mantle, broad and richly gemm'd
As purple heaven fringed with gold at sunset;
To wear a crown as dazzling as the sun,
And, holding up a scepter lightning-charged,
Stride out among the stars as I once strode
A barefoot boy among the buttercups.

Alas! I am so restless. There is that
Within me doth rebel and rise against
The all I am and half I see in others;
And were't not for contempt of coward act
Of flying all defeated from the world,
As if I feared and dared not face its ills,
I should ere this have known, known more or less

Than any flesh that frets this sullen earth.
I know not where such thoughts will lead me to:
I have had fear that they would drive me mad,
And then have flattered my weak self, and said
The soul's outgrown the body—yea, the soul
Aspires to the stars, and in its struggles upward
Make the dull flesh quiver as an aspen.

LAMONTE.

What waif is this cast here upon my shore,
From seas of subtle and most selfish men?

DON CARLOS.

Of subtle and most selfish men!—ah, that's the term!
And if you be but earnest in your spleen,
And other sex across man's shoulders lash,
I'll stand beside you on this crag and howl
And hurl my clenched fists down upon their heads,
Till I am hoarse as yonder cataract.

LAMONTE.

Why, no, my friend, I'll not consent to that.
No true man yet has ever woman cursed.
And I—I do not hate my fellow man,
For man by nature bears within himself
Nobility that makes him half a god;
But as in somewise he hath made himself,
His universal thirst for gold and pomp,
And purchased fleeting fame and bubble honors,
Forgetting good, so mocking helpless age,
And rushing roughshod o'er lowly merit,
I hold him but a sorry worm indeed;
And so have turn'd me quietly aside
To know the majesty of peaceful woods.

DON CARLOS (*as if alone*).

The fabled font of youth led many fools,
Zealous in its pursuit, to hapless death;
And yet this thirst for fame, this hot ambition,
This soft-toned syren-tongue, enchanting Fame,
Doth lead me headlong on to equal folly,
Like to a wild bird charm'd by shining coils
And swift mesmeric glance of deadly snake:
I would not break the charm, but win a world
Or die with curses blistering my lips.

LAMONTE.

Give up ambition, petty pride—
By pride the angels fell.

DON CARLOS.

By pride they reached a place from whence to fall.

LAMONTE.

You startle me! I am unused to hear
Men talk these fierce and bitter thoughts; and yet
In closed recesses of my soul was once
A dark and gloomy chamber where they dwelt.
Give up ambition — yea, crush such thoughts
As you would crush from hearth a scorpion brood;
For, mark me well, they'll get the mastery,
And drive you on to death—or worse, across
A thousand ruin'd homes and broken hearts.

DON CARLOS.

Give up ambition! Oh, rather than to die
And glide a lonely, nameless, shivering ghost

Down time's dark tide of utter nothingness,
I'd write a name in blood and orphans' tears.
The temple-burner wiser was than kings.

LAMONTE.

And would you dare the curse of man and—

DON CARLOS.

Dare the curse of man!
I'd dare the fearful curse of God!
I'd build a pyramid of whitest skulls,
And step therefrom unto the spotted moon,
And thence to stars, and thence to central suns.
Then with one grand and mighty leap would land
Unhinder'd on the shining shore of heaven,
And, sword in hand, unbared and unabash'd,
Would stand bold forth in presence of the God
Of gods, and on the jewel'd inner side
The walls of heaven, carve with keen Damascus steel,
And, highest up, a grand and titled name
That time nor tide could touch or tarnish ever.

LAMONTE.

Seek not to crop above the heads of men
To be a better mark for envy's shafts.
Come to my peaceful home, and leave behind
These stormy thoughts and daring aspirations.
All earthly power is but a thing comparative.
Is not a petty chief of some lone isle,
With half a dozen nude and starving subjects,
As much a king as he the Czar of Rusk?
In yonder sweet retreat and balmy place
I'll abdicate, and you be chief indeed.
There you will reign and tell me of the world,
Its life and lights, its sins and sickly shadows.
The pheasant will reveille beat at morn,
And rouse us to the battle of the day.
My swarthy subjects will in circle sit,
And, gazing on your noble presence, deem
You great indeed, and call you chief of chiefs;
And, knowing no one greater than yourself
In all the leafy borders of your realm,
'Gainst what can pride or poor ambition chafe?

'Twill be a kingdom without king, save you,
More broad than that the cruel Cortes won,
With subjects truer than he ever knew,
That know no law but only nature's law,
And no religion know but that of love.
There truth and beauty are, for there is Nature,
Serene and simple. She will be our priestess,
And in her calm and uncomplaining face
We two will read her rubric and be wise.

DON CARLOS.

Why, truly now, this fierce and broken land,
Seen through your eyes, assumes a fairer shape.
Lead up, for you are nearer God than I.

SCENE III.

INA, *in black, alone. Midnight.*

INA.

I weep? I weep? I laugh to think of it!
I lift my dark brow to the breath of the ocean,
Soft kissing me now like the lips of my mother,
And laugh low and long as I crush the brown grasses,

To think I should weep! Why, I never wept—never,
Not even in punishments dealt me in childhood!
Yea, all of my wrongs and my bitterness buried
In my brave baby heart, all alone and unfriended.
And I pitied, with proud and disdain fullest pity,
The weak who would weep, and I laugh'd at the folly
Of those who could laugh and make merry with playthings.

Nay, I will not weep now over that I desired.
Desired? Yes: I to myself dare confess it,
Ah, too, to the world should it question too closely,
And bathe me and sport in a deep sea of candor.
Let the world be deceived; it insists upon it:
Let it bundle me round in its black woe-garments;
But I, self with self—my free soul fearless—
Am frank as the sun, nor the toss of a copper
Care I if the world call it good or evil.
I am glad to-night, and in new-born freedom
Forget all earth with my old companions,—
The moon and the stars and the moon-clad ocean.
I am face to face with the stars that know me,
And gaze as I gazed in the eyes of my mother,
Forgetting the city and the coarse things in it;
For there's naught but God in the shape of mortal,
Save one—my wandering, wild boy-lover—
That I esteem worth a stale banana.

The hair hangs heavy and is warm on my shoulder,
And is thick with odors of balm and of blossom,
The great bay sleeps with the ships on her bosom;
Through the Golden Gate, to the left hand yonder,
The white sea lies in a deep sleep, breathing,
The father of melody, mother of measure.

SCENE IV

A wood by a rivulet on a spur of Mount Hood, overlooking the Columbia. LAMONTE *and* DON CARLOS, *on their way to the camp, are reposing under the shadow of the forest. Some deer are observed descending to the brook, and* DON CARLOS *seizes his rifle.*

LAMONTE.

Nay, nay, my friend, strike not from your covert,
Strike like a serpent in the grass well hidden?
What, steal into their homes, and, when they, thirsting,
And all unsuspecting, come down in couples
And dip brown muzzles in the mossy brink,
Then shoot them down without chance to fly—
The only means that God has given them,
Poor, unarm'd mutes, to baffle man's cunning?
Ah, now I see you had not thought of this!
The hare is fleet, and is most quick at sound,
His coat is changed with the changing fields;
Yon deer turn brown when the leaves turn brown;
The dog has teeth, the cat has talons,
And man has craft and sinewy arms:

All things that live have some means of defense
All, all—save only fair lovely woman.

DON CARLOS.

Nay, she has her tongue; is armed to the teeth.

LAMONTE.

Thou Timon, what can 'scape your bitterness?
But for this sweet content of Nature here,
Upon whose breast we now recline and rest,
Why, you might lift your voice and rail at her!

DON CARLOS.

Oh, I am out of patience with your faith!
What! She content and peaceful, uncomplaining?
I've seen her fretted like a lion caged,
Chafe like a peevish woman cross'd and churl'd,
Tramping and foaming like a whelpless bear;
Have seen her weep till earth was wet with tears,
Then turn all smiles—a jade that won her point?
Have seen her tear the hoary hair of ocean,
While he, himself full half a world, would moan
And roll and toss his clumsy hands all day
To earth like some great helpless babe,
Rude-rock'd and cradled by an unkind nurse,
Then stain her snowy hem with salt-sea tears;
And when the peaceful, mellow moon came forth,
To walk and meditate among the blooms
That make so blest the upper purple fields,
This wroth dyspeptic sea ran after her
With all his soul, as if to pour himself,
All sick and helpless, in her snowy lap.
Content! Oh, she has crack'd the ribs of earth
And made her shake poor trembling man from off
Her back, e'en as a grizzly shakes the hounds;
She has upheaved her rocky spine against
The flowing robes of the eternal God.

LAMONTE.

There once was one of nature like to this:
He stood a barehead boy upon a cliff
Pine-crown'd, that hung high o'er a bleak north sea
His long hair stream'd and flashed like yellow silk,
His sea-blue eyes lay deep and still as lakes
O'erhung by mountains arch'd in virgin snow;
And far astray, and friendless and alone,
A tropic bird blown through the north frost wind,
He stood above the sea in the cold white moon,
His thin face lifted to the flashing stars.
He talk'd familiarly and face to face
With the eternal God, in solemn night,
Confronting Him with free and flippant air
As one confronts a merchant o'er his counter,
And in vehement blasphemy did say:
"God, put aside this world—show me another!
God, this world's but a cheat—hand down another!
I will not buy—not have it as a gift.
Put this aside and hand me down another—
Another, and another, still another,

Till I have tried the fairest world that hangs
Upon the walls and broad dome of your shop.
For I am proud of soul and regal born,
And will not have a cheap and cheating world."

DON CARLOS.

The noble youth! So God gave him another?

LAMONTE.

A bear, as in old time, came from the woods
And tare him there upon that storm-swept cliff—
A grim and grizzled bear, like unto hunger.
A tall ship sail'd adown the sea next morn,
And, standing with his glass upon the prow,
The captain saw a vulture on a cliff,
Gorging, and pecking, stretching his long neck
Bracing his raven plumes against the wind,
Fretting the tempest with his sable feathers.

A Young POET *ascends the mountain and approaches.*

DON CARLOS.

Ho! ho! whom have we here? Talk of the devil,
And he's at hand. Say, who are you, and whence?

POET.

I am a poet, and dwell down by the sea.

DON CARLOS.

A poet! a poet, forsooth! A hungry fool!
Would you know what it means to be a poet now?
It is to want a friend, to want a home,
A country, money,—ay, to want a meal.
It is not wise to be a poet now,
For, oh, the world it has so modest grown
It will not praise a poet to his face,
But waits till he is dead some hundred years,
Then uprears marbles cold and stupid as itself. [POET *rises to go.*]

DON CARLOS.

Why, what's the haste? You'll reach there soon enough.

POET.

Reach where?

DON CARLOS.

The inn to which all earthly roads do tend:
The "neat apartments furnish'd—see within;"
The "furnish'd rooms for quiet, single gentlemen;"
The narrow six-by-two where you will lie
With cold blue nose up-pointing to the grass,
Labell'd and box'd, and ready all for shipment.

POET (*loosening hair and letting fall a mantle.*)

Ah me! my Don Carlos, look kindly upon me!
With my hand on your arm and my dark brow lifted
Full level to yours, do you not now know me?
'Tis I, your INA, whom you loved by the ocean,
In the warm-spiced winds from the far Cathay.

DON CARLOS (*bitterly*).

With the smell of the dead man still upon you!

Your dark hair wet from his death-damp forehead!
You are not my Ina, for she is a memory.
A marble chisell'd, in my heart's dark chamber
Set up for ever, and naught can change her;
And you are a stranger, and the gulf between us
Is wide as the plains, and as deep as Pacific.

And now, good night. In your serape folded
Hard by in the light of the pine-knot fire,
Sleep you as sound as you will be welcome;
And on the morrow — now mark me, madam—
When to-morrow comes, why, you will turn you
To the right or left as did Father Abram.
Good night, for ever and for aye, good by;
My bitter is sweet and your truth is a lie.

Ina *(letting go his arm and stepping back).*
Well, then! 'tis over, and 'tis well thus ended;
I am well escaped from my life's devotion.
The waters of bliss are a waste of bitterness;
The day of joy I did join hands over,
As a bow of promise when my years were weary,
And set high up as a brazen serpent
To look upon when I else had fainted
In burning deserts, while you sipp'd ices
And snowy sherbets, and roam'd unfetter'd,
Is a deadly asp in the fruit and flowers
That you in your bitterness now bear to me;
But its fangs unfasten and it glides down from me,
From a Cleopatra of cold white marble.

I have but done what I would do over,
Did I find one worthy of so much devotion;
And, standing here with my clean hands folded
Above a bosom whose crime is courage,
The only regret that my heart discovers
Is that I should do and have dared so greatly
For the love of one who deserved so little.

Nay! say no more, nor attempt to approach me!
This ten feet line lying now between us
Shall never be less while the land has measure.
See! night is forgetting the east in the heavens;
The birds pipe shrill and the beasts howl answer.

EVEN SO.

Sierras, and eternal tents
Of snow that flash o'er battlements
Of mountains! My land of the sun,
Am I not true? have I not done
All things for thine, for thee alone,
O sun-land, sea-land, thou mine own?
Be my reward some little place
To pitch my tent, some tree and vine
Where I may sit with lifted face,
And drink the sun as drinking wine:
Where sweeps the Oregon, and where
White storms caroused on perfumed air.

In the shadows a-west of the sunset mountains,
Where old-time giants had dwelt and peopled,
And built up cities and castled battlements,
And rear'd up pillars that pierced the heavens,
A poet dwelt, of the book of Nature—
An ardent lover of the pure and beautiful,
Devoutest lover of the true and beautiful.
Profoundest lover of the grand and beautiful—
With heart all impulse, and intensest passion,
Who believed in love as in God eternal—
A dream while the waken'd world went over,
An Indian summer of the singing seasons;
And he sang wild songs like the wind in cedars,
Was tempest-toss'd as the pines, yet ever
As fix'd in faith as they in the mountains.

He had heard a name as one hears of a princess,
Her glory had come unto him in stories;
From afar he had look'd as entranced upon her;
He gave her name to the wind in measures,
And he heard her name in the deep-voiced cedars,
And afar in the winds rolling on like the billows,
Her name in the name of another for ever
Gave all his numbers their grandest strophes;
Enshrined her image in his heart's high temple,
And saint-like held her, too sacred for mortal.

* * * * *

He came to fall like a king of the forest
Caught in the strong storm arms of the wrestler;
Forgetting his songs, his crags and his mountains,
And nearly his God, in his wild deep passion;
And when he had won her and turn'd him homeward,

With the holiest pledges love gives its lover,
The mountain route was as strewn with roses.

Can high love then be a thing unholy,
To make us better and bless'd supremely?
The day was fix'd for the feast and nuptials;
He crazed with impatience at the tardy hours;
He flew in the face of old Time as a tyrant;
He had fought the days that stood still between them,
Fought one by one, as you fight with a foeman,
Had they been animate and sensate beings.

At last then the hour came coldly forward.
When Mars was trailing his lance on the mountains
He rein'd his steed and look'd down in the cañon
To where she dwelt, with a heart of fire.
He kiss'd his hand to the smoke slow curling,
Then bow'd his head in devoutest blessing.
His spotted courser did plunge and fret him
Beneath his gay silken-fringed carona
And toss his neck in a black-mane banner'd;
Then all afoam, plunging iron-footed,
Dash'd him down with a wild impatience.

A coldness met him, like the breath of a cavern,
As he joyously hasten'd across the threshold.
She came, and coldly she spoke and scornful,
In answer to warm and impulsive passion.
All things did array them in shapes most hateful,
And life did seem but a jest intolerable.
He dared to question her why this estrangement:
She spoke with a strange and stiff indifference,
And bade him go on all alone life's journey.

Then stern and tall he did stand up before her,
And gaze dark-brow'd through the low narrow casement.
For a time, as if warring in thought with a passion;
Then, crushing hard down the hot welling bitterness,
He folded his form in a sullen silentness
And turned for ever away from her presence;
Bearing his sorrow like some great burden,
Like a black nightmare in his hot heart muffled;
With his faith in the truth of woman broken.

* * * * *

'Mid Theban pillars, where sang the Pindar,
Breathing the breath of the Grecian islands,
Breathing in spices and olive and myrtle,
Counting the caravans, curl'd and snowy,
Slow journeying over his head to Mecca
Or the high Christ land of most holy memory,
Counting the clouds through the boughs above him,
That brush'd white marbles that time had chisel'd
And rear'd as tombs on the great dead city,
Letter'd with solemn but unread moral—
A poet rested in the red-hot summer.
He took no note of the things about him,
But dream'd and counted the clouds above him;
His soul was troubled, and his sad heart's Mecca
Was a miner's home far over the ocean,
Banner'd by pines that did brush blue heaven.

When the sun went down on the bronzed Morea,
He read to himself from the lines of sorrow
That came as a wail from the one he worshipp'd,
Sent over the seas by an old companion:
They spoke no word of him, or remembrance.
And he was most sad, for he felt forgotten,
And said: "In the leaves of her fair heart's album
She has cover'd my face with the face of another.
Let the great sea lift like a wall between us,
High-back'd, with his mane of white storms for ever—
I shall learn to love, I shall wed my sorrow,
I shall take as a spouse the days that are perish'd;
I shall dwell in a land where the march of genius
Made tracks in marble in the days of giants;
I shall sit in the ruins where sat the Marius,
Gray with the ghosts of the great departed."
And then he said in the solemn twilight . . .

"Strangely wooing are yon worlds above us,
Strangely beautiful is the Faith of Islam,
Strangely sweet are the songs of Solomon,
Strangely tender are the teachings of Jesus,
Strangely cold is the sun on the mountains,
Strangely mellow is the moon on old ruins,
Strangely pleasant are the stolen waters,
Strangely lighted is the North night region,
Strangely strong are the streams in the ocean,
Strangely true are the tales of the Orient,
But stranger than all are the ways of women."

His head on his hands and his hands on the marble,
Alone in the midnight he slept in the ruins;
And a form was before him white mantled in moonlight,
And bitter he said to the one he had worshipp'd—

"Your hands in mine. your face, your eyes
Look level into mine, and mine
Are not abashed in anywise
As eyes were in an elden syne.
Perhaps the pulse is colder now,
And blood comes tamer to the brow
Because of hot blood long ago....
Withdraw your hand?....Well, be it so,
And turn your bent head slow sidewise,
For recollections are as seas
That come and go in tides, and these
Are flood tides filling to the eyes.

"How strange that you above the vale
And I below the mountain wall
Should walk and meet!..Why, you are pale!..
Strange meeting on the mountain fringe!..
....More strange we ever met at all!....
Tides come and go, we know their time;
The moon, we know her wane or prime;
But who knows how the heart may hinge?

"You stand before me here to-night,
But not beside me, not beside—
Are beautiful, but not a bride.
Some things I recollect aright,
Though full a dozen years are done
Since we two met one winter night—
Since I was crush'd as by a fall;
For I have watch'd and pray'd through all
The shining circles of the sun.

"I saw you where sad cedars wave;
I sought you in the dewy eve
When shining crickets trill and grieve;
You smiled, and I became a slave.
A slave! I worshipp'd you at night,
When all the blue field blossom'd red
With dewy roses overhead
In sweet and delicate delight.
I was devout. I knelt that night
To Him who doeth all things well.
I tried in vain to break the spell;
My prison'd soul refused to rise
And image saints in Paradise,
While one was here before my eyes.

"Some things are sooner marr'd than made.
A frost fell on a soul that night,
And one was black that erst was white.
And you forget the place—the night!
Forget that aught was done or said—
Say this has pass'd a long decade—
Say not a single tear was shed—
Say you forget these little things!
Is not your recollection loth?
Well, little bees have bitter stings,
And I remember for us both.

"No, not a tear. Do men complain?
The outer wound will show a stain,
And we may shriek at idle pain;
But pierce the heart, and not a word,
Or wail, or sign, is seen or heard.

"I did not blame—I do not blame,
My wild heart turns to you the same,
Such as it is; but oh, its meed
Of faithfulness and trust and truth,
And earnest confidence of youth,
I caution, you, is small indeed.

"I follow'd you, I worshipp'd you
And I would follow, worship still;
But if I felt the blight and chill
Of frosts in my uncheerful spring,
And show it now in riper years
In answer to this love you bring—
In answer to this second love,
This wail of an unmated dove,
In cautious answer to your tears—
You, you know who taught me disdain.
But deem you I would deal you pain?
I joy to know your heart is light,
I journey glad to know it thus,
And could I dare to make it less?
Yours—you are day, but I am night.

"God knows I would descend to-day
Devoutly on my knees, and pray
Your way might be one path of peace
Through bending boughs and blossom'd trees,
And perfect bliss through roses fair;
But know you, back—one long decade—
How fervently, how fond I pray'd?—
What was the answer to that prayer?

"The tale is old, and often told
And lived by more than you suppose—
The fragrance of a summer rose
Press'd down beneath the stubborn lid,
When sun and song are hush'd and hid,
And summer days are gray and old.

"We parted so. Amid the bays
And peaceful palms and song and shade
Your cheerful feet in pleasure stray'd
Through all the swift and shining days.

"You made my way another way,
You bade it should not be with thine—
A fierce and cheerless route was mine:
But we have met, to-night—to-day.

"You talk of tears—of bitter tears—
And tell of tyranny and wrong,
And I re-live some stinging jeers,
Back, far back, in the leaden years.
A lane without a turn is long,
I muse, and whistle a reply—
Then bite my lips and crush a sigh.

"You sympathize that I am sad,
I sigh for you that you complain,

I shake my yellow hair in vain,
I laugh with lips, but am not glad.
* * * * * * * *

...."His was a hot love of the hours,
And love and lover both are flown;
Now you walk, like a ghost, alone.
He sipp'd your sunny lips, and he
Took all their honey; now the bee
Bends down the heads of other flowers
And other lips lift up to kiss...
...I am not cruel, yet I find
A savage solace for the mind
And sweet delight in saying this...
Now you are silent, white, and you
Lift up your hands as making sign,
And your rich lips lie thin and blue
And ashen....and you writhe, and you
Breathe quick and tremble...is it true
The soul takes wounds, sheds blood like wine?
* * * * * * * *

..."You seem so most uncommon tall
Against the lonely ghostly moon,
That hurries homeward oversoon,
And hides behind you and the pines;
And your two hands hang cold and small,
And your two thin arms lie like vines,
Or winter moonbeams on a wall.
...What if you be a weary ghost,
And I but dream, and dream I wake?
Then wake me not, and my mistake
Is not so bad; let's make the most
Of all we get, asleep, awake—
And waste not one sweet thing at all.

God knows that, at the best, life brings
The soul's share so exceeding small
We weary for some better things,
And hunger even unto death.
Laugh loud, be glad with ready breath,
For after all are joy and grief
Not merely matters of belief?
And what is certain after all,
But death, delightful, patient death?
The cool and perfect, peaceful sleep,
Without one tossing hand, or deep
Sad sigh and catching in of breath!

"Be satisfied. The price of breath
Is paid in toil. But knowledge is
Bought only with a weary care,
And wisdom means a world of pain....
Well, we have suffered, will again,
And we can work and wait and bear,
Strong in the certainty of bliss.
Death is delightful: after death
Breaks in the dawn of perfect day.
Let question he who will: the May
Throws fragrance far beyond the wall.

"Death is delightful. Death is dawn.
Fame is not much, love is not much,
Yet what else is there worth the touch
Of lifted hand with dagger drawn?
So surely life is little worth:
Therefore I say, Look up; therefore
I say, One little star has more
Bright gold than all the earth of earth.

"Yea, we must labor, plant to reap—
Life knows no folding up of hands—
Must plow the soul, as plowing lands;
In furrows fashion'd strong and deep.
Life has its lesson. Let us learn
The hard, long lesson from the birth,
And be content; stand breast to breast,
And bear and battle till the rest.
Yet I look to yon stars, and say:
Thank Christ, ye are so far away
That when I win you I can turn
And look, and see no sign of earth.
* * * * * *

MYRRH.

Life knows no dead so beautiful
As is the white cold coffin'd past;
This I may love nor be betray'd:
The dead are faithful to the last.
I am not spouseless—I have wed
A memory—a life that 's dead.

Farewell! for here the ways at last
Divide—diverge, like delta'd Nile,
Which after desert dangers pass'd
Of many and many a thousand mile,
As constant as a column stone,
Seeks out the sea, divorced—alone.

And you and I have buried Love,
A red seal on the coffin's lid;
The clerk below, the court above,
Pronounce it dead: the corpse is hid
And I who never cross'd your will
Consent...that you may have it still.

Farewell! a sad word easy said
And easy sung, I think, by some....
....I clutch'd my hands, I turn'd my head
In my endeavor and was dumb;
And when I should have said, Farewell,
I only murmur'd, "This is hell."

What recks it now, whose was the blame?
But call it mine; for better used
Am I to wrong and cold disdain,
Can better bear to be accused
Of all that wears the shape of shame,
Than have you bear one touch of blame.

I set my face for power and place,
My soul is toned to sullenness,
My heart holds not one sign nor trace
Of love, or trust, or tenderness.
But you—your years of happiness
God knows I would not make them less.

And you will come some summer eve,
When wheels the white moon on her track,
And hear the plaintive night-bird grieve,
And heed the crickets clad in black;
Alone—not far—a little spell,
And say, "Well, yes, he loved me well;"

And sigh, "Well, yes, I mind me now,
None were so bravely true as he;
And yet his love was tame somehow,
It was so truly true to me;
I wish'd his patient love had less
Of worship and of tenderness:

"I wish it still, for thus alone
There comes a keen reproach or pain,
A feeling I dislike to own;
Half yearnings for his voice again,
Half longings for his earnest gaze,
To know him mine always—always."

* * * * *

I make no murmur; steady, calm,
Sphinxlike I gaze on days ahead.
No wooing word, no pressing palm,
No sealing love with lips seal-red,
No waiting for some dusk or dawn,
No sacred hour....all are gone.

I go alone; no little hands
To lead me from forbidden ways,
No little voice in other lands
To cheer through all the weary days,
Yet these are yours, and that to me
Is much indeed....So let it be....

....A last look from my mountain wall....
I watch the red sun wed the sea
Beside your home....the tides will fall
And rise, but nevermore shall we
Stand hand in hand and watch them flow,
As we once stood....Christ! this is so!

But, when the stately sea comes in
With measured tread and mouth afoam,
My darling cries above the din,
And asks, "Has father yet come home?"
Then look into the peaceful sky,
And answers, gently, "By and by."

* * * * *

One deep spring in a desert sand,
One moss'd and mystic pyramid,
A lonely palm on either hand,
A fountain in a forest hid,
Are all my life has realized
Of all I cherish'd, all I prized:

Of all I dream'd in early youth
Of love by streams and love-lit ways,
While my heart held its type of truth
Through all the tropic golden days,
And I the oak, and you the vine,
Clung palm in palm through cloud or shine.

Some time when clouds hang overhead,
(What weary skies without one cloud!)
You may muse on this love that's dead,
Muse calm when not so cold or proud,
And say, "At last it comes to me,
That none was ever true as he."

My sin was that I loved too much—
But I enlisted for the war,
Till we the deep-sea shore should touch,
Beyond Atlanta—near or far—
And truer soldier never yet
Bore shining sword or bayonet.

I did not blame you—do not blame.
The stormy elements of soul
That I did scorn to tone or tame,
Or bind down unto dull control
In full fierce youth, they all are yours,
With all their folly and their force.

God keep you pure, oh, very pure,
God give you grace to dare and do;
God give you courage to endure
The all He may demand of you,—
Keep time frosts from your raven hair,
And your young heart without a care.

I make no murmur nor complain;
Above me are the stars and blue
Alluring far to grand refrain;
Before, the beautiful and true,
To love or hate, to win or lose;
Lo! I will now arise, and choose.

But should you sometime read a sign,
In isles of song beyond the brine,
Then you will think a time, and you
Will turn and say, "He once was mine,
Was all my own; his smiles, his tears
Were mine—were mine for years and years."

KIT CARSON'S RIDE.

Room! room to turn round in, to breathe and be free,
To grow to be giant, to sail as at sea
With the speed of the wind on a steed with his mane
To the wind, without pathway or route or a rein.
Room! room to be free where the white border'd sea
Blows a kiss to a brother as boundless as he;
Where the buffalo come like a cloud on the plain,
Pouring on like the tide of a storm driven main,
And the lodge of the hunter to friend or to foe
Offers rest; and unquestion'd you come or you go.
My plains of America! Seas of wild lands!
From a land in the seas in a raiment of foam,
That has reached to a stranger the welcome of home,
I turn to you, lean to you, lift you my hands.
London, 1871.

Run? Run? See this flank, sir, and I do love him so!
But he's blind as a badger. Whoa, Pache, boy, whoa.
No, you wouldn't believe it to look at his eyes,
But he's blind, badger blind, and it happen'd this wise:

"We lay in the grass and the sunburnt clover
That spread on the ground like a great brown cover
Northward and southward, and west and away
To the Brazos, where our lodges lay,
One broad and unbroken level of brown.
We were waiting the curtains of night to come down
To cover us trio and conceal our flight
With my brown bride, won from an Indian town
That lay in the rear the full ride of a night.

"We lounged in the grass—her eyes were in mine,
And her hands on my knee, and her hair was as wine
In its wealth and its flood, pouring on and all over
Her bosom wine red, and press'd never by one.
Her touch was as warm as the tinge of the clover
Burnt brown as it reach'd to the kiss of the sun.
Her words they were low as the lute-throated dove,
And as laden with love as the heart when it beats
In its hot, eager answer to earliest love,
Or the bee hurried home by its burthen of sweets.

We lay low in the grass on the broad plain levels,
Old Revels and I, and my stolen brown bride;

"Forty full miles if a foot to ride!
Forty full miles if a foot, and the devils
Of red Comanches are hot on the track
When once they strike it. Let the sun go down
Soon, very soon," muttered bearded old Revels
As he peer'd at the sun, lying low on his back,
Holding fast to his lasso. Then he jerk'd at his steed
And he sprang to his feet, and glanced swiftly around,
And then dropp'd, as if shot, with an ear to the ground;
Then again to his feet, and to me, to my bride,
While his eyes were like flame, his face like a shroud,
His form like a king, and his beard like a cloud,
And his voice loud and shrill, as both trumpet and reed,—
"Pull, pull in your lassoes, and bridle to steed,
And speed you if ever for life you would speed.
Aye, ride for your lives, for your lives you must ride!
For the plain is aflame, the prairie on fire,
And the feet of wild horses hard flying before
I hear like a sea breaking high on the shore,
While the buffalo come like a surge of the sea,
Driven far by the flame, driving fast on us three
As a hurricane comes, crushing palms in his ire."

"We drew in the lassoes, seized saddle and rein,
Threw them on, cinched them on, cinched them over again,
And again drew the girth; and spring we to horse,
With head to the Brazos, with a sound in the air
Like the surge of a sea, with a flash in the eye,
From that red wall of flame reaching up to the sky;
A red wall of flame and a black rolling sea
Rushing fast upon us, as the wind sweeping free
And afar from the desert blown hollow and hoarse.

"Not a word, not a wail from a lip was let fall,
We broke not a whisper, we breathed not a prayer,
There was work to be done, there was death in the air,
And the chance was as one to a thousand for all.

Twenty miles!....thirty miles!....a dim distant speck....
Then a long reaching line, and the Brazos in sight!
And I rose in my seat with a shout of delight.
I stood in my stirrup and look'd to my right—
But Revels was gone; I glanced by my shoulder
And saw his horse stagger; I saw his head drooping
Hard down on his breast, and his naked breast stooping
Low down to the mane, as so swifter and bolder
Ran reaching out for us the red-footed fire.
He rode neck to neck with a buffalo bull,
That made the earth shake where he came in his course,
The monarch of millions, with shaggy mane full

Of smoke and of dust, and it shook with desire
Of battle, with rage and with bellowings hoarse.
His keen, crooked horns, through the storm of his mane,
Like black lances lifted and lifted again;
And I looked but this once, for the fire licked through,
And Revels was gone, as we rode two and two.

"I look'd to my left then—and nose, neck, and shoulder
Sank slowly, sank surely, till back to my thighs,
And up through the black blowing veil of her hair
Did beam full in mine her two marvelous eyes,
With a longing and love yet a look of despair
And of pity for me, as she felt the smoke fold her,
And flames leaping far for her glorious hair.
Her sinking horse falter'd, plunged, fell and was gone
As I reach'd through the flame and I bore her still on.
On! into the Brazos, she, Pache and I—
Poor, burnt, blinded Pache. I love him . . That's why.

With better fortunes when my first London book was out, I had taken rooms at Museum street, a few doors from the greatest storehouse of art and history on the globe, and I literally lived in the British Museum every day. But I had already overtaxed my strength, and my eyes were paining terribly. Never robust, I had always abhorred meat; and milk, from a child, had been my strongest drink. In the chill damp of London you must eat and drink. I was, without knowing it, starving and working myself to death. Always and wherever you are, when a hard bit of work is done, rest and refresh. Go to the fields, woods, to God and get strong. This is your duty as well as your right.

Letters—sweet, brave, good letters from the learned and great—were so many I could not read them with my poor eyes and had to leave them to friends. They found two from the Archbishop of Dublin. I was to breakfast with him to meet Browning, Dean Stanley, Houghton, and so on. I went to an old Jew close by to hire a dress suit, as Franklin had done for the Court of St. James. While fitting on the clothes I told him I was in haste to go to a great breakfast. He stopped, looked at me, looked me all over, and then told me I must not wear that, but he would hire me a suit of velvet. By degrees, as he fixed me up, he got at, or guessed at some facts, and when I asked to pay him he shook his head. I put some money down and he pushed it back. He said he had a son, his only family now, at Oxford, and he kept on fixing me up; cane, great, tall silk hat, gloves and all. Who would have guessed the heart to be found there?

Browning was just back from Italy, sunburnt and ruddy. "Robert, you are browning," smiled Lady Augusta. "And you are August—a," bowed the great poet grandly; and, by what coincidence—he, too, was in brown velvet, and so like my own that I was a bit uneasy.

Two of the Archbishop's beautiful daughters had been riding in the park with the Earl of Aberdeen. "And did you gallop?" asked Browning of the younger beauty. "I galloped, Joyce galloped, we galloped all three." Then we all laughed at the happy and hearty retort, and Browning, beating the time and clang of galloping horses' feet on the table with his fingers, repeated the exact measure in Latin from Virgil; and the Archbishop laughingly took it up, in Latin, where he left off. I then told Browning I had an order—it was my first—for a poem from the *Oxford Magazine*, and would like to borrow the measure and spirit of his "Good News" for a prairie fire on the plains, driving buffalo and all other life before it into a river. "Why not borrow from Virgil, as I did? He is as rich as one of your gold mines, while I am but a poor scribe." And this was my first of inner London.

Fast on top of this came breakfasts with Lord Houghton, lunch with Browning, a dinner with Rossetti to meet the great painters; the good old Jew garmenting me always, and always pushing back the pay. But still I could not or would not eat or drink. All the time, too, a dreadful sense of terror hung over me; for brother, at Easton, Pa., had written that our sister in Oregon was ill, and he far from well.

One evening Rossetti brought me Walt Whitman, new to me, and that night I lay in bed and read it through—the last book I ever read. I could not bear any light next morning, nor very much light ever since, nor have ever since looked upon any page long without intense pain. Hence the "eccentricity" of never having books or papers about me, of writing as few letters as possible, and these on colored or unruled paper. White paper hurts me so that I must look aside, and what with a crippled arm, too, I write a and hand. Pardon all this detail, but the facts may save pain to some young writers whom I surely would answer if I could.

Let me here note some things my new poets that you should not do; then some that you must. The random notes of this book will serve you better than all the letters I could ever write you. Spend no time or strength finding fault with a fellow scribe. I know but little of prize fighters or pirates of the high seas, but from what I am told they are far more courteous to one another than are American authors, except in sets and little circles.

If you feel a bitterness my young poet toward some one more favored at this time than yourself, pray God to send some good angel to lay you on your back and take the black drop from your heart, for it will make you not only weak and worthless if it remain, but it will make you certainly miserable. If you cannot learn to see beauty and love beauty in the life and work of Nature, then, believe me, you were not born to the sweetness of song. If you must find faults find them in your own work. I have done this, and it has kept me busy. Nor shall you to the extent of its newness, scorn a new character, mistake character for eccentricity. Our work, the calling of the poet is the highest under the stars, so are his triumphs the rarest; and he who would despoil him would despoil the dead.

Nor shall you bewail the afflictions of your flesh. That is old, old; and has been done perfectly. The man who intrudes the weakness of his body is a bore. Let him, if he must, sing the weakness of his mind. But when "he putteth off his armor," then, and not till then, may he tell the pain and peril of his fight.

And now fell the pending sword, just as my London life began. Sister was dead and my soldier brother dying—bleeding at the lungs. I took the first steamer, at Southampton for his bedside, so blinded that I had to be led to my berth.

This poem was not in any of my four first books, and so has not been rightly revised till now. It was too long for the tumultuous and swift action; and then the end was coarse and unworthy the brave spirit of Kit Carson. I have here cut and changed it much; as I cut and changed all the matter of my three preceding books in London when I cut and compressed all I had done worth preserving into the Songs of the Sierras.

WHEN LITTLE SISTER CAME.

We dwelt in the woods of the Tippecanoe,
In a lone lost cabin, with never a view
Of the full day's sun for a whole year through.
With strange half hints through the russet corn
We children were hurried one night. Next morn
There was frost on the trees, and a sprinkle of snow,
And tracks on the ground. Three boys below
The low eave listened. We burst through the door,
And a girl baby cried,—and then we were four.

We were not sturdy, and we were not wise
In the things of the world, and the ways men dare.
A pale browed mother with a prophet's eyes,
A father that dreamed and looked anywhere.
Three brothers—wild blossoms, tall-fashioned as men
And we mingled with none, but we lived as when
The pair first lived ere they knew the fall;
And, loving all things, we believed in all.

Ah! girding yourself and throwing your strength
On the front of the forest that stands in mail,
Sounds gallant, indeed, in a pioneer's tale,
But, God in heaven! the weariness
Of a sweet soul banished to a life like this!

This reaching of weary-worn arms full length;
This stooping all day to the cold stubborn soil—
This holding the heart! it is more than toil!
What loneless of heart! what wishings to die
In that soul in the earth, that was born for the sky!

We parted wood-curtains, pushed westward and we,
Why, we wandered and wandered a half year through,
We tented with herds as the Arabs do,
And at last sat down by the sundown sea.
Then there in that sun did my soul take fire!
It burned in its fervor, thou Venice, for thee!
My glad heart glowed with the one desire
To stride to the front, to live, to be!
To strow great thoughts through the world as I went,
As God sows stars through the firmament.

Venice, 1874.

We had been moving West and West from my birth, at Liberty, Union county, Ind., November 10, 1841 or 1842 (the Bible was burned and we don't know which year), and now were in the woods of the Miami Indian Reserve. My first recollection is of starting up from the trundle bed with my two little brothers and looking out one night at father and mother at work burning brush-heaps, which threw a lurid flare against the greased paper window. Late that autumn I was measured for my first shoes, and Papa led me to his school. Then a strange old woman came, and there was mystery and a smell of mint, and one night, as we three little ones were hurried away through the woods to a neighbor's, she was very cross. We three came back alone in the cold, early morning. There was a little snow, rabbit tracks in the trail, and some quail ran hastily from cover to cover. We three little ones were all alone and silent, so silent, We knew nothing, nothing at all, and yet we knew, intuitively, all; but truly the divine mystery of mother nature, God's relegation of His last great work to woman, her partnership with Him in creation—not one of us had ever dreamed of. Yet we three little lads huddled up in a knot near the ice-hung eaves of the log cabin outside the corner where mother's bed stood and —did the new baby hear her silent and awed little brothers? Did she feel them, outside there, huddled close together in the cold and snow, listening, listening? For lo! a little baby cry came through the cabin wall; and then we all rushed around the corner of the cabin, jerked the latch and all three in a heap tumbled up into the bed and peered down into the little pink face against mother's breast. Gentle, gentle, how more than ever gentle were we all six now in that little log cabin. Papa doing everything so gently, saying nothing, only doing, doing. And ever so and always toward the West, till 1852, when he had touched the sea of seas, and could go no farther. And so gentle always! Can you conceive how gentle? Seventy-two years he led and lived in the wilderness and yet never fired or even laid hand to a gun.

OLIVE LEAVES.

"In the desert a fountain is springing,
In the wild waste there still is a tree."

"Though the many lights dwindle to one light,
There is help if the heavens have one."

"Change lays not her hand upon truth."

AT BETHLEHEM.

With incense and myrrh and sweet spices,
Frankincense and sacredest oil
In ivory, chased with devices
Cut quaint and in serpentine coil;
Heads bared, and held down to the bosom;
Brows massive with wisdom and bronzed;
Beards white as the white May in blossom;
And borne to the breast and beyond,—
Came the Wise of the East, bending lowly
On staffs, with their garments girt round
With girdles of hair, to the Holy
Child Christ, in their sandals. The sound
Of song and thanksgiving ascended—
Deep night! Yet some shepherds afar
Heard a wail with the worshipping blended
And they then knew the sign of the star.

"LA NOTTE."

Is it night? And sits night at your pillow?
Sits darkness about you like death?
Rolls darkness above like a billow,
As drowning men catch in their breath?

Is it night, and deep night of dark errors,
Of crosses, of pitfalls and bars?
Then lift up your face from your terrors,
For heaven alone holds the stars!

Lo! shaggy beard shepherds, the fastness—
Lorn, desolate Syrian sod;
The darkness, the midnight, the vastness—
That vast, solemn night bore a God!

The night brought us God; and the Savior
Lay down in a cradle to rest;
A sweet cherub Babe in behavior,
So that all baby-world might be blest.

IN PALESTINE.

O Jebus! thou mother of prophets,
Of soldiers and heroes of song;
Let the crescent oppress thee and scoff its
Blind will, let the days do thee wrong;

But to me thou art sacred and splendid,
And to me thou art matchless and fair,
As the tawny sweet twilight, with blended
Sunlight and red stars in her hair.

Thy fair ships once came from sweet Cyprus,
And fair ships drew in from Cyrene,
With fruits and rich robes and sweet spices
For thee and thine, eminent queen;

And camels came in with the traces
Of white desert dust in their hair
As they kneel'd in the loud market places,
And Arabs with lances were there.

'Tis past, and the Bedouin pillows
His head where thy battlements fall,
And thy temples flash gold to the billows,
Never more over turreted wall.

'Tis past, and the green velvet mosses
Have grown by the sea, and now sore
Does the far billow mourn for his losses
Of lifted white ships to the shore.

Let the crescent uprise, let it flash on
Thy dust in the garden of death,
Thy chastened and passionless passion
Sunk down to the sound of a breath;

Yet you lived like a king on a throne and
You died like a queen of the south;
For you lifted the cup with your own hand
To your proud and your passionate mouth;

Like a splendid swift serpent surrounded
With fire and sword, in your side
You struck your hot fangs and confounded
Your foes; you struck deep, and so—died.

BEYOND JORDAN.

And they came to him, mothers of Judah,
Dark eyed and in splendor of hair,
Bearing down over shoulders of beauty,
And bosoms half hidden, half bare;

And they brought him their babes and besought him
Half kneeling, with suppliant air,
To bless the brown cherubs they brought him,
With holy hands laid in their hair.

Then reaching his hands he said, lowly,
"Of such is My Kingdom;" and then
Took the brown little babes in the holy
White hands of the Savior of men;

Held them close to his heart and caress'd them,
Put his face down to theirs as in prayer,
Put their hands to his neck, and so bless'd them
With baby hands hid in his hair.

FAITH.

There were whimsical turns of the waters,
There were rhythmical talks of the sea,—
There were gather'd the darkest eyed daughters
Of men, by the deep Galilee.

A blowing full sail, and a parting
From multitudes, living in Him,
A trembling of lips, and tears starting
From eyes that look'd downward and dim.

A mantle of night and a marching
Of storms, and a sounding of seas,
Of furrows of foam and of arching
Black billows; a bending of knees;

The rising of Christ—an entreating—
Hands reach'd to the seas as he saith,
"Have Faith!" And all seas are repeating,
"Have Faith! Have Faith! Have Faith!"

HOPE.

What song is well sung not of sorrow?
What triumph well won without pain?
What virtue shall be, and not borrow
Bright luster from many a stain?

What birth has there been without travail?
What battle well won without blood?

What good shall earth see without evil
  Ingarner'd as chaff with the good?

Lo! the Cross set in rocks by the Roman,
  And nourish'd by blood of the Lamb,
And water'd by tears of the woman,
  Has flourish'd, has spread like a palm;

Has spread in the frosts, and far regions
  Of snows in the North, and South sands,
Where never the tramp of his legions
  Was heard, or reach'd forth his red hands.

Be thankful; the price and the payment,
  The birth, the privations and scorn,
The cross, and the parting of raiment,
  Are finish'd. The star brought us morn.

Look starward; stand far and unearthy,
  Free soul'd as a banner unfurl'd.
Be worthy, O brother, be worthy!
  For a God was the price of the world.

CHARITY.

Her hands were clasped downward and doubled,
  Her head was held down and depress'd,
Her bosom, like white billows troubled,
  Fell fitful and rose in unrest;

Her robes were all dust, and disorder'd
  Her glory of hair, and her brow,
Her face, that had lifted and lorded,
  Fell pallid and passionless now.

She heard not accusers that brought her
  In mockery hurried to Him,
Nor heeded, nor said, nor besought her
  With eyes lifted doubtful and dim.

All crush'd and stone-cast in behavior,
  She stood as a marble would stand,
Then the Savior bent down, and the Savior
  In silence wrote on in the sand.

What wrote He? How fondly one lingers
  And questions, what holy command
Fell down from the beautiful fingers
  Of Jesus, like gems in the sand.

O better the Scian uncherish'd
  Had died ere a note or device
Of battle was fashion'd, than perish'd
  This only line written by Christ.

He arose and look'd on the daughter
  Of Eve, like a delicate flower,
And he heard the revilers that brought her;
  Men stormy, and strong as a tower;

And He said, "She has sinn'd; let the blameless
  Come forward and cast the first stone!"
But they, they fled shamed and yet shameless;
  And she, she stood white and alone.

Who now shall accuse and arraign us?
  What man shall condemn and disown?
Since Christ has said only the stainless
  Shall cast at his fellows a stone.

For what man can bare us his bosom,
  And touch with his forefinger there,
And say, 'Tis as snow, as a blossom?
  Beware of the stainless, beware!

O woman, born first to believe us;
  Yea, also born first to forget;
Born first to betray and deceive us;
  Yet first to repent and regret!

O first then in all that is human,
  Yea! first where the Nazarene trod,
O woman! O beautiful woman!
  Be then first in the kingdom of God!

THE LAST SUPPER.

"And when they had sung an hymn they went out into the Mount of Olives."

What song sang the twelve with the Savior
When finish'd the sacrament wine?
Were they bow'd and subdued in behavior,
Or bold as made bold with a sign?

Were the hairy breasts strong and defiant?
Were the naked arms brawny and strong?
Were the bearded lips lifted reliant,
Thrust forth and full sturdy with song!

What sang they? What sweet song of Zion
With Christ in their midst like a crown?
While here sat Saint Peter, the lion;
And there like a lamb, with head down,

Sat Saint John, with his silken and raven
Rich hair on his shoulders, and eyes
Lifting up to the faces unshaven
Like a sensitive child's in surprise.

Was the song as strong fishermen swinging
Their nets full of hope to the sea?
Or low, like the ripple wave, singing
Sea songs on their loved Galilee?

Were they sad with foreshadow of sorrows,
Like the birds that sing low when the breeze
Is tiptoe with a tale of to-morrows,—
Of earthquakes and sinking of seas?

Ah! soft was their song as the waves are
That fall in low musical moans;
And sad I should say as the winds are
That blow by the white gravestones.

A SONG FOR PEACE.

I.

As a tale that is told, as a vision,
Forgive and forget; for I say
That the true shall endure the derision
Of the false till the full of the day;

II.

Ay, forgive as you would be forgiven;
Ay, forget, lest the ill you have done
Be remember'd against you in heaven
And all the days under the sun.

III.

For who shall have bread without labor?
And who shall have rest without price?
And who shall hold war with his neighbor
With promise of peace with the Christ?

IV.

The years may lay hand on fair heaven;
May place and displace the red stars;
May stain them, as blood stains are driven
At sunset in beautiful bars;

V.

May shroud them in black till they fret us
As clouds with their showers of tears;
May grind us to dust and forget us,
May the years, O, the pitiless years!

VI.

But the precepts of Christ are beyond them;
The truths by the Nazarene taught,
With the tramp of the ages upon them,
They endure as though ages were naught;

VII.

The deserts may drink up the fountains,
The forests give place to the plain,
The main may give place to the mountains,
The mountains return to the main;

VIII.

Mutations of worlds and mutations
Of suns may take place, but the reign
Of Time, and the toils and vexations
Bequeath them, no, never a stain.

IX.

Go forth to the fields as one sowing,
Sing songs and be glad as you go,
There are seeds that take root without showing,
And bear some fruit whether or no.

X.

And the sun shall shine sooner or later,
Though the midnight breaks ground on the morn,
Then appeal you to Christ, the Creator,
And to gray bearded Time, His first born.

Jean Ingelow, London, had given a letter to a Boston publisher, who came to me there for my book in America, as I was more entirely a stranger in the Atlantic States than in Europe; and now returned I sat all summer at a bedside, editing the book and also trying to write the Life of Christ in verse for Brother. At last the revised edition for America was done. It came just in time. He took the book, still damp from the binders, said "It is a pretty book," and laid it down. He said some other things, sacred to us, and passed. Had he lived, with his better sense about all things, I surely should have done better, better in all ways. Death had broken in upon us cruelly, and I must go back to Oregon now. There was not time nor heart nor health to finish the Life of Christ; besides I had begun to see that the measure was monotonous. The greatest poem on earth probably is the Sermon on the Mount. I laid the few completed pages on my Brother's grave, and once more I was in Oregon. Care and toil had again brought on the painful snow blindness, and yet how fortunate this cruel misfortune now. For I could not see to read the fearfully coarse insults and falsehoods that now pursued me, simply because I had, at such cost, garmented my mountains with a new glory.

O boy at peace upon the Delaware!
O brother mine, that fell in battle front
Of life, so braver, nobler far than I,
The wanderer who vexed all gentleness,
Receive this song; I have but this to give.
I may not rear the rich man's ghostly stone;
But you, through all my follies loving still
And trusting me....nay, I shall not forget.

A failing hand in mine, and fading eyes
That look'd in mine as from another land,
You said: "Some gentler things; a song for Peace.
'Mid all your songs for men one song for God."
And then the dark-brow'd mother, Death, bent down
Her face to yours, and you were born to Him.

SONGS OF THE SUNLANDS.

THE SEA OF FIRE.

In a land so far that you wonder whether
If God would know it should you fall down dead;
In a land so far through the soft, warm weather
That the sun sinks red as a warrior sped,—
Where the sea and the sky seem closing together,
Seem closing together as a book that is read:

'Tis the half-finished world! Yon footfall retreating,—
It might be the Maker disturbed at his task.
But the footfall of God, or the far pheasant beating,
It is one and the same, whatever the mask
It may wear unto man. The woods keep repeating
The old sacred sermons, whatever you ask.

It is man in his garden, scarce wakened as yet
From the sleep that fell on him when woman was made.
The new-finished garden is plastic and wet
From the hand that has fashioned its unpeopled shade;
And the wonder still looks from the fair woman's eyes
As she shines through the wood like the light from the skies.

And a ship now and then for this far Ophir shore
Draws in from the sea. It lies close io the bank;
Then a dull, muffled sound on the slow shuffled plank
As they load the black ship; but you hear nothing more,
And the dark, dewy vines, and the tall, somber wood
Like twilight droop over the deep, sweeping flood.

The black masts are tangled with branches that cross,
The rich fragrant gums fall from branches to deck,
The thin ropes are swinging with streamers of moss
That mantle all things like the shreds of a wreck;
The long mosses swing, there is never a breath:
The river rolls still as the river of death.

I.

In the beginning,—ay, before
The six-days' labors were well o'er;
Yea, while the world lay incomplete,
Ere God had opened quite the door
Of this strange land for strong men's feet,—
There lay against that westmost sea,
A weird, wild land of mystery.

A far white wall, like fallen moon,
Girt out the world. The forest lay
So deep you scarcely saw the day,
Save in the high-held middle noon:
It lay a land of sleep and dreams,
And clouds drew through like shoreless streams
That stretch to where no man may say.

Men reached it only from the sea,
By black-built ships, that seemed to creep
Along the shore suspiciously,
Like unnamed monsters of the deep.
It was the weirdest land, I ween,
That mortal eye has ever seen.

A dim, dark land of bird and beast,
Black shaggy beasts with cloven claw,—
A land that scarce knew prayer or priest,
Or law of man, or Nature's law;
Where no fixed line drew sharp dispute
Twixt savage man and sullen brute.

II.

It hath a history most fit
For cunning hand to fashion on;
No chronicler hath mentioned it;
No buccaneer set foot upon.
'Tis of an outlawed Spanish Don,—
A cruel man, with pirate's gold
That loaded down his deep ship's hold.

A deep ship's hold of plundered gold!
The golden cruse, the golden cross,
From many a church of Mexico,
From Panama's mad overthrow,
From many a ransomed city's loss,
From many a follower fierce and bold,
And many a foeman stark and cold.

He found this wild, lost land. He drew
His ship to shore. His ruthless crew,
Like Romulus, laid lawless hand
On meek brown maidens of the land,
And in their bloody forays bore
Red firebrands along the shore.

III.

The red men rose at night. They came,
A firm, unflinching wall of flame;
They swept, as sweeps some fateful sea
O'er land of sand and level shore
That howls in far, fierce agony.
The red men swept that deep, dark shore
As threshers sweep a threshing floor.

And yet beside the slain Don's door
They left his daughter, as they fled:
They spared her life because she bore
Their Chieftain's blood and name. The red
And blood-stained hidden hoards of gold
They hollowed from the stout ship's hold,
And bore in many a slim canoe—
To where? The good priest only knew.

IV.

The course of life is like the sea;
Men come and go; tides rise and fall;
And that is all of history.
The tide flows in, flows out to-day—
And that is all that man may say;
Man is, man was,—and that is all.

Revenge at last came like a tide,—
'T was sweeping, deep and terrible;
The Christian found the land, and came
To take possession in Christ's name.
For every white man that had died
I think a thousand red men fell,—

A Christian custom; and the land
Lay lifeless as some burned-out brand.

V.

Ere while the slain Don's daughter grew
A glorious thing, a flower of spring,
A something more than mortals knew;
A mystery of grace and face,—
A silent mystery that stood
An empress in that sea-set wood,
Supreme, imperial in her place.

It might have been men's lust for gold,—
For all men knew that lawless crew
Left hoards of gold in that ship's hold,
That drew ships hence, and silent drew
Strange Jasons there to love or dare;
I never knew, nor need I care.

I say it might have been this gold
That ever drew and strangely drew
Strong men of land, strange men of sea
To seek this shore of mystery
With all its wondrous tales untold;
The gold or her, which of the two?
It matters not to me, or you.

But this I know, that as for me,
Between that face and the hard fate
That kept me ever from my own,
As some wronged monarch from his throne,
All heaped-up gold of land or sea
Had never weighed one feather's weight.

Her home was on the wooded height,—
A woody home, a priest at prayer,
A perfume in the fervid air,
And angels watching her at night.
I can but think upon the skies
That bound that other Paradise.

VI.

Below a star-built arch, as grand
As ever bended heaven spanned,
Tall trees like mighty columns grew—
They loomed as if to pierce the blue,
They reached, as reaching heaven through.

The shadowed stream rolled far below,
Where men moved noiseless to and fro
As in some vast cathedral, when
The calm of prayer comes to men,
And benedictions bless them so.

What wooded sea-banks, wild and steep!
What trackless wood! what snowy cone
That lifted from this wood alone!
What wild, wide river, dark and deep!
What ships against the shore asleep!

VII.

An Indian woman cautious crept
About the land the while it slept,
The relic of her perished race.
She wore rich, rudely-fashioned bands
Of gold above her bony hands;
She hissed hot curses on the place!

VIII.

Go seek the red man's last retreat!
What lonesome lands! what haunted lands!
Red mouths of beasts, red men's red hands;
Red prophet-priests, in mute defeat.
From Incan temples overthrown
To lorn Alaska's isles of bone
The red man lives and dies alone.

His boundaries in blood are writ!
His land is ghostland! That is his,
Whatever we may claim of this;
Beware how you shall enter it!
He stands God's guardian of ghostlands;
Yea, this same wrapped half-prophet stands
All nude and voiceless, nearer to
The dread, lone God than I or you.

IX.

This bronzed child, by that river's brink,
Stood fair to see as you can think,
As tall as tall reeds at her feet,

As fresh as flowers in her hair;
As sweet as flowers over-sweet,
As fair as vision more than fair!

How beautiful she was! How wild!
How pure as water-plant, this child,—
This one wild child of Nature here
Grown tall in shadows.

And how near
To God, where no man stood between
Her eyes and scenes no man hath seen,—
This maiden that so mutely stood,
The one lone woman of that wood.

Stop still, my friend, and do not stir,
Shut close your page and think of her.
The birds sang sweeter for her face;
Her lifted eyes were like a grace
To seamen of that solitude,
However rough, however rude.

The rippled river of her hair,
Flowed in such wondrous waves, somehow
Flowed down divided by her brow,—
It mantled her within its care,
And flooded all her form below,
In its uncommon fold and flow.

A perfume and an incense lay
Before her, as an incense sweet
Before blithe mowers of sweet May
In early morn. Her certain feet
Embarked on no uncertain way.

Come, think how perfect before men,
How sweet as sweet magnolia bloom
Embalmed in dews of morning, when
Rich sunlight leaps from midnight gloom
Resolved to kiss, and swift to kiss
Ere yet morn wakens man to bliss.

X.

The days swept on. Her perfect year
Was with her now. The sweet perfume
Of womanhood in holy bloom,
As when red harvest blooms appear,
Possessed her soul. The priest did pray
That saints alone should pass that way.

A red bird built beneath her roof,
Brown squirrels crossed her cabin sill,
And welcome came or went at will.
A hermit spider wove his web
Above her door and plied his trade,
With none to fright or make afraid.

The silly elk, the spotted fawn,
And all dumb beasts that came to drink,
That stealthy stole upon the brink
By coming night or going dawn,
On seeing her familiar face
Would fearless stop and stand in place.

She was so kind, the beasts of night
Gave her the road as if her right;
The panther crouching overhead
In sheen of moss would hear her tread,
And bend his eyes, but never stir
Lest he by chance might frighten her.

Yet in her splendid strength, her eyes,
There lay the lightning of the skies;
The love-hate of the lioness,
To kill the instant or caress:
A pent-up soul that sometimes grew
Impatient; why, she hardly knew.

At last she sighed, uprose, and threw
Her strong arms out as if to hand
Her love, sun-born and all complete
At birth, to some brave lover's feet
On some far, fair, and unseen land,
As knowing not quite what to do!

XI.

How beautiful she was! Why, she
Was inspiration! She was born
To walk God's sunlit hills at morn,
Nor waste her by this wood-dark sea.
What wonder, then, her soul's white wings
Beat at its bars, like living things!

Once more she sighed! She wandered
through
The sea-bound wood, then stopped and
drew
Her hand above her face, and swept
The lonesome sea, and all day kept
Her face to sea, as if she knew
Some day, some near or distant day.
Her destiny should come that way.

XII.

How proud she was! How darkly fair!
How full of faith, of love, of strength!
Her calm, proud eyes! Her great hair's
length,—
Her long, strong, tumbled, careless hair,
Half curled and knotted anywhere,—
By brow or breast, or cheek or chin,
For love to trip and tangle in!

XIII.

At last a tall strange sail was seen:
It came so slow, so wearily,
Came creeping cautious up the sea,
As if it crept from out between
The half-closed sea and sky that lay
Tight wedged together, far away.

She watched it, wooed it. She did pray
It might not pass her by but bring
Some love, some hate, some anything,
To break the awful loneliness
That like a nightly nightmare lay
Upon her proud and pent-up soul
Until it barely brooked control.

XIV.

The ship crept silent up the sea,
And came—
You cannot understand
How fair she was, how sudden she
Had sprung, full grown, to womanhood:
How gracious, yet how proud and grand;
How glorified, yet fresh and free,
How human, yet how more than good.

XV.

The ship stole slowly, slowly on;—
Should you in Californian field
In ample flower-time behold
The soft south rose lift like a shield
Against the sudden sun at dawn,
A double handful of heaped gold,
Why you, perhaps, might understand
How splendid and how queenly she
Uprose beside that wood-set sea.

The storm-worn ship scarce seemed to
creep
From wave to wave. It scarce could
keep—
How still this fair girl stood, how fair!
How tall her presence as she stood
Between that vast sea and west wood!
How large and liberal her soul,
How confident, how purely chare,
How trusting; how untried the whole
Great heart, grand faith, that blossomed
there.

XVI.

Ay, she was as Madonna to
The tawny, lawless, faithful few
Who touched her hand and knew her soul:
She drew them, drew them as the pole
Points all things to itself.
She drew
Men upward as a moon of spring
High wheeling, vast and bosom-full,
Half clad in clouds and white as wool,
Draws all the strong seas following.

Yet still she moved as sad, as lone
As that same moon that leans above,
And seems to search high heaven through
For some strong, all sufficient love,
For one brave love to be her own,
Be all her own and ever true.

Oh, I once knew a sad, sweet dove
That died for such sufficient love,

Such high, white love with wings to soar,
That looks love level in the face,
Nor wearies love with leaning o'er
To lift love level to her place.

XVII.

How slow before the sleeping breeze,
That stranger ship from under seas!
How like to Dido by her sea,
When reaching arms imploringly,—
Her large, round, rich, impassiond arms,
Tossed forth from all her storied charms—
This one lone maiden leaning stood
Above that sea, beneath that wood!

The ship crept strangely up the seas;
Her shrouds seemed shreds, her masts seemed trees,—
Strange tattered trees of toughest bough
That knew no cease of storm till now.
The maiden pitied her; she prayed
Her crew might come, nor feel afraid;
She prayed the winds might come,—they came,
As birds that answer to a name.

The maiden held her blowing hair
That bound her beauteous self about;
The sea-winds housed within her hair;
She let it go, it blew in rout
About her bosom full and bare.
Her round, full arms were free as air,
Her high hands clasped as clasped in prayer.

XVIII.

The breeze grew bold, the battered ship
Began to flap her weary wings;
The tall, torn masts began to dip
And walk the wave like living things.
She rounded in, moved up the stream,
She moved like some majestic dream.

The captain kept her deck. He stood
A Hercules among his men;
And now he watched the sea, and then
He peered as if to pierce the wood.
He now looked back, as if pursued,
Now swept the sea with glass as though
He fled, or feared some prowling foe.

Slow sailing up the river's mouth,
Slow tacking north, slow tacking south,
He touched the overhanging wood;
He kept his deck, his tall black mast
Touched tree-top mosses as he passed;
He touched the steep shore where she stood.

XIX.

Her hands still clasped as if in prayer,
Sweet prayer set to silentness;
Her sun-browned throat uplifted, bare
And beautiful.
Her eager face
Illumed with love and tenderness,
And all her presence gave such grace,
That she seemed more than mortal, fair.

XX.

He saw. He could not speak. No more
With lifted glass he swept the sea;
No more he watched the wild new shore.
Now foes might come, now friends might flee;
He could not speak, he would not stir,—
He saw but her, he feared but her.

The black ship ground against the shore,
With creak and groan and rusty clank,
And tore the mellow blossomed bank;
She ground against the bank as one
With long and weary journeys done,
That will not rise to journey more.

Yet still tall Jason silent stood
And gazed against that sea-washed wood,
As one whose soul is anywhere.
All seemed so fair, so wondrous fair!
At last aroused, he stepped to land
Like some Columbus; then laid hand
On lands and fruits, and rested there.

XXI

He found all fairer than fair morn
In sylvan land, where waters run
With downward leap against the sun,
And full-grown sudden May is born.
He found her taller than tall corn
Tiptoe in tassel; found her sweet
As vale where bees of Hybla meet.

An unblown rose, an unread book;
A wonder in her wondrous eyes;
A large, religious, steadfast look
Of faith, of trust,—the look of one
New fashioned in fair Paradise.

He read this book—read on and on
From title page to colophon:
As in cool woods, some summer day,
You find delight in one sweet lay,
And so entranced read on and on
From title page to colophon.

XXII.

And who was he that rested there,—
This giant of a grander day,
This Theseus of a nobler Greece,
This Jason of the golden fleece?
Aye, who was he? And who were they
That came to seek the hidden gold
Long hollowed from the pirate's hold?
I do not know. You need not care.

* * * * * *

They loved, this maiden and this man,
And that is all I surely know,—
The rest is as the winds that blow.
He bowed as brave men bow to fate,
Yet proud and resolute and bold;
She shy at first, and coyly cold,
Held back and tried to hesitate,—
Half frightened at this love that ran
Hard gallop till her hot heart beat
Like sounding of swift courser's feet.

XXIII.

Two strong streams of a land must run
Together surely as the sun
Succeeds the moon. Who shall gainsay
The gods that reign, that wisely reign?
Love is, love was, shall be again.
Like death, inevitable it is;
Perchance, like death, the dawn of bliss.
Let us, then, love the perfect day,
The twelve o'clock of life, and stop
The two hands pointing to the top,
And hold them tightly while we may.

XXIV.

How beautiful is love! The walks
By wooded ways; the silent talks
Beneath the broad and fragrant bough.
The dark deep wood, the dense black dell,
Where scarce a single gold beam fell
From out the sun.

They rested now
On mossy trunk. They wandered then
Where never fell the feet of men.
Then longer walks, then deeper woods,
Then sweeter talks, sufficient sweet,
In denser, deeper solitudes,—
Dear careless ways for careless feet;
Sweet talks of paradise for two,
And only two to watch or woo.

She rarely spake. All seemed a dream
She would not waken from. She lay
All night but waiting for the day,
When she might see his face, and deem
This man, with all his perils passed,
Had found sweet Lotus-land at last.

XXV.

The year waxed fervid, and the sun
Fell central down. The forest lay
A-quiver in the heat. The sea
Below the steep bank seemed to run
A molten sea of gold.

Away
Against the gray and rock-built isles
That broke the molten watery miles
Where lonesome sea-cows called all day,
The sudden sun smote angrily.

Therefore the need of deeper deeps,
Of denser shade for man and maid,
Of higher heights, of cooler steeps,
Where all day long the sea-wind stayed.

They sought the rock-reared steep. The breeze
Swept twenty thousand miles of seas;
Had twenty thousand things to say,
Of love, of lovers of Cathay,
To lovers 'mid these mossy trees.

XXVI.

To left, to right, below the height,
Below the wood by wave and stream,
Plumed pampas grass did wave and gleam
And bend their lordly plumes, and run
And shake, as if in very fright
Before sharp lances of the sun.

They saw the tide-bound, battered ship
Creep close below against the bank;
They saw it cringe and shrink; it shrank
As shrinks some huge black beast with fear
When some uncommon dread is near.
They heard the melting resin drip,
As drip the last brave blood-drops when
Red battle waxes hot with men.

XXVII.

Yet what to her were burning seas,
Or what to him was forest flame?
They loved; they loved the glorious trees;
The gleaming tides might rise or fall,—
They loved the lisping winds that came
From sea-lost spice-set isles unknown,
With breath not warmer than their own;
They loved, they loved,—and that was all.

XXVIII.

Full noon! Above, the ancient moss
From mighty boughs swang slow across,
As when some priest slow chants a prayer
And swings sweet smoke and perfumed air
From censer swinging—anywhere.

He spake of love, of boundless love,—
Of love that knew no other land,
Or face, or place, or anything;
Of love that like the wearied dove
Could light nowhere, but kept the wing
Till she alone put forth her hand
And so received it in her ark
From seas that shake against the dark!

Her proud breast heaved, her pure, bare breast
Rose like the waves in their unrest
When counter storms possess the seas.
Her mouth, her arch, uplifted mouth,
Her ardent mouth that thirsted so,—
No glowing love song of the South
Can say; no man can say or know
Such truth as lies beneath such trees.

Her face still lifted up. And she
Disdained the cup of passion he
Hard pressed her panting lips to touch.
She dashed it by, uprose, and she
Caught fast her breath. She trembled much,
Then sudden rose full height, and stood
An empress in high womanhood:
She stood a tower, tall as when
Proud Roman mothers suckled men
Of old-time truth and taught them such.

XXIX.

Her soul surged vast as space is. She
Was trembling as a courser when
His thin flank quivers, and his feet
Touch velvet on the turf, and he
Is all afoam, alert and fleet
As sunlight glancing on the sea,
And full of triumph before men.

At last she bended some her face,
Half leaned, then put him back a pace,
And met his eyes.

Calm, silently
Her eyes looked deep into his eyes,—
As maidens search some mossy well
And peer in hope by chance to tell
By image there what future lies
Before them, and what face shall be
The pole-star of their destiny.

Pure Nature's lover! Loving him
With love that made all pathways dim
And difficult where he was not,—
Then marvel not at forms forgot.
And who shall chide? Doth priest know
aught
Of sign, or holy unction brought
From over seas, that ever can
Make man love maid or maid love man
One whit the more, one bit the less,
For all his mummeries to bless?
Yea, all his blessings or his ban?

The winds breathed warm as Araby;
She leaned upon his breast, she lay
A wide-winged swan with folded wing.
He drowned his hot face in her hair,
He heard her great heart rise and sing;
He felt her bosom swell.

The air
Swooned sweet with perfume of her form.
Her breast was warm, her breath was warm,
And warm her warm and perfumed mouth
As summer journeys through the south.

XXX.

The argent sea surged steep below,
Surged languid in such tropic glow;
And two great hearts kept surging so!
The fervid kiss of heaven lay
Precipitate on wood and sea.
Two great souls glowed with ecstacy,
The sea glowed scarce as warm as they.

XXXI.

'Twas love's warm amber afternoon.
Two far-off pheasants thrummed a tune,
A cricket clanged a restful air.
The dreamful billows beat a rune
Like heart regrets.

Around her head
There shone a halo. Men have said
'Twas from a dash of Titian
That flooded all her storm of hair
In gold and glory. But they knew,
Yea, all men know there ever grew
A halo round about her head
Like sunlight scarcely vanishéd.

XXXII.

How still she was! She only knew
His love. She saw no life beyond.
She loved with love that only lives
Outside itself and selfishness,—
A love that glows in its excess;
A love that melts pure gold, and gives
Thenceforth to all who come to woo
No coins but this face stamped thereon,—
Ay, this one image stamped upon
Pure gold, with some dim date long gone.

XXXIII.

They kept the headland high; the ship
Below began to chafe her chain,
To groan as some great beast in pain:
While white fear leapt from lip to lip:
"The woods on fire! the woods in flame!
Come down and save us in God's name!"

He heard! he did not speak or stir,—
He thought of her, of only her,
While flames behind, before them lay
To hold the stoutest heart at bay!

Strange sounds were heard far up the
flood,
Strange, savage sounds that chilled the
blood!
Then sudden from the dense, dark wood

Above, about them where they stood
Strange, hairy beasts came peering out;
And now was thrust a long black snout,
And now a dusky mouth. It was
A sight to make the stoutest pause.

"Cut loose the ship!" the black mate cried;
"Cut loose the ship!" the crew replied.
They drove into the sea. It lay
As light as ever middle day.

And then a half-blind bitch that sat
All slobber-mouthed, and monkish cowled
With great, broad, floppy, leathern ears
Amid the men, rose up and howled,
And doleful howled her plaintive fears,
While all looked mute aghast thereat.
It was the grimmest eve, I think,
That ever hung on Hades' brink.
Great broad-winged bats possessed the air,
Bats whirling blindly everywhere;
It was such troubled twilight eve
As never mortal would believe.

XXXIV.

Some say the crazed hag lit the wood
In circle where the lovers stood;
Some say the gray priest feared the crew
Might find at last the hoard of gold
Long hidden from the black ship's hold,—
I doubt me if men ever knew.
But such mad, howling, flame-lit shore
No mortal ever knew before.

Huge beasts above that shining sea,
Wild, hideous beasts with shaggy hair,
With red mouths lifting in the air,
All piteous howled, and plaintively,—
The wildest sounds, the weirdest sight
That ever shook the walls of night.

How lorn they howled, with lifted head,
To dim and distant isles that lay
Wedged tight along a line of red,
Caught in the closing gates of day
'Twixt sky and sea and far away,—
It was the saddest sound to hear
That ever struck on human ear.

They doleful called; and answered they
The plaintiff sea-cows far away,—
The great sea-cows that called from isles,
Away across red flaming miles,
With dripping mouths and lolling tongue,
As if they called for captured young,—

The huge sea-cows that called the whiles
Their great wide mouths were mouthing moss;
And still they doleful called across
From isles beyond the watery miles.
No sound can half so doleful be
As sea-cows calling from the sea.

XXXV.

The sun, outdone, lay down. He lay
In seas of blood. He sinking drew
The gates of sunset sudden to,
And they in shattered fragments lay.
Then night came, moving in mad flame;
Then full night, lighted as he came,
As lighted by high summer sun
Descending through the burning blue.
It was a gold and amber hue,
Aye, all hues blended into one.

The moon came on, came leaning low.
The moon spilled splendor where she came,
And filled the world with yellow flame
Along the far sea-isles aglow;
She fell along that amber flood,
A silver flame in seas of blood.
It was the strangest moon, ah me!
That ever settled on God's sea,

XXXVI.

Slim snakes slid down from fern and grass,
From wood, from fen, from anywhere;
You could not step, you would not pass,

And you would hesitate to stir,
Lest in some sudden, hurried tread
Your foot struck some unbruiséd head:

It seemed like some infernal dream;
They slid in streams into the stream;
They curved, and sinuous curved across,
Like living streams of living moss,—
There is no art of man can make
A ripple like a swimming snake!

XXXVII.

Encompassed, lorn, the lovers stood,
Abandoned there, death in the air!
That beetling steep, that blazing wood—
Red flame! red flame, and everywhere!
Yet he was born to strive, to bear
The front of battle. He would die
In noble effort, and defy
The grizzled visage of despair.

He threw his two strong arms full length
As if to surely test their strength;
Then tore his vestments, textile things
That could but tempt the demon wings
Of flame that girt them round about,
Then threw his garments to the air
As one that laughed at death, at doubt,
And like a god stood thewed and bare.

She did not hesitate; she knew
The need of action; swift she threw
Her burning vestments by, and bound
Her wondrous wealth of hair that fell
An all-concealing cloud around
Her glorious presence, as he came
To seize and bear her through the flame,—
An Orpheus out of burning hell!

He leaned above her, wound his arm
About her splendor, while the noon
Of flood tide, manhood, flushed his face,
And high flames leapt the high headland!—
They stood as twin-hewn statues stand,
High lifted in some storied place.

He clasped her close, he spoke of death,—
Of death and love in the same breath.
He clasped her close; her bosom lay
Like ship safe anchored in some bay,
Where never rage or rack of main
Might even shake her anchor chain.

XXXVIII.

The flames! They could not stand or stay;
Beyond, the beetling steep, the sea!
But at his feet a narrow way,
A short steep path, pitched suddenly
Safe open to the river's beach,
Where lay a small white isle in reach,—
A small, white, rippled isle of sand
Where yet the two might safely land.

And there, through smoke and flame, behold
The priest stood safe, yet all appalled!
He reached the cross; he cried, he called;
He waved his high-held cross of gold.
He called and called, he bade them fly
Through flames to him, nor bide and die!

Her lover saw; he saw, and knew
His giant strength could bear her through.
And yet he would not start or stir.
He clasped her close as death can hold,
Or dying miser clasp his gold,—
His hold became a part of her.

He would not give her up! He would
Not bear her waveward though he could!
That height was heaven; the wave was hell.
He clasped her close,—what else had done
The manliest man beneath the sun?
Was it not well? was it not well?

O man, be glad! be grandly glad,
And king-like walk thy ways of death!
For more than years of bliss you had
That one brief time you breathed her breath,
Yea, more than years upon a throne
That one brief time you held her fast,
Soul surged to soul, vehement, vast,—
True breast to breast, and all your own.

Live me one day, one narrow night,
One second of supreme delight
Like that, and I will blow like chaff
The hollow years aside, and laugh
A loud triumphant laugh, and I,
King-like and crowned, will gladly die.

Oh, but to wrap my love with flame!
With flame within, with flame without!
Oh, but to die like this, nor doubt—
To die and know her still the same!
To know that down the ghostly shore
Snow-white she walks for ever more!

XXXIX.

He poised her, held her high in air,—
His great strong limbs, his great arm's length!—
Then turned his knotted shoulders bare
As birth-time in his splendid strength,
And strode with lordly, kingly stride
To where the high and wood-hung edge
Looked down, far down upon the molten tide.
The flames leaped with him to the ledge,
The flames leapt leering at his side.

XL.

He leaned above the ledge. Below
He saw the black ship grope and cruise,—
A midge below, a mile below.
His limbs were knotted as the thews
Of Hercules in his death-throe.

The flame! the flame! the envious flame!
She wound her arms, she wound her hair
About his tall form, grand and bare,
To stay the fierce flame where it came.

The black ship, like some moonlit wreck,
Below along the burning sea
Groped on and on all silently,
With silent pigmies on her deck.

That midge-like ship, far, far below;
That mirage lifting from the hill!
His flame-lit form began to grow,—
To glow and grow more grandly still.
The ship so small, that form so tall,
It grew to tower over all.

A tall Colossus, bronze and gold,
As if that flame-lit form were he
Who once bestrode the Rhodian sea,
And ruled the watery world of old:
As if the lost Colossus stood
Above that burning sea of wood.

And she ! that shapely form upheld,
Held high as if to touch the sky,
What airy shape, how shapely high,—
What goddess of the seas of eld!

Her hand upheld, her high right hand,
As if she would forget the land;
As if to gather stars, and heap
The stars like torches there to light
Her hero's path across the deep
To some far isle that fearful night.

XLI.

The envious flame, one moment leapt
Enraged to see such majesty,
Such scorn of death; such kingly scorn . . .

Then like some lightning-riven tree
They sank down in that flame—and slept.
Then all was hushed above that steep
So still that they might sleep and sleep,
As when a Summer's day is born.

At last! from out the embers leapt
Two shafts of light above the night,—
Two wings of flame that lifting swept
In steady, calm, and upward flight;
Two wings of flame against the white
Far-lifting, tranquil, snowy cone;
Two wings of love, two wings of light,
Far, far above that troubled night,
As mounting, mounting to God's throne.

XLII.

And all night long that upward light
Lit up the sea-cow's bed below:
The far sea-cows still calling so
It seemed as they must call all night.
All night! there was no night. Nay, nay,
There was no night. The night that lay
Between that awful eve and day,—
That nameless night was burned away.

Byron, Keats, Shelley, Browning, all poets, as a rule fled from the commercial centers, went out from under the mists and mirk into the sunlight to sing. I warn the coming poet that as a poet his place is not in any city. Be advised, or have done with' aspiration to do new work or true work. The Old World has been written, written fully and bravely and well. It is only the vast, far, New World that needs you. He who is aiming to sit down in New York, or any city, and eat dinners that are cooked and seasoned by servants who are not given even as much time to go to church as were the slaves of the South, may be good enough and write well enough to please the city in these headlong days, but the real poet would rather house with a half savage and live on a sixpence in some mountain village, as did Byron, than feast off the board of Madame Leo Hunter in a city. I now built a cabin on the edge of Washington, for I had written my longest and worst and only unkind book, "The Baroness ot New York," on such dinners. This longest poem has been destroyed, all except "The Sea of Fire," written years before in the wilderness of Honduras and by the Oregon sea bank. Nor is Washington a better place for work with soul or heart in it. Madame Leo Hunter is there also, persistent, numerous, superficial and soulless as in almost any great center. If I am cruel, O my coming poets, I am cruel to be kind. Go forth in the sun, away into the wilds or contentedly lay aside your aspirations of song. Now, mark you distinctly, I am not writing for nor of the poets of the Old World or the Atlantic seaboard. They have their work and their ways of work, great and good, but new no more. My notes are for the songless Alaskas, Canadas, Californias, the Aztec lands and the Argentines that patiently await their coming prophets. For come they will; but I warn them they will have to gird themselves mightily and pass through fire, and perish, many a man; for these new worlds will be whistling, out of time, the tunes of the old, and the rich and the proud will say in their insolence and ignorance, "Pipe thus, for thus piped the famous pipers of old; piping of perished kings, of wars, of castle walls, of battling knights, and of maids betrayed. Sing as of old or be silent, for we know not, we want not, and we will not, your seas of colors, your forests of perfumes, your mountains of melodies."

ISLES OF THE AMAZONS.

Part I.

Primeval forests! virgin sod!
That Saxon has not ravish'd yet,
Lo! peak on peak in stairways set—
In stepping stairs that reach to God!

Here we are free as sea or wind,
For here are set Time's snowy tents
In everlasting battlements
Against the march of Saxon mind.

Far up in the hush of the Amazon River,
And mantled and hung in the tropical trees,
There are isles as grand as the isles of seas.
And the waves strike strophes, and keen reeds quiver,
As the sudden canoe shoots past them and over
The strong, still tide to the opposite shore,
Where the blue-eyed men by the sycamore
Sit mending their nets 'neath the vine-twined cover;

Sit weaving the threads of long, strong grasses;
They wind and they spin on the clumsy wheel,
Into hammocks red-hued with the cochineal,
To trade with the single black ship that passes,
With foreign old freightage of curious old store,
And still and slow as if half asleep,—
A cunning old trader that loves to creep
Cautious and slow in the shade of the shore.

And the blue-eyed men that are mild as the dawns—
Oh, delicate dawns of the grand Andes!
Lift up soft eyes that are deep like seas,
And mild yet wild as the red-white fawns';

And they gaze into yours, then weave, then listen,
Then look in wonder, then again weave on,
Then again look wonder that you are not gone,
While the keen reeds quiver and the bent waves glisten;

But they say no word while they weave and wonder,
Though they sometimes sing, voiced low like the dove,
And as deep and as rich as their tropical love,
A-weaving their net threads through and under.

A pure, true people you may trust are these
That weave their threads where the quick leaves quiver;
And this is their tale of the Isles of the river,
And the why that their eyes are so blue like seas:

The why that the men draw water and bear
The wine or the water in the wild boar skin,
And do hew the wood and weave and spin,
And so bear with the women full burthen and share.

A curious old tale of a curious old time,
That is told you betimes by a quaint old crone,
Who sits on the rim of an island alone,
As ever was told you in story or rhyme.

Her brown, bare feet dip down to the river,
And dabble and plash to her monotone,
As she holds in her hands a strange green stone,
And talks to the boat where the bent reeds quiver.

And the quaint old crone has a singular way
Of holding her head to the side and askew,
And smoothing the stone in her palms all day
As saying "I've nothing at all for you,"
Until you have anointed her palm, and you
Have touched on the delicate spring of a door
That silver has opened perhaps before;
For woman is woman the wide world through.

The old near truth on the far new shore,
I bought and I paid for it; so did you;
The tale may be false or the tale may be true;
I give as I got it, and who can more?

If I have made journeys to difficult shores,
And woven delusions in innocent verse,
If none be the wiser, why, who is the worse?
The field it was mine, the fruit it is yours.

A sudden told tale. You may read as you run.
A part of it hers, some part is my own,
Crude, and too carelessly woven and sown,
As I sail'd on the Mexican seas in the sun.

'Twas nations ago, when the Amazons were,
That a fair young knight—says the quaint old crone,
With her head sidewise, as she smooths at the stone—
Came over the seas, with his golden hair,
And a great black steed, and glittering spurs,
With a woman's face, with a manly frown,
A heart as tender and as true as hers,
And a sword that had come from crusaders down.

And fairest, and foremost in love as in war
Was the brave young knight of the brave old days.
Of all the knights, with their knightly ways,
That had journey'd away to this world afar
In the name of Spain; of the splendid few
Who bore her banner in the new-born world,

From the sea rim up to where clouds are curl'd,
And condors beat with black wings the blue.

He was born, says the crone, where the brave are fair,
And blown from the banks of the Guadalquiver,
And yet blue-eyed, with the Celt's soft hair,
With never a drop of the dark deep river
Of Moorish blood that had swept through Spain,
And plash'd the world with its tawny stain.

He sat on his steed, and his sword was bloody
With heathen blood: the battle was done;
His heart rebell'd and rose with pity.
For crown'd with fire, wreathed and ruddy
Fell antique temples built up to the sun.
Below on the plain lay the burning city
At the conqueror's feet; the red street strown
With dead, with gold, and with gods overthrown.

And the heathen pour'd, in a helpless flood,
With never a wail and with never a blow,
At last, to even provoke a foe,
Through gateways, wet with the pagan's blood.

"Ho, forward! smite!" but the minstrel linger'd,
He reach'd his hand and he touch'd the rein,
He humm'd an air, and he toy'd and finger'd
The arching neck and the glossy mane.
He rested the heel, he rested the hand,
Though the thing was death to the man to dare
To doubt, to question, to falter there,
Nor heeded at all to the hot command.

He wiped his steel on his black steed's mane,
He sheathed it deep, then look'd at the sun,
Then counted his comrades, one by one,
With booty returning from the plunder'd plain.

He lifted his face to the flashing snow,
He lifted his shield of steel as he sang,
And he flung it away till it clang'd and rang
On the granite rocks in the plain below.

He cross'd his bosom. Made overbold,
He lifted his voice and sang, quite low
At first, then loud in the long ago,
When the loves endured though the days grew old.

They heard his song, the chief on the plain
Stood up in his stirrups, and, sword in hand,
He cursed and he call'd with a loud command
To the blue-eyed boy to return again;
To lift his shield again to the sky,
And come and surrender his sword or die.

He wove his hand in the stormy mane,
He lean'd him forward, he lifted the rein,
He struck the flank, he wheel'd and sprang,
And gaily rode in the face of the sun,
And bared his sword and he bravely sang,
"Ho! come and take it!" but there came not one.

And so he sang with his face to the south:
"I shall go; I shall search for the Amazon shore,
Where the curses of man they are heard no more,
And kisses alone shall embrace the mouth.

"I shall journey in search of the Incan Isles,
Go far and away to traditional land,
Where love is queen in a crown of smiles,
And battle has never imbrued a hand;

"Where man has never despoil'd or trod;
Where woman's hand with a woman's heart
Has fashion'd an Eden from man apart,
And walks in her garden alone with God.

"I shall find that Eden, and all my years
Shall sit and repose, shall sing in the sun;
And the tides may rest or the tides may run,
And men may water the world with tears;

"And the years may come and the years may go,
And men make war, may slay and be slain,
But I not care, for I never shall know
Of man, or of aught that is man's again.

"The waves may battle, the winds may blow,
The mellow rich moons may ripen and fall,
The seasons of gold they may gather or go,
The mono may chatter, the paroquet call,
And I shall not heed, take note, or know,
If the Fates befriend, or if ill befall,
Of worlds without, or of worlds at all,
Of heaven above, or of hades below."

'Twas the song of a dream and the dream of a singer,
Drawn fine as the delicate fibers of gold,
And broken in two by the touch of a finger,
And blown as the winds blow, rent and roll'd
In dust, and spent as a tale that is told.

Alas! for his dreams and the songs he sung;
The beasts beset him; the serpents they hung,
Red-tongued and terrible, over his head.
He clove and he thrust with his keen, quick steel,
He coax'd with his hand, he urged with his heel,
Till his steel was broken, and his steed lay dead.

He toil'd to the river, he lean'd intent
To the wave, and away to the islands fair,
From beasts that pursued, and he breathed a prayer;
For soul and body were well-nigh spent.

'Twas the king of rivers, and the Isles were near;
Yet it moved so strange, so still, so strong,
It gave no sound, not even the song
Of a sea-bird screaming defiance or fear.

It was dark and dreadful! Wide like an ocean,
Much like a river but more like a sea,
Save that there was naught of the turbulent motion
Of tides, or of winds blown abaft, or a-lee.

Yea, strangely strong was the wave and slow,
And half-way hid in the dark, deep tide,
Great turtles, they paddled them to and fro,
And away to the Isles and the opposite side.

The nude black boar through abundant grass
Stole down to the water and buried his nose,
And crunch'd white teeth till the bubbles rose
As white and as bright as are globes of glass.

Yea, steadily moved it, mile upon mile,
Above and below and as still as the air;
The bank made slippery here and there
By the slushing slide of the crocodile.

The great trees bent to the tide like slaves;
They dipp'd their boughs as the stream swept on,
And then drew back, then dipp'd and were gone
Away to the sea with the resolute waves.

The land was the tide's; the shore was undone;
It look'd as the lawless, unsatisfied seas
Had thrust up an arm through the tangle of trees,
And clutch'd at the citrons that grew in the sun;

And clutch'd at the diamonds that hid in the sand,
And laid heavy hand on the gold, and a hand
On the redolent fruits, on the ruby-like wine,
On the stones like the stars when the stars are divine;

Had thrust through the rocks of the ribb'd Andes;
Had wrested and fled; and had left a waste
And a wide way strewn in precipitate haste,
As he bore them away to the buccaneer seas.

O, heavens, the eloquent song of the silence!
Asleep lay the sun in the vines, on the sod,
And asleep in the sun lay the green-girdled islands,
As rock'd to their rest in the cradle of God.

God's poet is silence! His song is unspoken,
And yet so profound, so loud, and so far,
It fills you, it thrills you with measures unbroken,
And as still, and as fair, and as far as a star.

The shallow seas moan. From the first they have mutter'd,
As a child that is fretted, and weeps at its will.
The poems of God are too grand to be utter'd:
The dreadful deep seas they are loudest when still.

"I shall fold my hands, for this is the river
Of death," he said, "and the sea-green isle
Is an Eden set by the Gracious Giver
Wherein to rest." He listen'd the while,
Then lifted his head, then lifted a hand
Arch'd over his brow, and he lean'd and listen'd,—

'Twas only a bird on a border of sand,—
The dark stream eddied and gleam'd and glisten'd,
And the martial notes from the isle were gone,—
Gone as a dream dies out with the dawn.

'Twas only a bird on a border of sand,
Slow piping, and diving it here and there,

Slim, gray, and shadowy, light as the air,
That dipp'd below from a point of the land.

"Unto God a prayer and to love a tear,
And I die," he said, "in a desert here,
So deep that never a note is heard
But the listless song of that soulless bird.

"The strong trees lean in their love unto trees.
Lock arms in their loves, and are so made strong,
Stronger than armies; aye, stronger than seas
That rush from their caves in a storm of song.

"A miser of old, his last great treasure
Flung far in the sea, and he fell and he died;
And so shall I give, O terrible tide,
To you my song and my last sad measure."

He blew on a reed by the still, strong river,
Blew low at first, like a dream, then long,
Then loud, then loud as the keys that quiver,
And fret and toss with their freight of song.

He sang and he sang with a resolute will,
Till the mono rested above on his haunches,
And held his head to the side and was still,—
Till a bird blown out of the night of branches
Sang sadder than love, so sweeter than sad,
Till the boughs did burthen and the reeds did fill
With beautiful birds, and the boy was glad.

Our loves they are told by the myriad-eyed stars,
And love it is grand in a reasonable way,
And fame it is good in its way for a day,
Borne dusty from books and bloody from wars;
And death, I say, is an absolute need,
And a calm delight, and an ultimate good;
But a song that is blown from a watery reed
By a soundless deep from a boundless wood,
With never a hearer to heed or to prize
But God and the birds and the hairy wild beasts,
Is sweeter than love, than fame, or than feasts,
Or any thing else that is under the skies.

The quick leaves quiver'd, and the sunlight danced;
As the boy sang sweet, and the birds said, "Sweet;"
And the tiger crept close, and lay low at his feet,
And he sheathed his claws as he listened entranced.

The serpent that hung from the sycamore bough,
And sway'd his head in a crescent above,
Had folded his neck to the white limb now,
And fondled it close like a great black love.

But the hands grew weary, the heart wax'd faint,
The loud notes fell to a far-off plaint,
The sweet birds echo'd no more, "Oh, sweet,"
The tiger arose and unsheathed his claws,
The serpent extended his iron jaws,
And the frail reed shiver'd and fell at his feet.

A sound on the tide! and he turn'd and cried,
"Oh, give God thanks, for they come, they come!"
He look'd out afar on the opaline tide,
Then clasp'd his hands, and his lips were dumb.

A sweeping swift crescent of sudden canoes!
As light as the sun of the south and as soon,
And true and as still as a sweet half-moon
That leans from the heavens, and loves and woos!

The Amazons came in their martial pride,
As full on the stream as a studding of stars,
All girded in armor as girded in wars,
In foamy white furrows dividing the tide.

With a face as brown as the boatmen's are,
Or the brave, brown hand of a harvester;
The Queen on a prow stood splendid and tall,
As the petulant waters did lift and fall;

Stood forth for the song, half lean'd in surprise,
Stood fair to behold, and yet grand to behold,
And austere in her face, and saturnine-soul'd,
And sad and subdued, in her eloquent eyes.

And sad were they all; yet tall and serene
Of presence, but silent, and brow'd severe;
As for some things lost, or for some fair, green,
And beautiful place, to the memory dear.

"O Mother of God! Thrice merciful saint!
I am saved!" he said, and he wept outright;
Ay, wept as even a woman might,
For the soul was full and the heart was faint.

"Stay! stay!" cried the Queen, and she leapt to the land,
And she lifted her hand, and she lowered their spears,
"A woman! a woman! ho! help! give a hand!
A woman! a woman! I know by the tears."

Then gently as touch of the truest of woman,
They lifted him up from the earth where he fell,
And into the boat, with a half hidden swell
Of the heart that was holy and tenderly human.

They spoke low-voiced as a vesper prayer;
They pillow'd his head as only the hand
Of woman can pillow, and push'd from the land,
And the Queen she sat threading the gold of his hair.

PART II.

Forsake those People. What are they
That laugh, that live, that love by rule?
Forsake the Saxon. Who are these
That shun the shadows of the trees;
The perfumed forests? . . . Go thy way,
We are not one. I will not please
You:—fare you well, O wiser fool!

But ye who love me:—Ye who love
The shaggy forests, fierce delights
Of sounding waterfalls, of heights
That hang like broken moons above,
With brows of pine that brush the sun,
Believe and follow. We are one:
The wild man shall to us be tame,
The woods shall yield their mysteries;
The stars shall answer to a name,
And be as birds above the trees.

They swept to their Isles through the furrows of foam;
They alit on the land, as love hastening home,
And below the banana, with leaf like a tent,
They tenderly laid him, they bade him take rest,
They brought him strange fishes and fruits of the best,
And he ate and took rest with a patient content.

They watched so well that he rose up strong,
And stood in their midst, and they said, "How fair!"
And they said, "How tall!" And they toy'd with his hair.
And they touched his limbs and they said, "How long
And how strong they are; and how brave she is,
That she made her way through the wiles of man,
That she braved his wrath that she broke the ban
Of his desolate life for the love of this!"

They wrought for him armor and cunning attire,
They brought him a sword and a great shell shield,
And implored him to shiver the lance on the field,
And to follow their beautiful Queen in her ire.

But he took him apart; then the Amazons came
And entreated of him with their eloquent eyes
And their earnest and passionate souls of flame,
And the soft, sweet words that are broken of sighs,
To be one of their own, but he still denied
And bow'd and abash'd he stole further aside.

He stood by the Palms and he lean'd in unrest,
And standing alone, looked out and afar,
For his own fair land where the castles are,
With irresolute arms on a restless breast.

He re-lived his loves, he recall'd his wars,
He gazed and he gazed with a soul distress'd,
Like a far sweet star that is lost in the west,
Till the day was broken to a dust of stars.

They sigh'd, and they left him alone in the care
Of faithfullest matron; they moved to the field
With the lifted sword and the sounding shield
High fretting magnificent storms of hair.

And, true as the moon in her march of stars,
The Queen stood forth in her fierce attire
Worn as they trained or worn in the wars,
As bright and as chaste as a flash of fire.

With girdles of gold and of silver cross'd,
And plaited, and chased, and bound together,
Broader and stronger than belts of leather,
Cunningly fashion'd and blazon'd and boss'd—

With diamonds circling her, stone upon stone,
Above the breast where the borders fail,
Below the breast where the fringes zone,
She moved in a glittering garment of mail.

The form made hardy and the waist made spare
From athlete sports and adventures bold,
The breastplate; fasten'd with clasps of gold,
Was clasp'd, as close as the breasts could bear,—

And bound and drawn to a delicate span,
It flash'd in the red front ranks of the field—
Was fashion'd full trim in its intricate plan
And gleam'd as a sign, as well as a shield,

That the virgin Queen was unyielding still,
And pure as the tides that around her ran;
True to her trust, and strong in her will
Of war, and hatred to the touch of man.

The field it was theirs in storm or in shine,
So fairly they stood that the foe came not
To battle again, and the fair forgot
The rage of battle; and they trimm'd the vine,

They tended the fields of the tall green corn,

They crush'd the grape and they drew
the wine
In the great round gourds and the bended
horn—
And they lived as the gods in the days
divine.

They bathed in the wave in the amber
morn,
They took repose in the peaceful shade
Of eternal palms, and were never afraid;
Yet oft did they sigh, and look far and
forlorn.

Where the rim of the wave was weaving a
spell,
And the grass grew soft where it hid
from the sun,
Would the Amazons gather them every
one
At the call of the Queen or the sound of
her shell:

Would come in strides through the kingly
trees,
And train and marshal them brave and
well
In the golden noon, in the hush of peace
Where the shifting shades of the fan-
palms fell;
Would train till flush'd and as warm as
wine:
Would reach with their limbs, would
thrust with the lance,
Attack, retire, retreat and advance,
Then wheel in column, then fall in line;
Stand thigh and thigh with the limbs
made hard
And rich and round as the swift limb'd
pard,
Or a racer train'd, or a white bull caught
In the lasso's toils, where the tame are
not:

Would curve as the waves curve, swerve
in line;
Would dash through the trees, would
train with the bow,
Then back to the lines, now sudden,
then slow,
Then flash their swords in the sun at a
sign:

Would settle the foot right firmly afront,
Then sound the shield till the sound
was heard
Afar, as the horn in the black boar
hunt;
Yet, strangest of all, say never one
word.

When shadows fell far from the westward,
and when
The sun had kiss'd hands and set forth
for the east,
They would kindle campfires and gather
them then,
Well-worn and most merry with song,
to the feast.

They sang of all things, but the one,
sacred one,
That could make them most glad, as
they lifted the gourd
And pass'd it around, with its rich purple
hoard,
From the island that lay with its face to
the sun.

Though lips were most luscious, and eyes
as divine
As the eyes of the skies that bend down
from above;
Though hearts were made glad and
most mellow with love,
As dripping gourds drain'd of their bur-
thens of wine;
Though brimming, and dripping, and bent
of their shape
Were the generous gourds from the juice
of the grape,

They could sing not of love, they could breathe not a thought
Of the savor of life; of love sought, or unsought.

Their loves they were not; they had banished the name
Of man, and the uttermost mention of love,—
The moonbeams about them, the quick stars above,
The mellow-voiced waves, they were ever the same,
In sign, and in saying, of the old true lies;
But they took no heed; no answering sign,
Save glances averted and half-hush'd sighs,
Went back from the breasts with their loves divine.

They sang of free life with a will, and well,
They had paid for it well when the price was blood;
They beat on the shield, and they blew on the shell,
When their wars were not, for they held it good
To be glad, and to sing till the flush of the day,
In an annual feast, when the broad leaves fell;
Yet some sang not, and some sighed, "Ah, well!"—
For there's far less left you to sing or to say,
When mettlesome love is banish'd, I ween—
To hint at as hidden, or to half disclose
In the swift sword-cuts of the tongue, made keen
With wine at a feast,—than one would suppose.

So the days wore by, but they brought no rest
To the minstrel knight, though the sun was as gold,
And the Isles were green, and the great Queen blest
In the splendor of arms, and as pure as bold.

He would now resolve to reveal to her all,
His sex and his race in a well-timed song;
And his love of peace, his hatred of wrong,
And his own deceit, though the sun should fall.

Then again he would linger, and knew not how
He could best proceed, and deferr'd him now
Till a favorite day, then the fair day came,
And still he delay'd, and reproached him the same.

And he still said nought, but, subduing his head,
He wander'd one day in a dubious spell
Of unutterable thought of the truth unsaid,
To the indolent shore, and he gather'd a shell,
And he shaped its point to his passionate mouth,
And he turn'd to a bank and began to blow,
While the Amazons trained in a troop below—
Blew soft and sweet as a kiss of the south.

The Amazons lifted with glad surprise,
Stood splendid and glad and look'd far and fair,

Set forward a foot, and shook back their hair,
Like clouds push'd back from the sun-lit skies.

It stirr'd their souls, and they ceased to train
In troop by the shore, as the tremulous strain
Fell down from the hill through the tasselling trees;
And a murmur of song, like the sound of bees
In the clover crown of a queenly spring,
Came back unto him, and he laid the shell
Aside on the bank, and began to sing
Of eloquent love; and the ancient spell
Of passionate song was his, and the Isle,
As waked to delight from its slumber long,
Came back in echoes; yet all this while
He knew not at all the sin of his song.

PART III.

Come, lovers, come, forget your pains!
I know upon this earth a spot
Where clinking coins, that clank as chains,
Upon the souls of men, are not;
Nor man is measured for his gains
Of gold that stream with crimson stains.

There snow-topp'd towers crush the clouds
And break the still abode of stars,
Like sudden ghosts in snowy shrouds,
New broken through their earthly bars,
And condors whet their crooked beaks
On lofty limits of the peaks.

O men that fret as frets the main!
You irk me with your eager gaze
Down in the earth for fat increase—
Eternal talks of gold and gain,
Your shallow wit, your shallow ways,
And breaks my soul across the shoal
As breakers break on shallow seas.

They bared their brows to the palms above,
But some look'd level into comrades' eyes,
And they then remember'd that the thought of love
Was the thing forbidden, and they sank in sighs.

They turned from the training, to heed in throng
To the old, old tale; and they trained no more,
As he sang of love; and some on the shore,
And full in the sound of the eloquent song,

With womanly air and an irresolute will
Went listlessly onward as gathering shells;
Then gazed in the waters, as bound by spells;
Then turned to the song and so sigh'd, and were still.

And they said no word. Some tapp'd on the sand
With the sandal'd foot, keeping time to the sound,
In a sort of dream; some timed with the hand,
And one held eyes full of tears to the ground.

She thought of the days when their wars
they were not,
As she lean'd and listened to the old, old
song,
When they sang of their loves, and she
well forgot
Man's hard oppressions and a world of
wrong.

Like a pure true woman, with her trust in
tears
And the things that are true, she re-
lived them in thought,
Though hush'd and crush'd in the fall of
the years;
She lived but the fair, and the false she
forgot.

As a tale long told, or as things that are
dreams
The quivering curve of the lip it confest
The silent regrets, and the soul that teems
With a world of love in a brave true
breast.

Then this one, younger, who had known
no love,
Nor look'd upon man but in blood on
the field,
She bow'd her head, and she leaned on
her shield,
And her heart beat quick as the wings of
a dove
That is blown from the sea, where the rests
are not
In the time of storms; and by instinct
taught
Grew pensive, and sigh'd; as she thought
and she thought
Of some wonderful things, and—she knew
not of what.

Then this one thought of a love forsaken,
She thought of a brown sweet babe,
and she thought
Of the bread-fruits gather'd, of the swift
fish taken
In intricate nets, like a love well sought.

She thought of the moons of her maiden
dawn,
Mellow'd and fair with the forms of man;
So dearer indeed to dwell upon
Than the beautiful waves that around
her ran:

So fairer indeed than the fringes of light
That lie at rest on the west of the sea
In furrows of foam on the borders of night,
And dearer indeed than the songs to be—

Than calling of dreams from the opposite
land,
To the land of life, and of journeys
dreary,
When the soul goes over from the form
grown weary,
And walks in the cool of the trees on the
sand.

But the Queen was enraged and would
smite him at first
With the sword unto death, yet it seemed
that she durst
Not touch him at all; and she moved as to
chide,
And she lifted her face, and she frown'd
at his side,
Then she touch'd on his arm; then she
looked in his eyes
And right full in his soul, but she saw
no fear,
In the pale fair face, and with frown
severe
She press'd her lips as suppressing her
sighs.

She banish'd her wrath, she unbended her
face,
She lifted her hand and put back his
hair

From his fair sad brow, with a penitent air,
And forgave him all with unuttered grace.

But she said no word, yet no more was severe;
She stood as subdued by the side of him still,
Then averted her face with a resolute will,
As to hush a regret, or to hide back a tear.

She sighed to herself: "A stranger is this,
And ill and alone, that knows not at all
That a throne shall totter and the strong shall fall,
At the mention of love and its banefullest bliss.

"O life that is lost in bewildering love—
But a stranger is sacred!" She lifted a hand
And she laid it as soft as the breast of a dove
On the minstrel's mouth. It was more than the wand
Of the tamer of serpents, for she did no more
Than to bid with her eyes and to beck with her hand,
And the song drew away to the waves of the shore;
Took wings, as it were, to the verge of the land.

But her heart was oppress'd. With penitent head
She turned to her troop, and retiring, she said:
"Alas! and alas! shall it come to pass
That the panther shall die from a blade of grass?

That the tiger shall yield at the bent-horn's blast?
That we, who have conquer'd a world and all
Of men and of beasts in the world must fall
Ourselves at the mention of love at last?"

The tall Queen turn'd with her troop;
She led minstrel and all to the innermost part
Of the palm-crowned Isle, where great trees group
In armies, to battle when black-storms start,
And made a retreat from the sun by the trees
That are topp'd like tents, where the fire-flies
Are a light to the feet, and a fair lake lies,
As cool as the coral-set centers of seas.

The palm-trees lorded the copse like kings,
Their tall tops tossing the indolent clouds
That folded the Isle in the dawn, like shrouds,
Then fled from the sun like to living things.

The cockatoo swung in the vines below,
And muttering hung on a golden thread,
Or moved on the moss'd bough to and fro,
In plumes of gold and array'd in red.

The lake lay hidden away from the light,
As asleep in the Isle from the tropical noon,
And narrow and bent like a new-born moon,
And fair as a moon in the noon of the night.

'Twas shadow'd by forests, and fringed by ferns,
And fretted anon by red fishes that leapt
At indolent flies that slept or kept
Their drowsy tones on the tide by turns.

And here in the dawn when the Day was strong
And newly aroused from leafy repose,
With dews on his feet and tints of the rose
In his great flush'd face was a sense of song
That the tame old world has nor known nor heard.

The soul was filled with the soft perfumes,
The eloquent wings of the humming bird
Beguiled the heart, they purpled the air
And allured the eye, as so everywhere
On the rim of the wave or across it in swings,
They swept or they sank in a sea of blooms,
And wove and wound in a song of wings.

A bird in scarlet and gold, made mad
With sweet delights, through the branches slid
And kiss'd the lake on a drowsy lid
Till the ripples ran and the face was glad;

Was glad and lovely as lights that sweep
The face of heaven when the stars are forth
In autumn time through the sapphire north,
Or the face of a child when it smiles in sleep.

And here came the Queen, in the tropical noon,
When the wars and the world and all were asleep,
And nothing look'd forth to betray or to peep
Through the glories of jungle in garments of June,
To bathe with her court in the waters that bent
In the beautiful lake through tasseling trees,
And the tangle of blooms in a burden of bees,
As bold and as sharp as a bow unspent.

And strangely still, and more strangely sweet,
Was the lake that lay in its cradle of fern,
As still as a moon with her horns that turn
In the night, like lamps to white delicate feet.

They came and they stood by the brink of the tide,
They hung their shields on the boughs of the trees,
They lean'd their lances against the side,
Unloosed their sandals, and busy as bees
Ungather'd their robes in the rustle of leaves
That wound them as close as the wine-vine weaves.

The minstrel then falter'd, and further aside
Than ever before he averted his head;
He pick'd up a pebble and fretted the tide
Afar, with a countenance flushed and red.

He feign'd him ill, he wander'd away,
He sat him down by the waters alone,
And pray'd for pardon, as a knight should pray,
And rued an error not all his own.

The Amazons press'd to the girdle of reeds,
Two and by two they advanced to the tide,
They challenged each other, they laughed in their pride,
And banter'd, and vaunted of valorous deeds.

They push'd and they parted the curtains of green,
All timid at first; then looked in the wave

And laugh'd; retreated, then came up brave
To the brink of the water, led on by their Queen.

Again they retreated, again advanced,
Then parted the boughs in a proud disdain,
Then bent their heads to the waters, and glanced
Below, then blush'd, and then laughed again.

A bird awaken'd; then all dismayed
With a womanly sense of a beautiful shame
That strife and changes had left the same,
They shrank to the leaves and the somber shade.

At last, press'd forward a beautiful pair
And leapt to the wave, and laughing they blushed
As rich as their wines; when the waters rush'd
To the dimpled limbs, and laugh'd in their hair.

The fair troop follow'd with shouts and cheers,
They cleft the wave, and the friendly ferns
Came down in curtains and curves by turns,
And a brave palm lifted a thousand spears.

From under the ferns and away from the land,
And out in the wave until lost below,
There lay, as white as a bank of snow,
A long and beautiful border of sand.

Here clothed alone in their clouds of hair
And curtain'd about by the palm and fern,
And made as their maker had made them, fair,
And splendid of natural curve and turn;
Untrammel'd by art and untroubled by man
They tested their strength, or tried their speed:
And here they wrestled, and there they ran,
As supple and lithe as the watery reed.

The great trees shadow'd the bow-tipp'd tide,
And nodded their plumes from the opposite side,
As if to whisper, Take care! take care!
But the meddlesome sunshine here and there
Kept pointing a finger right under the trees,—
Kept shifting the branches and wagging a hand
At the round brown limbs on the border of sand,
And seem'd to whisper, Fie! what are these?

The gold-barr'd butterflies to and fro
And over the waterside wander'd and wove
As heedless and idle as clouds that rove
And drift by the peaks of perpetual snow.

A monkey swung out from a bough in the skies,
White-whisker'd and ancient, and wisest of all
Of his populous race, when he heard them call
And he watch'd them long, with his head sidewise.

He wondered much and he watched them all
From under his brows of amber and brown,
All patient and silent, and never once stirr'd
Till he saw two wrestle, and wrestling fall;
Then he arched his brows and he hasten'd him down
To his army below and said never a word.

PART IV.

There is many a love in the land, my love,
But never a love like this is;
Then kill me dead with your love, my love,
And cover me up with kisses.

Yea, kill me dead and cover me deep
Where never a soul discovers;
Deep in your heart to sleep, to sleep,
In the darlingest tomb of lovers.

The wanderer took him apart from the place;
Look'd up in the boughs at the gold birds there,
He envied the humming-birds fretting the air,
And frowned at the butterflies fanning his face.

He sat him down in a crook of the wave
And away from the Amazons, under the skies
Where great trees curved to a leaf-lined cave,
And he lifted his hands and he shaded his eyes:

And he held his head to the north when they came
To run on the reaches of sand from the south,
And he pull'd at his chin, and he pursed his mouth,
And he shut his eyes, with a sense of shame.

He reach'd and he shaped a bamboo reed
From the brink below, and began to blow
As if to himself; as the sea sometimes
Does soothe and soothe in a low, sweet song,
When his rage is spent, and the beach swells strong
With sweet repetitions of alliterate rhymes.

The echoes blew back from the indolent land;
Silent and still sat the tropical bird,
And only the sound of the reed was heard,
As the Amazons ceased from their sports on the sand.

They rose from the wave, and inclining the head,
They listened intent, with the delicate tip
Of the finger touch'd to the pouting lip,
Till the brown Queen turn'd in the tide, and led
Through the opaline lake, and under the shade,
To the shore where the chivalrous singer played.

He bended his head and he shaded his eyes
As well as he might with his lifted fingers,

And ceased to sing. But in mute surprise
He saw them linger as a child that lingers
Allured by a song that has ceased in the street,
And looks bewilder'd about from its play,
For the last loved notes that fell at its feet.

How the singer was vexed; he averted his head;
He lifted his eyes, looked far and wide
For a brief, little time; but they bathed at his side
In spite of his will, or of prayers well said.

He press'd four fingers against each lid,
Till the light was gone; yet for all that he did
It seem'd that the lithe forms lay and beat
Afloat in his face and full under his feet.

He seem'd to behold the billowy breasts,
And the rounded limbs in the rest or unrests—
To see them swim as the mermaid swims,
With the drifting, dimpled delicate limbs,
Folded or hidden or reach'd or caress'd.

It seems to me there is more that sees
Than the eyes in man; you may close your eyes,
You may turn your back, and may still be wise
In sacred and marvelous mysteries.
He saw as one sees the sun of a noon
In the sun-kiss'd south, when the eyes are closed—
He saw as one sees the bars of a moon
That fall through the boughs of the tropical trees,
When he lies at length, and is all composed,
And asleep in his hammock by the sundown seas.

He heard the waters beat, bubble and fret;
He lifted his eyes, yet forever they lay
Afloat in the tide; and he turn'd him away
And resolved to fly and for aye to forget.

He rose up strong, and he cross'd him twice,
He nerved his heart and he lifted his head,
He crush'd the treacherous reed in a trice,
With an angry foot, and he turn'd and fled.
Yet flying, he hurriedly turn'd his head
With an eager glance, with meddlesome eyes,
As a woman will turn; and he saw arise
The beautiful Queen from the silvery bed.

She toss'd back her hair, and she turn'd her eyes
With all of their splendor to his as he fled;
Ay, all their glory, and a strange surprise,
And a sad reproach, and a world unsaid.

Then she struck their shields, they rose in array,
As roused from a trance, and hurriedly came
From out of the wave. He wander'd away,
Still fretting his sensitive soul with blame.

Alone he sat in the shadows at noon,
Alone he sat by the waters at night;
Alone he sang, as a woman might,
With pale. kind face to the pale, cold moon.

He would here advance, and would there retreat,
As a petulant child that has lost its way
In the redolent walks of a sultry day,
And wanders around with irresolute feet.

He made him a harp of mahogany wood,
He strung it well with the sounding strings
Of a strong bird's thews, and from ostrich wings,
And play'd and sang in a sad, sweet rune.
He hang'd his harp in the vines, and stood
By the tide at night, in the palms at noon,
And lone as a ghost in the shadowy wood.

Then two grew sad, and alone sat she
By the great, strong stream, and she bow'd her head,
Then lifted her face to the tide, and said,
"O, pure as a tear and as strong as a sea,
Yet tender to me as the touch of a dove,
I had rather sit sad and alone by thee,
Than to go and be glad, with a legion in love."

She sat one time at the wanderer's side
As the kingly water went wandering by;
And the two once look'd, and they knew not why,
Full sad in each other's eyes, and they sigh'd.

She courted the solitude under the rim
Of the trees that reach'd to the resolute stream,
And gazed in the waters as one in a dream,
Till her soul grew heavy and her eyes grew dim.

She bow'd her head with a beautiful grief
That grew from her pity; she forgot her arms,
And she made neglect of the battle alarms
That threaten'd the land; the banana's leaf
Made shelter; he lifted his harp again,
She sat, she listen'd intent and long,
Forgetting her care and forgetting her pain—
Made sad for the singer, made glad for his song.

And the women waxed cold; the white moons waned,
And the brown Queen marshall'd them never once more,
With sword and with shield, in the palms by the shore;
But they sat them down to repose, or remain'd
Apart and scatter'd in the tropic-leaf'd trees,
As sadden'd by song, or for loves delay'd;
Or away in the Isle in couples they stray'd,
Not at all content in their Isles of peace.

They wander'd away to the lakes once more,
Or walk'd in the moon, or they sigh'd, or slept,
Or they sat in pairs by the shadowy shore,
And silent song with the waters kept.

There was one who stood by the waters one eve,
With the stars on her hair, and the bars of the moon
Broken up at her feet by the bountiful boon
Of extending old trees, who did questioning grieve;

"The birds they go over us two and by two;
The mono is mated; his bride in the boughs
Sits nursing his babe, and his passionate vows

Of love, you may hear them the whole day
through.

"The lizard, the cayman, the white-
tooth'd boar,
The serpents that glide in the sword-
leaf'd grass,
The beasts that abide or the birds that
pass,
They are glad in their loves as the green-
leaf'd shore.

"There is nothing that is that can yield
one bliss
Like an innocent love; the leaves have
tongue
And the tides talk low in the reeds, and
the young
And the quick buds open their lips but
for this.

"In the steep and the starry silences,
On the stormy levels of the limitless
seas,
Or here in the deeps of the dark-brow'd
trees,
There is nothing so much as a brave
man's kiss.

"There is nothing so strong, in the
stream, on the land,
In the valley of palms, on the pinnacled
snow,
In the clouds of the gods, on the grasses
below,
As the silk-soft touch of a baby's brown
hand.

"It were better to sit and to spin on a
stone
The whole year through with a babe at
the knee,
With its brown hands reaching caress-
ingly,
Than to sit in a girdle of gold and alone.

"It were better indeed to be mothers of
men,
And to murmur not much; there are
clouds in the sun.
Can a woman undo what the gods have
done?
Nay, the things must be as the things
have been."

They wander'd well forth, some here and
some there,
Unsatisfied some and irresolute all.
The sun was the same, the moonlight
did fall
Rich-barr'd and refulgent; the stars were
as fair
As ever were stars; the fruitful clouds
cross'd
And the harvest fail'd not; yet the fair
Isles grew
As a prison to all, and they search d on
through
The magnificent shades as for things that
were lost.

The minstrel, more pensive, went deep in
the wood,
And oft-time delay'd him the whole day
through,
As charm'd by the deeps, or the sad
heart drew
Some solaces sweet from the solitude.

The singer forsook them at last, and the
Queen
Came seldom then forth from the fierce
deep wood,
And her warriors, dark-brow'd and be-
wildering stood
In bands by the wave in the complicate
screen
Of overbent boughs. They would lean on
their spears
And would sometimes talk, low-voiced
and by twos,

As allured by longings they could not refuse,
And would sidewise look, as beset by their fears.

Once, wearied and sad, by the shadowy trees
In the flush of the sun they sank to their rests,
The dark hair veiling the beautiful breasts
That arose in billows, as mists veil seas.

Then away to the dream-world one by one;
The great red sun in his purple was roll'd,
And red-wing'd birds and the birds of gold
Were above in the trees like the beams of the sun.

Then the sun came down, on his ladders of gold
Built up of his beams, and the souls arose
And ascended on these, and the fair repose
Of the negligent forms was a feast to behold.

The round brown limbs they were reach'd or drawn,
The grass made dark with the fervour of hair;
And here were the rose-red lips and there
A flush'd breast rose like a sun at a dawn.

Then black-wing'd birds flew over in pair,
Listless and slow, as they call'd of the seas
And sounds came down through the tangle of trees
As lost, and nestled, and hid in their hair.

They started disturb'd, they sprang as at war
To lance and to shield; but the dolorous sound
Was gone from the wood; they gazed around
And saw but the birds, black-wing'd and afar.

They gazed at each other, then turn'd them unheard,
Slow trailing their lances, in long single line;
They moved through the forest, all dark as the sign
Of death that fell down from the ominous bird

Then the great sun died, and a rose-red bloom
Grew over his grave in a border of gold,
And a cloud with a silver-white rim was roll'd
Like a cold gray stone at the door of his tomb.

Strange voices were heard, sad visions were seen,
By sentries, betimes, on the opposite shore,
Where broad boughs bended their curtains of green
Far over the wave with their tropical store.

A sentry bent low on her palms and she peer'd
Suspiciously through; and, heavens! a man,
Low-brow'd and wicked, looked backward, and jeer'd
And taunted right full in her face as he ran:

A low crooked man, with eyes like a bird,—
As round and as cunning,—who came from the land
Of lakes, where the clouds lie low and at hand,
And the songs of the bent black swans are heard;
Where men are most cunning and cruel withal,
And are famous as spies, and are supple and fleet,
And are webb'd like the water-fowl under the feet,
And they swim like the swans, and like pelican's call.

And again, on a night when the moon she was not,
A sentry saw stealing, as still as a dream,
A sudden canoe down the mid of the stream,
Like the dark boat of death, and as still as a thought.

And lo! as it pass'd, from the prow there arose
A dreadful and gibbering, hairy old man,
Loud laughing as only a maniac can,
And shaking a lance at the land of his foes;
Then sudden it vanish'd, as still as it came,
Far down through the walls of the shadowy wood,
And the great moon rose like a forest aflame,
All threat'ning, sullen, and red like blood.

PART V.

Well, we have threaded through and through
The gloaming forests, Fairy Isles,
Afloat in sun and summer smiles,
As fallen stars in fields of blue;
Some futile wars with subtile love
That mortal never vanquish'd yet,
Some symphonies by angels set
In wave below, in bough above,
Were yours and mine; but here adieu.

And if it come to pass some days
That you grow weary, sad, and you
Lift up deep eyes from dusty ways
Of mart and moneys to the blue
And pure cold waters, isle and vine,
And bathe you there, and then arise
Refresh'd by one fresh thought of mine,
I rest content: I kiss your eyes,
I kiss your hair, in my delight:
I kiss my hand, and say, "Good-night."

I tell you that love is the bitterest sweet
That ever laid hold on the heart of a man;
A chain to the soul, and to cheer as a ban,
And a bane to the brain and a snare to the feet.

Aye! who shall ascend on the hollow white wings
Of love but to fall; to fall and to learn,
Like a moth, or a man, that the lights lure to burn,
That the roses have thorns and the honey-bee stings?

I say to you surely that grief shall befall;
I lift you my finger, I caution you true,
And yet you go forward, laugh gaily, and you
Must learn for yourself, then lament for us all.

You had better be drown'd than to love and to dream.
It were better to sit on a moss-grown stone,
And away from the sun, forever alone,
Slow pitching white pebbles at trout in a stream.

Alas for a heart that must live forlorn!
If you live you must love; if you love, regret—
It were better, perhaps, had you never been born,
Or better, at least, you could well forget.

The clouds are above us and snowy and cold,
And what is beyond but the steel gray sky,
And the still far stars that twinkle and lie
Like the eyes of a love or delusions of gold!

Ah! who would ascend? The clouds are above.
Aye! all things perish; to rise is to fall.
And alack for lovers, and alas for love,
And alas that we ever were born at all.

* * * * * *

The minstrel now stood by the border of wood,
But now not alone; with a resolute heart
He reach'd his hand, like to one made strong,
Forgot his silence and resumed his song,
And aroused his soul, and assumed his part
With a passionate will, in the palms where he stood.

"She is sweet as the breath of the Castile rose,
She is warm to the heart as a world of wine,
And as rich to behold as the rose that grows
With its red heart bent to the tide of the Rhine.

"I shall sip her lips as the brown bees sup
From the great gold heart of the buttercup!
I shall live and love! I shall have my day,
And die in my time, and who shall gainsay?
"What boots me the battles that I have have fought
With self for honor? My brave resolves?
And who takes note? The soul dissolves
In a sea of love, and the wars are forgot.

"The march of men, and the drift of ships,
The dreams of fame, and desires for gold,
Shall go for aye as a tale that is told,
Nor divide for a day my lips from her lips.

"And a knight shall rest, and none shall say nay,
In a green Isle wash'd by an arm of the seas,
And walled from the world by the white Andes:
The years are of age and can go their way."

A sentinel stood on the farthermost land,
And struck her shield, and her sword in hand,
She cried, "He comes with his silver spears,
With flint-tipp'd arrows and bended bows,
To take our blood though we give him tears,
And to flood our Isle in a world of woes!

"He comes, O Queen of the sun-kiss'd Isle,
He comes as a wind comes, blown from the seas,
In a cloud of canoes, on the curling breeze,
With his shields of tortoise and of crocodile!"

* * * * * *

Sweeter than swans' are a maiden's graces!
Sweeter than fruits are the kisses of morn!
Sweeter than babies' is a love new-born,
But sweeter than all are a love's embraces.

The Queen was at peace. Her terms of surrender
To love, who knows? and who can defend her?
She slept at peace, and the sentry's warning
Could scarce awaken the love-conquer'd Queen;
She slept at peace in the opaline
Hush and blush of that tropical morning;

And bound about by the twining glory,
Vine and trellis in the vernal morn,
As still and sweet as a babe new-born,
The brown Queen dream'd of the old new story.

But hark! her sentry's passionate words,
The sound of shields, and the clash of swords!
And slow she came, her head on her breast,
And her two hands held as to plead for rest.

Where, O where, were the Juno graces?
Where, O where was the glance of Jove,
As the Queen came forth from the sacred places,
Hidden away in the heart of the grove?

They rallied around as of old,—they besought her,
With swords to the sun and the sounding shield,
To lead them again to the glorious field,
So sacred to Freedom; and, breathless, they brought her
Her buckler and sword, and her armor all bright
With a thousand gems enjewell'd in gold.
She lifted her head with the look of old
An instant only; with all of her might
She sought to be strong and majestic again:
She bared them her arms and her ample brown breast;
They lifted her armor, they strove to invest
Her form in armor, but they strove in vain.
It could close no more, but it clang'd on the ground,
Like the fall of a knight, with an ominous sound,
And she shook her hair and she cried "Alas!
That love should come and liberty pass;"
And she cried, "Alas! to be cursed.... and bless'd
For the nights of love and noons of rest."

Her warriors wonder'd; they wander'd apart,
And trail'd their swords, and subdued their eyes
To earth in sorrow and in hush'd surprise,
And forgot themselves in their pity of heart.

"O Isles of the sun," sang the blue-eyed youth,
"O Edens new-made and let down from above!
Be sacred to peace and to passionate love,
Made happy in peace and made holy with truth."

The fair Isle fill'd with the fierce invader;
They form'd on the strand, they lifted their spears,
Where never was man for years and for years,
And moved on the Queen. She lifted and laid her
Finger-tip to her lips. For O sweet
Was the song of love as the love new-born,

That the minstrel blew in the virgin morn,
Away where the trees and the soft sands meet.

The strong men lean'd and their shields let fall,
And slowly they came with their trailing spears,
And heads bow'd down as if bent with years,
And an air of gentleness over them all.

The men grew glad as the song ascended,
They lean'd their lances against the palms,
They reach'd their arms as to reach for alms,
And the Amazons came—and their reign was ended.

* * * * * *

The tawny old crone here lays her stone
On the leaning grass and reaches a hand;
The day like a beautiful dream has flown,
The curtains of night come down on the land,
And I dip to the oars; but ere I go,
I tip her an extra bright pesos or so,
And I smile my thanks, for I think them due:
But, reader, fair reader, now what think you?

I do not like this, although I have cut it up and cut it down, and worked it over and over more than anything else. I had seen this vast and indescribable country, but not absorbed it; and that, most likely, is the reason it seems artificial and foolish, with knights and other things that I know nothing about. The only thing that I like in it is the water. I can handle water, and water is water the world over. But had it not been for the water and some of the wild tangles and jungles the whole thing would, ere this, have gone where the biggest half went long since. It was written in San Francisco, and was published at the same time in the *Overland* there and the *Gentleman's Magazine* in London. It was written at the instance of the Emperor, who translated it and to the last was brave and courtly enough to insist that it was good work. I had hoped to induce people to pour out of crowded London and better their fortunes there; for there is great wealth far, far up the Amazon. Aye, what exultant praise swelled my heart one happy day in Rome when Partridge, our minister to Brazil, gave me that message of thanks from the good Emperor, with a request to make his home my own while he lived.

AN INDIAN SUMMER.

The world it is wide; men go their ways
But love he is wise, and of all the hours,
And of all the beautiful sun-born days,
He sips their sweets as the bee sips flowers.

The sunlight lay in gather'd sheaves
Along the ground, the golden leaves
Possess'd the land and lay in bars
Above the lifted lawn of green
Beneath the feet, or fell, as stars
Fall, slantwise, shimmering and still
Upon the plain, upon the hill,
And heaving hill and plain between.

Some steeds in panoply were seen,
Strong, martial trained, with manes in air,
And tassell'd reins and mountings rare;
Some silent people here and there,
That gather'd leaves with listless will,
Or moved adown the dappled green,
Or look'd awa with idle gaze
Against the gold and purple haze.
You might have heard red leaflets fall,
The pheasant on the farther hill,
A single, lonely, locust trill,
Or sliding, sable cricket call
From out the grass, but that was all.

A wanderer of many lands
Was I, a weary Ishmaelite,
That knew the sign of lifted hands;
Had seen the Crescent-mosques, had seen
The Druid oaks of Aberdeen—
Recross'd the hilly seas, and saw
The sable pines of Mackinaw,
And lakes that lifted cold and white.

I saw the sweet Miami, saw
The swift Ohio bent and roll'd
Between his woody walls of gold,
The Wabash banks of gray pawpaw,
The Mississippi's ash; at morn
Of autumn, when the oak is red,
Saw slanting pyramids of corn,
The level fields of spotted swine,
The crooked lanes of lowing kine,
And in the burning bushes saw
The face of God, with bended head.

But when I saw her face, I said,
"Earth has no fruits so fairly red
As these that swing above my head;
No purpled leaf, no poppied land,
Like this that lies in reach of hand."

And, soft, unto myself I said:
"O soul, inured to rue and rime,
To barren toil and bitter bread,
To biting rime, to bitter rue,
Earth is not Nazareth; be good.
O sacred Indian-summer time
Of scarlet fruits, of fragrant wood,
Of purpled clouds, of curling haze—
O days of golden dreams, and days
Of banish'd, vanish'd tawny men,
Of martial songs of manly deeds—
Be fair to-day, and bear me true."
We mounted, turn'd the sudden steeds
Toward the yellow hills and flew.

My faith! but she rode fair, and she
Had scarlet berries in her hair,
And on her hands white starry stones.
The satellites of many thrones

Fall down before her gracious air
In that full season. Fair to see
Are pearly shells, red, virgin gold,
And yellow fruits, and sun-down seas,
And babes sun-brown; but all of these,
And all fair things of sea besides,
Before the matchless, manifold
Accomplishments of her who rides
With autumn summer in her hair,
And knows her steed and holds her fair
And stately in her stormy seat,
They lie like playthings at her feet.

By heaven! she was more than fair,
And more than good, and matchless wise,
With all the lovelight in her eyes,
And all the midnight in her hair.

Through leafy avenues and lanes,
And lo! we climb'd the yellow hills,
With russet leaves about the brows
That reach'd from over-reaching trees.
With purpled briars to the knees
Of steeds that fretted foamy thews.
We turn'd to look a time below
Beneath the ancient arch of boughs,
That bent above us as a bow
Of promise, bound in many hues.

I reach'd my hand. I could refuse
All fruits but this, the touch of her
At such a time. But lo! she lean'd
With lifted face and soul, and leant
As leans devoutest worshipper,
Beyond the branches scarlet screen'd
And look'd above me and beyond,
So fix'd and silent, still and fond,
She seem'd the while she look'd to lose
Her very soul in such intent.
She look'd on other things, but I,
I saw nor scarlet leaf nor sky;
I look'd on her, and only her.

Afar the city lay in smokes
Of battle, and the martial strokes
Of Progress thunder'd through the land
And struck against the yellow trees,
And roll'd in hollow echoes on
Like sounding limits of the seas
That smite the shelly shores at dawn.

Beyond, below, on either hand
There reach'd a lake in belt of pine,
A very dream; a distant dawn
Asleep in all the autumn shine,
Some like one of another land
That I once laid a hand upon,
And loved too well, and named as mine.

She sometimes touch'd with dimpl'd hand
The drifting mane with dreamy air,
She sometimes push'd aback her hair;
But still she lean'd and look'd afar,
As silent as the statues stand,—
For what? For falling leaf? For star,
That runs before the bride of death?....
The elements were still; a breath
Stirr'd not, the level western sun
Pour'd in his arrows every one;
Spill'd all his wealth of purpled red
On velvet poplar leaf below,
On arching chestnut overhead
In all the hues of heaven's bow.

She sat the upper hill, and high.
I spurr'd my black steed to her side;
"The bow of promise, lo!" I cried,
And lifted up my eyes to hers
With all the fervid love that stirs
The blood of men beneath the sun,
And reach'd my hand, as one undone,
In suppliance to hers above:
"The bow of promise! give me love!
I reach a hand, I rise or fall,
Henceforth from this: put forth a hand
From your high place and let me stand—
Stand soul and body, white and tall!
Why, I would live for you, would die
To-morrow, but to live to-day,

Give me but love, and let me live
To die before you. I can pray
To only you, because I know,
If you but give what I bestow,
That God has nothing left to give."

Christ! still her stately head was raised,
And still she silent sat and gazed
Beyond the trees, beyond the town,
To where the dimpled waters slept,
Nor splendid eyes once bended down
To eyes that lifted up and wept.

She spake not, nor subdued her head
To note a hand or heed a word;
And then I question'd if she heard
My life-tale on that leafy hill,
Or any fervid word I said,
And spoke with bold, vehement will.

She moved, and from her bridle hand
She slowly drew the dainty glove,
Then gazed again upon the land.
The dimpled hand, a snowy dove
Alit, and moved along the mane
Of glossy skeins; then, overbold,
It fell across the mane, and lay
Before my eyes a sweet bouquet
Of cluster'd kisses, white as snow.
I should have seized it reaching so,
But something bade me back,—a ban;
Around the third fair finger ran
A shining, hateful hoop of gold.

Ay, then I turn'd, I look'd away,
I sudden felt forlorn and chill;
I whistled, like, for want to say,
And then I said, with bended head,
"Another's ship from other shores,
With richer freight, with fairer stores,
Shall come to her some day instead;"
Then turn'd about,—and all was still.

Yea, you had chafed at this, and cried,
And laugh'd with bloodless lips, and said
Some bitter things to sate your pride,
And toss'd aloft a lordly head,
And acted well some wilful lie,
And, most like, cursed yourself—but I...
Well, you be crucified, and you
Be broken up with lances through
The soul, then you may turn to find
Some ladder-rounds in keenest rods,
Some solace in the bitter rind,
Some favor with the gods irate—
The everlasting anger'd gods—
And ask not overmuch of fate.

I was not born, was never bless'd,
With cunning ways, nor wit, nor skill
In woman's ways, nor words of love,
Nor fashion'd suppliance of will.
A very clown, I think, had guess'd
How out of place and plain I seem'd;
I, I, the idol-worshiper,
Who saw nor maple-leaves nor sky
But took some touch and hue of her.

I am a pagan, heathen, lo!
A savage man, of savage lands;
Too quick to love, too slow to know
The sign that tame love understands.

* * * * * *

Some heedless hoofs went sounding down
The broken way. The woods were brown,
And homely now; some idle talk
Of folk and town; a broken walk;
But sounding feet made song no more
For me along that leafy shore.

The sun caught up his gather'd sheaves;
A squirrel caught a nut and ran;
A rabbit rustled in the leaves,
A whirling bat, black-wing'd and tan,
Blew swift between us; sullen night
Fell down upon us; mottled kine,
With lifted heads, went lowing down
The rocky ridge toward the town,
And all the woods grew dark as wine.

* * * * * *

Yea, bless'd Ohio's banks are fair;
A sunny clime and good to touch,
For tamer men of gentler mien,
But as for me, another scene.
A land below the Alps I know,
Set well with grapes and girt with much
Of woodland beauty; I shall share
My rides by night below the light
Of Mauna Loa, ride below
The steep and Starry Hebron height;
Shall lift my hands in many lands,
See South Sea palm, see Northland fir,
See white-winged swans, see red-bill'd
doves;
See many lands and many loves,
But never more the face of her.

And what her name or now the place
Of her who makes my Mecca's prayer,
Concerns you not; not any trace
Of entrance to my temple's shrine
Remains. The memory is mine,
And none shall pass the portals there.

I see the gold and purple gleam
Of autumn leaves, a reach of seas,
A silent rider like a dream
Moves by, a mist of mysteries,
And these are mine, and only these,
Yet they be more in my esteem,
Than silver'd sails on corall'd seas.

The present! take it, hold it thine,
But that one hour out from all
The years that are, or yet shall fall,
I pluck it out, I name it mine;
That hour bound in sunny sheaves,
With tassell'd shocks of golden shine,
That hour wound in scarlet leaves,
Is mine. I stretch a hand and swear
An oath that breaks into a prayer;
By heaven, it is wholly mine!

* I wrote, or rather lived, this bit of color at Cleveland, Ohio, giving to it the entire autumn of gold. The prime purpose was to get the atmosphere of an Ohio Saint Martin's summer, but it grew to be a very serious matter. The story, what little there is of it, is literally true. In fact we must in some sort at least, live what we write if what we write is to live.

FROM SEA TO SEA.

Lo! here sit we by the sun-down seas
And the White Sierras. The sweet sea-breeze
Is about us here; and a sky so fair
Is bending above, so cloudless, blue,
That you gaze and you gaze and you dream, and you
See God and the portals of heaven there.

Shake hands! kiss hands in haste to the sea,
Where the sun comes in, and mount with me
The matchless steed of the strong New World,
As he champs and chafes with a strength untold,—
And away to the West, where the waves are curl'd,
As they kiss white palms to the capes of gold!

A girth of brass and a breast of steel,
A breath of flame and a flaming mane,
An iron hoof and a steel-clad heel,
A Mexican bit and a massive chain
Well tried and wrought in an iron rein;
And away! away! with a shout and yell
That had stricken a legion of old with fear,
They had started the dead from their graves while're,
And startled the damn'd in hell as well.

Stand up! stand out! where the wind comes in.
And the wealth of the seas pours over you,
As its health floods up to the face like wine,
And a breath blows up from the Delaware
And the Susquehanna. We feel the might
Of armies in us; the blood leaps through
The frame with a fresh and a keen delight
As the Alleghanies have kiss'd the hair,
With a kiss blown far through the rush and din,
By the chestnut burrs and through boughs of pine.

O seas in a land! O lakes of mine!
By the love I bear and the songs I bring
Be glad with me! lift your waves and sing
A song in the reeds that surround your isles!—
A song of joy for this sun that smiles,
For this land I love and this age and sign;
For the peace that is and the perils pass'd;
For the hope that is and the rest at last!

O heart of the world's heart! West! my West!
Look up! look out! There are fields of kine,
There are clover-fields that are red as wine;
And a world of kine in the fields take rest,
As they ruminate in the shade of trees
That are white with blossoms or brown with bees.

There are emerald seas of corn and cane;
There are isles of oak on the harvest plain,
Where brown men bend to the bending
 grain;
There are temples of God and towns new
 born,
And beautiful homes of beautiful brides;
And the hearts of oak and the hands of
 horn
Have fashion'd all these and a world be-
 sides...

A rush of rivers and a brush of trees,
A breath blown far from the Mexican seas,
And over the great heart-vein of earth!
... By the South-Sun-land of the Chero-
 kee,
By the scalp-lock-lodge of the tall Pawnee,
And up La Platte. What a weary dearth
Of the homes of men! What a wild delight
Of space! Of room! What a sense of seas,
Where the seas are not! What a salt-like
 breeze!
What dust and taste of quick alkali!
...Then hills! green, brown, then black
 like night,
All fierce and defiant against the sky!

At last! at last! O steed new-born,
Born strong of the will of the strong New
 World,
We shoot to the summit, with the shafts
 of morn,
On the mount of Thunder, where clouds
 are curl'd,
Below in a splendor of the sun-clad seas.
A kiss of welcome on the warm west breeze
Blows up with a smell of the fragrant
 pine,
And a faint, sweet fragrance from the far-
 off seas
Comes in through the gates of the great
 South Pass,
And thrills the soul like a flow of wine.
The hare leaps low in the storm-bent grass,
The mountain ram from his cliff looks
 back,
The brown deer hies to the tamarack;
And afar to the South with a sound of the
 main,
Roll buffalo herds to the limitless plain . . .

On, on, o'er the summit; and onward
 again,
And down like the sea-dove the billow en-
 shrouds,
And down like the swallow that dips to
 the sea,
We dart and we dash and we quiver and we
Are blowing to heaven white billows of
 clouds.

Thou "City of Saints!" O antique men,
And men of the Desert as the men of old!
Stand up! be glad! When the truths are
 told,
When Time has utter'd his truths and
 when
His hand has lifted the things to fame
From the mass of things to be known no
 more,
A monument set in the desert sand,
A pyramid rear'd on an inland shore,
And their architects shall have place and
 name.

The Humboldt desert and the alkaline
 land,
And the seas of sage and of arid sand
That stretch away till the strain'd eye
 carries
The soul where the infinite spaces fill,
Are far in the rear, and the fierce Sierras
Are under our feet, and the hearts beat
 high
And the blood comes quick; but the lips
 are still
With awe and wonder, and all the will
Is bow'd with a grandeur that frets the
 sky.

A flash of lakes through the fragrant trees,
A song of birds and a sound of bees
Above in the boughs of the sugar-pine.
The pick-ax stroke in the placer mine,
The boom of blasts in the gold-ribbed hills,
The grizzly's growl in the gorge below
Are dying away, and the sound of rills
From the far-off shimmering crest of snow,
The laurel green and the ivied oak,
A yellow stream and a cabin's smoke,
The brown bent hills and the shepherd's call,
The hills of vine and of fruits, and all
The sweets of Eden are here, and we
Look out and afar to a limitless sea.

We have lived an age in a half-moon-wane!
We have seen a world! We have chased the sun
From sea to sea; but the task is done.
We here descend to the great white main—
To the King of Seas, with its temples bare
And a tropic breath on the brow and hair.

We are hush'd with wonder, we stand apart,
We stand in silence; the heaving heart
Fills full of heaven, and then the knees
Go down in worship on the golden sands.
With faces seaward, and with folded hands
We gaze on the boundless, white Balboa seas.

This was written during my first railroad ride from New York to San Francisco, at a time when this was the greatest ride on the globe and parties came to California in great crowds to look upon the Pacific. It is to be deplored that zeal and interest have so nearly perished with the novelty of the great journey.

A SONG OF THE SOUTH.

Part I.

Rhyme on, rhyme on, in reedy flow,
O river, rhymer ever sweet!
The story of thy land is meet;
The stars stand listening to know.

Rhyme on, O river of the earth!
Gray father of the dreadful seas,
Rhyme on! the world upon its knees
Invokes thy songs, thy wealth, thy worth.

Rhyme on! the reed is at thy mouth,
O kingly minstrel, mighty stream!
Thy Crescent City, like a dream,
Hangs in the heaven of my South.

Rhyme on, rhyme on! these broken strings
Sing sweetest in this warm south wind;
I sit thy willow banks and bind
A broken harp that fitful sings.

I.

And where is my silent, sweet blossom-sown town?
And where is her glory, and what has she done?
By her Mexican seas in the path of the sun,
Sit you down; in her crescent of seas, sit you down.

Aye, glory enough by her Mexican seas!
Aye, story enough in that battle-torn town,
Hidden down in her crescent of seas, hidden down
In her mantle and sheen of magnolia-white trees.

But mine is the story of souls; of a soul
That barter'd God's limitless kingdom for gold,—
Sold stars and all space for a thing he did hold
In his palm for a day; and then hid with the mole:

Sad soul of a rose-land, of moss-mantled oak—
Gray, Druid-old oaks; and the moss that sways
And swings in the wind is the battle-smoke
Of duelists dead, in her storied days:

Sad soul of a love-land, of church-bells and chimes;

A love-land of altars and orange flowers;
And that is the reason for all these rhymes—
That church-bells are ringing through all
these hours!

This sun-land has churches, has priests
at prayer,
White nuns, that are white as the far north
snow:
They go where duty may bid them go,—
They dare when the angel of death is there.

This land has ladies so fair, so fair,
In their Creole quarter, with great black
eyes—
So fair that the Mayor must keep them
there
Lest troubles, like troubles of Troy, arise.

This sun-land has ladies with eyes held
down,
Held down, because if they lifted them,
Why, you would be lost in that old French
town,
Though even you held to God's garment
hem.

This love-land has ladies so fair, so fair,
That they bend their eyes to the holy book,
Lest you should forget yourself, your
prayer,
And never more cease to look and to look.

And these are the ladies that no men
see,
And this is the reason men see them not;
Better their modest, sweet mystery—
Better by far than red battle-shot.

And so, in this curious old town of
tiles,
The proud French quarter of days long
gone,
In castles of Spain and tumble-down piles,
These wonderful ladies live on and on.

I sit in the church where they come and
go;
I dream of glory that has long since gone;
Of the low raised high, of the high brought
low
As in battle-torn days of Napoleon.

These grass-plaited places, so rich, so
poor!
One quaint old church at the edge of the
town
Has white tombs laid to the very church
door—
White leaves in the story of life turn'd
down:

White leaves in the story of life are
these,
The low white slabs in the long, strong
grass,
Where glory has emptied her hour-glass,
And dreams with the dreamers beneath
the trees.

I dream with the dreamers beneath the
sod,
Where souls pass by to the great white
throne;
I count each tomb as a mute mile-stone
For weary, sweet souls on their way to
God.

I sit all day by the vast, strong stream,
'Mid low white slabs in the long, strong
grass,
Where time has forgotten for aye to pass,
To dream, and ever to dream and to dream.

This quaint old church, with its dead to
the door,
By the cypress swamp at the edge of the
town,
So restful it seems that you want to sit
down
And rest you, and rest you for evermore.

And one white stone is a lowliest tomb
That has crept up close to the crumbling door,—
Some penitent soul, as imploring room
Close under the cross that is leaning o'er.

'T is a low white slab, and 't is nameless, too,—
Her untold story, why, who should know?
Yet God, I reckon, can read right through
That nameless stone to the bosom below.

And the roses know, and they pity her, too;
They bend their heads in the sun or rain,
And they read, and they read, and then read again,
As children reading strange pictures through.

Why, surely her sleep it should be profound;
For oh, the apples of gold above!
And oh, the blossoms of bridal love!
And oh, the roses that gather around!

The sleep of a night or a thousand morns—
Why, what is the difference here, to-day?
Sleeping and sleeping the years away,
With all earth's roses and none of its thorns.

Magnolias white, white rose and red—
The palm-tree here and the cypress there:
Sit down by the palm at the feet of the dead,
And hear a penitent's midnight prayer.

II.

The old churchyard is still as death;
A stranger passes to and fro,
As if to church—he does not go;
The dead night does not draw a breath.

A lone sweet lady prays within.
The stranger passes by the door—
Will he not pray? Is he so poor
He has no prayer for his sin?

Is he so poor? Why, two strong hands
Are full and heavy, as with gold;
They clasp as clasp two iron bands
About two bags with eager hold.

Will he not pause and enter in,
Put down his heavy load and rest,
Put off his garmenting of sin,
As some black mantle from his breast?

Ah me! the brave alone can pray,
The church-door is as cannon's mouth
For crime to face, or North or South,
More dreaded than dread battle-day.

* * * * * *

Now two men pace. They pace apart:
And one with youth and truth is fair,
The fervid sun is in his heart,
The tawny South is in his hair.

Aye, two men pace—pace left and right—
The lone sweet lady prays within;
Aye, two men pace; the silent night
Kneels down in prayer for some sin.

Lo! two men pace; and one is gray,
A blue-eyed man from snow-clad land,
With something heavy in each hand,—
With heavy feet, as feet of clay.

Aye, two men pace; and one is light
Of step, but still his brow is dark;
His eyes are as a kindled spark
That burns beneath the brow of night!

And still they pace. The stars are red,
The tombs are white as frosted snow;
The silence is as if the dead
Did pace in couples to and fro.

III.

The azure curtain of God's house
Draws back, and hangs star-pinned to space;
I hear the low, large moon arouse,
And slowly lift her languid face.

I see her shoulder up the east,
Low-necked, and large as womanhood—
Low-necked, as for some ample feast
Of gods, within yon orange-wood.

She spreads white palms, she whispers peace,—
Sweet peace on earth forevermore;
Sweet peace for two beneath the trees,
Sweet peace for one within the door.

The bent stream, as God's scimitar,
Flashed in the sun, sweeps on and on,
Till sheathed, like some great sword new-drawn,
In seas beneath the Carib's star.

The high moon climbs the sapphire hill,
The lone sweet lady prays within;
The crickets keep such clang and din—
They are so loud, earth is so still!

And two men glare in silence there!
The bitter, jealous hate of each
Has grown too deep for deed or speech—
The lone sweet lady keeps her prayer.

The vast moon high through heaven's field
In circling chariot is rolled;
The golden stars are spun and reeled,
And woven into cloth of gold.

The white magnolia fills the night
With perfume, as the proud moon fills
The glad earth with her ample light
From out her awful sapphire hills.

White orange-blossoms fill the boughs
Above, about the old church-door;
They wait the bride, the bridal vows,—
They never hung so fair before.

The two men glare as dark as sin!
And yet all seem so fair, so white,
You would not reckon it was night,—
The while the lady prays within.

IV.

She prays so very long and late,—
The two men, weary, waiting there,—
The great magnolia at the gate
Bends drowsily above her prayer.

The cypress in his cloak of moss,
That watches on in silent gloom,
Has leaned and shaped a shadow cross
Above the nameless, lowly tomb.

* * * * *

What can she pray for? What her sin?
What folly of a maid so fair?
What shadows bind the wondrous hair
Of one who prays so long within?

The palm-trees guard in regiment,
Stand right and left without the gate;
The myrtle-moss trees wait and wait;
The tall magnolia leans intent.

The cypress-trees, on gnarled old knees,
Far out the dank and marshy deep
Where slimy monsters groan and creep,
Kneel with her in their marshy seas.

What can her sin be? Who shall know?
The night flies by,—a bird on wing;
The men no longer to and fro
Stride up and down, or anything.

For one, so weary and so old,
Has hardly strength to stride or stir;
He can but hold his bags of gold,—
But hug his gold and wait for her.

The two stand still,—stand face to face.
The moon slides on, the midnight air
Is perfumed as a house of prayer,—
The maiden keeps her holy place.

Two men! And one is gray, but one
Scarce lifts a full-grown face as yet;
With light foot on life's threshold set,—
Is he the other's sun-born son?

And one is of the land of snow,
And one is of the land of sun;
A black-eyed, burning youth is one,
But one has pulses cold and slow:

Aye, cold and slow from clime of snow
Where Nature's bosom, icy bound,
Holds all her forces, hard, profound,—
Holds close where all the South lets go.

Blame not the sun, blame not the snows,—
God's great schoolhouse for all is clime;
The great school teacher, Father Time,
And each has borne as best he knows.

At last the elder speaks,—he cries,—
He speaks as if his heart would break;
He speaks out as a man that dies,—
As dying for some lost love's sake:

"Come, take this bag of gold, and go!
Come, take one bag! See, I have two!
Oh, why stand silent, staring so,
When I would share my gold with you?

"Come, take this gold! See how I pray!
See how I bribe, and beg, and buy,—
Aye, buy! and beg, as you, too, may
Some day before you come to die.

"God! take this gold, I beg, I pray!
I beg as one who thirsting cries
For but one drop of drink, and dies
In some lone, loveless desert way.

"You hesitate? Still hesitate?
Stand silent still and mock my pain?
Still mock to see me wait and wait,
And wait her love, as earth waits rain?"

V.

O broken ship! O starless shore!
O black and everlasting night!
Where love comes never any more
To light man's way with heaven's light.

A godless man with bags of gold
I think a most unholy sight;
Ah, who so desolate at night,
Amid death's sleepers still and cold?

A godless man on holy ground
I think a most unholy sight.
I hear death trailing, like a hound,
Hard after him, and swift to bite.

VI.

The vast moon settles to the west;
Yet still two men beside that tomb,
And one would sit thereon to rest,—
Aye, rest below, if there were room.

VII.

What is this rest of death, sweet friend?
What is the rising up, and where?
I say, death is a lengthened prayer,
A longer night, a larger end.

Hear you the lesson I once learned:
I died; I sailed a million miles
Through dreamful, flowery, restful isles,—
She was not there, and I returned.

I say the shores of death and sleep
Are one; that when we, wearied, come
To Lethe's waters, and lie dumb,
'Tis death, not sleep, holds us to keep.

Yea, we lie dead for need of rest,
And so the soul drifts out and o'er
The vast still waters to the shore
Beyond, in pleasant, tranquil quest:

It sails straight on, forgetting pain,
Past isles of peace, to perfect rest,—
Now were it best abide, or best
Return and take up life again?

And that is all of death there is,
Believe me. If you find your love
In that far land, then, like the dove,
Pluck olive boughs, nor back to this.

But if you find your love not there;
Or if your feet feel sure, and you
Have still allotted work to do,—
Why, then haste back to toil and care.

Death is no mystery. 'T is plain
If death be mystery, then sleep
Is mystery thrice strangely deep,—
For oh, this coming back again!

Austerest ferryman of souls!
I see the gleam of shining shores;
I hear thy steady stroke of oars
Above the wildest wave that rolls.

O Charon, keep thy somber ships!
I come, with neither myrrh nor balm,
Nor silver piece in open palm,—
Just lone, white silence on my lips.

VIII.

She prays so long! she prays so late!
What sin in all this flower land
Against her supplicating hand
Could have in heaven any weight?

Prays she for her sweet self alone?
Prays she for some one far away,
Or some one near and dear to-day,
Or some poor lorn, lost soul unknown?

It seems to me a selfish thing
To pray forever for one's self;
It seems to me like heaping pelf,
In heaven by hard reckoning.

Why, I would rather stoop and bear
My load of sin, and bear it well
And bravely down to your hard hell,
Than pray and pray a selfish prayer!

IX.

The swift chameleon in the gloom—
This gray morn silence so profound!—
Forsakes its bough, glides to the ground,
Then up, and lies across the tomb.

It erst was green as olive-leaf;
It then grew gray as myrtle moss
The time it slid the tomb across;
And now 't is marble-white as grief.

The little creature's hues are gone
Here in the gray and ghostly light;
It lies so pale, so panting white,—
White as the tomb it lies upon.

The two still by that nameless tomb!
And both so still! You might have said,
These two men, they are also dead,
And only waiting here for room.

How still beneath the orange-bough!
How tall was one, how bowed was one!
The one was as a journey done,
The other as beginning now.

And one was young,—young with that youth
Eternal that belongs to truth;
And one was old,—old with the years
That follow fast on doubts and fears.

And yet the habit of command
Was his, in every stubborn part;

No common knave was he at heart,
Nor his the common coward's hand.

He looked the young man in the face,
So full of hate, so frank of hate;
The other, standing in his place,
Stared back as straight and hard as fate.

And now he sudden turned away,
And now he paced the path, and now
Came back beneath the orange bough,
Pale-browed, with lips as cold as clay.

As mute as shadows on a wall,
As silent still, as dark as they,
Before that stranger, bent and gray,
The youth stood scornful, proud and tall.

He stood a clean palmetto tree
With Spanish daggers guarding it;
Nor deed, nor word, to him seemed fit
While she prayed on so silently

He slew his rival with his eyes
His eyes were daggers piercing deep,—
So deep that blood began to creep
From their deep wounds and drop word-wise.

His eyes so black, so bright, that they
Might raise the dead, the living slay,
If but the dead, the living bore
Such hearts as heroes had of yore.

Two deadly arrows barbed in black,
And feathered, too, with raven's wing;
Two arrows that could silent sting,
And with a death-wound answer back.

How fierce he was! how deadly still
In that mesmeric, searching stare
Turned on the pleading stranger there
That drew to him, despite his will!

So like a bird down-fluttering,
Down, down, beneath a snake's bright eyes,
He stood, a fascinated thing,
That hopeless, unresisting, dies.

He raised a hard hand as before,
Reached out the gold, and offered it
With hand that shook as ague-fit,—
The while the youth but scorned the more.

"You will not touch it? In God's name,
Who are you, and what are you, then?
Come, take this gold, and be of men,—
A human form with human aim.

"Yea, take this gold,—she must be mine!
She shall be mine! I do not fear
Your scowl, your scorn, your soul austere,
The living, dead, or your dark sign.

"I saw her as she entered there;
I saw her, and uncovered stood;
The perfume of her womanhood
Was holy incense on the air.

"She left behind sweet sanctity,
Religion went the way she went;
I cried I would repent, repent!
She passed on, all unheeding me.

"Her soul is young, her eyes are bright
And gladsome, as mine own are dim;
But oh, I felt my senses swim
The time she passed me by to-night!—

"The time she passed, nor raised her eyes
To hear me cry I would repent,
Nor turned her head to hear my cries,
But swifter went the way she went,—

"Went swift as youth, for all these years!
And this the strangest thing appears,

That lady there seems just the same,—
Sweet Gladys—Ah! you know her name?

"You hear her name and start that I
Should name her dear name trembling so?
Why, boy, when I shall come to die
That name shall be the last I know.

"That name shall be the last sweet name
My lips shall utter in this life!
That name is brighter than bright flame,—
That lady is mine own sweet wife!

"Ah, start and catch your burning breath!
Ah, start and clutch your deadly knife!
If this be death, then be it death,—
But that loved lady is my wife!

"Yea, you are stunned! your face is white,
That I should come confronting you,
As comes a lorn ghost of the night
From out the past, and to pursue.

"You thought me dead? You shake your head,
You start back horrified to know
That she is loved, that she is wed,
That you have sinned in loving so.

"Yet what seems strange, that lady there,
Housed in the holy house of prayer,
Seems just the same for all her tears,—
For all my absent twenty years.

"Yea, twenty years to-night, to-night,—
Just twenty years this day, this hour,
Since first I plucked that perfect flower,
And not one witness of the rite.

"Nay, do not doubt,—I tell you true!
Her prayers, her tears, her constancy
Are all for me, are all for me,—
And not one single thought for you!

"I knew, I knew she would be here
This night of nights to pray for me!
And how could I for twenty year
Know this same night so certainly?

"Ah me! some thoughts that we would drown,
Stick closer than a brother to
The conscience, and pursue, pursue,
Like baying hound, to hunt us down.

"And, then, that date is history;
For on that night this shore was shelled,
And many a noble mansion felled,
With many a noble family.

"I wore the blue; I watched the flight
Of shells, like stars tossed through the air
To blow your hearth-stones—anywhere,
That wild, illuminated night.

"Nay, rage befits you not so well;
Why, you were but a babe at best;
Your cradle some sharp bursted shell
That tore, maybe, your mother's breast!

"Hear me! We came in honored war.
The risen world was on your track!
The whole North-land was at our back,
From Hudson's bank to the North Star!

"And from the North to palm-set sea
The splendid fiery cyclone swept.
Your fathers fell, your mothers wept,
Their nude babes clinging to the knee.

"A wide and desolated track:
Behind, a path of ruin lay;
Before, some women by the way
Stood mutely gazing, clad in black.

'From silent women waiting there
White tears came down like still, small rain;
Their own sons of the battle-plain
Were now but viewless ghosts of air.

"Their own dear, daring boys in gray,—
They should not see them any more;
Our cruel drums kept telling o'er
The time their own sons went away

"Through burning town, by bursting shell—
Yea, I remember well that night;
I led through orange-lanes of light,
As through some hot outpost of hell!

"That night of rainbow shot and shell
Sent from yon surging river's breast
To waken me, no more to rest,—
That night I should remember well!

"That night, amid the maimed and dead—
A night in history set down
By light of many a burning town,
And written all across in red,—

"Her father dead, her brothers dead,
Her home in flames,—what else could she
But fly all helpless here to me,
A fluttered dove, that night of dread?

"Short time, hot time had I to woo
Amid the red shells' battle-chime;
But women rarely reckon time,
And perils waken love anew.

"Aye, then I wore a captain's sword;
And, too, had oftentime before
Doffed cap at her dead father's door,
And passed a lover's pleasant word.

"And then—ah, I was comely then!
I bore no load upon my back,
I heard no hounds upon my track,
But stood the tallest of tall men.

"Her father's and her mother's shrine,
This church amid the orange-wood;
So near and so secure it stood,
It seemed to beckon as a sign.

"Its white cross seemed to beckon me;
My heart was strong, and it was mine
To throw myself upon my knee,
To beg to lead her to this shrine.

"She did consent. Through lanes of light
I led through this church-door that night—
Let fall your hand! Take back your face
And stand,—stand patient in your place!

"She loved me; and she loves me still.
Yea, she clung close to me that hour
As honey-bee to honey-flower,—
And still is mine through good or ill.

"The priest stood there. He spake the prayer;
He made the holy, mystic sign,
And she was mine, was wholly mine,—
Is mine this moment, I can swear!

"Then days, then nights of vast delight,—
Then came a doubtful later day;
The faithful priest, now far away,
Watched with the dying in the fight:

"The priest amid the dying, dead,
Kept duty on the battle-field,—
That midnight marriage unrevealed
Kept strange thoughts running thro' my head.

"At last a stray ball struck the priest;
This vestibule his chancel was;

And now none lived to speak her cause,
Record, or champion her the least.

"Hear me! I had been bred to hate
All priests, their mummeries and all.
Ah, it was fate,—ah, it was fate
That all things tempted to my fall!

"And then the dashing songs we sang
Those nights when rudely reveling,—
Such songs that only soldiers sing,—
Until the very tent-poles rang!

"What is the rhyme that rhymers say,
Of maidens born to be betrayed
By epaulettes and shining blade,
While soldiers love and ride away?

"And then my comrades spake her name
Half taunting, with a touch of shame;
Taught me to hold that lily-flower
As some light pastime of the hour.

"And then the ruin in the land,
The death, dismay, the lawlessness!
Men gathered gold on every hand,—
Heaped gold: and why should I do less?

"The cry for gold was in the air,—
For Creole gold, for precious things;
The sword kept prodding here and there,
Through bolts and sacred fastenings.

"'Get gold! get gold!' This was the cry.
And I loved gold. What else could I
Or you, or any earnest one,
Born in this getting age, have done?

"With this one lesson taught from youth,
And ever taught us, to get gold,—
To get and hold, and ever hold,—
What else could I have done, forsooth?

"She, seeing how I crazed for gold,—
This girl, my wife, one late night told
Of treasures hidden close at hand,
In her dead father's mellow land;

"Of gold she helped her brothers hide
Beneath a broad banana-tree
The day the two in battle died,
The night she, dying, fled to me.

"It seemed too good; I laughed to scorn
Her trustful tale. She answered not;
But meekly on the morrow morn
These two great bags of bright gold brought.

"And when she brought this gold to me,—
Red Creole gold, rich, rare, and old,—
When I at last had gold, sweet gold,
I cried in very ecstasy.

"Red gold! rich gold! two bags of gold!
The two stout bags of gold she brought
And gave, with scarce a second thought,—
Why, her two hands could scarcely hold!

"Now I had gold! two bags of gold!
Two wings of gold, to fly, and fly
The wide world's girth; red gold to hold
Against my heart for aye and aye!

"My country's lesson: 'Gold! get gold!'
I learned it well in land of snow;
And what can glow, so brightly glow,
Long winter nights of northern cold?

"Aye, now at last, at last I had
The one thing, all fair things above,
My land had taught me most to love!
A miser now! and I grew mad.

"With these two bags of gold my own,
I soon began to plan some night
For flight, for far and sudden flight,—
For flight; and, too, for flight alone.

"I feared! I feared! My heart grew
    cold,—
Some one might claim this gold of me!
I feared her,—feared her purity—
Feared all things but my bags of gold.

"I grew to hate her face, her creed,—
That face the fairest ever yet
That bowed o'er holy cross or bead,
Or yet was in God's image set.

"I fled,—nay, not so knavish low,
As you have fancied, did I fly:
I sought her at this shrine, and I
Told her full frankly I should go.

"I stood a giant in my power,—
And did she question or dispute?
I stood a savage, selfish brute,—
She bowed her head, a lily-flower.

"And when I sudden turned to go,
And told her I should come no more,
She bowed her head so low, so low,
Her vast black hair fell pouring o'er.

"And that was all; her splendid face
Was mantled from me, and her night
Of hair half hid her from my sight,
As she fell moaning in her place.

"And there, through her dark night of
    hair,
She sobbed, low moaning in hot tears,
That she would wait, wait all the years,—
Would wait and pray in her despair.

"Nay, did not murmur, not deny,—
She did not cross me one sweet word!
I turned and fled; I thought I heard
A night-bird's piercing low death-cry!"

PART II.

How soft the moonlight of my South!
How sweet the South in soft moonlight!
I want to kiss her warm, sweet mouth
As she lies sleeping here to-night.

How still! I do not hear a mouse.
I see some bursting buds appear;
I hear God in his garden,—hear
Him trim some flowers for His house.

I hear some singing stars; the mouth
Of my vast river sings and sings,
And pipes on reeds of pleasant things,—
Of splendid promise for my South:

My great South-woman, soon to rise
And tiptoe up and loose her hair;
Tiptoe, and take from out the skies
God's stars and glorious moon to wear!

I.

The poet shall create or kill,
Bid heroes live, bid braggarts die.
I look against a lurid sky,—
My silent South lies proudly still.

The fading light of burning lands
Still climbs to God's house overhead;
Mute women wring white, withered hands;
Their eyes are red, their skies are red.

And we still boast our bitter wars!
Still burn and boast, and boast and lie
But God's white finger spins the stars
In calm dominion of the sky.

And not one ray of light the less
Comes down to bid the grasses spring;
No drop of dew nor anything
Shall fail for all our bitterness.

If man grows large, is God the less?
The moon shall rise and set the same,
The great sun spill his splendid flame,
And clothe the world in queenliness.

Yea, from that very blood-soaked sod
Some large-souled, seeing youth shall come
Some day, and he shall not be dumb
Before the awful court of God.

II.

The weary moon had turned away,
The far North Star was turning pale
To hear the stranger's boastful tale
Of blood and flame that battle-day.

And yet again the two men glared,
Close face to face above that tomb;
Each seemed as jealous of the room
The other, eager waiting shared.

Again the man began to say,—
As taking up some brôken thread,
As talking to the patient dead,—
The Creole was as still as they:

"That night we burned yon grass-grown town,—
The grasses, vines are reaching up;
The ruins they are reaching down,
As sun-browned soldiers when they sup.

"I knew her,—knew her constancy.
She said this night of every year
She here would come, and kneeling here,
Would pray the livelong night for me.

"This praying seems a splendid thing!
It drives old Time the other way;
It makes him lose all reckoning
Of years that I have had to pay.

"This praying seems a splendid thing!
It makes me stronger as she prays—
But oh, those bitter, bitter days,
When I became a banished thing!

"I fled, took ship,—I fled as far
As far ships drive tow'rd the North Star:
For I did hate the South, the sun
That made me think what I had done.

"I could not see a fair palm-tree
In foreign land, in pleasant place,
But it would whisper of her face
And shake its keen, sharp blades at me.

"Each black-eyed woman would recall
A lone church-door, a face, a name,
A coward's flight, a soldier's shame:
I fled from woman's face, from all.

"I hugged my gold, my precious gold,
Within my strong, stout buckskin vest.
I wore my bags against my breast
So close I felt my heart grow cold.

"I did not like to see it now;
I did not spend one single piece;
I traveled, traveled without cease
As far as Russian ship could plow.

"And when my own scant hoard was gone,
And I had reached the far North-land,
I took my two stout bags in hand
As one pursued, and journeyed on.

"Ah, I was weary! I grew gray;
I felt the fast years slip and reel,
As slip bright beads when maidens kneel
At altars when outdoor is gay.

"At last I fell prone in the road,—
Fell fainting with my cursèd load.
A skin-clad Cossack helped me bear
My bags, nor would one shilling share.

"He looked at me with proud disdain,—
He looked at me as if he knew;
His black eyes burned me thro' and thro';
His scorn pierced like a deadly pain.

"He frightened me with honesty;
He made me feel so small, so base,
I fled, as if a fiend kept chase,—
A fiend that claimed my company!

"I bore my load alone; I crept
Far up the steep and icy way;

And there, before a cross there lay
A barefoot priest, who bowed and wept.

"I threw my gold right down and sped
Straight on. And oh, my heart was light!
A springtime bird in springtime flight
Flies scarce more happy than I fled.

"I felt somehow this monk would take
My gold, my load from off my back;
Would turn the fiend from off my track,
Would take my gold for sweet Christ's sake!

"I fled; I did not look behind;
I fled, fled with the mountain wind.
At last, far down the mountain's base
I found a pleasant resting-place.

"I rested there so long, so well,
More grateful than all tongues can tell.
It was such pleasant thing to hear
That valley's voices calm and clear:

"That valley veiled in mountain air,
With white goats on the hills at morn;
That valley green with seas of corn,
With cottage-islands here and there.

"I watched the mountain girls. The hay
They mowed was not more sweet than they;
They laid brown hands in my white hair;
They marveled at my face of care.

"I tried to laugh; I could but weep.
I made these peasants one request,—
That I with them might toil or rest,
And with them sleep the long, last sleep.

"I begged that I might battle there,
In that fair valley-land, for those
Who gave me cheer, when girt with foes,
And have a country loved as fair.

"Where is that spot that poets name
Our country? name the hallowed land?
Where is that spot where man must stand
Or fall when girt with sworn and flame?

Where is that one permitted spot?
Where is the one place man must fight?
Where rests the one God-given right
To fight, as ever patriots fought?

"I say 'tis in that holy house
Where God first set us down on earth;
Where mother welcomed us at birth,
And bared her breasts, a happy spouse.

"The simple plowboy from his field
Looks forth. He sees God's purple wall
Encircling him. High over all
The vast sun wheels his shining shield.

"This King, who makes earth what it is,—
King David bending to his toil!
O lord and master of the soil,
How envied in thy loyal bliss!

"Long live the land we loved in youth
That world with blue skies bent about,
Where never entered ugly doubt!
Long live the simple, homely truth!

"Can true hearts love some far snow-land,
Some bleak Alaska bought with gold?
God's laws are old as love is old;
And Home is something near at hand.

"Yea, change yon river's course; estrange
The seven sweet stars; make hate divide
The full moon from the flowing tide,—
But this old truth ye cannot change.

"I begged a land as begging bread;
I begged of these brave mountaineers

To share their sorrows, share their tears;
To weep as they wept with their dead.

"They did consent. The mountain town
Was mine to love, and valley lands.
That night the barefoot monk came down
And laid my two bags in my hands!

"On! on! And oh, the load I bore!
Why, once I dreamed my soul was lead;
Dreamed once it was a body dead!
It made my cold, hard bosom sore.

"I dragged that body forth and back—
O conscience, what a baying hound!
Nor frozen seas nor frosted ground
Can throw this bloodhound from his track.

"In farthest Russia I lay down,
A dying man, at last to rest;
I felt such load upon my breast
As seamen feel, who, sinking, drown.

"That night, all chill and desperate,
I sprang up, for I could not rest;
I tore the two bags from my breast,
And dashed them in the burning grate.

"I then crept back into my bed;
I tried, I begged, I prayed to sleep;
But those red, restless coins would keep
Slow dropping, dropping, and blood-red.

"I heard them clink, and clink, and clink,—
They turned, they talked within that grate.
They talked of her; they made me think
Of one who still did pray and wait.

"And when the bags burned crisp and black,
Two coins did start, roll to the floor,—
Roll out, roll on, and then roll back,
As if they needs must journey more.

"Ah, then I knew nor change nor space,
Nor all the drowning years that rolled
Could hide from me her haunting face,
Nor still that red-tongued, talking gold!

"Again I sprang forth from my bed!
I shook as in an ague fit;
I clutched that red gold, burning red,
I clutched as if to strangle it.

"I clutched it up—you hear me, boy?—
I clutched it up with joyful tears!
I clutched it close with such wild joy
I had not felt for years and years?

"Such joy! for I should now retrace
My steps, should see my land, her face;
Bring back her gold this battle-day,
And see her, hear her, hear her pray!

"I brought it back—you hear me, boy?
I clutch it, hold it, hold it now;
Red gold, bright gold that giveth joy
To all, and anywhere or how;

"That giveth joy to all but me,—
To all but me, yet soon to all.
It burns my hands, it burns! but she
Shall ope my hands and let it fall.

"For oh, I have a willing hand
To give these bags of gold; to see
Her smile as once she smiled on me
Here in this pleasant warm palm-land."

He ceased, he thrust each hard-clenched fist,—
He threw his gold hard forth again,
As one impelled by some mad pain
He would not or could not resist.

The Creole, scorning, turned away,
As if he turned from that lost thief,—
The one who died without belief
That dark, dread crucifixion day.

III.

Believe in man nor turn away.
Lo! man advances year by year;
Time bears him upward, and his sphere
Of life must broaden day by day.

Believe in man with large belief;
The garnered grain each harvest-time
Hath promise, roundness, and full prime
For all the empty chaff and sheaf.

Believe in man with brave belief;
Truth keeps the bottom of her well;
And when the thief peeps down, the thief
Peeps back at him perpetual.

Faint not that this or that man fell;
For one that falls a thousand rise
To lift white Progress to the skies:
Truth keeps the bottom of her well.

Fear not for man, nor cease to delve
For cool, sweet truth, with large belief.
Lo! Christ himself chose only twelve,
Yet one of these turned out a thief.

IV.

Down through the dark magnolia leaves,
Where climbs the rose of Cherokee
Against the orange-blossomed tree,
A loom of morn-light weaves and weaves,—

A loom of morn-light, weaving clothes
From snow-white rose of Cherokee,
And bridal blooms of orange-tree,
For fairy folk housed in red rose.

Down through the mournful myrtle crape,
Thro' moving moss, thro' ghostly gloom,
A long, white morn-beam takes a shape
Above a nameless, lowly tomb;

A long white finger through the gloom
Of grasses gathered round about,—
As God's white finger pointing out
A name upon that nameless tomb.

V.

Her white face bowed in her black hair,
The maiden prays so still within
That you might hear a falling pin,—
Aye, hear her white, unuttered prayer.

The moon has grown disconsolate,
Has turned her down her walk of stars:
Why, she is shutting up her bars,
As maidens shut a lover's gate.

The moon has grown disconsolate;
She will no longer watch and wait.
But two men wait; and two men will
Wait on till full morn, mute and still.

Still wait and walk among the trees.
Quite careless if the moon may keep
Her walk along her starry steep
Or drown her in the Southern seas.

They know no moon, or set or rise
Of sun, or anything to light
The earth or skies, save her dark eyes,
This praying, waking, watching night.

They move among the tombs apart,
Their eyes turn ever to that door;
They know the worn walks there by heart—
They turn and walk them o'er and o'er.

They are not wide, these little walks
For dead folk by this crescent town:
They lie right close when they lie down,
As if they kept up quiet talks.

VI.

The two men keep their paths apart;
But more and more begins to stoop
The man with gold, as droop and droop
Tall plants with something at their heart.

Now once again, with eager zest,
He offers gold with silent speech;
The other will not walk in reach,
But walks around, as round a pest.

His dark eyes sweep the scene around,
His young face drinks the fragrant air,
His dark eyes journey everywhere,—
The other's cleave unto the ground.

It is a weary walk for him,
For oh, he bears such weary load!
He does not like that narrow road
Between the dead—it is so dim:

It is so dark, that narrow place,
Where graves lie thick, like yellow leaves:
Give us the light of Christ and grace;
Give light to garner in the sheaves.

Give light of love; for gold is cold,—
Aye, gold is cruel as a crime;
It gives no light at such sad time
As when man's feet wax weak and old.

Aye, gold is heavy, hard, and cold!
And have I said this thing before?
Well, I will say it o'er and o'er,
'T were need be said ten thousand fold.

"Give us this day our daily bread,"—
Get this of God; then all the rest
Is housed in thine own earnest breast,
If you but lift an honest head.

VII.

Oh, I have seen men tall and fair,
Stoop down their manhood with disgust,—
Stoop down God's image to the dust,
To get a load of gold to bear:

Have seen men selling day by day
The glance of manhood that God gave:
To sell God's image, as a slave
Might sell some little pot of clay!

Behold! here in this green graveyard
A man with gold enough to fill
A coffin, as a miller's till;
And yet his path is hard, so hard!

His feet keep sinking in the sand,
And now so near an opened grave!
He seems to hear the solemn wave
Of dread oblivion at hand.

The sands, they grumble so, it seems
As if he walks some shelving brink;
He tries to stop, he tries to think,
He tries to make believe he dreams:

Why, he was free to leave the land,—
The silver moon was white as dawn;
Why, he has gold in either hand,
Had silver ways to walk upon.

And who should chide, or bid him stay?
Or taunt, or threat, or bid him fly?
"The world 's for sale," I hear men say,
And yet this man had gold to buy.

Buy what? Buy rest? He could not rest!
Buy gentle sleep? He could not sleep,
Though all these graves were wide and deep
As their wide mouths with the request.

Buy Love, buy faith, buy snow-white truth?
Buy moonlight, sunlight, present, past?
Buy but one brimful cup of youth
That true souls drink of to the last?

O God! 't was pitiful to see
This miser so forlorn and old!
O God! how poor a man may be
With nothing in this world but gold!

VIII.

The broad magnolia's blooms were white;
Her blooms were large, as if the moon
Quite lost her way that dreamful night,
And lodged to wait the afternoon.

Oh, vast white blossoms, breathing love!
White bosom of my lady dead,
In your white heaven overhead
I look, and learn to look above.

IX.

The dew-wet roses wept; their eyes
All dew, their breath as sweet as prayer.
And as they wept, the dead down there
Did feel their tears and hear their sighs.

The grass uprose, as if afraid
Some stranger foot might press too near;
Its every blade was like a spear,
Its every spear a living blade.

The grass above that nameless tomb
Stood all arrayed, as if afraid
Some weary pilgrim, seeking room
And rest, might lay where she was laid.

X.

'T was morn, and yet it was not morn;
'T was morn in heaven, not on earth:
A star was singing of a birth,—
Just saying that a day was born.

The marsh hard by that bound the lake,—
The great stork sea-lake, Ponchartrain,
Shut off from sultry Cuban main,—
Drew up its legs, as half awake:

Drew long, thin legs, stork-legs that steep
In slime where alligators creep,—
Drew long, green legs that stir the grass,
As when the lost, lorn night winds pass.

Then from the marsh came croakings low;
Then louder croaked some sea-marsh beast;
Then, far away against the east,
God's rose of morn began to grow.

From out the marsh against that east,
A ghostly moss-swept cypress stood;
With ragged arms, above the wood
It rose, a God-forsaken beast.

It seemed so frightened where it rose!
The moss-hung thing, it seemed to wave
The worn-out garments of a grave,—
To wave and wave its old grave-clothes.

Close by, a cow rose up and lowed
From out a palm-thatched milking-shed;
A black boy on the river road
Fled sudden, as the night had fled:

A nude black boy,—a bit of night
That had been broken off and lost
From flying night, the time it crossed
The soundless river in its flight:

A bit of darkness, following
The sable night on sable wing,—
A bit of darkness, dumb with fear,
Because that nameless tomb was near.

Then holy bells came pealing out;
Then steamboats blew, then horses neighed;
Then smoke from hamlets round about
Crept out, as if no more afraid.

Then shrill cocks here, and shrill cocks there,
Stretched glossy necks and filled the air;—
How many cocks it takes to make
A country morning well awake!

Then many boughs, with many birds,—
Young boughs in green, old boughs in gray;

These birds had very much to say,
In their soft, sweet, familiar words.

And all seemed sudden glad; the gloom
Forgot the church, forgot the tomb;
And yet, like monks with cross and bead,
The myrtles leaned to read and read.

And oh, the fragrance of the sod!
And oh, the perfume of the air!
The sweetness, sweetness everywhere,
That rose like incense up to God!

* * * * * *

I like a cow's breath in sweet spring;
I like the breath of babes new-born;
A maid's breath is a pleasant thing,—
But oh, the breath of sudden morn!—

Of sudden morn, when every pore
Of Mother Earth is pulsing fast
With life, and life seems spilling o'er
With love, with love too sweet to last:

Of sudden morn beneath the sun,
By God's great river wrapped in gray,
That for a space forgets to run,
And hides his face, as if to pray.

XI.

The black-eyed Creole kept his eyes
Turned to the door, as eyes might turn
To see the holy embers burn
Some sin away at sacrifice.

Full dawn! but yet he knew no dawn,
Nor song of bird, nor bird on wing,
Nor breath of rose, nor anything
Her fair face lifted not upon.

And yet he taller stood with morn;
His bright eyes, brighter than before,
Burned fast against that favored door,
His proud lips lifting still with scorn,—

With lofty, silent scorn for one
Who all night long had plead and plead,
With none to witness but the dead
How he for gold had been undone.

O ye who feed a greed for gold
And barter truth, and trade sweet youth
For cold, hard gold, behold, behold!
Behold this man! behold this truth!

Why what is there in all God's plan
Of vast creation, high or low,
By sea or land, by sun or snow,
So mean, so miserly as man?

* * * * * *

Lo, earth and heaven all let go
Their garnered riches, year by year!
The treasures of the trackless snow,
Ah, hast thou seen how very dear?

The wide earth gives, gives golden grain,
Gives fruits of gold, gives all, gives all!
Hold forth your hand, and these shall fall
In your full palm as free as rain.

Yea, earth is generous. The trees
Strip nude as birth-time without fear;
And their reward is year by year
To feel their fullness but increase.

The law of Nature is to give,
To give, to give! and to rejoice
In giving with a generous voice,
And so trust God and truly live.

* * * * * *

But see this miser at the last,—
This man who loved, who worshipped gold,
Who grasped gold with such eager hold,
He fain must hold forever fast:

As if to hold what God lets go;
As if to hold, while all around
Lets go and drops upon the ground
All things as generous as snow.

Let go your hold! let go or die!
Let go poor soul! Do not refuse
Till death comes by and shakes you loose,
And sends you shamed to hell for aye!

What if the sun should keep his gold?
The rich moon lock her silver up?
What if the gold-clad buttercup
Became such miser, mean and old?

Ah, me! the coffins are so true
In all accounts, the shrouds so thin
That down there you might sew and sew,
Nor ever sew one pocket in.

And all that you can hold of lands
Down there, below the grass, down there,
Will only be that little share
You hold in your two dust-full hands.

XII.

She comes! she comes! The stony floor
Speaks out! And now the rusty door
At last has just one word this day,
With mute, religious lips, to say.

She comes! she comes! And lo, her face
Is upward, radiant, fair as prayer!
So pure here in this holy place,
Where holy peace is everywhere.

Her upraised face, her face of light
And loveliness, from duty done,
Is like a rising orient sun
That pushes back the brow of night.

* * * * * *

How brave, how beautiful is truth!
Good deeds untold are like to this.
But fairest or all fair things is
A pious maiden in her youth:

A pious maiden as she stands
Just on the threshold of the years
That throb and pulse with hopes and fears,
And reaches God her helpless hands.

* * * * * *

How fair is she! How fond is she!
Her foot upon the threshold there.
Her breath is as a blossomed tree,—
This maiden mantled in her hair!

Her hair, her black abundant hair,
Where night inhabited, all night
And all this day, will not take flight,
But finds content and houses there.

Her hands are clasped, her two small hands:
They hold the holy book of prayer
Just as she steps the threshold there,
Clasped downward where she silent stands.

XIII

Once more she lifts her lowly face,
And slowly lifts her large, dark eyes
Of wonder, and in still surprise
She looks full forward in her place.

She looks full forward on the air
Above the tomb, and yet below
The fruits of gold, the blooms of snow,
As looking—looking anywhere.

She feels—she knows not what she feels;
It is not terror, is not fear.
But there is something that reveals
A presence that is near and dear.

She does not let her eyes fall down,
They lift against the far profound:
Against the blue above the town
Two wide-winged vultures circle round.

Two brown birds swim above the sea,—
Her large eyes swim as dreamily,
And follow far, and follow high,
Two circling black specks in the sky.

One forward step,—the closing door
Creaks out, as frightened or in pain;
Her eyes are on the ground again—
Two men are standing close before.

"My love," sighs one, "my life, my all!"
Her lifted foot across the sill
Sinks down,—and all things are so still
You hear the orange-blossoms fall.

But fear comes not where duty is,
And purity is peace and rest;
Her cross is close upon her breast,
Her two hands clasp hard hold of this.

Her two hands clasp cross, book, and she
Is strong in tranquil purity,—
Aye, strong as Samson when he laid
His two hands forth and bowed and prayed.

One at her left, one at her right,
And she between, the steps upon,—
I can but see that Syrian night,
The women there at early dawn.

XIV.

The sky is like an opal sea,
The air is like the breath of kine;
But oh, her face is white, and she
Leans faint to see a lifted sign,—

To see two hands lift up and wave,—
To see a face so white with woe,
So ghastly, hollow, white as though
It had that moment left the grave.

Her sweet face at that ghostly sign,
Her fair face in her weight of hair,
Is like a white dove drowning there,—
A white dove drowned in Tuscan wine.

He tries to stand, to stand erect;
'T is gold, 't is gold that holds him down!
And soul and body both must drown,—
Two millstones tied about his neck.

Now once again his piteous face
Is raised to her face reaching there
He prays such piteous silent prayer,
As prays a dying man for grace.

It is not good to see him strain
To lift his hands, to gasp, to try
To speak. His parched lips are so dry
Their sight is as a living pain,

I think that rich man down in hell
Some like this old man with his gold,—
To gasp and gasp perpetual,
Like to this minute I have told.

XV.

At last the miser cries his pain,—
A shrill, wild cry, as if a grave
Just op'd its stony lips and gave
One sentence forth, then closed again.

"'T was twenty years last night, last night!"
His lips still moved, but not to speak;
His outstretched hands, so trembling weak,
Were beggar's hands in sorry plight.

His face upturned to hers; his lips
Kept talking on, but gave no sound;
His feet were cloven to the ground;
Like iron hooks his finger tips.

"Aye, twenty years," she sadly sighed;
"I promised mother every year,
That I would pray for father here,
As she still prayed the night she died:

"To pray as she prayed, fervently,
As she had promised she would pray
The sad night that he turned away,
For him, wherever he might be."

Then she was still; then sudden she
Let fall her eyes, and so outspake,
As if her very heart would break,
Her proud lips trembling piteously:

"And whether he comes soon or late
To kneel beside this nameless grave,
May God forgive my father's hate
As I forgive, as she forgave!"

He saw the stone; he understood,
With that quick knowledge that will come
Most quick when men are made most dumb
With terror that stops still the blood.

And then a blindness slowly fell
On soul and body; but his hands
Held tight his bags, two iron bands,
As if to bear them into hell.

He sank upon the nameless stone
With oh! such sad, such piteous moan
As never man might seek to know
From man's most unforgiving foe.

He sighed at last, so long, so deep,
As one heart breaking in one's sleep,—
One long, last, weary, willing sigh,
As if it were a grace to die.

And then his hands, like loosened bands,
Hung down, hung down, on either side;
His hands hung down, hung open wide:
Wide empty hung the dead man's hands.

I had long aspired, too selfishly, perhaps, to associate my name in song with the father of waters, and finally, under the wing of Captain James Eades, of the jetties, gave the year of the Cotton Centennial to the endeavor. Frankly I was not equal to the stupendous task. I found nothing all the way from Saint Paul down, down to where Eades bitted and bridled the mighty river's mouth in the Mexican seas that I could master or lay hand upon. Yes, majesty, majesty, majesty, thousands of miles of majesty, movement, color; corn, cotton, cane, cane and cotton and corn, green, gray and golden; but it was the monotonous majesty of eternity; an eternity of monotony.

However the work was done and published as "The Rhyme of the Great River." Several revisions and publications followed. This is the fifth. Each time I got further and further away from the mighty theme until at last De Soto's river is no longer the subject, and a new name is fit.

But, believe me, I do not disparage what is written here, as it now stands, shorn of half its verbiage. Indeed, were the lesson of this poem not needed in this age of getting and getting, it would find no place here. As said elsewhere, I never work without some foundation for story, character, and scene. The little church at the edge of the city—a shrine for the devout who wait miraculous cures—is, as well as the environments, described literally.

When the great poet comes who can bend these mighty waters to his will, and make melody of this eternal majesty which awed me to silence, he will find endless material for his story in this brave, cultured, and classic old French city of New Orleans. As for myself, I can better value gold in the rough ore than the glittering coins. And, too, I must have mountains, mountains, the wilderness, not these polished, civilized levels, even though never so stately and vast.

THE SHIP IN THE DESERT.

A wild, wide land of mysteries,
Of sea-salt lakes and dried up seas,
And lonely wells and pools; a land
That seems so like dead Palestine,
Save that its wastes have no confine
Till push'd against the levell'd skies.
A land from out whose depths shall rise
The new-time prophets. Yea, the land
From out whose awful depths shall come,
A lowly man, with dusty feet,
A man fresh from his Maker's hand,
A singer singing oversweet,
A charmer charming very wise;
And then all men shall not be dumb.
Nay, not be dumb; for he shall say,
"Take heed, for I prepare the way
For weary feet." Lo! from this land
Of Jordan streams and dead sea sand,
The Christ shall come when next the race
Of man shall look upon His face

I.

A man in middle Aridzone
Stood by the desert's edge alone,
And long he look'd, and lean'd and peer'd,
And twirl'd and twirl'd his twist'd beard,
Beneath a black and slouchy hat—
Nay, nay, the tale is not of that.

A skin-clad trapper, toe-a-tip,
Stood on a mountain top; and he
Look'd long, and still, and eagerly.
"It looks so like some lonesome ship
That sails this ghostly, lonely sea,—
This dried-up desert sea," said he,
"These tawny sands of buried seas"—
Avaunt! this tale is not of these!

A chief from out the desert's rim
Rode swift as twilight swallows swim,
And O! his supple steed was fleet!
About his breast flapped panther skins,
About his eager flying feet
Flapp'd beaded, braided moccasins:
He stopp'd, stock still, as still as stone,
He lean'd, he look'd, there glisten'd bright,
From out the yellow, yielding sand,
A golden cup with jewell'd rim.

He lean'd him low, he reach'd a hand,
He caught it up, he gallop'd on,

He turn'd his head, he saw a sight—
His panther-skins flew to the wind,
He rode into the rim of night;
The dark, the desert lay behind;
The tawny Ishmaelite was gone.

He reach'd the town, and there held up
Above his head a jewel'd cup.
He put two fingers to his lip,
He whisper'd wild, he stood a-tip,
And lean'd the while with lifted hand,
And said, "A ship lies yonder dead,"
And said, "Such things lie sown in sand
In yon far desert dead and brown,
Beyond where wave-wash'd walls look down,
As thick as stars set overhead."
"'Tis from that desert ship," they said,
"That sails with neither sail nor breeze
The lonely bed of dried-up seas,—
A galleon that sank below
White seas ere Red men drew the bow."

By Arizona's sea of sand
Some bearded miners, gray and old,
And resolute in search of gold,
Sat down to tap the savage land.
A miner stood beside the mine,
He pull'd his beard, then looked away
Across the level sea of sand,
Beneath his broad and hairy hand,
A hand as hard as knots of pine.
"It looks so like a sea," said he.
He pull'd his beard, and he did say,
"It looks just like a dried-up sea."
Again he pull'd that beard of his,
But said no other thing than this.

A stalwart miner dealt a stroke,
And struck a buried beam of oak.
The miner twisted, twirl'd his beard,
Lean'd on his pick-ax as he spoke:
"'Tis that same long-lost ship," he said,
"Some laden ship of Solomon
That sail'd these lonesome seas upon
In search of Ophir's mine, ah me!
That sail'd this dried-up desert sea."

II.

Now this the tale. Along the wide
Missouri's stream some silent braves,
That stole along the farther side
Through sweeping wood that swept the waves
Like long arms reach'd across the tide,
Kept watch and every foe defied.

A low, black boat that hugg'd the shores,
An ugly boat, an ugly crew,
Thick-lipp'd and woolly-headed slaves,
That bow'd, and bent the white-ash oars,
That cleft the murky waters through,
Slow climb'd the swift Missouri's waves.

A grand old Neptune in the prow,
Gray-hair'd, and white with touch of time,
Yet strong as in his middle prime,
Stood up, turn'd suddenly, look'd back
Along his low boat's wrinkled track,
Then drew his mantle tight, and now
He sat all silently. Beside
The grim old sea-king sat his bride,
A sun land blossom, rudely torn
From tropic forests to be worn
Above as stern a breast as e'er
Stood king at sea, or anywhere.

Another boat with other crew
Came swift and cautious in her track,
And now shot shoreward, now shot back,
And now sat rocking fro and to,
But never once lost sight of her.
Tall, sunburnt, southern men were these
From isles of blue Carribbean seas,
And one, that woman's worshiper,
Who look'd on her, and loved but her.

And one, that one, was wild as seas
That wash the far, dark Oregon.
And one, that one, had eyes to teach

The art of love, and tongue to preach
Life's hard and sober homilies,
While he stood leaning, urging on.

II.

Pursuer and pursued. And who
Are these that make the sable crew;
These mighty Titans, black and nude,
Who dare this Red man's solitude?

And who is he that leads them here,
And breaks the hush of wave and wood?
Comes he for evil or for good?
Brave Jesuit or bold buccaneer?

Nay, these be idle themes. Let pass.
These be but men. We may forget
The wild sea-king, the tawny brave,
The frowning wold, the woody shore,
The tall-built, sunburnt man of Mars.
But what and who was she, the fair?
The fairest face that ever yet
Look'd in a wave as in a glass;
That look'd, as look the still, far stars,
So woman-like, into the wave
To contemplate their beauty there?

I only saw her, heard the sound
Of murky waters gurgling round
In counter-currents from the shore,
But heard the long, strong stroke of oar
Against the water gray and vast;
I only saw her as she pass'd—
A great, sad beauty, in whose eyes
Lay all the peace of Paradise.

O you had loved her sitting there,
Half hidden in her loosen'd hair;
Yea, loved her for her large dark eyes,
Her push'd out mouth, her mute surprise—
Her mouth! 'twas Egypt's mouth of old,
Push'd out and pouting full and bold
With simple beauty where she sat.
Why, you had said, on seeing her,
This creature comes from out the dim,
Far centuries, beyond the rim
Of time's remotest reach or stir;
And he who wrought Semiramis
And shaped the Sibyls, seeing this,
Had kneeled and made a shrine thereat,
And all his life had worshipp'd her.

IV.

The black men bow'd, the long oars bent,
They struck as if for sweet life's sake,
And one look'd back, but no man spake,
And all wills bent to one intent.
On, through the golden fringe of day
Into the deep, dark night, away
And up the wave 'mid walls of wood
They cleft, they climb'd, they bow'd, they bent,
But one stood tall, and restless stood,
And one sat still all night, all day,
And gazed in helpless wonderment.

Her hair pour'd down like darkling wine,
The black men lean'd a sullen line,
The bent oars kept a steady song,
And all the beams of bright sunshine
That touch'd the waters wild and strong,
Fell drifting down and out of sight
Like fallen leaves, and it was night.

And night and day, and many days
They climb'd the sullen, dark gray tide.
And she sat silent at his side,
And he sat turning many ways;
Sat watching for his wily foe.
At last he baffled him. And yet
His brow gloom'd dark, his lips were set;
He lean'd, he peer'd through boughs, as though
From heart of forests deep and dim
Grim shapes might come confronting him.

A stern, uncommon man was he,
Broad-shoulder'd, as of Gothic form,

Strong-built, and hoary like a sea;
A high sea broken up by storm.
His face was brown and over-wrought
By seams and shadows born of thought,
Not over-gentle. And his eyes,
Bold, restless, resolute and deep,
Too deep to flow like shallow fount
Of common men where waters mount;—
Fierce, lumined eyes, where flames might rise
Instead of flood, and flash and sweep—
Strange eyes, that look'd unsatisfied
With all things fair or otherwise;
As if his inmost soul had cried
All time for something yet unseen,
Some long-desired thing denied.

V.

Below the overhanging boughs
The oars lay idle at the last;
Yet long he look'd for hostile prows
From out the wood and down the stream.
They came not, and he came to dream
Pursuit abandon'd, danger past.

He fell'd the oak, he built a home
Of new-hewn wood with busy hand,
And said, "My wanderings are told,"
And said, "No more by sea, by land,
Shall I break rest, or drift, or roam,
For I am worn, and I grow old."

And there, beside that surging tide,
Where gray waves meet, and wheel, and strike,
The man sat down as satisfied
To sit and rest unto the end;
As if the strong man here had found
A sort of brother in this sea,—
This surging, sounding majesty,
Of troubled water, so profound,
So sullen, strong, and lion-like,
So lawless in its every round.

Hast seen Missouri cleave the wood
In sounding whirlpools to the sea?
What soul hath known such majesty?
What man stood by and understood?

VI.

Now long the long oars idle lay.
The cabin's smoke came forth and curl'd
Right lazily from river brake,
And Time went by the other way.
And who was she, the strong man's pride,
This one fair woman of his world,
A captive? Bride, or not a bride?
Her eyes, men say, grew sad and dim
With watching from the river's rim,
As waiting for some face denied.

Yea, who was she? none ever knew.
The great, strong river swept around
The cabins nestled in its bend,
But kept its secrets. Wild birds flew
In bevies by. The black men found
Diversion in the chase: and wide
Old Morgan ranged the wood, nor friend
Nor foeman ever sought his side,
Or shared his forests deep and dim,
Or cross'd his path or question'd him.

He stood as one who found and named
The middle world. What visions flamed
Athwart the west! What prophecies
Were his, the gray old man, that day
Who stood alone and look'd away,—
Awest from out the waving trees,
Against the utter sundown seas.

Alone ofttime beside the stream
He stood and gazed as in a dream,—
As if he knew a life unknown
To those who knew him thus alone.
His eyes were gray and overborne
By shaggy brows, his strength was shorn,
Yet still he ever gazed awest,
As one that would not, could not rest.

And had he fled with bloody hand?
Or had he loved some Helen fair,
And battling lost both land and town?
Say, did he see his walls go down,
Then choose from all his treasures there
This one, and seek some other land?

VII.

The squirrels chatter'd in the leaves,
The turkeys call'd from pawpaw wood,
The deer with lifted nostrils stood,
'Mid climbing blossoms sweet with bee,
'Neath snow-white rose of Cherokee.

Then frosts hung ices on the eaves,
Then cushion snows possess'd the ground,
And so the seasons kept their round;
Yet still old Morgan went and came
From cabin door through forest dim,
Through wold of snows, through wood of
flame,
Through golden Indian-summer days,
Hung red with soft September haze,
And no man cross'd or questioned him.

Nay, there was that in his stern air
That held e'en these rude men aloof;
None came to share the broad-built roof
That rose so fortress-like beside
The angry, rushing, sullen tide,
And only black men gather'd there,
The old man's slaves in dull content,
Black, silent, and obedient.

Then men push'd westward through his
wood,
His wild beasts fled, and now he stood
Confronting men. He had endear'd
No man, but still he went and came
Apart, and shook his beard and strode
His ways alone, and bore his load,
If load it were, apart, alone.
Then men grew busy with a name
That no man loved, that many fear'd,
And rude men stoop'd, and cast a stone,
As at some statue overthrown.

Some said, a stolen bride was she,
And that her lover from the sea
Lay waiting for his chosen wife,
And that a day of reckoning
Lay waiting for this grizzled king.

Some said that looking from her place
A love would sometimes light her face,
As if sweet recollections stirr'd
Like far, sweet songs that come to us,
So soft, so sweet, they are not heard,
So far, so faint, they fill the air,
A fragrance falling anywhere.

So, wasting all her summer years
That utter'd only through her tears,
The seasons went, and still she stood
For ever watching down the wood.

Yet in her heart there held a strife
With all this wasting of sweet life,
That none who have not lived and died—
Held up the two hands crucified
Between two ways—can understand.

Men went and came, and still she stood
In silence watching down the wood—
Adown the wood beyond the land,
Her hollow face upon her hand,
Her black, abundant hair all down
About her loose, ungather'd gown.

And what her thought? her life unsaid?
Was it of love? of hate? of him,
The tall, dark Southerner? Her head
Bow'd down. The day fell dim
Upon her eyes. She bowed, she slept.
She waken'd then, and waking wept.

VIII.

The black-eyed bushy squirrels ran
Like shadows scattered through the
boughs;

The gallant robin chirp'd his vows,
The far-off pheasant thrumm'd his fan,
A thousand blackbirds kept on wing
In walnut-top, and it was Spring.

Old Morgan sat his cabin door,
And one sat watching as of yore,
But why turn'd Morgan's face as white
As his white beard? A bird aflight,
A squirrel peering through the trees,
Saw some one silent steal away
Like darkness from the face of day,
Saw two black eyes look back, and these
Saw her hand beckon through the trees.

Ay! they have come, the sun-brown'd men,
To beard old Morgan in his den.
It matters little who they are,
These silent men from isles afar;
And truly no one cares or knows
What be their merit or demand;
It is enough for this rude land—
At least, it is enough for those,
The loud of tongue and rude of hand—
To know that they are Morgan's foes.

Proud Morgan! More than tongue can tell
He loved that woman watching there,
That stood in her dark storm of hair,
That stood and dream'd as in a spell,
And look'd so fix'd and far away;
And who that loveth woman well,
Is wholly bad? be who he may.

IX.

Ay! we have seen these Southern men,
These sun-brown'd men from island shore,
In this same land, and long before.
They do not seem so lithe as then,
They do not look so tall, and they
Seem not so many as of old.
But that same resolute and bold
Expression of unbridled will,
That even Time must half obey,
Is with them and is of them still.

They do not counsel the decree
Of court or council, where they drew
Their breath, nor law nor order knew,
Save but the strong hand of the strong;
Where each stood up, avenged his wrong,
Or sought his death all silently.
They watch along the wave and wood,
They heed, but haste not. Their estate,
Whate'er it be, can bide and wait,
Be it open ill or hidden good.
No law for them! For they have stood
With steel, and writ their rights in blood;
And now, whatever 't is they seek,
Whatever be their dark demand,
Why, they will make it, hand to hand,
Take time and patience: Greek to Greek.

X.

Like blown and snowy wintry pine,
Old Morgan stoop'd his head and pass'd
Within his cabin door. He cast
A great arm out to men, made sign,
Then turn'd to Sybal; stood beside
A time, then turn'd and strode the floor,
Stopp'd short, breathed sharp, threw wide the door,
Then gazed beyond the murky tide,
Past where the forky peaks divide.

He took his beard in his right hand,
Then slowly shook his grizzled head
And trembled, but no word he said.
His thought was something more than pain;
Upon the seas, upon the land
He knew he should not rest again.

He turn'd to her; and then once more
Quick turn'd, and through the oaken door
He sudden pointed to the west.
His eye resumed its old command,

The conversation of his hand
It was enough; she knew the rest.

He turn'd, he stoop'd, and smooth'd her
hair,
As if to smooth away the care
From his great heart, with his left hand.
His right hand hitch'd the pistol round
That dangled at his belt. The sound
Of steel to him was melody
More sweet than any song of sea.
He touch'd his pistol, push'd his lips,
Then tapp'd it with his finger tips,
And toy'd with it as harper's hand
Seeks out the chords when he is sad
And purposeless. At last he had
Resolved. In haste he touch'd her hair,
Made sign she should arise—prepare
For some long journey, then again
He look'd awest toward the plain;
Against the land of boundless space,
The land of silences, the land
Of shoreless deserts sown with sand,
Where Desolation's dwelling is;
The land where, wondering, you say,
What dried-up shoreless sea is this?
Where, wandering, from day to day
You say, To-morrow sure we come
To rest in some cool resting place,
And yet you journey on through space
While seasons pass, and are struck dumb
With marvel at the distances.

Yea, he would go. Go utterly
Away, and from all living kind;
Pierce through the distances, and find
New lands. He had outlived his race.
He stood like some eternal tree
That tops remote Yosemite,
And cannot fall. He turn'd his face
Again and contemplated space.

And then he raised his hand to vex
His beard, stood still, and there fell down
Great drops from some unfrequent spring,
And streak'd his chanell'd cheeks sun-
brown,
And ran uncheck'd, as one who recks
Nor joy, nor tears, nor anything.

And then, his broad breast heaving deep,
Like some dark sea in troubled sleep,
Blown round with groaning ships and
wrecks,
He sudden roused himself, and stood
With all the strength of his stern mood,
Then call'd his men, and bade them go
And bring black steeds with banner'd
necks,
And strong, like burly buffalo.

XI.

The bronzen, stolid, still, black men
Their black-maned horses silent drew
Through solemn wood. One midnight
when
The curl'd moon tipp'd her horn, and
threw
A black oak's shadow slant across
A low mound hid in leaves and moss,
Old Morgan cautious came and drew
From out the ground, as from a grave,
Great bags, all copper-bound and old,
And fill'd, men say, with pirates' gold.
And then they, silent as a dream,
In long black shadow cross'd the stream.

XII.

And all was life at morn, but one,
The tall old sea-king, grim and gray,
Look'd back to where his cabins lay,
And seem'd to hesitate. He rose
At last, as from his dream's repose,
From rest that counterfeited rest,
And set his blown beard to the west;
And rode against the setting sun,
Far up the levels vast and dun.

His steeds were steady, strong and fleet,
The best in all the wide west land,

Their manes were in the air, their feet
Seem'd scarce to touch the flying sand.

They rode like men gone mad, they fled
All day and many days they ran,
And in the rear a gray old man
Kept watch, and ever turn'd his head
Half eager and half angry, back
Along their dusty desert track.

And she look'd back, but no man spoke,
They rode, they swallowed up the plain;
The sun sank low, he look'd again,
With lifted hand and shaded eyes.
Then far, afar, he saw uprise,
As if from giant's stride or stroke,
Dun dust, like puffs of battle-smoke.

He turn'd, his left hand clutched the rein,
He struck hard west his high right hand,
His limbs were like the limbs of oak;
All knew too well the man's command.
On, on they spurred, they plunged again,
And one look'd back, but no man spoke.

They climb'd the rock-built breasts of earth,
The Titan-fronted, blowy steeps
That cradled Time. Where freedom keeps
Her flag of bright, blown stars unfurl'd,
They climbed and climbed. They saw the birth
Of sudden dawn upon the world;
Again they gazed; they saw the face
Of God, and named it boundless space.

And they descended and did roam
Through levell'd distances set round
By room. They saw the Silences
Move by and beckon; saw the forms,
The very beards, of burly storms,
And heard them talk like sounding seas.
On unnamed heights, bleak-blown and brown,
And torn-like battlements of Mars,
They saw the darknesses come down,
Like curtains loosen'd from the dome
Of God's cathedral, built of stars.

They pitch'd the tent where rivers run
All foaming to the west, and rush
As if to drown the falling sun.
They saw the snowy mountains roll'd,
And heaved along the nameless lands
Like mighty billows; saw the gold
Of awful sunsets; felt the hush
Of heaven when the day sat down,
And drew about his mantle brown,
And hid his face in dusky hands.

The long and lonesome nights! the tent
That nestled soft in sweep of grass,
The hills against the firmament
Where scarce the moving moon could pass;
The cautious camp, the smother'd light,
The silent sentinel at night!

The wild beasts howling from the hill;
The savage prowling swift and still,
And bended as a bow is bent.
The arrow sent; the arrow spent
And buried in its bloody place;
The dead man lying on his face!

The clouds of dust, their cloud by day;
Their pillar of unfailing fire
The far North Star. And high, and higher,
They climb'd so high it seemed eftsoon
That they must face the falling moon,
That like some flame-lit ruin lay
High built before their weary way.

They learn'd to read the sign of storms,
The moon's wide circles, sunset bars,
And storm-provoking blood and flame;
And, like the Chaldean shepherds, came
At night to name the moving stars.
In heaven's face they pictured forms
Of beasts, of fishes of the sea.

They watch'd the Great Bear wearily
Rise up and drag his clinking chain
Of stars around the starry main

XIII.

And why did these worn, sun-burnt men
Let Morgan gain the plain, and then
Pursue him ever where he fled?
Some say their leader sought but her;
Unlike each swarthy follower.
Some say they sought his gold alone,
And fear'd to make their quarrel known
Lest it should keep its secret bed;
Some say they thought to best prevail
And conquer with united hands
Alone upon the lonesome sands;
Some say they had as much to dread;
Some say—but I must tell my tale.

And still old Morgan sought the west;
The sea, the utmost sea, and rest.
He climb'd, descended, climb'd again,
Until pursuit seemed all in vain;
Until they left him all alone,
As unpursued and as unknown,
As some lost ship upon the main.

O there was grandeur in his air,
An old-time splendor in his eye,
When he had climb'd at last the high
And rock-built bastions of the plain,
Thrown back his beard and blown white
hair,
And halting turn'd to look again.

Dismounting in his lofty place,
He look'd far down the fading plain
For his pursuers, but in vain.
Yea, he was glad. Across his face
A careless smile was seen to play,
The first for many a stormy day.

He turn'd to Sybal, dark, yet fair
As some sad twilight; touch'd her hair,
Stoop'd low, and kiss'd her gently there,
Then silent held her to his breast;
Then waved command to his black men,
Look'd east, then mounted slow and then
Led leisurely against the west.

And why should he who dared to die,
Who more than once with hissing breath
Had set his teeth and pray'd for death?
Why fled these men, or wherefore fly
Before them now? why not defy?

His midnight men were strong and true,
And not unused to strife, and knew
The masonry of steel right well,
And all such signs that lead to hell.

It might have been his youth had
wrought
Some wrongs his years would now repair,
That made him fly and still forbear;
It might have been he only sought
To lead them to some fatal snare,
And let them die by piecemeal there.

I only know it was not fear
Of any man or any thing
That death in any shape might bring.
It might have been some lofty sense
Of his own truth and innocence,
And virtues lofty and severe—
Nay, nay! what room for reasons here?

And now they pierced a fringe of trees
That bound a mountain's brow like bay.
Sweet through the fragrant boughs a breeze
Blew salt-flood freshness. Far away,
From mountain brow to desert base
Lay chaos, space; unbounded space.

The black men cried, "The sea!" They
bow'd
Black, woolly heads in hard black hands.
They wept for joy. They laugh'd, they
broke
The silence of an age, and spoke
Of rest at last; and, grouped in bands,

They threw their long black arms about
Each other's necks, and laugh'd aloud,
Then wept again with laugh and shout.

Yet Morgan spake no word, but led
His band with oft-averted head
Right through the cooling trees, till he
Stood out upon the lofty brow
And mighty mountain wall. And now
The men who shouted, "Lo, the sea!"
Rode in the sun; sad, silently,
Rode in the sun, and look'd below.
They look'd but once, then look'd away,
Then look'd each other in the face.
They could not lift their brows, nor say,
But held their heads, nor spake, for lo!
Nor sea, nor voice of sea, nor breath
Of sea, but only sand and death,
The dread mirage, the fiend of space!

XIV.

Old Morgan eyed his men, look'd back
Against the groves of tamarack,
Then tapp'd his stirrup foot, and stray'd
His broad left hand along the mane
Of his strong steed, and careless play'd
His fingers through the silken skein.

And then he spurr'd him to her side,
And reach'd his hand and leaning wide,
He smiling push'd her falling hair
Back from her brow, and kiss'd her there.
Yea, touch'd her softly, as if she
Had been some priceless, tender flower;
Yet touch'd her as one taking leave
Of his one love in lofty tower
Before descending to the sea
Of battle on his battle eve.

A distant shout! quick oaths! alarms!
The black men start, turn suddenly,
Stand in the stirrup, clutch their arms,
And bare bright arms all instantly.
But he, he slowly turns, and he
Looks all his full soul in her face.
He does not shout, he does not say,
But sits serenely in his place
A time, then slowly turns, looks back
Between the trim-boughed tamarack,
And up the winding mountain way,
To where the long, strong grasses lay,
And there they came, hot on his track!

He raised his glass in his two hands,
Then in his left hand let it fall,
Then seem'd to count his fingers o'er,
Then reached his glass, waved his commands,
Then tapped his stirrup as before,
Stood in the stirrup stern and tall,
Then ran a hand along the mane
Half-nervous like, and that was all.

And then he turn'd, and smiled half sad,
Half desperate, then hitch'd his steel;
Then all his stormy presence had,
As if he kept once more his keel,
On listless seas where breakers reel.

At last he tossed his iron hand
Above the deep, steep desert space,
Above the burning seas of sand,
And look'd his black men in the face.
They spake not, nor look'd back again,
They struck the heel, they clutch'd the rein,
And down the darkling plunging steep
They dropp'd into the dried-up deep.

Below! It seem'd a league below,
The black men rode, and she rode well,
Against the gleaming, sheening haze
That shone like some vast sea ablaze—
That seem'd to gleam, to glint, to glow,
As if it mark'd the shores of hell.

Then Morgan reined alone, look'd back
From off the high wall where he stood,
And watch'd his fierce approaching foe.
He saw him creep along his track,

Saw him descending from the wood,
And smiled to see how worn and slow.

And Morgan heard his oath and shout,
And Morgan turned his head once more,
And wheel'd his stout steed short about,
Then seem'd to count their numbers o'er.
And then his right hand touch'd his steel,
And then he tapp'd his iron heel,
And seemed to fight with thought. At last
As if the final die was cast,
And cast as carelessly as one
Would toss a white coin in the sun,
He touched his rein once more, and then
His right hand laid with idle heed
Along the toss'd mane of his steed.

Pursuer and pursued! who knows
The why he left the breezy pine,
The fragrant tamarack and vine,
Red rose and precious yellow rose!
Nay, Vasques held the vantage ground
Above him by the wooded steep,
And right nor left no passage lay,
And there was left him but that way,—
The way through blood, or to the deep
And lonesome deserts far profound,
That knew not sight of man, nor sound.

Hot Vasques reined upon the rim,
High, bold, and fierce with crag and spire.
He saw a far gray eagle swim,
He saw a black hawk wheel, retire,
And shun that desert's burning breath
As shunning something more than death.

Ah, then he paused, turn'd, shook his head.
"And shall we turn aside," he said,
"Or dare this Death?" The men stood still
As leaning on his sterner will.
And then he stopp'd and turn'd again,
And held his broad hand to his brow,
And look'd intent and eagerly.
The far white levels of the plain
Flash'd back like billows. Even now
He thought he saw rise up 'mid sea,
'Mid space, 'mid wastes, 'mid nothingness
A ship becalm'd as in distress.

The dim sign pass'd as suddenly,
And then his eager eyes grew dazed,—
He brought his two hands to his face.
Again he raised his head, and gazed
With flashing eyes and visage fierce
Far out, and resolute to pierce
The far, far, faint receding reach
Of space and touch its farther beach.
He saw but space, unbounded space;
Eternal space and nothingness.

Then all wax'd anger'd as they gazed
Far out upon the shoreless land,
And clench'd their doubled hands and raised
Their long bare arms, but utter'd not.
At last one rode from out the band,
And raised his arm, push'd back his sleeve,
Push'd bare his arm, rode up and down,
With hat push'd back. Then flush'd and hot
He shot sharp oaths like cannon shot.

Then Vasques was resolved; his form
Seem'd like a pine blown rampt with storm.
He clutch'd his rein, drove spur, and then
Turn'd sharp and savage to his men,
And then led boldly down the way
To night that knows not night or day.

XV.

How broken plunged the steep descent!
How barren! Desolate, and rent
By earthquake's shock, the land lay dead,
With dust and ashes on its head.

'Twas as some old world overthrown
Where Thesus fought and Sappho dream'd

In æons ere they touch'd this land,
And found their proud souls foot and hand
Bound to the flesh and stung with pain.
An ugly skeleton it seem'd
Of its old self. The fiery rain
Of red volcanoes here had sown
The desolation of the plain.
Ay, vanquish'd quite and overthrown,
And torn with thunder-stroke, and strown
With cinders, lo! the dead earth lay
As waiting for the judgment day.
Why, tamer men had turn'd and said,
On seeing this, with start and dread,
And whisper'd each with gather'd breath,
"We come on the abode of death."

They wound below a savage bluff
That lifted, from its sea-mark'd base,
Great walls with characters cut rough
And deep by some long-perish'd race;
And great, strange beasts unnamed, unknown,
Stood hewn and limn'd upon the stone.

A mournful land as land can be
Beneath their feet in ashes lay,
Beside that dread and dried-up sea;
A city older than that gray
And sand sown tower builded when
Confusion cursed the tongues of men.

Beneath, before, a city lay
That in her majesty had shamed
The wolf-nursed conqueror of old;
Below, before, and far away,
There reach'd the white arm of a bay,
A broad bay shrunk to sand and stone,
Where ships had rode and breakers roll'd
When Babylon was yet unnamed,
And Nimrod's hunting-fields unknown.

Where sceptered kings had sat at feast
Some serpents slid from out the grass
That grew in tufts by shatter'd stone,
Then hid beneath some broken mass
That time had eaten as a bone
Is eaten by some savage beast.

A dull-eyed rattlesnake that lay
All loathsome, yellow-skinn'd, and slept,
Coil'd tight as pine-knot, in the sun,
With flat head through the center run,
Struck blindly back, then rattling crept
Flat-bellied down the dusty way . . .
'Twas all the dead land had to say.

Two pink-eyed hawks, wide-wing'd and gray,
Scream'd savagely, and, circling high,
And screaming still in mad dismay,
Grew dim and died against the sky . . .
'Twas all the heavens had to say.

Some low-built junipers at last,
The last that o'er the desert look'd,
Where dumb owls sat with bent bills hook'd
Beneath their wings awaiting night,
Rose up, then faded from the sight.

What dim ghosts hover on this rim:
What stately-manner'd shadows swim
Along these gleaming wastes of sands
And shoreless limits of dead lands?

Dread Azteckee! Dead Azteckee!
White place of ghosts, give up thy dead;
Give back to Time thy buried hosts!
The new world's tawny Ishmaelite,
The roving tent-born Shoshonee,
Hath shunned thy shores of death, at night
Because thou art so white, so dread,
Because thou art so ghostly white,
And named thy shores "the place of ghosts."

Thy white, uncertain sands are white
With bones of thy unburied dead,
That will not perish from the sight.
They drown, but perish not—ah me!

What dread unsightly sights are spread
Along this lonesome, dried-up sea?

Old, hoar, and dried-up sea! so old
So strown with wealth, so sown with gold!
Yea, thou art old and hoary white
With time, and ruin of all things;
And on thy lonesome borders night
Sits brooding as with wounded wings.

The winds that toss'd thy waves and blew
Across thy breast the blowing sail,
And cheer'd the hearts of cheering crew
From farther seas, no more prevail.
Thy white-wall'd cities all lie prone,
With but a pyramid, a stone,
Set head and foot in sands to tell
The thirsting stranger where they fell.

The patient ox that bended low
His neck, and drew slow up and down
Thy thousand freights through rock-built town
Is now the free-born buffalo.
No longer of the timid fold,
The mountain ram leaps free and bold
His high-built summit, and looks down
From battlements of buried town.

Thine ancient steeds know not the rein;
They lord the land; they come, they go
At will; they laugh at man; they blow
A cloud of black steeds o'er the plain.
The winds, the waves, have drawn away—
The very wild man dreads to stay.

XVI.

Away! upon the sandy seas,
The gleaming, burning, boundless plain;
How solemn-like, how still, as when
The mighty minded Genoese
Drew three slim ships and led his men
From land they might not meet again.

The black men rode in front by two,
The fair one follow'd close, and kept
Her face held down as if she wept;
But Morgan kept the rear, and threw
His flowing, swaying beard still back
In watch along their lonesome track.

The weary day fell down to rest,
A star upon his mantled breast,
Ere scarce the sun fell out of space,
And Venus glimmer'd in his place.
Yea, all the stars shone just as fair,
And constellations kept their round,
And look'd from out the great profound,
And march'd, and countermarch'd, and shone
Upon that desolation there—
Why, just the same as if proud man
Strode up and down array'd in gold
And purple as in days of old,
And reckon'd all of his own plan,
Or made at least for man alone.

Yet on push'd Morgan silently,
And straight as strong ship on a sea;
And ever as he rode there lay—
To right, to left, and in his way,
Strange objects looming in the dark,
Some like tall mast, or ark, or bark.

And things half-hidden in the sand
Lay down before them where they pass'd—
A broken beam, half-buried mast,
A spar or bar, such as might be
Blown crosswise, tumbled on the strand
Of some sail-crowded, stormy sea.

All night by moon, by morning star,
The still, black men still kept their way;
All night till morn, till burning day
Hard Vasques follow'd fast and far.

The sun is high, the sands are hot
To touch, and all the tawny plain
Sinks white and open as they tread
And trudge, with half-averted head,

As if to swallow them in sand.
They look, as men look back to land
When standing out to stormy sea,
But still keep pace and murmur not;
Keep stern and still as destiny.

It was a sight! A slim dog slid
White-mouth'd and still along the sand,
The pleading picture of distress.
He stopp'd, leap'd up to lick a hand,
A hard, black hand that sudden chid
Him back, and check'd his tenderness.
Then when the black man turn'd his head,
His poor, mute friend had fallen dead.

The very air hung white with heat,
And white, and fair, and far away
A lifted, shining snow-shaft lay
As if to mock their mad retreat.
The white, salt sands beneath their feet
Did make the black men loom as grand,
From out the lifting, heaving heat,
As they rode sternly on and on,
As any bronze men in the land
That sit their statue steeds upon.

The men were silent as men dead.
The sun hung centered overhead,
Nor seem'd to move. It molten hung
Like some great central burner swung
From lofty beams with golden bars
In sacristy set round with stars.

Why, flame could hardly be more hot;
Yet on the mad pursuer came
Across the gleaming, yielding ground,
Right on, as if he fed on flame,
Right on until the mid-day found
The man within a pistol-shot.

He hail'd, but Morgan answered not;
He hail'd, then came a feeble shot,
And strangely, in that vastness there,
It seem'd to scarcely fret the air,
But fell down harmless anywhere.

He fiercely hail'd; and then there fell
A horse. And then a man fell down,
And in the sea-sand seem'd to drown.
Then Vasques cursed, but scarce could tell
The sound of his own voice, and all
In mad confusion seem'd to fall.

Yet on pushed Morgan, silent on,
And as he rode, he lean'd and drew
From his catenas gold, and threw
The bright coins in the glaring sun.
But Vasques did not heed a whit,
He scarcely deign'd to scowl at it.

Again lean'd Morgan. He uprose,
And held a high hand to his foes,
And held two goblets up, and one
Did shine as if itself a sun.
Then leaning backward from his place,
He hurl'd them in his foeman's face;
Then drew again, and so kept on,
Till goblets, gold, and all were gone.

Yea, strew'd them out upon the sands
As men upon a frosty morn,
In Mississippi's fertile lands,
Hurl out great yellow ears of corn,
To hungry swine with hurried hands.

Yet still hot Vasques urges on,
With flashing eye and flushing cheek.
What would he have? what does he seek?
He does not heed the gold a whit,
He does not deign to look at it;
But now his gleaming steel is drawn,
And now he leans, would hail again,—
He opes his swollen lips in vain.

But look you! See! A lifted hand,
And Vasques beckons his command.
He cannot speak, he leans, and he
Bends low upon his saddle-bow.
And now his blade drops to his knee,
And now he falters, now comes on,
And now his head is bended low;

And now his rein, his steel, is gone;
Now faint as any child is he;
And now his steed sinks to the knee.

The sun hung molten in mid-space,
Like some great star fix'd in its place.
From out the gleaming spaces rose
A sheen of gossamer and danced,
As Morgan slow and still advanced
Before his far-receding foes.
Right on, and on, the still, black line
Drove straight through gleaming sand and shine,
By spar and beam and mast, and stray
And waif of sea and cast away.

The far peaks faded from their sight,
The mountain walls fell down like night,
And nothing now was to be seen
Except the dim sun hung in sheen
Of gory garments all blood-red,—
The hell beneath, the hell o'erhead.

A black man tumbled from his steed.
He clutch'd in death the moving sands,
He caught the hot earth in his hands,
He gripp'd it, held it hard and grim—
The great, sad mother did not heed
His hold, but pass'd right on from him.

XVII.

The sun seem'd broken loose at last.
And settled slowly to the west,
Half-hidden as he fell to rest,
Yet, like the flying Parthian, cast
His keenest arrows as he pass'd.

On, on, the black men slowly drew
Their length like some great serpent through
The sands, and left a hollow'd groove:
They moved, they scarcely seem'd to move.
How patient in their muffled tread!
How like the dead march of the dead!

At last the slow, black line was check'd,
An instant only; now again
It moved, it falter'd now, and now
It settled in its sandy bed,
And steeds stood rooted to the plain.
Then all stood still, and men somehow
Look'd down and with averted head;
Look'd down, nor dared look up, nor reck'd
Of anything, of ill or good,
But bow'd and stricken still they stood.

Like some brave band that dared the fierce
And bristled steel of gather'd host,
These daring men had dared to pierce
This awful vastness, dead and gray.
And now at last brought well at bay
They stood,—but each stood to his post.

Then one dismounted, waved a hand,
'Twas Morgan's stern and still command.
There fell a clank, like loosen'd chain,
As men dismounting loosed the rein.
Then every steed stood loosed and free;
And some stepp'd slow and mute aside,
And some sank to the sands and died;
And some stood still as shadows be.

Old Morgan turn'd and raised his hand
And laid it level with his eyes,
And looked far back along the land.
He saw a dark dust still uprise,
Still surely tend to where he lay.
He did not curse, he did not say—
He did not even look surprise.

Nay, he was over-gentle now;
He wiped a time his Titan brow,
Then sought dark Sybal in her place,
Put out his arms, put down his face
And look'd in hers. She reach'd her hands,
She lean'd, she fell upon his breast;
He reach'd his arms around; she lay
As lies a bird in leafy nest.

And he look'd out across the sands
And bearing her, he strode away.

Some black men settled down to rest,
But none made murmur or request.
The dead were dead, and that were best;
The living, leaning, follow'd him,
A long dark line of shadow dim.

The day through high mid-heaven rode
Across the sky, the dim, red day;
And on, the war-like day-god strode
With shoulder'd shield away, away.
The savage, war-like day bent low,
As reapers bend in gathering grain,
As archer bending bends yew bow,
And flush'd and fretted as in pain.

Then down his shoulder slid his shield,
So huge, so awful, so blood-red
And batter'd as from battle-field:
It settled, sunk to his left hand,
Sunk down and down, it touch'd the sand;
Then day along the land lay dead,
Without one candle, foot or head.

And now the moon wheel'd white and vast,
A round, unbroken, marbled moon,
And touch'd the far, bright buttes of snow,
Then climb'd their shoulders over soon;
And there she seem'd to sit at last,
To hang, to hover there, to grow,
Grow grander than vast peaks of snow.

She sat the battlements of time;
She shone in mail of frost and rime
A time, and then rose up and stood
In heaven in sad widowhood.

The faded moon fell wearily,
And then the sun right suddenly
Rose up full arm'd, and rushing came
Across the land like flood of flame.

And now it seemed that hills uprose,
High push'd against the arching skies,
As if to meet the sudden sun—
Rose sharp from out the sultry dun,
And seem'd to hold the free repose
Of lands where flow'ry summits rise,
In unfenced fields of Paradise.

The black men look'd up from the sands
Against the dim, uncertain skies,
As men that disbelieved their eyes,
And would have laugh'd; they wept instead,
With shoulders heaved, with bowing head
Hid down between the two black hands.

They stood and gazed. Lo! like the call
Of spring-time promises, the trees
Lean'd from their lifted mountain wall,
And stood clear cut against the skies,
As if they grew in pistol-shot;
Yet all the mountains answer'd not,
And yet there came no cooling breeze,
Nor soothing sense of wind-wet trees.

At last old Morgan, looking through
His shaded fingers, let them go,
And let his load fall down as dead.
He groan'd, he clutch'd his beard of snow
As was his wont, then bowing low,
Took up his life, and moaning said,
"Lord Christ! 'tis the mirage, and we
Stand blinded in a burning sea."

XVIII.

Again they move, but where or how
It recks them little, nothing now.
Yet Morgan leads them as before,
But totters now; he bends, and he
Is like a broken ship a-sea,—
A ship that knows not any shore,
Nor rudder, nor shall anchor more.

Some leaning shadows crooning crept
Through desolation, crown'd in dust.

And had the mad pursuer kept
His path, and cherish'd his pursuit?
There lay no choice. Advance, he must:
Advance, and eat his ashen fruit.

Again the still moon rose and stood
Above the dim, dark belt of wood,
Above the buttes, above the snow,
And bent a sad, sweet face below.
She reach'd along the level plain
Her long, white fingers. Then again
She reach'd, she touch'd the snowy sands.
Then reach'd far out until she touch'd
A heap that lay with doubled hands,
Reach'd from its sable self, and clutch'd
With patient death. O tenderly
That black, that dead and hollow face
Was kiss'd at midnight.... What if I say
The long, white moonbeams reaching there,
Caressing idle hands of clay,
And resting on the wrinkled hair
And great lips push'd in sullen pout,
Were God's own fingers reaching out
From heaven to that lonesome place?

XIX.

By waif and stray and cast-away,
Such as are seen in seas withdrawn,
Old Morgan led in silence on;
And sometimes lifting up his head,
To guide his footsteps as he led,
He deem'd he saw a great ship lay
Her keel along the sea-wash'd sand,
As with her captain's old command.

The stars were seal'd; and then a haze
Of gossamer fill'd all the west,
So like in Indian summer days,
And veil'd all things. And then the moon
Grew pale, and faint, and far. She died,
And now nor star nor any sign
Fell out of heaven. Oversoon
A black man fell. Then at his side
Some one sat down to watch, to rest—
To rest, to watch, or what you will,
The man sits resting, watching still.

XX.

The day glared through the eastern rim
Of rocky peaks, as prison bars,
With light as dim as distant stars.
The sultry sunbeams filter'd down
Through misty phantoms weird and dim,
Through shifting shapes bat-wing'd and brown.

Like some vast ruin wrapp'd in flame
The sun fell down before them now.
Behind them wheel'd white peaks of snow,
As they proceeded. Gray and grim
And awful objects went and came
Before them all. They pierced at last
The desert's middle depths, and lo!
There loom'd from out the desert vast
A lonely ship, well-built and trim,
And perfect all in hull and mast.

No storm had stain'd it any whit,
No seasons set their teeth in it.
Her masts were white as ghosts, and tall;
Her decks were as of yesterday.
The rains, the elements, and all
The moving things that bring decay
By fair green lands or fairer seas,
Had touch'd not here for centuries.
Lo! date had lost all reckoning,
And time had long forgotten all
In this lost land, and no new thing
Or old could anywise befall,
For Time went by the other way.

What dreams of gold or conquest drew
The oak-built sea-king to these seas,
Ere earth, old earth, unsatisfied,
Rose up and shook man in disgust
From off her wearied breast, and threw
His high-built cities down, and dried
These unnamed ship-sown seas to dust?

Who trod these decks? What captain knew
The straits that led to lands like these?

Blew south-sea breeze or north-sea breeze?
What spiced-winds whistled through this sail?
What banners stream'd above these seas?
And what strange seaman answer'd back
To other sea-king's beck and hail,
That blew across his foamy track?

Sought Jason here the golden fleece?
Came Trojan ship or ships of Greece?
Came decks dark-mann'd from sultry Ind,
Woo'd here by spacious wooing wind?
So like a grand, sweet woman, when
A great love moves her soul to men?

Came here strong ships of Solomon
In quest of Ophir by Cathay?....
Sit down and dream of seas withdrawn,
And every sea-breath drawn away.
Sit down, sit down! What is the good
That we go on still fashioning
Great iron ships or walls of wood,
High masts of oak, or anything?

Lo! all things moving must go by.
The seas lie dead. Behold, this land
Sits desolate in dust beside
His snow-white, seamless shroud of sand;
The very clouds have wept and died,
And only God is in the sky.

XXI.

The sands lay heaved, as heaved by waves,
As fashioned in a thousand graves:
And wrecks of storm blown here and there,
And dead men scatter'd everywhere;
And strangely clad they seem'd to be
Just as they sank in that dread sea.

The mermaid with her golden hair
Had clung about a wreck's beam there,
And sung her song of sweet despair,
The time she saw the seas withdrawn
And all her pride and glory gone:
Had sung her melancholy dirge
Above the last receding surge,
And, looking down the rippled tide,
Had sung, and with her song had died.

The monsters of the sea lay bound
In strange contortions. Coil'd around
A mast half heaved above the sand
The great sea-serpent's folds were found,
As solid as ship's iron band;
And basking in the burning sun
There rose the great whale's skeleton.

A thousand sea things stretch'd across
Their weary and bewilder'd way:
Great unnamed monsters wrinkled lay
With sunken eyes and shrunken form.
The strong sea-horse that rode the storm
With mane as light and white as floss,
Lay tangled in his mane of moss.

And anchor, hull, and cast-away,
And all things that the miser deep
Doth in his darkling locker keep,
To right and left around them lay.
Yea, golden coin and golden cup,
And golden cruse, and golden plate,
And all that great seas swallow up,
Right in their dreadful pathway lay.
The hoary sea made white with time,
And wrinkled cross with many a crime,
With all his treasured thefts lay there,
His sins, his very soul laid bare,
As if it were the Judgment Day.

XXII.

And now the tawny night fell soon,
And there was neither star nor moon;
And yet it seem'd it was not night.

There fell a phosphorescent light,
There rose from white sands and dead men
A soft light, white and strange as when
The Spirit of Jehovah moved
Upon the water's conscious face,
And made it His abiding place.

Remote, around the lonesome ship,
Old Morgan môved, but knew it not,
For neither star nor moon fell down....
I trow that was a lonesome spot
He found, where boat and ship did dip
In sands like some half-sunken town.

At last before the leader lay
A form that in the night did seem
A slain Goliath. As in a dream,
He drew aside in his slow pace,
And look'd. He saw a sable face!
A friend that fell that very day,
Thrown straight across his wearied way.

He falter'd now. His iron heart,
That never yet refused its part,
Began to fail him; and his strength
Shook at his knees, as shakes the wind
A shatter'd ship. His shatter'd mind
Ranged up and down the land. At length
He turn'd, as ships turn, tempest toss'd,
For now he knew that he was lost!
He sought in vain the moon, the stars,
In vain the battle-star of Mars.

Again he moved. And now again
He paused, he peer'd along the plain,
Another form before him lay.
He stood, and statue-white he stood,
He trembled like a stormy wood,—
It was a foeman brawn and gray.

He lifted up his head again,
Again he search'd the great profound
For môon, for star, but sought in vain.
He kept his circle round and round
The great ship lifting from the sand,
And pointing heavenward like a hand.

And still he crept along the plain,
Yet where his foeman dead again
Lay in his way he moved around,
And soft as if on sacred ground,
And did not touch him anywhere.
It might have been he had a dread,
In his half-crazed and fever'd brain,
His fallen foe might rise again
If he should dare to touch him there.

He circled round the lonesome ship
Like some wild beast within a wall,
That keeps his paces round and round.
The very stillness had a sound;
He saw strange somethings rise and dip;
He felt the weirdness like a pall
Come down and cover him. It seem'd
To take a form, take many forms,
To talk to him, to reach out arms;
Yet on he kept, and silent kept,
And as he led he lean'd and slept,
And as he slept he talk'd and dream'd.

Two shadows follow'd, stopp'd, and stood
Bewilder'd, wander'd back again,
Came on and then fell to the sand,
And sinking died. Then other men
Did wag their woolly heads and laugh,
Then bend their necks and seem to quaff
Of cooling waves that careless flow
Where woods and long, strong grasses grow.

Yet on wound Morgan, leaning low,
With her upon his breast, and slow
As hand upon a dial plate.
He did not turn his course or quail,
He did not falter, did not fail,
Turn right or left or hesitate.

Some far-off sounds had lost their way,
And seem'd to call to him and pray

For help, as if they were affright.
It was not day, it seem'd not night,
But that dim land that lies between
The mournful, faithful face of night,
And loud and gold-bedazzled day;
A night that was not felt but seen.

There seem'd not now the ghost of sound,
He stepp'd as soft as step the dead;
Yet on he led in solemn tread,
Bewilder'd, blinded, round and round,
About the great black ship that rose
Tall-masted as that ship that blows
Her ghost below lost Panama,—
The tallest mast man ever saw.

Two leaning shadows follow'd him:
Their eyes were red, their teeth shone white,
Their limbs did lift as shadows swim.
Then one went left and one went right,
And in the night pass'd out of sight;
Pass'd through the portals black, unknown,
And Morgan totter'd on alone.

And why he still survived the rest,
Why still he had the strength to stir,
Why still he stood like gnarlèd oak
That buffets storm and tempest stroke,
One cannot say, save but for her,
That helpless being on his breast.

She did not speak, she did not stir;
In rippled currents over her,
Her black, abundant hair pour'd down
Like mantle or some sable gown.
That sad, sweet dreamer; she who knew
Not anything of earth at all,
Nor cared to know its bane or bliss;
That dove that did not touch the land,
That knew, yet did not understand.
And this may be because she drew
Her all of life right from the hand
Of God, and did not choose to learn
The things that make up man's concern.

Ah ! there be souls none understand;
Like clouds, they cannot touch the land.
Unanchored ships, they blow and blow,
Sail to and fro, and then go down
In unknown seas that none shall know,
Without one ripple of renown.

Call these not fools; the test of worth
Is not the hold you have of earth.
Ay, there be gentlest souls sea-blown
That know not any harbor known.
Now it may be the reason is,
They touch on fairer shores than this.

At last he touch'd a fallen group,
Dead fellows tumbled in the sands,
Dead foemen, gather'd to their dead.
And eager now the man did stoop,
Lay down his load and reach his hands,
And stretch his form and look steadfast
And frightful, and as one aghast.
He lean'd, and then he raised his head,
And look'd for Vasques, but in vain
He peer'd along the deadly plain.

Now, from the night another face
The last that follow'd through the deep,
Comes on, falls dead within a pace.
Yet Vasques still survives! But where?
His last bold follower lies there,
Thrown straight across old Morgan's track,
As if to check him, bid him back.
He stands, he does not dare to stir,
He watches by his charge asleep,
He fears for her: but only her.
The man who ever mock'd at death,
He only dares to draw his breath.

XXIII.

Beyond, and still as black despair,
A man rose up, stood dark and tall,
Stretch'd out his neck, reach'd forth, let fall
Dark oaths, and Death stood waiting there.

He drew his blade, came straight as death
For Morgan's last and most endear'd.
I think no man there drew a breath,
I know that no man quail'd or fear'd.

A tawny dead man stretch'd between,
And Vasques set his foot thereon.
The stars were seal'd, the moon was gone,
The very darkness cast a shade.
The scene was rather heard than seen,
The rattle of a single blade....

A right foot rested on the dead,
A black hand reach'd and clutch'd a beard,
Then neither pray'd, nor dream'd of hope.
A fierce face reach'd, a black face peer'd....
No bat went whirling overhead,
No star fell out of Ethiope.

The dead man lay between them there,
The two men glared as tigers glare,—
The black man held him by the beard.
He wound his hand, he held him fast,
And tighter held, as if he fear'd
The man might 'scape him at the last.
Whiles Morgan did not speak or stir,
But stood in silent watch with her.

Not long....A light blade lifted, thrust,
A blade that leapt and swept about,
So wizard-like, like wand in spell,
So like a serpent's tongue thrust out....
Thrust twice, thrust thrice, thrust as he fell,
Thrust through until it touched the dust.

Yet ever as he thrust and smote,
A black hand like an iron band
Did tighten round a gasping throat.
He fell, but did not loose his hand;
The two lay dead upon the sand.

Lo! up and from the fallen forms
Two ghosts came, dark as gathered storms;
Two gray ghosts stood, then looking back;
With hands all empty, and hands clutch'd,
Strode on in silence. Then they touch'd,
Along the lonesome, chartless track,
Where dim Plutonian darkness fell,
Then touch'd the outer rim of hell;
And looking back their great despair
Sat sadly down, as resting there.

XXIV.

As if there was a strength in death
The battle seem'd to nerve the man
To superhuman strength. He rose,
Held up his head, began to scan
The heavens and to take his breath
Right strong and lustily. He now
Resumed his part, and with his eye
Fix'd on a star that filter'd through
The farther west, push'd bare his brow,
And kept his course with head held high,
As if he strode his deck and drew
His keel below some lofty light
That watch'd the rocky reef at night.

How lone he was, how patient she
Upon that lonesome sandy sea!
It were a sad, unpleasant sight
To follow them through all the night,

Until the time they lifted hand,
And touch'd at last a water'd land.

* * * * * *

The turkeys walk'd the tangled grass,
And scarcely turn'd to let them pass,
There was no sign of man, nor sign
Of savage beast. 'Twas so divine,
It seem'd as if the bended skies
Were rounded for this Paradise.

The large-eyed antelope came down
From off their windy hills, and blew
Their whistles as they wander'd through
The open groves of water'd wood;
They came as light as if on wing,
And reached their noses wet and brown
And stamp'd their little feet and stood
Close up before them wondering.

What if this were that Eden old,
They found in this heart of the new
And unnamed westmost world of gold,
Where date and history had birth,
And man began first wandering
To go the girdle of the earth,
And find the beautiful and true?

It lies a little isle mid land,
An island in a sea of sand;
With reedy waters and the balm
Of an eternal summer air;
Some blowy pines toss tall and fair;
And there are grasses long and strong,
And tropic fruits that never fail:
The Manzanita pulp, the palm,
The prickly pear, with all the song
Of summer birds. And there the quail
Makes nest, and you may hear her call
All day from out the chaparral.

A land where white man never trod,
And Morgan seems some demi-god,
That haunts the red man's spirit land.
A land where never red man's hand
Is lifted up in strife at all,
But holds it sacred unto those
Who bravely fell before their foes,
And rarely dares its desert wall.

Here breaks nor sound of strife nor sign;
Rare times a chieftain comes this way,
Alone, and battle-scarr'd and gray,
And then he bends devout before
The maid who keeps the cabin-door,
And deems her something all divine.

Within the island's heart 'tis said,
Tall trees are bending down with bread,
And that a fountain pure as Truth,
And deep and mossy-bound and fair,
Is bubbling from the forest there,—
Perchance the fabled fount of youth!
An isle where skies are ever fair,
Where men keep never date nor day,
Where Time has thrown his glass away.

This isle is all their own. No more
The flight by day, the watch by night.
Dark Sybal twines about the door
The scarlet blooms, the blossoms white
And winds red berries in her hair,
And never knows the name of care.

She has a thousand birds; they blow
In rainbow clouds, in clouds of snow;
The birds take berries from her hand;
They come and go at her command.

She has a thousand pretty birds,
That sing her summer songs all day;
Small, black-hoof'd antelope in herds,
And squirrels bushy-tail'd and gray,

With round and sparkling eyes of pink,
And cunning-faced as you can think.

She has a thousand busy birds:
And is she happy in her isle,
With all her feather'd friends and herds?
For when has Morgan seen her smile?

She has a thousand cunning birds,
They would build nestings in her hair,
She has brown antelope in herds;
She never knows the name of care;
Why, then, is she not happy there?

All patiently she bears her part;
She has a thousand birdlings there,
These birds they would build in her
hair;
But not one bird builds in her heart.

She has a thousand birds; yet she
Would give ten thousand cheerfully,
All bright of plume and pure of tongue,
And sweet as ever trilled or sung,
For one small flutter'd bird to come
And build within her heart, though
dumb.

She has a thousand birds; yet one
Is lost, and, lo! she is undone.
She sighs sometimes. She looks away,
And yet she does not weep or say.

"The Ship in the Desert" was first published in London—Chapman and Hall, 1876. It was nearly twice its present length and was dedicated TO MY PARENTS IN OREGON, as follows:

With deep reverence I inscribe these lines, my dear parents, to you. I see you now, away beyond the seas—beyond the lands where the sun goes down in the Pacific like some great ship of fire, resting still on the green hills, waiting

"Where rolls the Oregon
And hears no sound save its own dashing."

Nearly a quarter of a century ago you took me the long and lonesome half-year's journey across the mighty continent, wild and rent and broken up and sown with sand and ashes and crossed by tumbling wooded rivers that ran as if glad to get away, fresh and strange and new, as if but half-fashioned from the hand of God. All the time as I tread this strange land I re-live those scenes, and you are with me. How dark and deep, how sullen, strong and lionlike the mighty Missouri rolled between his walls of untracked wood and cleft the unknown domain of the middle world before us! Then the frail and buffeted rafts on the river, the women and children huddled together, the shouts of the brawny men as they swam with the bellowing cattle, the cows in the stormy stream eddying, whirling, spinning about, calling to their young, their bright horns shining in the sun. The wild men waiting on the other side; painted savages, leaning on their bows, despising our weakness, opening a way, letting us pass on to the unknown distances, where they said the sun and moon lay down together and brought forth the stars. The long and winding lines of wagons, the graves by the wayside, the women weeping together as they passed on. Then hills, then plains, parched lands like Syria, dust and alkali, cold streams with woods, camps by night, great wood fires in circles, tents in the center like Cæsar's battle camps, painted men that passed like shadows, showers of arrows, the wild beasts howling from the hills. You, my dear parents, will pardon the thread of fiction on which I have strung these scenes and descriptions of a mighty land of mystery, and wild and savage grandeur, for the world will have its way, and, like a spoiled child, demands a tale—

"Yea,
We who toil and earn our bread, still have our masters."

A ragged and broken story it is, with long deserts, with alkali and ashes, yet it may, like the land it deals of, have some green places, and woods and running waters, where you can rest.

Three times now I have ranged the great West in fancy, as I did in fact for twenty years and gathered unknown and unnamed blossoms from mountain top, from desert land, where man never ranged before, and asked the West to receive my weeds, my grasses and blue-eyed blossoms. But here it ends. Good or bad, I have done enough of this work on the border. The Orient promises a more grateful harvest I have been true to my West. She has been my only love. I have remembered her greatness. I have done my work to show to the world her vastness, her riches, her resources. her valor and her dignity, her poetry and her grandeur. Yet while I was going on working so in silence, what were the things she said of me? But let that pass, my dear parents. Others will come after us. Possibly I have blazed out the trail for great minds over this field, as you did across the deserts and plains for great men a quarter of a century ago. JOAQUIN MILLER.

LAKE COMO, ITALY.

I had bought land near Naples, along with a young Englishman intending to settle down there: but we both were stricken with malarial fever; he died, and I, broken and sick at heart for my mountains, finally came home.

The author of Cleopatra, a man of great and varied endowments, laid a strong hand to the fashioning of this poem, and in return I made mention of his Sybals and Semiramis. We knew, in Rome, and loved much the woman herein described. In truth, I never created any one of my men or women or scenes entirely.

As for the story of the ship in the desert, it is old, old. You can see the tide marks of an ocean even from your car window as you glide around Salt Lake, hundreds of feet up the steeps. The mighty Colorado Cañon was made by the breaking away of this ocean, you find oyster shells and petrified salt water fish in the Rocky Mountains, and a stranded ship in the desert is quite in line with these facts.

The body of this poem was first published in the *Atlantic Monthly*. The purpose of it was the same as induced the Isles of the Amazons, but the work is better because more true and nearer to the heart. Bear in mind it was done when the heart of the continent was indeed a desert, or at least a wilderness. How much or how little it may have had to do in bringing Europe this way to seek for the lost Edens, and to make the desert blossom as the rose, matters nothing now; but, "He hath brought many captives home to Rome whose ransom did the generous coffers fill."

THE HIGHTS, May, '97.

PICTURES.

My brave world-builders of the West!
Why, who doth know ye? Who shall know
But I, that on thy peaks of snow
Brake bread the first? Who loves ye best?
Who holds ye still, of more stern worth
Than all proud peoples of the earth?

Yea, I, the rhymer of wild rhymes,
Indifferent of blame or praise,
Still sing of ye, as one who plays
The same sweet air in all strange climes—
The same wild, piercing highland air,
Because—because, his heart is there.

THE SIERRAS FROM THE SEA.

I.

Like fragments of an uncompleted world,
From bleak Alaska, bound in ice and spray,
To where the peaks of Darien lie curl'd
In clouds, the broken lands loom bold and gray.
The seamen nearing San Francisco Bay
Forget the compass here; with sturdy hand
They seize the wheel, look up, then bravely lay
The ship to shore by rugged peaks that stand
The stern and proud patrician fathers of the land.

II.

They stand white stairs of heaven,—stand a line
Of lifting, endless, and eternal white.
They look upon the far and flashing brine,
Upon the boundless plains, the broken height
Of Kamiakin's battlements. The flight
Of time is underneath their untopp'd towers.
They seem to push aside the moon at night,
To jostle and to loose the stars. The flowers
Of heaven fall about their brows in shining showers.

III.

They stand in line of lifted snowy isles
High held above the toss'd and tumbled sea,—
A sea of wood in wild unmeasured miles:
White pyramids of Faith where man is free;
White monuments of Hope that yet shall be
The mounts of matchless and immortal song....

I look far down the hollow days; I see
The bearded prophets, simple-soul'd and strong,
That strike the sounding harp and thrill the heeding throng.

IV.

Serene and satisfied! supreme! as lone
As God, they loom like God's archangels churl'd;
They look as cold as kings upon a throne;
The mantling wings of night are crush'd and curl'd
As feathers curl. The elements are hurl'd
From off their bosoms, and are bidden go,
Like evil spirits, to an under-world.
They stretch from Cariboo to Mexico,
A line of battle-tents in everlasting snow.

WHERE ROLLS THE OREGON.

See once these stately scenes, then roam no more;
No more remains on earth to cultured eyes;
The cataract comes down, a broken roar,
The palisades defy approach, and rise
Green moss'd and dripping to the clouded skies.
The cañon thunders with its full of foam,
And calls loud-mouth'd, and all the land defies;
The mounts make fellowship and dwell at home
In snowy brotherhood beneath their purpled dome.

The rainbows swim in circles round, and rise
Against the hanging granite walls till lost
In drifting dreamy clouds and dappled skies,
A grand mosaic intertwined and toss'd
Along the mighty cañon, bound and cross'd
By storms of screaming birds of sea and land;
The salmon rush below, bright red and boss'd
In silver. Tawny, tall, on either hand
You see the savage spearman nude and silent stand.

Here sweep the wide wild waters cold and white
And blue in their far depths; divided now
By sudden swift canoe as still and light
As feathers nodding from the painted brow
That lifts and looks from out the imaged prow.
Ashore you hear the papoose shout at play;
The curl'd smoke comes from underneath the bough
Of leaning fir: the wife looks far away
And sees a swift slim bark divide the dashing spray.

Slow drift adown the river's level'd deep,
And look above; lo, columns! woods! the snow!
The rivers rush upon the brink and leap
From out the clouds three thousand feet below,
And land afoam in tops of firs that grow
Against your river's rim: they plash, they play
In clouds, now loud and now subdued and slow,
A thousand thunder tones; they swing and sway
In idle winds, long leaning shafts of shining spray.

An Indian summer-time it was, long past,
We lay on this Columbia, far below
The stormy water falls, and God had cast
Us heaven's stillness. Dreamily and slow

We drifted as the light bark chose to go.
An Indian girl with ornaments of shell
Began to sing.... The stars may hold such flow
Of hair, such eyes, but rarely earth. There fell
A sweet enchantment that possess'd me as a spell.

We saw the elk forsake the sable wood,
Step quick across the rim of shining sand,
Breast out unscared against the flashing flood,
Then brisket deep with lifted antlers stand,
And ears alert, look sharp on either hand,
Then whistle shrill to dam and doubting fawn
To cross, then lead with black nose to the land.
They cross'd, they climb'd the heaving hills, were gone,
A sturdy charging line with crooked sabers drawn.

Then black swans cross'd us slowly low and still;
Then other swans, wide-wing'd and white as snow,
Flew overhead and topp'd the timber'd hill,
And call'd and sang afar, coarse-voiced and slow,
Till sounds roam'd lost in somber firs below....
Then clouds blew in, and all the sky was cast
With tumbled and tumultuous clouds that grow
Red thunderbolts.... A flash! A thunder-blast!
The clouds were rent, and lo! Mount Hood hung white and vast.

PICTURE OF A BULL.

Once, morn by morn, when snowy mountains flamed
With sudden, shafts of light that shot a flood
Into the vale like fiery arrows aim'd
At night from mighty battlements, there stood
Upon a cliff high-limn'd against Mount Hood,
A matchless bull, fresh forth from sable wold,
And standing so seem'd grander 'gainst the wood
Than wingéd bull that stood with tips of gold
Beside the brazen gates of Nineveh of old.

A time he toss'd the dewy turf, and then
Stretch'd forth his wrinkled neck, and loud
He call'd above the far abodes of men
Until his breath became a curling cloud
And wreathed about his neck a misty shroud.
He then as sudden as he came pass'd on
With lifted head, majestic and most proud,
And lone as night in deepest wood withdrawn
He roamed in silent rage until another dawn.

What drove the hermit from the valley herd,
What cross of love, what cold neglect of kind,
Or scorn of unpretending worth had stirr'd
The stubborn blood and drove him forth to find
A fellowship in mountain cloud and wind,
I ofttime wonder'd much; and ofttime thought

The beast betray'd a royal monarch's
mind,
To lift above the low herd's common lot,
And make them hear him still when they
had fain forgot.

VAQUERO.

His broad-brimm'd hat push'd back with
careless air,
The proud vaquero sits his steed as free
As winds that toss his black abundant
hair.
No rover ever swept a lawless sea
With such a haught and heedless air as he
Who scorns the path, and bounds with
swift disdain
Away, a peon born, yet born to be
A splendid king; behold him ride, and
reign.

How brave he takes his herds in brand-
ing days,
On timber'd hills that belt about the plain;
He climbs, he wheels, he shouts through
winding ways
Of hiding ferns and hanging fir; the rein
Is loose, the rattling spur drives swift;
the mane
Blows free; the bullocks rush in storms
before;
They turn with lifted heads, they rush
again,
Then sudden plunge from out the wood,
and pour
A cloud upon the plain with one terrific
roar.

Now sweeps the tawny man on stormy
steed,
His gaudy trappings toss'd about and
blown
About the limbs as lithe as any reed;
The swift long lasso twirl'd above is thrown
From flying hand; the fall, the fearful
groan
Of bullock toil'd and tumbled in the dust—
The black herds onward sweep, and all
disown
The fallen, struggling monarch that has
thrust
His tongue in rage and roll'd his red eyes
in disgust.

IN THE GREAT EMERALD LAND.

A morn in Oregon! The kindled camp
Upon the mountain brow that broke below
In steep and grassy stairway to the damp
And dewy valley, snapp'd and flamed aglow
With knots of pine. Above, the peaks of
snow,
With under-belts of sable forests, rose
And flash'd in sudden sunlight. To and
fro
And far below, in lines and winding
rows,
The herders drove their bands, and broke
the deep repose.

I heard their shouts like sounding hun-
ter's horn,
The lowing herds made echoes far away;
When lo! the clouds came driving in with
morn
Toward the sea, as fleeing from the day.
The valleys fill'd with curly clouds. They
lay
Below, a levell'd sea that reach'd and
roll'd
And broke like breakers of a stormy bay
Against the grassy shingle fold on fold,
So like a splendid ocean, snowy white and
cold.

The peopled valley lay a hidden world,
The shouts were shouts of drowning men
that died,

The broken clouds along the border
curl'd,
And bent the grass with weighty freight
of tide.
A savage stood in silence at my side,
Then sudden threw aback his beaded
strouds
And stretch'd his hand above the scene,
and cried,
As all the land lay dead in snowy shrouds:
"Behold! the sun bathes in a silver sea
of clouds."

Here lifts the land of clouds! Fierce
mountain forms,
Made white with everlasting snows, look
down
Through mists of many cañons, mighty
storms
That stretch from Autumn's purple, drench
and drown
The yellow hem of Spring. Tall cedars
frown
Dark-brow'd, through banner'd clouds that
stretch and stream
Above the sea from snowy mountain
crown.
The heavens roll, and all things drift or
seem
To drift about and drive like some majestic
dream.

In waning Autumn time, when purpled
skies
Begin to haze in indolence below
The snowy peaks, you see black forms
arise,
In rolling thunder banks above, and
throw
Quick barricades about the gleaming
snow.
The strife begins! The battling seasons
stand
Broad breast to breast. A flash! Conten-
tions grow
Terrific. Thunders crash, and lightnings
brand
The battlements. The clouds possess the
conquered land.

The clouds blow by, the swans take
loftier flight,
The yellow blooms burst out upon the hill,
The purple camas comes as in a night,
Tall spiked and dripping of the dews that
fill
The misty valley. Sunbeams break and
spill
Their glory till the vale is full of noon.
The roses belt the streams, no bird is still.
The stars, as large as lilies, meet the moon
And sing of summer, born thus sudden
full and soon.

PILGRIMS OF THE PLAINS.

A tale half told and hardly understood;
The talk of bearded men that chanced to
meet,
That lean'd on long quaint rifles in the
wood,
That look'd in fellow faces, spoke dis-
creet
And low, as half in doubt and in defeat
Of hope; a tale it was of lands of gold
That lay toward the sun. Wild wing'd
and fleet
It spread among the swift Missouri's bold
Unbridled men, and reach'd to where Ohio
roll'd.

Then long chain'd lines of yoked and
patient steers;
Then long white trains that pointed to the
west,
Beyond the savage west; the hopes and
fears
Of blunt, untutor'd men, who hardly
guess'd

Their course; the brave and silent women, dress'd
In homely spun attire, the boys in bands,
The cheery babes that laugh'd at all, and bless'd
The doubting hearts with laughing lifted hands!....
What exodus for far untraversed lands!

The Plains! The shouting drivers at the wheel;
The crash of leather whips; the crush and roll
Of wheels; the groan of yokes and grinding steel
And iron chain, and lo! at last the whole
Vast line, that reach'd as if to touch the goal,
Began to stretch and stream away and wind
Toward the west, as if with one control;
Then hope loom'd fair, and home lay far behind;
Before, the boundless plain, and fiercest of their kind.

At first the way lay green and fresh as seas,
And far away as any reach of wave;
The sunny streams went by in belt of trees;
And here and there the tassell'd tawny brave
Swept by on horse, look'd back, stretch'd forth and gave
A yell of hell, and then did wheel and rein
Awhile, and point away, dark-brow'd and grave,
Into the far and dim and distant plain
With signs and prophecies, and then plunged on again.

Some hills at last began to lift and break;
Some streams began to fail of wood and tide,
The somber plain began betime to take
A hue of weary brown, and wild and wide
It stretch'd its naked breast on every side.
A babe was heard at last to cry for bread
Amid the deserts; cattle low'd and died,
And dying men went by with broken tread,
And left a long black serpent line of wreck and dead.

Strange hunger'd birds, black-wing'd and still as death,
And crown'd of red with hooked beaks, blew low
And close about, till we could touch their breath—
Strange unnamed birds, that seem'd to come and go
In circles now, and now direct and slow,
Continual, yet never touch the earth;
Slim foxes shied and shuttled to and fro
At times across the dusty weary dearth
Of life, look'd back, then sank like crickets in a hearth.

Then dust arose, a long dim line like smoke
From out of riven earth. The wheels went groaning by,
The thousand feet in harness and in yoke,
They tore the ways of ashen alkali,
And desert winds blew sudden, swift and dry.
The dust! it sat upon and fill'd the train!
It seem'd to fret and fill the very sky.
Lo! dust upon the beasts, the tent, the plain,
And dust, alas! on breasts that rose not up again.

They sat in desolation and in dust
By dried-up desert streams; the mother's hands
Hid all her bended face; the cattle thrust
Their tongues and faintly call'd across the lands.

The babes, that knew not what the way through sands
Could mean, did ask if it would end to-day....
The panting wolves slid by, red-eyed, in bands
To pools beyond. The men look'd far away,
And silent deemed that all a boundless desert lay.

They rose by night; they struggled on and on
As thin and still as ghosts; then here and there
Beside the dusty way before the dawn,
Men silent laid them down in their despair,
And died. But woman! Woman, frail as fair!
May man have strength to give to you your due;
You falter'd not, nor murmur'd anywhere,
You held your babes, held to your course, and you
Bore on through burning hell your double burdens through.

Men stood at last, the decimated few,
Above a land of running streams, and they?
They push'd aside the boughs, and peering through
Beheld afar the cool, refreshing bay;
Then some did curse, and some bend hands to pray;
But some look'd back upon the desert, wide
And desolate with death, then all the day
They mourned. But one, with nothing left beside
His dog to love, crept down among the ferns and died.

THE HEROES OF MY WEST.

I stand upon the green Sierra's wall;
Toward the east, beyond the yellow grass,
I see the broken hill-tops lift and fall,
Then sands that shimmer like a sea of glass....
There lies the nation's great high road of dead.
Forgotten aye, unnumber'd, and, alas!
Unchronicled in deed or death; instead,
The new aristocrat lifts high a lordly head.

My brave and unremember'd heroes, rest;
You fell in silence, silent lie and sleep.
Sleep on unsung, for this, I say, were best:
The world to-day has hardly time to weep;
The world to-day will hardly care to keep
In heart her plain and unpretending brave.
The desert winds, they whistle by and sweep
About you; brown'd and russet grasses wave
Along a thousand leagues that lie one common grave.

The proud and careless pass in palace car
Along the line you blazon'd white with bones;
Pass swift to people, and possess and mar
Your lands with monuments and letter'd stones
Unto themselves. Thank God! this waste disowns
Their touch. His everlasting hand has drawn
A shining line around you. Wealth bemoans

The waste your splendid grave employs.
Sleep on,
No hand shall touch your dust this side
of God and dawn.

I let them stride across with grasping
hands
And strive for brief possession; mark and
line
With lifted walls the new divided lands,
And gather growing herds of lowing kine.
I could not covet these, could not confine
My heart to one; all seem'd to me the
same,
And all below my mountain home, divine
And beautiful, held in another's name,
As if the herds and lands were mine,
All mine or his, all beautiful the same.

I have not been, shall not be, under-
stood;
I have not wit, nor will, to well explain,
But that which men call good I find not
good.
The lands the savage held, shall hold again,
The gold the savage spurn'd in proud dis-
dain
For centuries; go, take them all; build
high
Your gilded temples; strive and strike and
strain
And crowd and controvert and curse and
lie
In church and State, in town and citadel,
and....die.

And who shall grow the nobler from it
all?
The mute and unsung savage loved as
true,—
He felt, as grateful felt, God's blessings
fall
About his lodge and tawny babes as you
In temples,—Moslem, Christian, infidel, or
Jew.

....The sea, the great white, braided,
bounding sea,
Is laughing in your face; the arching blue
Remains to God; the mountains still are
free,
A refuge for the few remaining tribes and
me.

Your cities! from the first the hand of
God
Has been against them; sword and flood
and flame,
The earthquake's march, and pestilence,
have trod
To undiscerning dust the very name
Of antique capitals; and still the same
Sad destiny besets the battlefields
Of Mammon and the harlot's house of
shame.
Lo! man with monuments and lifted
shields
Against his city's fate. A flame! his city
yields.

ENGLAND.

Thou, mother of brave men, of nations!
Thou,
The white-brow'd Queen of bold white-
bearded Sea!
Thou wert of old ever the same as now,
So strong, so weak, so tame, so fierce, so
bound, so free,
A contradiction and a mystery;
Serene, yet passionate, in ways thine own.
Thy brave ships wind and weave earth's
destiny.
The zones of earth, aye, thou hast set and
sown
All seas in bed of blossom'd sail, as some
great garden blown.

London.

Above yon inland populace the skies
Are pink and mellow'd soft in rosy light.

The crown of earth! A halo seems to rise
And hang perpetual above by night,
And dash by day the heavens, till the sight
Betrays the city's presence to the wave...
You hear a hollow sound as of the might
Of seas; you see the march of fair and brave
In millions; moving, moving, moving toward—a grave.

St. Paul's.

I see above a crowded world a cross
Of gold. It grows like some great cedar tree
Upon a peak in shroud of cloud and moss,
Made bare and bronzed in far antiquity.
Stupendous pile! The grim Yosemite
Has rent apart his granite wall, and thrown
Its rugged front before us.... Here I see
The strides of giant men in cryptic stone,
And turn, and slow descend where sleep the great alone.

The mighty captains have come home to rest;
The brave return'd to sleep amid the brave.
The sentinel that stood with steely breast
Before the fiery hosts of France, and gave
The battle-cry that roll'd, receding wave
On wave, the foeman flying back and far,
Is here. How still! Yet louder now the grave
Than ever-crashing Belgian battle-car
Or blue and battle-shaken seas of Trafalgar.

The verger stalks in stiff importance o'er
The hollow, deep, and strange responding stones;
He stands with lifted staff unchid before
The forms that once had crush'd or fashion'd thrones,
And coldly points you out the coffin'd bones:
He stands composed where armies could not stand
A little time before.... The hand disowns
The idle sword, and now instead the grand
And golden cross makes sign and takes austere command.

Westminster Abbey.

The Abbey broods beside the turbid Thames;
Her mother heart is filled with memories;
Her every niche is stored with storied names;
They move before me like a mist of seas.
I am confused, and made abash'd by these
Most kingly souls, grand, silent, and severe.
I am not equal, I should sore displease
The living....dead. I dare not enter; drear
And stain'd in storms of grander days all things appear.

I go! but shall I not return again
When art has taught me gentler, kindlier skill,
And time has given force and strength of strain?
I go! O ye that dignify and fill
The chronicles of earth! I would instil
Into my soul somehow the atmosphere
Of sanctity that here usurps the will;
But go; I seek the tomb of one—a peer
Of peers—whose dust a fool refused to cherish here.

At Lord Byron's Tomb.

O Master, here I bow before a shrine;
Before the lordliest dust that ever yet
Moved animate in human form divine.
Lo! dust indeed to dust. The mold is set
Above thee and the ancient walls are wet,
And drip all day in dank and silent gloom,
As if the cold gray stones could not forget

Thy great estate shrunk to this somber
room,
But lean to weep perpetual tears above
thy tomb.

Before me lie the oak-crown'd Annesley
hills,
Before me lifts the ancient Annesley Hall
Above the mossy oaks.... A picture fills
With forms of other days. A maiden
tall
And fair; a fiery restless boy, with all
The force of man! a steed that frets without;
A long thin sword that rusts upon the
wall....
The generations pass.... Behold! about
The ivied hall the fair-hair'd children
sport and shout.

A bay wreath, wound by Ina of the
West,
Hangs damp and stain'd upon the dark
gray wall,
Above thy time soil'd tomb and tatter'd
crest;
A bay wreath gather'd by the seas that
call
To orient Cathay, that break and fall
On shell-lined shores before Tahiti's
breeze.
A slab, a crest, a wreath, and these are
all
Neglected, tatter'd, torn; yet only these
The world bestows for song that rivall'd
singing seas.

A bay-wreath wound by one more truly
brave
Than Shastan; fair as thy eternal fame,
She sat and wove above the sunset wave,
And wound and sang thy measures and
thy name.
'Twas wound by one, yet sent with one
acclaim
By many, fair and warm as flowing wine,
And purely true, and tall as growing
flame,
That list and lean in moonlight's mellow
shine
To tropic tales of love in other tongues
than thine.

I bring this idle reflex of thy task,
And my few loves, to thy forgotten tomb;
I leave them here; and here all pardon ask
Of thee, and patience ask of singers whom
Thy majesty hath silenced. I resume
My staff, and now my face is to the West;
My feet are worn; the sun is gone, a gloom
Has mantled Hucknall, and the minstrel's
zest
For fame is broken here, and here he pleads
for rest.

TO REST AT LAST.*

What wonder that I swore a prophet's
oath
Of after days.... I push'd the boughs
apart,
I stood, look'd forth, and then look'd back,
all loath
To leave my shadow'd wood. I gather'd
heart
From very fearfulness; with sudden start
I plunged in the arena; stood a wild
Uncertain thing, all artless, all in art....
The brave approved, the fair lean'd fair and
smiled,—

---

* These final verses are peculiarly descriptive of the home I have built here on the Hights for my declining years; although written and published in London—Songs of the Sunlands—in 1873. True, my strong love of a home of my own, woods, and "a careless ordered garden" led me to settle down in other lands more than

The lions touch with velvet-touch a timid
child.

But now enough of men. Enough, brief
day
Of tamer life. The court, the castle gate
That open'd wide along the pleasant way,
The gracious converse of the kingly great
Had made another glad and well elate
With hope. A world of thanks; but I am
grown
Aweary.... I am not of this estate;
The poor, the plain brave border-men
alone
Were my first love, and these I will not
now disown.

I know a grassy slope above the sea,
The utmost limit of the westmost land.
In savage, gnarl'd, and antique majesty
The great trees belt about the place, and
stand
In guard, with mailéd limb and lifted
hand,
Against the cold approaching civic pride.
The foamy brooklets seaward leap; the
bland
Still air is fresh with touch of wood and
tide,
And peace, eternal peace, possesses wild
and wide.

Here I return, here I abide and rest;
Some flocks and herds shall feed along the
stream;
Some corn and climbing vines shall make
us blest
With bread and luscious fruit.... The sun-
ny dream
Of wampum men in moccasins that seem
To come and go in silence, girt in shell,
Before a sun-clad cabin-door, I deem
The harbinger of peace. Hope weaves her
spell
Again about the wearied heart, and all is
well.

Here I shall sit in sunlit life's decline
Beneath my vine and somber verdant
tree.
Some tawny maids in other tongues than
mine
Shall minister. Some memories shall be
Before me. I shall sit and I shall see,
That last vast day that dawn shall rein-
spire,
The sun fall down upon the farther sea,
Fall wearied down to rest, and so retire,
A splendid sinking isle of far-off fading
fire.

BEFORE CORTEZ CAME!

But see! The day-king hurls a dart
At darkness, and his cold black heart
Is pierced; and now, compell'd to flee,
Flies bleeding to the hollow'd sea.
And now, behold, she radiant stands,
And lifts her round brown jewell'd hands
Unto the broad, unfolding sun,
And hails him Tonatiu and King
With hallow'd mien and holy prayer.
Her fingers o'er some symbols run,
Her knees are bow'd in worshipping
Her God, beheld when thine is not,
In form of faith long, long forgot.

Again she lifts her brown arms bare,
Far flashing in their bands of gold
And precious stones, rare, rich, and old.
Was ever mortal half so fair?

---

once and in places widely different from this which I had fancied and pictured long, long ago, but I was never well or at all content in any place till now. Even the people about me, unworldly, dreamful, silent and of other lands and tongues are, like my home, the same I had pictured more than a quarter of a century ago, and I joy in this, that I have been thus true to myself. The only departure from my dear first plan is in finding my ideal home by the glorious gate of San Francisco instead of the somber fir set sea bank far to the north, "Where Rolls the Oregon."

Was ever such a wealth of hair?
Was ever such a plaintive air?
Was ever such a sweet despair?

Still humbler now her form she bends;
Still higher now the flame ascends:
She bares her bosom to the sun.
Again her jewell'd fingers run
In signs and sacred form and prayer.
She bows with awe and holy air
In lowly worship to the sun;
Then rising calls her lover's name,
And leaps into the leaping flame.

I do not hear the faintest moan,
Or sound, or syllable, or tone.
The red flames stoop a moment down,
As if to raise her from the ground;
They whirl, they swirl, they sweep around
With lightning feet and fiery crown;
Then stand up, tall, tip-toed, as one
Would hand a soul up to the sun.

IN THE SIERRAS.

"No, not so lonely now—I love
A forest maiden: she is mine
And on Sierras' slopes of pine,
The vines below, the snows above,
A solitary lodge is set
Within a fringe of water'd firs;
And there my wigwam fires burn,
Fed by a round brown patient hand,
That small brown faithful hand of hers
That never rests till my return.
The yellow smoke is rising yet;
Tiptoe, and see it where you stand
Lift like a column from the land.

"There are no sea-gems in her hair,
No jewels fret her dimpled hands,
And half her bronzen limbs are bare.
Her round brown arms have golden bands,
Broad, rich, and by her cunning hands
Cut from the yellow virgin ore,
And she does not desire more.
I wear the beaded wampum belt
That she has wove—the sable pelt
That she has fringed red threads around;
And in the morn, when men are not,
I wake the valley with the shot
That brings the brown deer to the ground.
And she beside the lodge at noon
Sings with the wind, while baby swings
In sea-shell cradle by the bough—
Sings low, so like the clover sings
With swarm of bees; I hear her now,
I see her sad face through the moon....
Such songs!—would earth had more of such!
She has not much to say, and she
Lifts never voice to question me
In aught I do....and that is much.
I love her for her patient trust,
And my love's forty-fold return—
A value I have not to learn
As you....at least, as many must....

...."She is not over tall or fair;
Her breasts are curtain'd by her hair,
And sometimes, through the silken fringe,
I see her bosom's wealth, like wine
Burst through in luscious ruddy tinge—
And all its wealth and worth are mine.
I know not that one drop of blood
Of prince or chief is in her veins:
I simply say that she is good,
And loves me with pure womanhood.
.... When that is said, why, what remains?"

MOUNT SHASTA, 1872.

PROPHECY.

When spires shall shine on the Amazon's shore,
From temples of God, and time shall have roll'd

Like a scroll from the border the limitless
wold;
When the tiger is tamed, and the mono no
more
Swings over the waters to chatter and call
To the crocodile sleeping in rushes and
fern;
When cities shall gleam, and their battle-
ments burn
In the sunsets of gold, where the cocoa-
nuts fall,
'Twill be something to lean from the
stars and to know
That the engine, red-mouthing with tur-
bulent tongue,
The white ships that come, and the cargoes
that go,
We invoked them of old when the nations
were young:

'Twill be something to know that we
named them of old,—
That we said to the nations, Lo! here is
the fleece
That allures to the rest, and the perfectest
peace,
With its foldings of sunlight shed mellow
like gold:

That we were the Carsons in kingdoms
untrod,
And follow'd the trail through the rustle of
leaves,
And stood by the wave where solitude
weaves
Her garments of mosses and lonely as
God:

That we did make venture when singers
were young,
Inviting from Europe, from long-trodden
lands
That are easy of journeys, and holy from
hands
Laid upon by the Masters when giants had
tongue:

The prophet should lead us, —and lifting
a hand
To the world on the way, like a white
guiding star,
Point out and allure to the fair and un-
known,
And the far, and the hidden delights of a
land.

Behold my Sierras! there singers shall
throng;
Their white brows shall break through the
wings of the night
As the fierce condor breaks through the
clouds in his flight;
And I here plant the cross and possess
them with song.

QUESTION?

In the days when my mother, the Earth,
was young,
And you all were not, nor the likeness of
you,
She walk'd in her maidenly prime
among
The moonlit stars in the boundless
blue.

Then the great sun lifted his shining
shield,
And he flash'd his sword as the soldiers
do,
And he moved like a king full over the
field,
And he look'd, and he loved her brave and
true.

And looking afar from the ultimate
rim,
As he lay at rest in a reach of light,
He beheld her walking alone at night,
When the buttercup stars in their beauty
swim.

So he rose up flush'd in his love, and he ran,
And he reach'd his arms, and around her waist
He wound them strong like a love-struck man,
And he kiss'd and embraced her, brave and chaste.

So he nursed his love like a babe at its birth,
And he warm'd in his love as the long years ran,
Then embraced her again, and sweet mother Earth
Was a mother indeed, and her child was man.

The sun is the sire, the mother is earth!
What more do you know? what more do I need?
The one he begot, and the one gave birth,
And I love them both, and let laugh at your creed.

And who shall say I am all unwise
In my great, warm faith? Time answers us not:
The quick fool questions; but who replies?
The wise man hesitates, hushed in thought.

THOMAS OF TIGRE.*

King of Tigre, comrade true
Where in all thine isles art thou?
Sailing on Fonseca blue?
Nearing Amapala now?
King of Tigre, where art thou?

Battling for Antilles' queen?
Saber hilt, or olive bough?
Crown of dust, or laurel green?
Roving love, or marriage vow?
King and comrade, where art thou?

Sailing on Pacific seas?
Pitching tent in Pimo now?
Underneath magnolia trees?
Thatch of palm, or cedar bough?
Soldier singer, where art thou?

Coasting on the Oregon?
Saddle bow, or birchen prow?
Round the Isles of Amazon?
Pampas, plain, or mountain brow?
Prince of rovers, where art thou?

MRS. FRANK LESLIE.

I dream'd, O Queen, of thee, last night;
I can but dream of thee to-day.
But dream? Oh! I could kneel and pray
To one, who, like a tender light,

---

*This was a brave old boyhood friend in the Mount Shasta Days. You will find him there as the Prince in my "Life Among the Modocs," "Unwritten History, Paquita," "My Life Among the Indians," "My Own Story," or whatever other name enterprising or piratical publishers, Europe or America, may have chosen to give the one prose book Mulford and I put out in London during the Modoc war. This man, Prince Thomas, now of Leon, Nicaragua, was a great favorite and my best friend, in one sense for years in Europe. He had passed the most adventurous life conceivable, at one time having been king of an island. He gloried in the story of his wild life, spent money like a real prince, and was the envy and admiration of fashionable club men.

"Where in all the world, and when, did he get so much money?" once asked the president of the Savage Club.

"Well, I am not certain whether it was as a pirate of the South Seas or merely as a brigand of Mexico," I answered.

This answer coming to the ears of Thomas, he so far from being angered was greatly pleased and laughed heartily over it with some friends at Lord Houghton's table.

Leads ever on my lonesome way,
And will not pass—yet will not stay.

I dream'd we roam'd in elden land;
I saw you walk in splendid state,
With lifted head and heart elate,
And lilies in your white right hand,
Beneath your proud Saint Peter's dome
That, silent, lords almighty Rome.

A diamond star was in your hair,
Your garments were of gold and snow;
And men did turn and marvel so,
And men did say, How matchless fair!
And all men follow'd as you pass'd;
But I came silent, lone, and last.

And holy men in sable gown,
And girt with cord, and sandal shod,
Did look to thee, and then to God.
They cross'd themselves, with heads held down;
They chid themselves, for fear that they
Should, seeing thee, forget to pray.

Men pass'd, men spake in wooing word;
Men pass'd, ten thousand in a line.
You stood before the sacred shrine,
You stood as if you had not heard.
And then you turn'd in calm command,
And laid two lilies in my hand.

O Lady, if by sea or land
You yet might weary of all men,
And turn unto your singer then,
And lay one lily in his hand,
Lo! I would follow true and far
As seamen track the polar star.

My soul is young, my heart is strong;
O Lady, reach a hand to-day,
And thou shalt walk the milky way,
For I will give thy name to song.
Yea, I am of the kings of thought,
And thou shalt live when kings are not.

THE POET.

Yes, I am a dreamer. Yet while you dream,
Then I am awake. When a child, back through
The gates of the past I peer'd, and I knew
The land I had lived in. I saw a broad stream,
Saw rainbows that compass'd a world in their reach;
I saw my belovéd go down on the beach;
Saw her lean to this earth, saw her looking for me
As shipmen look for loved ship at sea....
While you seek gold in the earth, why, I
See gold in the steeps of the starry sky;
And which do you think has the fairer view
Of God in heaven—the dreamer or you?

DYSPEPTIC.

I am as lone as lost winds on some height;
As lone as yonder leaning moon at night,
That climbs, like some sad, noiseless-footed nun,
Far up against the steep and starry height,
As if on holy mission. Yea, as one
That knows no ark, or isle, or resting-place,
Or chronicle of time, or wheeling sun,
I drive for ever on through endless space.
Like some lone bird in everlasting flight,
My lonesome soul sails on through seas of night.

Alone in sounding hollows of the sea;
Alone on lifted, heaving hills of foam!
To never rest; to ever rise and roam
Where never kind or kindred soul may be;
To roam where ships of commerce never ride,
Sail on, and so forget the rest of shore;

To hear the waves complain, as if they died;
To see the vast waves heave for evermore;
To know that no ships cross or measure these,
My shoreless, strange, and most uncommon seas.

Oh! who art thou, veil'd shape? My soul cries out
Through mist and storm. Lean thou to me!
Come nearer, thou, that I may feel and see
Thy wounded side, and so forget all doubt!
How terrible the night! I kneel to thee;
I clasp thy knees: would clamber to thy hair.
As one shipwreck'd on some broad, broken sea
Through intermingled oaths and awful shout,
Uplifts white hands and prays in his despair,—
So now my curses break into a prayer.

The long days through I sit and sigh, alas!
For love! Lone, beggar-like, beside the way
I sit forlorn in lanes where Day must pass.
I stretch imploring palms toward the Day,
And cry, "O Day! but give me love! I die
For love! I let all other gifts go by.
Yea, bring me but one love that runs to waste,
One love that men pass by in heedless haste,
And I will kiss thy feet and ask no more
From all To-morrow's rich, mysterious store."
The drear days mock me in my mute request;
The dark years roll like breakers on the shore,
And die in futile thunder. As in jest,
They bring bright, empty shells,—bring nothing more.
Oh, say! is sweet Love dead and hid from all
Who would disdain a colder touch than his?
Then show me where Love lies. Put back the pall.
Lo! I will fall upon his face and kiss
Sweet Love to life again; or I will lie,
Lamenting, prone beside his dust, and die.

Behold! my love has brought but rue and rime!
I loved the blushing, bounding, singing Spring:
She scarce would pause a day to hear me sing.
I loved her sister, golden Summer-time:
She gather'd close her robes and rustled past,
Through yellow fields of corn. She scorn'd to cast
One tender look of love or hope behind;
But, sighing, died upon the Autumn wind.
Oh, then I loved the vast, the lonesome Night!
She, too, pass'd on, and perish'd from my sight.

Say! lives there naught on all the girdled world,
That may survive one day its sorry birth?
The very Moon grows thin and hunger-curl'd;
The ardent Sun forgets his love of Earth,
And turns, dark-brow'd, and draws his reach'd arms back,

The while she, mourning, moves on clad in black.
But list! I once did hear the good priest tell
That hell is everlasting. Oh, my friend,
To think that there is aught that will not end!
Now let us kneel and give God thanks that hell is hell.

VALE! AMERICA.*

Let me rise and go forth. A far, dim spark
Illumes my path. The light of my day
Hath fled, and yet am I far away.
The bright, bent moon has dipp'd her horn
In the darkling sea. High up in the dark
The wrinkled old lion, he looks away
To the east, and impatient as if for morn....
I have gone the girdle of earth, and say,
What have I gain'd but a temple gray,
Two crow's feet, and a heart forlorn?

A star starts yonder like a soul afraid!
It falls like a thought through the great profound.
Fearfully swift and with never a sound,
It fades into nothing, as all things fade;
Yea, as all things fail. And where is the leaven
In the pride of a name or a proud man's nod?
Oh, tiresome, tiresome stairs to heaven!
Weary, oh, wearisome ways to God!
'Twere better to sit with the chin on the palm,
Slow tapping the sand, come storm, come calm.

I have lived from within and not from without;
I have drunk from a fount, have fed from a hand
That no man knows who lives upon land;
And yet my soul it is crying out.
I care not a pin for the praise of men;
But I hunger for love. I starve, I die,
Each day of my life. Ye pass me by
Each day, and laugh as ye pass; and when
Ye come, I start in my place as ye come,
And lean, and would speak,—but my lips are dumb.

Yon sliding stars and the changeful moon....
Let me rest on the plains of Lombardy for aye,
Or sit down by this Adrian Sea and die.
The days that do seem as some afternoon
They all are here. I am strong and true
To myself; can pluck and could plant anew
My heart, and grow tall; could come to be
Another being; lift bolder hand
And conquer. Yet ever will come to me
The thought that Italia is not my land.

Could I but return to my woods once more,
And dwell in their depths as I have dwelt,
Kneel in their mosses as I have knelt,
Sit where the cool white rivers run,
Away from the world and half hid from the sun,
Hear winds in the wood of my storm-torn shore,
To tread where only the red man trod,
To say no word, but listen to God!
Glad to the heart with listening,—

---

* I do not like this bit of impatience, nor do I expect any one else to like it and only preserve it here as a sort of landmark or journal in my journey through life. It is only an example of almost an entire book, written in Italy. I had, after a long struggle with myself, settled down in Italy to remain, as I believed, and as you can see was very miserable, and wrote accordingly.

It seems to me that I then could sing,
And sing as never sung man before.

But deep-tangled woodland and wild waterfall,
O farewell for aye, till the Judgment Day!
I shall see you no more, O land of mine,
O half-aware land, like a child at play!
O voiceless and vast as the push'd-back skies!
No more, blue seas in the blest sunshine,
No more, black woods where the white peaks rise,
No more, bleak plains where the high winds fall,
Or the red man keeps or the shrill birds call!

I must find diversion with another kind:
There are roads on the land and roads on the sea;
Take ship and sail, and sail till I find
The love that I sought from eternity;
Run away from oneself, take ship and sail
The middle white seas; see turban'd men,—
Throw thought to the dogs for aye. And when
All seas are travel'd and all scenes fail,
Why, then this doubtful, cursed gift of verse
May save me from death—or something worse.

My hand it is weary, and my harp unstrung;
And where is the good that I pipe or sing,
Fashion new notes, or shape any thing?
The songs of my rivers remain unsung
Henceforward for me....But a man shall arise
From the far, vast valleys of the Occident,
With hand on a harp of gold, and with eyes
That lift with glory and a proud intent;
Yet so gentle indeed, that his sad heart-strings
Shall thrill to the heart of your heart as he sings.

Let the wind sing songs in the lake-side reeds,
Lo, I shall be less than the indolent wind!
Why should I sow, when I reap and bind
And gather in nothing but the thistle weeds?
It is best I abide, let what will befall;
To rest if I can, let time roll by:
Let others endeavor to learn, while I,
With naught to conceal, with much to regret,
Shall sit and endeavor, alone, to forget.

Shall I shape pipes from these seaside reeds,
And play for the children, that shout and call?
Lo! men they have mock'd me the whole year through!
I shall sing no more ...I shall find in old creeds,
And in quaint old tongues, a world that is new;
And these, I will gather the sweets of them all.
And the old-time doctrines and the old-time signs,
I will taste of them all, as tasting old wines.

I will find new thought, as a new-found vein
Of rock-lock'd gold in my far, fair West.
I will rest and forget, will entreat to be blest;
Take up new thought and again grow young;
Yea, take a new world as one born again,
And never hear more mine own mother tongue;

Nor miss it. Why should I? I never once
heard,
In my land's language, love's one sweet
word.

Did I court fame, or the favor of
man?
Make war upon creed, or strike hand with
clan?
I sang my songs of the sounding
trees,
As careless of name or of fame as the
sea;
And these I sang for the love of these,
And the sad sweet solace they brought to
me.
I but sang for myself, touch'd here, touch'd
there,
As a strong-wing'd bird that flies any-
where.

....How I do wander! And yet why
not?
I once had a song, told a tale in rhyme;
Wrote books, indeed, in my proud young
prime;
I aim'd at the heart like a musket
ball;
I struck cursed folly like a cannon
shot,—
And where is the glory or good of it
all?
Yet these did I write for my land, but
this
I write for myself,—and it is as it is.

Yea, storms have blown counter and
shaken me.
And yet was I fashion'd for strife, and
strong
And daring of heart, and born to en-
dure;
My soul sprang upward, my feet felt
sure;
My faith was as wide as a wide-bough'd
tree.
But there be limits; and a sense of
wrong
Forever before you will make you less
A man, than a man at first would guess.

Good men can forgive—and, they say,
forget....
Far less of the angel than Indian was
set
In my fierce nature. And I look
away
To a land that is dearer than this, and
say,
"I shall remember, though you may for-
get.
Yea, I shall remember for aye and a
day
The keen taunts thrown in a boy face,
when
He cried unto God for the love of men."

Enough, ay and more than enough, of
this!
I know that the sunshine must follow the
rain;
And if this be the winter, why spring
again
Must come in its season, full blossom'd
with bliss.
I will lean to the storm, though the winds
blow strong....
Yea, the winds they have blown and have
shaken me—
As the winds blow songs through a shat-
tered tree,
They have blown this broken and careless
set song.

They have sung this song, be it never
bad;
Have blown upon me and play'd upon
me,

Have broken the notes,—blown sad, blown glad;
Just as the winds blow fierce and free
A barren, a blighted, and a cursed fig tree.
And if I grow careless and heed no whit
Whether it please or what comes of it,
Why, talk to the winds, then, and not to me.

VENICE, 1874.

THE QUEST OF LOVE.*

The quest of love? 'Tis the quest of troubles;
'Tis the wind through the woods of the Oregon.
Sit down, sit down, for the world goes on
Precisely the same; and the rainbow bubbles
Of love, they gather, or break, or blow,
Whether you bother your brain or no;
And for all your troubles and all your tears,
'Twere just the same in a hundred years.

By the populous land, or the lonesome sea,
Lo! these were the gifts of the gods to men,—
Three miserable gifts, and only three:
To love, to forget, and to die—and then?
To love in peril, and bitter-sweet pain,
And then, forgotten, lie down and die:
One moment of sun, whole seasons of rain,
Then night is roll'd to the door of the sky.

To love? To sit at her feet and to weep;
To climb to her face, hide your face in her hair;
To nestle you there like a babe in its sleep,
And, too, like a babe, to believe—it stings there!
To love! 'Tis to suffer, "Lie close to my breast,
Like a fair ship in haven, O darling!" I cried.
"Your round arms outreaching to heaven for rest
Make signal to death."....Death came, and love died.
To forget? To forget, mount horse and clutch sword;
Take ship and make sail to the ice-prison'd seas,
Write books and preach lies; range lands; or go hoard
A grave full of gold, and buy wines—and drink lees:
Then die; and die cursing, and call it a prayer!
Is earth but a top—a boy-god's delight,
To be spun for his pleasure, while man's despair
Breaks out like a wail of the damn'd through the night?

Sit down in the darkness and weep with me
On the edge of the world. Lo, love lies dead!
And the earth and the sky, and the sky and the sea,
Seem shutting together as a book that is read.

* Fragment from a long poem done in Italy.

Yet what have we learn'd? We laugh'd with delight
In the morning at school, and kept toying with all
Time's silly playthings. Now, wearied ere night,
We must cry for dark-mother, her cradle the pall.

'Twere better blow trumpets 'gainst love, keep away
That traitorous urchin with fire or shower,
Than have him come near you for one little hour.
Take physic, consult with your doctor, as you
Would fight a contagion; carry all through
The populous day some drug that smells loud,
As you pass on your way, or make way through the crowd.
Talk war, or carouse; only keep off the day
Of his coming, with every hard means in your way.

Blow smoke in the eyes of the world, and laugh
With the broad-chested men, as you loaf at your inn,
As you crowd to your inn from your saddle and quaff
Red wine from a horn; while your dogs at your feet,
Your slim spotted dogs, like the fawn, and as fleet,
Crouch patiently by and look up at your face,
As they wait for the call of the horn to the chase;
For you shall not suffer, and you shall not sin,
Until peace goes out just as love comes in.

Love horses and hounds, meet many good men—
Yea, men are most proper, and keep you from care.
There is strength in a horse. There is pride in his will;
It is sweet to look back as you climb the steep hill.
There is room. You have movement of limb; you have air,
Have the smell of the wood, of the grasses; and then
What comfort to rest, as you lie thrown full length
All night and alone, with your fists full of strength!
Go away, go away with your bitter-sweet pain
Of love; for love is the story of troubles,
Of troubles and love, that travel together
The round world round. Behold the bubbles
Of love! Then troubles and turbulent weather.
Why, man had all Eden! Then love, then Cain!

AFRICA.

Oh! she is very old. I lay,
Made dumb with awe and wonderment,
Beneath a palm before my tent,
With idle and discouraged hands,
Not many days ago, on sands
Of awful, silent Africa.
Long gazing on her ghostly shades,
That lift their bare arms in the air,

I lay. I mused where story fades
From her dark brow and found her fair.

A slave, and old, within her veins
There runs that warm, forbidden blood
That no man dares to dignify
In elevated song. The chains
That held her race but yesterday
Hold still the hands of men. Forbid
Is Ethiop. The turbid flood
Of prejudice lies stagnant still,
And all the world is tainted. Will
And wit lie broken as a lance
Against the brazen mailèd face
Of old opinion. None advance,
Steel-clad and glad, to the attack,
With trumpet and with song. Look back!
Beneath yon pyramids lie hid
The histories of her great race....
Old Nilus rolls right sullen by,
With all his secrets. Who shall say:
My father rear'd a pyramid;
My brother clipp'd the dragon's wings;
My mother was Semiramis?
Yea, harps strike idly out of place;
Men sing of savage Saxon kings
New-born and known but yesterday,
And Norman blood presumes to say....

Nay, ye who boast ancestral name
And vaunt deeds dignified by time
Must not despise her. Who hath worn
Since time began a face that is
So all-enduring, old like this—
A face like Africa's? Behold!
The Sphinx is Africa. The bond
Of silence is upon her. Old
And white with tombs, and rent and shorn;
With raiment wet with tears, and torn,
And trampled on, yet all untamed;
All naked now, yet not ashamed,—
The mistress of the young world's prime,
Whose obelisks still laugh at time,
And lift to heaven her fair name,
Sleeps satisfied upon her fame.

Beyond the Sphinx, and still beyond,
Beyond the tawny desert-tomb
Of Time; beyond tradition, loom
And lifts, ghost-like, from out the gloom,
Her thousand cities, battle-torn
And gray with story and with Time.
Her humblest ruins are sublime;
Her thrones with mosses overborne
Make velvets for the feet of Time.

She points a hand and cries: "Go read
The letter'd obelisks that lord
Old Rome, and know my name and deed.
My archives these, and plunder'd when
I had grown weary of all men."
We turn to these; we cry: "Abhorr'd
Old Sphinx, behold, we cannot read!"

CROSSING THE PLAINS.

What great yoked brutes with briskets low,
With wrinkled necks like buffalo,
With round, brown, liquid, pleading eyes,
That turn'd so slow and sad to you,
That shone like love's eyes soft with tears,
That seem'd to plead, and make replies,
The while they bow'd their necks and drew
The creaking load; and look'd at you.
Their sable briskets swept the ground,
Their cloven feet kept solemn sound.

Two sullen bullocks led the line,
Their great eyes shining bright like wine;

Two sullen captive kings were they,
That had in time held herds at bay,
And even now they crush'd the sod
With stolid sense of majesty,
And stately stepp'd and stately trod,
As if 'twere something still to be
Kings even in captivity.

THE MEN OF FORTY-NINE.

Those brave old bricks of forty-nine!
What lives they lived! what deaths they died!
A thousand cañons, darkling wide
Below Sierra's slopes of pine,
Receive them now. And they who died
Along the far, dim, desert route—
Their ghosts are many. Let them keep
Their vast possessions. The Piute,
The tawny warrior, will dispute
No boundary with these. And I
Who saw them live, who felt them die,
Say, let their unplow'd ashes sleep,
Untouch'd by man, on plain or steep.

The bearded, sunbrown'd men who bore
The burden of that frightful year,
Who toil'd, but did not gather store,
They shall not be forgotten. Drear
And white, the plains of Shoshonee
Shall point us to that farther shore,
And long, white, shining lines of bones,
Make needless sign or white mile-stones.

The wild man's yell, the groaning wheel;
The train that moved like drifting barge;
The dust that rose up like a cloud—
Like smoke of distant battle! Loud
The great whips rang like shot, and steel
Of antique fashion, crude and large,
Flash'd back as in some battle charge.

They sought, yea, they did find their rest.
Along that long and lonesome way,
These brave men buffet'd the West
With lifted faces. Full were they
Of great endeavor. Brave and true
As stern Crusader clad in steel,
They died a-field as it was fit.
Made strong with hope, they dared to do
Achievement that a host to-day
Would stagger at, stand back and reel,
Defeated at the thought of it.

What brave endeavor to endure!
What patient hope, when hope was past!
What still surrender at the last,
A thousand leagues from hope! how pure
They lived, how proud they died!
How generous with life! The wide
And gloried age of chivalry
Hath not one page like this to me.

Let all these golden days go by,
In sunny summer weather. I
But think upon my buried brave,
And breathe beneath another sky.
Let Beauty glide in gilded car,
And find my sundown seas afar,
Forgetful that 'tis but one grave
From eastmost to the westmost wave.

Yea, I remember! The still tears
That o'er uncoffin'd faces fell!
The final, silent, sad farewell!
God! these are with me all the years!
They shall be with me ever. I
Shall not forget. I hold a trust.
They are part of my existence. When

Swift down the shining iron track
You sweep, and fields of corn flash back,
And herds of lowing steers move by,
And men laugh loud, in mute mistrust,
I turn to other days, to men
Who made a pathway with their dust.

NAPLES, 1874.

THE HEROES OF AMERICA.

O perfect heroes of the earth,
That conquer'd forests, harvest set!
O sires, mothers of my West!
How shall we count your proud bequest?
But yesterday ye gave us birth;
We eat your hard-earn'd bread to-day,
Nor toil nor spin nor make regret,
But praise our petty selves and say
How great we are. We all forget
The still endurance of the rude
Unpolish'd sons of solitude.

What strong, uncommon men were these,
These settlers hewing to the seas!
Great horny-handed men and tan;
Men blown from many a barren land
Beyond the sea; men red of hand,
And men in love, and men in debt,
Like David's men in battle set;
And men whose very hearts had died,
Who only sought these woods to hide
Their wretchedness, held in the van;
Yet every man among them stood
Alone, along that sounding wood,
And every man somehow a man.
They push'd the mailéd wood aside,
They toss'd the forest like a toy,
That grand forgotten race of men—
The boldest band that yet has been
Together since the siege of Troy.

SAN FRANCISCO, 1871.

ATTILA'S THRONE: TORCELLO.

I do recall some sad days spent
By borders of the Orient,
'Twould make a tale. It matters not.
I sought the loneliest seas; I sought
The solitude of ruins, and forgot
Mine own life and my littleness
Before this fair land's mute distress.

Slow sailing through the reedy isles,
Some sunny summer yesterdays,
I watched the storied yellow sail,
And lifted prow of steely mail
'Tis all that's left Torcello now,—
A pirate's yellow sail, a prow.

I touch'd Torcello. Once on land,
I took a sea-shell in my hand,
And blew like any trumpeter.
I felt the fig leaves lift and stir
On trees that reach from ruin'd wall
Above my head,—but that was all.
Back from the farther island shore
Came echoes trooping—nothing more.

By cattle paths grass-grown and worn,
Through marbled streets all stain'd and torn
By time and battle, lone I walk'd.
A bent old beggar, white as one
For better fruitage blossoming,
Came on. And as he came he talk'd
Unto himself; for there were none
In all his island, old and dim,
To answer back or question him.
I turn'd, retraced my steps once more.
The hot miasma steam'd and rose
In deadly vapor from the reeds
That grew from out the shallow shore,
Where peasants say the sea-horse feeds,
And Neptune shapes his horn and blows

Yet here stood Adria once, and here
Attila came with sword and flame,

And set his throne of hollow'd stone
In her high mart. And it remains
Still lord o'er all. Where once the tears
Of mute petition fell, the rains
Of heaven fall. Lo! all alone
There lifts this massive empty throne.

I climb'd and sat that throne of stone
To contemplate, to dream, to reign—
Ay, reign above myself; to call
The people of the past again
Before me as I sat alone
In all my kingdom. There were kine
That browsed along the reedy brine,
And now and then a tusky boar
Would shake the high reeds of the shore,
A bird blow by,—but that was all.

I watch'd the lonesome sea-gull pass.
I did remember and forget,—
The past roll'd by; I lived alone.
I sat the shapely, chisell'd stone
That stands in tall, sweet grasses set;
Ay, girdle deep in long, strong grass,
And green alfalfa. Very fair
The heavens were, and still and blue,
For Nature knows no changes there.
The Alps of Venice, far away,
Like some half-risen late moon lay.

How sweet the grasses at my feet!
The smell of clover over-sweet.
I heard the hum of bees. The bloom
Of clover-tops and cherry-trees
Was being rifled by the bees,
And these were building in a tomb.
The fair alfalfa—such as has
Usurp'd the Occident, and grows
With all the sweetness of the rose
On Sacramento's sundown hills—
Is there, and that dead island fills
With fragrance. Yet the smell of death
Comes riding in on every breath.

That sad, sweet fragrance. It had sense,
And sound, and voice. It was a part
Of that which had possess'd my heart,
And would not of my will go hence.
'Twas Autumn's breath; 'twas sad as kiss
Of some sweet worshipp'd woman is.

Some snails had climb'd the throne and writ
Their silver monograms on it
In unknown tongues. I sat thereon,
I dream'd until the day was gone;
I blew again my pearly shell,—
Blew long and strong, and loud and well;
I puff'd my cheeks, I blew as when
Horn'd satyrs piped and danced as men.

Some mouse-brown cows that fed within
Look'd up. A cowherd rose hard by,
My single subject, clad in skin,
Nor yet half-clad. I caught his eye,—
He stared at me, then turn'd and fled.
He frighten'd fled, and as he ran,
Like wild beast from the face of man,
Back o'er his shoulder threw his head.
He stopp'd, and then this subject true,
Mine only one in all the isle,
Turn'd round, and, with a fawning smile,
Came back and ask'd me for a *sou!*

WESTWARD HO!

What strength! what strife! what rude unrest!
What shocks! what half-shaped armies met!
A mighty nation moving west,
With all its steely sinews set
Against the living forests. Hear
The shouts, the shots of pioneer,

The rended forests, rolling wheels,
As if some half-check'd army reels,
Recoils, redoubles, comes again,
Loud sounding like a hurricane.

O bearded, stalwart, westmost men,
So tower-like, so Gothic built!
A kingdom won without the guilt
Of studied battle, that hath been
Your blood's inheritance.... Your heirs
Know not your tombs: The great plow-shares
Cleave softly through the mellow loam
Where you have made eternal home,
And set no sign. Your epitaphs
Are writ in furrows. Beauty laughs
While through the green ways wandering
Beside her love, slow gathering
White starry-hearted May-time blooms
Above your lowly level'd tombs;
And then below the spotted sky
She stops, she leans, she wonders why
The ground is heaved and broken so,
And why the grasses darker grow
And droop and trail like wounded wing.

Yea, Time, the grand old harvester,
Has gather'd you from wood and plain.
We call to you again, again;
The rush and rumble of the car
Comes back in answer. Deep and wide
The wheels of progress have passed on;
The silent pioneer is gone.
His ghost is moving down the trees,
And now we push the memories
Of bluff, bold men who dared and died
In foremost battle, quite aside.

VENICE.

City at sea, thou art surely an ark,
Sea-blown and a-wreck in the rain and dark,
Where the white sea-caps are so toss'd and curl'd.
Thy sins they were many—and behold the flood!
And here and about us are beasts in stud.
Creatures and beasts that creep and go,
Enough, ay, and wicked enough I know,
To populate, or devour, a world.

O wrinkled old lion, looking down
With brazen frown upon mine and me,
From tower a-top of your watery town,
Old king of the desert, once king of the sea:
List! here is a lesson for thee to-day.
Proud and immovable monarch, I say,
Lo! here is a lesson to-day for thee,
Of the things that were and the things to be.

Dank palaces held by the populous sea
For the good dead men, all cover'd with shell,—
We will pay them a visit some day; and we,
We may come to love their old palaces well.
Bah! toppled old columns all tumbled across,
Toss'd in the waters that lift and fall,
Waving in waves long masses of moss,
Toppled old columns,—and that will be all.

I know you, lion of gray Saint Mark;
You flutter'd all seas beneath your wing.
Now, over the deep, and up in the dark,
High over the girdles of bright gaslight,
With wings in the air as if for flight,
And crouching as if about to spring
From top of your granite of Africa,—

Say, what shall be said of you some
day?

What shall be said, O grim Saint Mark,
Savage old beast so cross'd and churl'd,
By the after-men from the under-world?
What shall be said as they search along
And sail these seas for some sign or spark
Of the old dead fires of the dear old days,
When men and story have gone their
ways,
Or even your city and name from song?

Why, sullen old monarch of still'd Saint
Mark,
Strange men of my West, wise-mouth'd
and strong,
Will come some day and, gazing long
And mute with wonder, will say of thee:
"This is the Saint! High over the dark,
Foot on the Bible and great teeth bare,
Tail whipp'd back and teeth in the air—
Lo! this is the Saint, and none but he!"

A HAILSTORM IN VENICE.

The hail like cannon-shot struck the
sea
And churn'd it white as a creamy foam;
Then hail like battle-shot struck where we
Stood looking a-sea from a sea-girt home—
Came shooting askance as if shot at the
head;
Then glass flew shiver'd and men fell
down
And pray'd where they fell, and the gray
old town
Lay riddled and helpless as if shot dead.

Then lightning right full in the eyes!
and then
Fair women fell down flat on the face,
And pray'd their pitiful Mother with tears,
And pray'd black death as a hiding-place;
And good priests pray'd for the sea-bound
men
As never good priests had pray'd for
years....
Then God spake thunder! And then the
rain!
The great, white, beautiful, high-born
rain!

SANTA MARIA: TORCELLO.

And yet again through the watery miles
Of reeds I row'd, till the desolate isles
Of the black-bead makers of Venice were
not.
I touch'd where a single sharp tower is
shot
To heaven, and torn by thunder and rent
As if it had been Time's battlement.
A city lies dead, and this great grave-
stone
Stands on its grave like a ghost alone.

Some cherry-trees grow here, and here
An old church, simple and severe
In ancient aspect, stands alone
Amid the ruin and decay, all grown
In moss and grasses. Old and quaint,
With antique cuts of martyr'd saint,
The gray church stands with stooping
knees,
Defying the decay of seas.

Her pictured hell, with flames blown
high,
In bright mosaics wrought and set
When man first knew the Nubian art;
Her bearded saints as black as jet;
Her quaint Madonna, dim with rain
And touch of pious lips of pain,
So touch'd my lonesome soul, that I

Gazed long, then came and gazed again,
And loved, and took her to my heart.

Nor monk in black, nor Capucin,
Nor priest of any creed was seen.
A sunbrown'd woman, old and tall,
And still as any shadow is,
Stole forth from out the mossy wall
With massive keys to show me this:
Came slowly forth, and, following,
Three birds—and all with drooping wing.

Three mute brown babes of hers; and they—
Oh, they were beautiful as sleep,
Or death, below the troubled deep!
And on the pouting lips of these,
Red corals of the silent seas,
Sweet birds, the everlasting seal
Of silence that the God has set
On this dead island sits for aye.

I would forget, yet not forget
Their helpless eloquence. They creep
Somehow into my heart, and keep
One bleak, cold corner, jewel set.
They steal my better self away
To them, as little birds that day
Stole fruits from out the cherry-trees.

So helpless and so wholly still,
So sad, so wrapt in mute surprise,
That I did love, despite my will.
One little maid of ten—such eyes,
So large and lovely, so divine!
Such pouting lips, such pearly cheek!
Did lift her perfect eyes to mine,
Until our souls did touch and speak—
Stood by me all that perfect day,
Yet not one sweet word could she say.

She turn'd her melancholy eyes
So constant to my own, that I
Forgot the going clouds, the sky;
Found fellowship, took bread and wine:
And so her little soul and mine
Stood very near together there.
And oh, I found her very fair!
Yet not one soft word could she say:
What did she think of all that day?

CARMEN.

Not that I deem'd she loved me. Nay,
I dared not even dream of that.
I do but say I knew her; say
She sat in dreams before me, sat
All still and voiceless as love is—
But say her soul was warm as wine,
But say it overflow'd in mine,
And made itself a part of this.

The conversation of her eyes
Was language of the gods. Her breast
Was their abiding place of rest;
Her heart their gate to Paradise.
Her heart, her heart! 'Tis shut, ah me!
'Tis shut, and I have lost the key.

The prayer of love breaks to an oath...
No matter if she loved or no,
God knows I loved enough for both,
That day of days, so dear, so fond;
And knew her, as you shall not know
Till you have known sweet death, and you
Have cross'd the dark; gone over to
The great majority beyond.

TO THE JERSEY LILY.

If all God's world a garden were,
And women were but flowers.
If men were bees that busied there,
Through endless summer hours,
O I would hum God's garden through
For honey till I came to you.

IN A GONDOLA.

Twas night in Venice. Then down to the
tide,
Where a tall and a shadowy gondolier
Lean'd on his oar, like a lifted spear;—
'Twas night in Venice; then side by side
We sat in his boat. Then oar a-trip
On the black boat's keel, then dip and dip,
These boatmen should build their boats
more wide,
For we were together, and side by side.

The sea it was level as seas of light,
As still as the light ere a hand was laid
To the making of lands, or the seas were
made.
'Twas fond as a bride on her bridal night
When a great love swells in her soul like a
sea,
And makes her but less than divinity.
'Twas night,—The soul of the day, I wis.
A woman's face hiding from her first kiss.

....Ah, how one wanders! Yet after it
all,
To laugh at all lovers and to learn to
scoff....
When you really have naught of account
to say,
It is better, perhaps, to pull leaves by the
way;
Watch the round moon rise, or the red
stars fall;
And then, too, in Venice! dear, moth-
eaten town;
One palace of pictures; great frescoes
spill'd down
Outside the walls from the fullness there-
of:—

'Twas night in Venice. On o'er the
tide—
These boats they are narrow as they can
be,
These crafts they are narrow enough, and
we,
To balance the boat, sat side by side—
Out under the arch of the Bridge of Sighs,
On under the arch of the star-sown skies;
We two were together on the Adrian Sea,—
The one fair woman of the world to me.

I was vain enough to be persuaded—London, 1877-8—into publishing two fat volumes of my "complete" poems. The work was dedicated to Lord Houghton, who generously gave permission without looking it over. But he had the good taste to dislike the empty verbosity, imitations and all such weaknesses of the mass, and had the gentility to promptly tell me so. Better still, he took a pencil and struck out much. Braver still, he heartily indorsed many descriptions of men and things in the West, and here and there wrote "Pictures! Pictures." And so in memory of the most helpful friend I ever had I have put these bits together here, along with some others of like character, and called them Pictures.

Yet Houghton was not so stoutly my friend at first, and came forward only tardily as the rightful and undisputed head of literary and social London, after I had my first success. But on my third and fourth visits to Europe, and when the pitiful jackals were loud in my land, then he took me to his heart and to his hearthstone. So that I am indebted to the small enmities of America for his great friendship. You may remember it was he who was first to know Keats; and the last, too. For he it was who set up that stone with the poetical inscription, Here lies one whose name was writ in water." And for half a century Houghton kept that lowly grave the greenest and pleasantest in all Rome; literally kept "The daisies growing over me."

I see in the first volume of his biography, newly out, that he and Gladstone had some exchange of letters about myself; and from this I suspect I owe this brave nobleman far more than he ever let me know. In his last letter, written from Greece when no longer strong, he says: "I command you accept the invitation to spend a season with Mr. Gladstone at Hawarden Castle. It is your duty to yourself and your great country to learn how the real king of England lives."

Here ends, as a rule, my earlier poems; that is such as were written or outlined before going abroad; also such as were written in or of other lands. Of course no sharp lines can be drawn between old and new, if we follow date of production, nor is that important. I only wish to point out that the place for a man to write is in his own country, of his own land and out of his own heart. He must have a home and he must have a heart for that home. True, some of these last and best poems were begun and even published in Italy, but they never could have been finished there. Much of this foreign work is left out entirely, as beyond repair; for it was nearly all sad, even sickly. Song should be glad, lofty, beautiful. Besides some of it was bitter. As to whether I had a right to feel so utterly miserable in my exile does not matter now. I am thankful for the strength that kept me silent and the courage that brought me home to the brave and bright young lovers of the beautiful Truth by the sea of seas. Those of the new generation who gather about me see no reason why a man may not win fame or friends abroad if he can, and I would not have them see one word of bitterness in this book. For truly there is nothing of the sort in my heart now at the last.

LATER POEMS.

My Mountains still are free!
They hurl oppression back;
They keep the boon of liberty.

THE GOLD THAT GREW BY SHASTA TOWN.

From Shasta town to Redding town
The ground is torn by miners dead;
The manzanita, rank and red,
Drops dusty berries up and down
Their grass-grown trails. Their silent mines
Are wrapped in chaparral and vines;
Yet one gray miner still sits down
'Twixt Redding and sweet Shasta town.

The quail pipes pleasantly. The hare
Leaps careless o'er the golden oat
That grows below the water moat;
The lizard basks in sunlight there.
The brown hawk swims the perfumed air
Unfrightened through the livelong day;
And now and then a curious bear
Comes shuffling down the ditch by night,
And leaves some wide, long tracks in clay
So human-like, so stealthy light,
Where one lone cabin still stoops down
'Twixt Redding and sweet Shasta town.

That great graveyard of hopes! of men
Who sought for hidden veins of gold;
Of young men suddenly grown old—
Of old men dead, despairing when
The gold was just within their hold!
That storied land, whereon the light
Of other days gleams faintly still;
Somelike the halo of a hill
That lifts above the falling night;
That warm, red, rich and human land,
That flesh-red soil, that warm red sand,
Where one gray miner still sits down!
'Twixt Redding and sweet Shasta town!

"I know the vein is here!" he said;
For twenty years, for thirty years!
While far away fell tears on tears
From wife and babe who mourned him dead.
No gold! No gold! And he grew old
And crept to toil with bended head
Amid a graveyard of his dead,
Still seeking for that vein of gold.

Then lo, came laughing down the years
A sweet grandchild! Between his tears
He laughed. He set her by the door
The while he toiled; his day's toil o'er
He held her chubby cheeks between
His hard palms, laughed; and laughing cried.
You should have seen, have heard and seen
His boyish joy, his stout old pride,
When toil was done and he sat down
At night, below sweet Shasta town!

At last his strength was gone. "No more!
I mine no more. I plant me now
A vine and fig-tree; worn and old,
I seek no more my vein of gold.

But, oh, I sigh to give it o'er;
These thirty years of toil! somehow
It seems so hard; but now, no more."

And so the old man set him down
To plant, by pleasant Shasta town.
And it was pleasant; piped the quail
The full year through. The chipmunk stole,
His whiskered nose and tossy tail
Full buried in the sugar-bowl.

And purple grapes and grapes of gold
Swung sweet as milk. While orange-trees
Grew brown with laden honey-bees.
Oh! it was pleasant up and down
That vine-set hill of Shasta town.

* * * * * * *

And then that cloud-burst came! Ah, me!
That torn ditch there! The mellow land
Rolled seaward like a rope of sand,
Nor left one leafy vine or tree
Of all that Eden nestling down
Below that moat by Shasta town!

* * * * * * *

The old man sat his cabin's sill,
His gray head bowed to hands and knee;
The child went forth, sang pleasantly,
Where burst the ditch the the day before,
And picked some pebbles from the hill.
The old man moaned, moaned o'er and o'er:
"My babe is dowerless, and I
Must fold my helpless hands and die!
Ah, me! What curse comes ever down
On me and mine at Shasta town."

"Good Grandpa, see!" the glad child said,
And so leaned softly to his side,—
Laid her gold head to his gray head,
And merry voiced and cheery cried,
"Good Grandpa, do not weep, but see!
I've found a peck of orange seeds!
I searched the hill for vine or tree;
Not one!—not even oats or weeds;
But, oh! such heaps of orange seeds!

"Come, good Grandpa! Now, once you said
That God is good. So this may teach
That we must plant each seed, and each
May grow to be an orange tree.
Now, good Grandpa, please raise your head,
And please come plant the seeds with me."
And prattling thus, or like to this,
The child thrust her full hands in his.

He sprang, sprang upright as of old.
"'Tis gold! 'tis gold! my hidden vein!
'Tis gold for you, sweet babe, 'tis gold!
Yea, God is good; we plant again!"
So one old miner still sits down
By pleasant, sunlit Shasta town.

THE SIOUX CHIEF'S DAUGHTER.

Two gray hawks ride the rising blast;
Dark cloven clouds drive to and fro
By peaks pre-eminent in snow;
A sounding river rushes past,
So wild, so vortex-like, and vast.

A lone lodge tops the windy hill;
A tawny maiden, mute and still,
Stands waiting at the river's brink,
As eager, fond as you can think.
A mighty chief is at her feet;
She does not heed him wooing so—
She hears the dark, wild waters flow;
She waits her lover, tall and fleet,
From out far beaming hills of snow.

He comes! The grim chief springs in air—
His brawny arm, his blade is bare.

She turns; she lifts her round, brown
hand;
She looks him fairly in the face;
She moves her foot a little pace
And says, with calmness and command,
"There's blood enough in this lorn land.

"But see! a test of strength and skill,
Of courage and fierce fortitude;
To breast and wrestle with the rude
And storm-born waters, now I will
Bestow you both.

".......... Stand either side!
And you, my burly chief, I know
Would choose my right. Now peer you low
Across the waters wild and wide.
See! leaning so this morn I spied
Red berries dip yon farther side.

"See, dipping, dripping in the stream!
Twin boughs of autumn berries gleam!

"Now this, brave men, shall be the test:
Plunge in the stream, bear knife in teeth
To cut yon bough for bridal wreath.
Plunge in! and he who bears him best,
And brings yon ruddy fruit to land
The first, shall have both heart and hand."

Two tawny men, tall, brown and thewed
Like antique bronzes rarely seen,
Shot up like flame.

She stood between
Like fixed, impassive fortitude.
Then one threw robes with sullen air,
And wound red fox-tails in his hair;
But one with face of proud delight
Entwined a wing of snowy white.

She stood between. She sudden gave
The sign and each impatient brave
Shot sudden in the sounding wave;
The startled waters gurgled round;
Their stubborn strokes kept sullen sound.

Oh, then uprose the love that slept!
Oh, then her heart beat loud and strong!
Oh, then the proud love pent up long
Broke forth in wail upon the air!
And leaning there she sobbed and wept,
With dark face mantled in her hair

She sudden lifts her leaning brow.
He nears the shore, her love! and now
The foam flies spouting from the face
That laughing lifts from out the race.

The race is won, the work is done!
She sees the kingly crest of snow;
She knows her tall, brown Idaho.
She cries aloud, she laughing cries,
And tears are streaming from her eyes:
"O splendid, kingly Idaho!
I kiss thy lifted crest of snow.

"My tall and tawny king, come back!
Come swift, O sweet! why falter so?
Come! Come! What thing has crossed
your track?
I kneel to all the gods I know....
Great Spirit, what is this I dread?
Why, there is blood! the wave is red!
That wrinkled chief, outstripped in race,
Dives down, and, hiding from my face,
Strikes underneath.

" . . . He rises now!
Now plucks my hero's berry bough,
And lifts aloft his red fox head,
And signals he has won for me. . . .
Hist, softly! Let him come and see.

"Oh, come! my white-crowned hero,
come!
Oh, come! and I will be your bride,

Despite yon chieftain's craft and might.
Come back to me! my lips are dumb,
My hands are helpless with despair;
The hair you kissed, my long, strong hair,
Is reaching to the ruddy tide,
That you may clutch it when you come.

"How slow he buffets back the wave!
O God, he sinks! O Heaven! save
My brave, brave king! He rises! see!
Hold fast, my hero! Strike for me.
Strike straight this way! Strike firm and strong!
Hold fast your strength. It is not long—
O God, he sinks! He sinks! Is gone!

"And did I dream and do I wake?
Or did I wake and now but dream?
And what is this crawls from the stream?
Oh, here is some mad, mad mistake!
What, you! the red fox at my feet?
You first, and failing from the race?
What! You have brought me berries red?
What! You have brought your bride a wreath?
You sly red fox with wrinkled face—
That blade has blood between your teeth!

"Lie low! lie low! while I lean o'er
And clutch your red blade to the shore. . .
Ha! ha! Take that! take that and that!
Ha! ha! So, through your coward throat
The full day shines!.... Two fox-tails float
Far down, and I but mock thereat.

"But what is this? What snowy crest
Climbs out the willows of the west,
All dripping from his streaming hair?
'Tis he! My hero brave and fair!
His face is lifting to my face,
And who shall now dispute the race?

"The gray hawks pass, O love! and doves
O'er yonder lodge shall coo their loves.
My hands shall heal your wounded breast,
And in yon tall lodge two shall rest."

TO THE CZAR.

Down from her high estate she stept,
A maiden, gently born,
And by the icy Volga kept
Sad watch, and waited morn;
And peasants say that where she slept
The new moon dipt her horn.
Yet on and on, through shoreless snows,
Far tow'rd the bleak north pole,
The foulest wrong the good God knows
Rolled as dark rivers roll;
While never once for all their woes
Upspake your ruthless soul.

She toiled, she taught the peasant, taught
The dark-eyed Tartar. He,
Illumined with her lofty thought,
Rose up and sought to be,
What God at the creation wrought,
A man! God-like and free.
Yet still before him yawned the black
Siberian mines! And oh,
The knout upon the bare white back!
The blood upon the snow!
The gaunt wolves, close upon the track,
Fought o'er the fallen so!

And this that one might wear a crown
Snatched from a strangled sire!
And this that two might mock or frown,
From high thrones climbing higher—
From where the Parricide looked down
With harlot in desire!
Yet on, beneath the great north star,
Like some lost, living thing,
That long dread line stretched, black and far

Till buried by death's wing!
And great men praised the goodly Czar—
But God sat pitying.

* * * * * *

A storm burst forth! From out the storm
The clean, red lightning leapt,
And lo, a prostrate royal form....
And Alexander slept!
Down through the snow, all smoking, warm
Like any blood, his crept.
Yea, one lay dead, for millions dead!
One red spot in the snow
For one long damning line of red,
Where exiles endless go—
The babe at breast, the mother's head
Bowed down, and dying so.

And did a woman do this deed?
Then build her scaffold high,
That all may on her forehead read
The martyr's right to die!
Ring Cossack round on royal steed!
Now lift her to the sky!
But see! From out the black hood shines
A light few look upon!
Lorn exiles, see, from dark, deep mines,
A star at burst of dawn!....
A thud! A creak of hangman's lines!—
A frail shape jerked and drawn!....

* * * * * *

The Czar is dead; the woman dead,
About her neck a cord.
In God's house rests his royal head—
Her's in a place abhorred;
Yet I had rather have her bed
Than thine, most royal lord!
Aye, rather be that woman dead,
Than thee, dead-living Czar,
To hide in dread, with both hands red,
Behind great bolt and bar....
You may control to the North Pole,
But God still guides the star.

TO RUSSIA.

"Where wast thou when I laid the foundations of the earth?"—Bible.

Who tamed your lawless Tartar blood?
What David bearded in her den
The Russian bear in ages when
You strode your black, unbridled stud,
A skin-clad savage of your steppes?
Why, one who now sits low and weeps,
Why one who now wails out to you—
The Jew, the Jew, the homeless Jew.

Who girt the thews of your young prime
And bound your fierce divided force?
Why, who but Moses shaped your course
United down the grooves of time?
Your mighty millions all to-day
The hated, homeless Jew obey.
Who taught all poetry to you?
The Jew, the Jew, the hated Jew.

Who taught you tender Bible tales
Of honey-lands, of milk and wine?
Of happy, peaceful Palestine?
Of Jordan's holy harvest vales?
Who gave the patient Christ? I say,
Who gave your Christian creed? Yea, yea,
Who gave your very God to you?
Your Jew! Your Jew! Your hated Jew!

TO RACHEL IN RUSSIA.

"To bring them unto a good land and a large; unto a land flowing with milk and honey."

O thou, whose patient, peaceful blood
Paints Sharon's roses on thy cheek,

And down thy breasts played hide and seek,
Six thousand years a stainless flood,
Rise up and set thy sad face hence.
Rise up and come where Freedom waits
Within these white, wide ocean gates
To give thee God's inheritance;
To bind thy wounds in this despair;
To braid thy long, strong, loosened hair.

O Rachel, weeping where the flood
Of icy Volga grinds and flows
Against his banks of blood-red snows—
White banks made red with children's blood—
Lift up thy head, be comforted;
For, as thou didst on manna feed,
When Russia roamed a bear in deed,
And on her own foul essence fed,
So shalt thou flourish as a tree
When Russ and Cossack shall not be.

Then come where yellow harvests swell;
Forsake that savage land of snows;
Forget the brutal Russian's blows;
And come where Kings of Conscience dwell.
Oh come, Rebecca to the well!
The voice of Rachel shall be sweet!
The Gleaner rest safe at the feet
Of one who loves her; and the spell
Of Peace that blesses Paradise
Shall kiss thy large and lonely eyes.

THE BRAVEST BATTLE.

The bravest battle that ever was fought;
Shall I tell you where and when?
On the maps of the world you will find it not;
It was fought by the mothers of men.

Nay, not with cannon or battle shot,
With sword or nobler pen;
Nay not with eloquent word or thought,
From mouths of wonderful men,

But deep in a walled-up woman's heart—
Of woman that would not yield,
But patiently, silently bore her part—
Lo! there in that battlefield.

No marshaling troop, no bivouac song;
No banner to gleam and wave;
And oh! these battles they last so long—
From babyhood to the grave!

Yet, faithful still as a bridge of stars,
She fights in her walled-up town—
Fights on and on in the endless wars,
Then silent, unseen—goes down.

RIEL, THE REBEL.

He died at dawn in the land of snows;
A priest at the left, a priest at the right;
The doomed man praying for his pitiless foes,
And each priest holding a low dim light,
To pray for the soul of the dying.
But Windsor Castle was far away;
And Windsor Castle was never so gay
With her gorgeous banners flying!

The hero was hung in the windy dawn—
'Twas splendidly done, the telegraph said;
A creak of the neck, then the shoulders drawn;
A heave of the breast—and the man hung dead,
And, oh! never such valiant dying!
While Windsor Castle was far away
With its fops and fools on that windy day,
And its thousand banners flying!

Some starving babes where a stark stream flows
'Twixt windy banks by an Indian town,

A frenzied mother in the freezing snows,
While softly the pitying snow came down
To cover the dead and the dying.
But Windsor Castle was gorgeous and gay
With lion banners that windy day—
With lying banners flying.

A CHRISTMAS EVE IN CUBA.

Their priests are many, for many their sins,
Their sins are many, for their land is fair;
The perfumed waves and the perfumed winds,
The cocoa-palms and the perfumed air;
The proud old Dons, so poor and so proud,
So poor their ghosts can scarce wear a shroud—
This town of Columbus has priests and prayer;
And great bells pealing in the palm land.

A proud Spanish Don lies shriven and dead;
The cross on his breast, a priest at his prayer;
His slave at his feet, his son at his head—
A slave's white face in her midnight hair;
A slave's white face, why, a face as white,
As white as that dead man's face this night—
This town of Columbus can pray for the dead;
Such great bells booming in the palm land.

The moon hangs dead up at heaven's white door;
As dead as the isle of the great, warm seas;
As dead as the Don, so proud and so poor,
With two quite close by the bed on their knees;
The slave at his feet, the son at his head,
And both in tears for the proud man dead—
This town of Columbus has tears, if you please;
And great bells pealing in the palm land.

Aye, both are in tears; for a child might trace
In the face of the slave, as the face of the son,
The same proud look of the dead man's face—
The beauty of one; and the valor of one—
The slave at his feet, the son at his head,
This night of Christ, where the Don lies dead—
This town of Columbus, this land of the sun
Keeps great bells clanging in the palm land.

The slave is so fair, and so wonderful fair!
A statue stepped out from some temple of old;
Why, you could entwine your two hands in her hair,
Nor yet could encompass its ample, dark fold.
And oh, that pitiful, upturned face;
Her master lies dead—she knows her place.
This town of Columbus has hundreds at prayer,
And great bells booming in the palm land.

The proud Don dead, and this son his heir;
This slave his fortune. Now, what shall he do?
Why, what should he do? or what should he care,
Save only to cherish a pride as true?—

To hide his shame as the good priests hide

Black sins confessed when the damned
have died.
This town of Columbus has pride with
her prayer—
And great bells pealing in the palm land!

Lo, Christ's own hour in the argent seas,
And she, his sister, his own born slave!
His secret is safe; just master and she;
These two, and the dead at the door of
the grave....
And death, whatever our other friends do,
Why, death, my friend, is a friend most
true—
This town of Columbus keeps pride and
keeps prayer,
And great bells booming in the palm land.

COMANCHE.

A blazing home, a blood-soaked hearth;
Fair woman's hair with blood upon!
That Ishmaelite of all the earth
Has like a cyclone, come and gone—
His feet are as the blighting dearth;
His hands are daggers drawn.

"To horse! to horse!" the rangers shout,
And red revenge is on his track!
The black-haired Bedouin en route
Looks like a long, bent line of black.
He does not halt nor turn about;
He scorns to once look back.

But on! right on that line of black,
Across the snow-white, sand-sown pass;
The bearded rangers on their track
Bear thirsty sabers bright as glass.
Yet not one red man there looks back;
His nerves are braided brass.

* * * * * *

At last, at last, their mountain came
To clasp its children in their flight!
Up, up from out the sands of flame
They clambered, bleeding to their height;
This savage summit, now so tame,
Their lone star, that dread night!

"Huzzah! Dismount!" the captain
cried.
"Huzzah! the rovers cease to roam!
The river keeps yon farther side,
A roaring cataract of foam.
They die, they die for those who died
Last night by hearth and home!"

His men stood still beneath the steep;
The high, still moon stood like a nun.
The horses stood as willows weep;
Their weary heads drooped every one.
But no man there had thought of sleep;
Each waited for the sun.

Vast nun-white moon! Her silver rill
Of snow-white peace she ceaseless poured;
The rock-built battlement grew still,
The deep-down river roared and roared.
But each man there with iron will
Leaned silent on his sword.

Hark! See what light starts from the
steep!
And hear, ah, hear that piercing sound.
It is their lorn death-song they keep
In solemn and majestic round.
The red fox of these deserts deep
At last is run to ground.

* * * * * *

Oh, it was weird,—that wild, pent
horde!
Their death-lights, their death-wails each
one.
The river in sad chorus roared
And boomed like some great funeral gun.
The while each ranger nursed his sword
And waited for the sun.

Then sudden star-tipped mountains topt
With flame beyond! And watch-fires ran
To where white peaks high heaven propt;
And stars and lights left scarce a span.
Why none could say where death-lights stopt
Or where red stars began!

And then such far, wild wails that came
In tremulous and pitying flight
From star-lit peak and peak of flame!
Wails that had lost their way that night
And knocked at each heart's door to claim
Protection in their flight.

O, chu-lu-le! O, chu-lu-lo!
A thousand red hands reached in air,
O, chu-lu-le! O, chu-lu-lo!
While midnight housed in midnight hair—
O, chu-lu-le! O, chu-lu-lo!
Their one last wailing prayer.

And all night long, nude Rachels poured
Melodious pity one by one
From mountain tops....The river roared
Sad requiem for his braves undone.
The while each ranger nursed his sword
And waited for the sun.

THE SOLDIERS' HOME, WASHINGTON.

The monument, tipped with electric fire,
Blazed high in a halo of light below
My low cabin door in the hills that inspire;
And the dome of the Capitol gleamed like snow
In a glory of light, as higher and higher
This wondrous creation of man was sent
To challenge the lights of the firmament.

A tall man, tawny and spare as bone,
With battered old hat and with feet half bare,
With the air of a soldier that was all his own—
Aye, something more than a soldier's air—
Came clutching a staff, with a face like stone;
Limped in through my gate—and I thought to beg—
Tight clutching a staff, slow dragging a leg.

The bent new moon, like a simitar,
Kept peace in Heaven. All earth lay still.
Some sentinel stars stood watch afar,
Some crickets kept clanging along the hill,
As the tall, stern relic of blood and war
Limped in, and, with hand up to brow half raised,
Limped up, looked about, as one dazed or crazed.

His gaunt face pleading for food and rest,
His set lips white as a tale of shame,
His black coat tight to a shirtless breast,
His black eyes burning in mine-like flame;
But never a word from his set lips came
As he whipped in line his battered old leg,
And his knees made mouths, and as if to beg.

Aye! black were his eyes; but doubtful and dim
Their vision of beautiful earth, I think.
And I doubt if the distant, dear worlds to him
Were growing brighter as he neared the brink
Of dolorous seas where phantom ships swim.
For his face was as hard as the hard, thin hand
That clutched that staff like an iron band.

"Sir, I am a soldier!" The battered old hat

Stood up as he spake, like to one on
parade—
Stood taller and braver as he spake out
that—
And the tattered old coat, that was tightly
laid
To the battered old breast, looked so trim
thereat
That I knew the mouths of the battered
old leg
That had opened wide were not made to
beg.

"I have wandered and wandered this
twenty year:
Searched up and down for my regiments.
Have they gone to that field where no foes
appear?
Have they pitched in Heaven their cloud-
white tents?
Or, tell me, my friend, shall I find them
here
On the hill beyond, at the Soldiers' Home,
Where the weary soldiers have ceased to
roam?

"Aye, I am a soldier and a brigadier;
Is this the way to the Soldiers' Home?
There is plenty and rest for us all, I hear,
And a bugler, bidding us cease to roam,
Rides over the hill all the livelong year—
Rides calling and calling the brave to come
And rest and rest in that Soldiers' Home.

"Is this, sir, the way? I wandered in
here
Just as one oft will at the close of day.
Aye, I am a soldier and a brigadier!
Now, the Soldiers' Home, sir. Is this the
way?
I have wandered and wandered this twenty
year,
Seeking some trace of my regiments
Sabered and riddled and torn to rents.

"Aye, I am a soldier and a brigadier!
A battered old soldier in the dusk of his
day;
But you don't seem to heed, or you don't
seem to hear,
Though, meek as I may, I ask for the
way
To the Soldiers' Home, which must be
quite near,
While under your oaks, in your easy
chair,
You sit and you sit, and you stare and
you stare.

"What battle? What deeds did I do in
the fight?
Why, sir, I have seen green fields turn as
red
As yonder red town in that marvelous
light!
Then the great blazing guns! Then the
ghastly white dead—
But, tell me, I faint, I must cease to
roam!
This battered leg aches! Then this sa-
bered old head—
Is—*is* this the way to the Soldiers' Home?

"Why, I hear men say 't is a Paradise
On the green oak hills by the great red
town;
That many old comrades shall meet my
eyes;
That a tasseled young trooper rides up
and rides down,
With bugle horn blowing to the still blue
skies,
Rides calling and calling us to rest and to
stay
In that Soldiers' Home. Sir, is this the
way?

"My leg is so lame! Then this sabered
old head—
Ah! pardon me. sir, I never complain;

But the road is so rough, as I just now said;
And then there is this something that troubles my brain.
It makes the light dance from yon Capitol's dome;
It makes the road dim as I doubtfully tread—
And—sir, *is* this the way to the Soldier's Home?

"From the first to the last in that desperate war—
Why, I did my part. If I did not fall,
A hair's breadth measure of this skull-bone scar
Was all that was wanting; and then this ball—
But what cared I? Ah! better by far
Have a sabered old head and a shattered old knee
To the end, than not had the praise of Lee—

"What! What do I hear? No home there for me?
Why, I heard men say that the war was at end!
Oh, my head swims so; and I scarce can see!
But a soldier's a soldier, I think, my friend,
Wherever that soldier may chance to be!
And wherever a soldier may chance to roam,
Why, a Soldiers' Home is a soldier's home!"

He turned as to go; but he sank to the grass;
And I lifted my face to the firmament;
For I saw a sentinel white star pass,
Leading the way the old soldier went.
And the light shone bright from the Capitol's dome,
Ah, brighter from Washington's monument,
Lighting his way to the Soldiers' Home.

THE CABIN, Washington, D. C.

OLIVE.

Dove-borne symbol, olive bough;
Dove-hued sign from God to men,
As if still the dove and thou
Kept companionship as then.

Dove-hued, holy branch of peace,
Antique, all-enduring tree;
Deluge and the floods surcease—
Deluge and Gethsemane.

THE BATTLE FLAG AT SHENANDOAH.

The tented field wore a wrinkled frown,
And the emptied church from the hill looked down
On the emptied road and the emptied town,
That summer Sunday morning.

And here was the blue, and there was the gray;
And a wide green valley rolled away
Between where the battling armies lay,
That sacred Sunday morning.

And Custer sat, with impatient will,
His restless horse, 'mid his troopers still,
As he watched with glass from the oak-set hill,
That silent Sunday morning.

Then fast he began to chafe and to fret;
"There's a battle flag on a bayonet

Too close to my own true soldiers set
For peace this Sunday morning!"

"Ride over, some one," he haughtily said,
"And bring it to me! Why, in bars blood red
And in stars I will stain it, and overhead
Will flaunt it this Sunday morning!"

Then a West-born lad, pale-faced and slim,
Rode out, and touching his cap to him,
Swept down, swept swift as Spring swallows swim,
That anxious Sunday morning.

On, on through the valley! up, up, anywhere!
That pale-faced lad like a bird through the air
Kept on till he climbed to the banner there
That bravest Sunday morning!

And he caught up the flag, and around his waist
He wound it tight, and he turned in haste,
And swift his perilous route retraced
That daring Sunday morning.

All honor and praise to the trusty steed!
Ah! boy, and banner, and all God speed!
God's pity for you in your hour of need
This deadly Sunday morning.

O, deadly shot! and O, shower of lead!
O, iron rain on the brave, bare head!
Why, even the leaves from the trees fall dead
This dreadful Sunday morning!

But he gains the oaks! Men cheer in their might!
Brave Custer is laughing in his delight!
Why, he is embracing the boy outright
This glorious Sunday morning!

But, soft! Not a word has the pale boy said.
He unwinds the flag. It is starred, striped, red
With his heart's best blood; and he falls down dead,
In God's still Sunday morning.

So, wrap this flag to his soldier's breast;
Into stars and stripes it is stained and blest;
And under the oaks let him rest and rest
Till God's great Sunday morning.

THE LOST REGIMENT.*

The dying land cried; they heard her death-call,
These bent old men stopped, listened intent;
Then rusty old muskets rushed down from the wall,

*In a pretty little village of Louisiana, destroyed by shells toward the end of the war, on a bayou back from the river, a great number of very old men had been left by their sons and grandsons, while they went to the war. And these old men, many of them veterans of other wars, formed themselves into a regiment, made for themselves uniforms, picked up old flintlock guns, even mounted a rusty old cannon, and so prepared to go to battle if ever the war came within their reach. Toward the close of the war some gunboats came down the river shelling the shore. The old men heard the firing, and, gathering together, they set out with their old muskets and rusty old cannon to try to reach the river over the corduroy road through the cypress swamp. They marched out right merrily that hot day, shouting and bantering to encourage each other, the dim fires of their old eyes burning with desire of battle, although not one of them was young enough to stand erect. And they never came back any more. The shells from the gunboats set the dense and sultry woods on fire. The old men were shut in by the flames—the gray beards and the gray moss and the gray smoke together.

And squirrel-guns gleamed in that regiment,
And grandsires marched, old muskets in hand—
The last men left in the old Southland.

The gray grandsires! They were seen to reel,
Their rusty old muskets a wearisome load;
They marched, scarce tall as the cannon's wheel,
Marched stooping on up the corduroy road;
These gray old boys, all broken and bent,
Marched out, the gallant last regiment.

But oh! that march through the cypress trees,
When zest and excitement had died away!
That desolate march through the marsh to the knees—
The gray moss mantling the battered and gray—
These gray grandsires all broken and bent—
The gray moss mantling the regiment.

The gray bent men and the mosses gray;
The dull dead gray of the uniform!
The dull dead skies, like to lead that day,
Dull, dead, heavy and deathly warm!
Oh, what meant more than the cypress meant,
With its mournful moss, to that regiment?

That deadly march through the marshes deep!
That sultry day and the deeds in vain!
The rest on the cypress roots, the sleep—
The sleeping never to rise again!
The rust on the guns; the rust and the rent—
That dying and desolate regiment!

The muskets left leaning against the trees,
The cannon wheels clogged from the moss o'erhead,
The cypress trees bending on obstinate knees
As gray men kneeling by the gray men dead!
A lone bird rising, long legged and gray,
Slow rising and rising and drifting away.

The dank dead mosses gave back no sound,
The drums lay silent as the drummers there;
The sultry stillness it was so profound
You might have heard an unuttered prayer;
And ever and ever and far away,
Kept drifting that desolate bird in gray.

The long gray shrouds of that cypress wood,
Like vails that sweep where the gray nuns weep—
That cypress moss o'er the dankness deep,
Why, the cypress roots they were running blood;
And to right and to left lay an old man dead—
A mourning cypress set foot and head.

'Twas man hunting men in the wilderness there;
'Twas man hunting man and hunting to slay,
But nothing was found but death that day,

And possibly God—and that bird in
gray
Slow rising and rising and drifting away.

Now down in the swamp where the gray
men fell
The fireflies volley and volley at night,
And black men belated are heard to tell
Of the ghosts in gray in a mimic fight—
Of the ghosts of the gallant old men in
gray
Who silently died in the swamp that day.

CUSTER.

Oh, it were better dying there
On glory's front, with trumpet's blare,
And battle's shout blent wild about—
The sense of sacrifice, the roar
Of war! The soul might well leap out—
The brave, white soul leap boldly out
The door of wounds, and up the stair
Of heaven to God's open door,
While yet the knees were bent in prayer.

THE WORLD IS A BETTER WORLD.

Aye, the world is a better old world to-
day!
And a great good mother this earth of
ours;
Her white to-morrows are a white stair-
way
To lead us up to the star-lit flowers—
The spiral to-morrows that one by one
We climb and we climb in the face of the
sun.

Aye, the world is a braver old world to-
day!
For many a hero dares bear with wrong—
Will laugh at wrong and will turn away;
Will whistle it down the wind with a
song—
Dares slay the wrong with his splendid
scorn!
The bravest old hero that ever was born!

OUTSIDE OF CHURCH.

It seems to me a grandest thing
To save the soul from perishing
By planting it where heaven's rain
May reach and make it grow again.

It seems to me the man who leaves
The soul to perish is as one
Who gathers up the empty sheaves
When all the golden grain is done.

DOWN THE MISSISSIPPI AT NIGHT.

Sowing the waves with a fiery rain,
Leaving behind us a lane of light,
Weaving a web in the woof of night,
Cleaving a continent's wealth in twain.

Lighting the world with a way of flame,
Writing, even as the lightnings write
High over the awful arched forehead of
night,
Jehovah's dread, unutterable name.

A NUBIAN FACE ON THE NILE.

One night we touched the lily shore,
And then passed on, in night indeed,
Against the far white waterfall.
I saw no more, shall know no more
Of her for aye. And you who read
This broken bit of dream will smile,
Half vexed that I saw aught at all.

The waves struck strophes on the shore
And all the sad song of the oar
That long, long night against the Nile,
Was: Nevermore and nevermore
This side that shadowy shore that lies
Below the leafy Paradise.

LA EXPOSICION.

NEW ORLEANS.

The banners! The bells! The red banners!
The rainbows of banners! The chimes!
The music of stars! The sweet manners
Of peace in old pastoral times!

The coming of nations! Kings bringing
Rich gifts to Republics! The trees
Of paradise, and birds singing
By the bank of De Soto's swift seas!

LINCOLN PARK.

Unwalled it lies, and open as the sun
When God swings wide the dark doors of the East.
Oh, keep this one spot, still keep this one,
Where tramp or banker, laymen or high priest,
May equal meet before the face of God:
Yea, equals stand upon that common sod
Where they shall one day equals be
Beneath, for aye, and all eternity.

THE RIVER OF REST.

A beautiful stream is the River of Rest;
The still, wide waters sweep clear and cold,
A tall mast crosses a star in the west,
A white sail gleams in the west world's gold:
It leans to the shore of the River of Rest—
The lily-lined shore of the River of Rest.

The boatman rises, he reaches a hand,
He knows you well, he will steer you true,
And far, so far, from all ills upon land,
From hates, from fates that pursue and pursue;
Far over the lily-lined River of Rest—
Dear mystical, magical River of Rest.

A storied, sweet stream is this River of Rest;
The souls of all time keep its ultimate shore;
And journey you east or journey you west,
Unwilling, or willing, sure footed or sore,
You surely will come to this River of Rest—
This beautiful, beautiful River of Rest.

THE NEW PRESIDENT.

Granite and marble and granite,
Corridor, column and dome!
A capitol huge as a planet
And massive as marble-built Rome.

Stair steps of granite to glory!
Go up with thy face to the sun;
They are stained with the footsteps and story
Of giants and battles well won.

Stop—stand on this stairway of granite,
Lo! Arlington, storied and still,

With a lullaby hush. But the land it
Springs fresh as that sun-fronted hill.

Beneath us stout-hearted Potomac
In majesty moves to the sea—
Beneath us a sea of proud people
Moves on, undivided as he.

Yea, strife it is over and ended
For all the days under the sun;
The banners unite and are blended
As moonlight and sunlight in one.

Lo! banners and banners and banners,
Broad star-balanced banners of blue—
If a single star fell from fair heaven,
Why, what would befall us, think you?

MONTGOMERY AT QUEBEC.

Sword in hand he was slain;
The snow his winding sheet;
The grinding ice at his feet—
The river moaning in pain.

Pity and peace at last;
Flowers for him to-day
Above on the battlements gray—
And the river rolling past.

BY THE BALBOA SEAS.

The golden fleece is at our feet,
Our hills are girt in sheen of gold;
Our golden flower-fields are sweet
With honey hives. A thousand-fold
More fair our fruits on laden stem
Than Jordan tow'rd Jerusalem.

Behold this mighty sea of seas!
The ages pass in silence by.
Gold apples of Hesperides
Hang at our God-land gates for aye.
Our golden shores have golden keys
Where sound and sing the Balboa seas.

MAGNOLIA BLOSSOMS.

The broad magnolia's blooms are white;
Her blooms are large, as if the moon
Had lost her way some lazy night,
And lodged here till the afternoon.

Oh, vast white blossoms breathing love!
White bosom of my lady dead,
In your white heaven overhead
I look, and learn to look above.

CALIFORNIA'S CHRISTMAS.

The stars are large as lilies! Morn
Seems some illumined story—
The story of our Savior born,
Told from old turrets hoary—
The full moon smiling tips a horn
And hies to bed in glory!

My sunclad city walks in light
And lasting summer weather;
Red roses bloom on bosoms white
And rosy cheeks together.
If you should smite one cheek, still smite
For she will turn the other.

The thronged warm street tides to and fro
And Love, roseclad, discloses.
The only snowstorm we shall know
Is this white storm of roses—
It seems like Maytime, mating so,
And—Nature counting noses.

Soft sea winds sleep on yonder tide;
You hear some boatmen rowing.

Their sisters' hands trail o'er the side;
They toy with warm waves flowing;
Their laps are laden deep and wide
From rose-trees green and growing.

Such roses white! such roses red!
Such roses richly yellow!
The air is like a perfume fed
From autumn fruits full mellow—
But see! a brother bends his head,
An oar forgets its fellow!

Give me to live in land like this,
Nor let me wander further;
Some sister in some boat of bliss
And I her only brother—
Sweet paradise on earth it is;
I would not seek another.

THOSE PERILOUS SPANISH EYES.

Some fragrant trees,
Some flower-sown seas
Where boats go up and down,
And a sense of rest
To the tired breast
In this beauteous Aztec town.

But the terrible thing in this Aztec town
That will blow men's rest to the stormiest skies,
Or whether they journey or they lie down—
Those perilous Spanish eyes!

Snow walls without,
Drawn sharp about
To prop the sapphire skies!
Two huge gate posts,
Snow-white like ghosts—
Gate posts to paradise!

But, oh! turn back from the high-walled town!
There is trouble enough in this world, I surmise,
Without men riding in regiments down—
Oh, perilous Spanish eyes!

MEXICO CITY, 1880.

NEWPORT NEWS.

The huge sea monster, the "Merrimac;"
The mad sea monster, the "Monitor;"
You may sweep the sea, peer forward and back,
But never a sign or a sound of war.
A vulture or two in the heavens blue;
A sweet town building, a boatman's call:
The far sea-song of a pleasure crew;
The sound of hammers. And that is all.

And where are the monsters that tore this main?
And where are the monsters that shook this shore?
The sea grew mad! And the shore shot flame!
The mad sea monsters they are no more.
The palm, and the pine, and the sea sands brown;
The far sea songs of the pleasure crews;
The air like balm in this building town—
And that is the picture of Newport News.

THE COMING OF SPRING.

My own and my only Love some night
Shall keep her tryst, shall come from the South,
And oh, her robe of magnolia white!
And oh, and oh, the breath of her mouth!

And oh, her grace in the grasses sweet!
And oh, her love in the leaves new born!
And oh, and oh, her lily-white feet
Set daintily down in the dew-wet morn!

The drowsy cattle at night shall kneel
And give God thanks, and shall dream and rest;
The stars slip down and a golden seal
Be set on the meadows my Love has blest.

Come back, my Love, come sudden, come soon.
The world lies waiting as the cold dead lie;
The frightened winds wail and the crisp-curled moon
Rides, wrapped in clouds, up the cold gray sky.

Oh, Summer, my Love, my first, last Love!
I sit all day by Potomac here,
Waiting and waiting the voice of the dove;
Waiting my darling, my own, my dear.

THE CABIN, Washington, D. C.

OUR HEROES OF TO-DAY.

I.

With high face held to her ultimate star,
With swift feet set to her mountains of gold,
This new-built world, where the wonders are,
She has built new ways from the ways of old.

II.

Her builders of worlds are workers with hands;
Her true world-builders are builders of these,
The engines, the plows; writing poems in sands
Of gold in our golden Hesperides.

III.

I reckon these builders as gods among men:
I count them creators, creators who knew
The thrill of dominion, of conquest, as when
God set His stars spinning their spaces of blue.

IV.

A song for the groove, and a song for the wheel,
And a roaring song for the rumbling car;
But away with the pomp of the soldier's steel,
And away forever with the trade of war.

V.

The hero of time is the hero of thought;
The hero who lives is the hero of peace;
And braver his battles than ever were fought,
From Shiloh back to the battles of Greece.

VI.

The hero of heroes is the engineer;
The hero of height and of gnome-built deep,
Whose only fear is the brave man's fear
That some one waiting at home might weep.

VII.

The hero we love in this land to-day
Is the hero who lightens some fellow-man's load—

Who makes of the mountain some pleasant highway;
Who makes of the desert some blossom-sown road.

VIII.

Then hurrah! for the land of the golden downs,
For the golden land of the silver horn;
Her heroes have built her a thousand towns,
But never destroyed her one blade of corn.

BY THE LOWER MISSISSIPPI.

The king of rivers has a dolorous shore,
A dreamful dominion of cypress-trees,
A gray bird rising forever more,
And drifting away toward the Mexican seas—
A lone bird seeking for some lost mate,
So dolorous, lorn and desolate.

The shores are gray as the sands are gray;
And gray are the trees in their cloaks of moss;—
That gray bird rising and drifting away,
Slow dragging its weary long legs across—
So weary, just over the gray wood's brink;
It wearies one, body and soul, to think.

These vast gray levels of cypress wood,
The gray soldiers' graves; and so, God's will—
These cypress-trees' roots are still running blood;
The smoke of battle in their mosses still—
That gray bird wearily drifting away
Was startled some long-since battle day.

HER PICTURE.

I see her now—the fairest thing
That ever mocked man's picturing,
I picture her as one who drew
Aside life's curtain and looked through
The mists of all life's mystery
As from a wood to open sea.

I picture her as one who knew
How rare is truth to be untrue—
As one who knew the awful sign
Of death, of life, of the divine
Sweet pity of all loves, all hates,
Beneath the iron-footed fates.

I picture her as seeking peace,
And olive leaves and vine-set land;
While strife stood by on either hand,
And wrung her tears like rosaries.
I picture her in passing rhyme
As of, yet not a part of, these—
A woman born above her time.

The soft, wide eyes of wonderment
That trusting looked you through and through;
The sweet, arched mouth, a bow new bent,
That sent love's arrow swift and true.

That sweet, arched mouth! The Orient
Hath not such pearls in all her stores,
Nor all her storied, spice-set shores
Have fragrance such as it hath spent.

DROWNED.

A fig for her story of shame and of pride!
She strayed in the night and her feet fell astray;
The great Mississippi was glad that day,
And that is the reason the poor girl died;
The great Mississippi was glad, I say,
And splendid with strength in his fierce, full pride—
And that is the reason the poor girl died.

And that was the reason, from first to last;
Down under the dark, still cypresses there
The Father of Waters he held her fast.
He kissed her face, he fondled her hair,
No more, no more an unloved outcast,
He clasped her close to his great, strong breast,
Brave lover that loved her last and best:

Around and around in her watery world,
Down under the boughs where the bank was steep,
And cypress trees kneeled all gnarly and curled,
Where woods were dark as the waters were deep,
Where strong, swift waters were swept and swirled,
Where the whirlpool sobbed and sucked in its breath,
As some great monster that is choking to death:

Where sweeping and swirling around and around
That whirlpool eddied so dark and so deep
That even a populous world might have drowned,
So surging, so vast, and so swift its sweep—
She rode on the wave. And the trees that weep,
The solemn gray cypresses leaning o'er;
The roots that ran blood as they leaned from the shore!

She surely was drowned! But she should have lain still;
She should have lain dead as the dead under ground;
She should have kept still as the dead on the hill!
But ever and ever she eddied around,
And so nearer and nearer she drew me there
Till her eyes met mine in their cold dead stare.

Then she looked, and she looked as to look me through;
And she came so close to my feet on the shore;
And her large eyes, larger than ever before,
They never grew weary as dead men's do.
And her hair! as long as the moss that swept
From the cypress trees as they leaned and wept.

Then the moon rose up, and she came to see,
Her long white fingers slow pointing there;
Why, shoulder to shoulder the moon with me
On the bank that night, with her shoulders bare,
Slow pointing and pointing that white face out,
As it swirled and it swirled, and it swirled about.

There ever and ever, around and around,
Those great sad eyes that refused to sleep!
Reproachful sad eyes that had ceased to weep!

And the great whirlpool with its gurgling sound!
The reproachful dead that was not yet dead!
The long strong hair from that shapely head!

Her hair was so long! so marvelous long,
As she rode and she rode on that whirlpool's breast;
And she rode so swift, and she rode so strong,
Never to rest as the dead should rest.
Oh, tell me true, could her hair in the wave
Have grown, as grow dead men's in the grave?

For, hist! I have heard that a virgin's hair
Will grow in the grave of a virgin true,
Will grow and grow in the coffin there,
Till head and foot it is filled with hair
All silken and soft—but what say you?
Yea, tell me truly can this be true?

For oh, her hair was so strangely long
That it bound her about like a veil of night,
With only her pitiful face in sight!
As she rode so swift, and she rode so strong,
That it wrapped her about, as a shroud had done,
A shroud, a coffin, and a veil in one.

And oh, that ride on the whirling tide!
That whirling and whirling it is in my head,
For the eyes of my dead they are not yet dead,
Though surely the lady had long since died:
Then the mourning wood by the watery grave;
The moon's white face to the face in the wave.

That moon I shall hate! For she left her place
Unasked up in heaven to show me that face.
I shall hate forever the sounding tide;
For oh, that swirling it is in my head
As it swept and it swirled with my dead not dead,
As it gasped and it sobbed as a God that died.

AFTER THE BATTLE.

Sing banners and cannon and roll of drum!
The shouting of men and the marshaling!
Lo! cannon to cannon and earth struck dumb!
Oh, battle, in song, is a glorious thing!

Oh, glorious day, riding down to the fight!
Oh, glorious battle in story and song!
Oh, godlike man to die for the right!
Oh, manlike God to revenge the wrong!

Yea, riding to battle, on battle day—
Why, a soldier is something more than a king!
But after the battle! The riding away!
Ah, the riding away is another thing!

BY THE PACIFIC OCEAN.

Here room and kingly silence keep
Companionship in state austere,
The dignity of death is here,
The large, lone vastness of the deep.

Here toil has pitched his camp to rest,
The west is banked against the west.

Above yon gleaming skies of gold
One lone imperial peak is seen;
While gathered at his feet in green
Ten thousand foresters are told.
And all so still! so still the air
That duty drops the web of care.

Beneath the sunset's golden sheaves
The awful deep walks with the deep,
Where silent sea doves slip and sweep,
And commerce keeps her loom and weaves.
The dead red men refuse to rest;
Their ghosts illume my lurid West.

CHRISTMAS BY THE GREAT RIVER.

Oh, lion of the ample earth,
What sword can cleave thy sinews through?
The south forever cradles you;
And yet the great North gives you birth.

Go find an arm so strong, so sure,
Go forge a sword so keen, so true,
That it can thrust thy bosom through;
Then may this union not endure!

In orange lands I lean to-day
Against thy warm tremendous mouth,
Oh, tawny lion of the South,
To hear what story you shall say.

What story of the stormy North,
Of frost-bound homes, of babes at play—
What tales of twenty States the day
You left your lair and leapt forth:

The day you tore the mountain's breast
And in the icy North uprose,
And shook your sides of rains and snows,
And rushed against the South to rest:

Oh, tawny river, what of they,
The far North folk? The maiden sweet—
The ardent lover at her feet—
What story of thy States to-day!

* * * * * *

The river kissed my garment's hem,
And whispered as it swept away:
"*God's story in all States to-day*
Is of a babe of Bethlehem."

GRANT AT SHILOH.

The blue and the gray! Their work was well done!
They lay as to listen to the water's flow.
Some lay with their faces upturned to the sun,
As seeking to know what the gods might know.
Their work was well done, each soldier was true.
But what is the question that comes to you?

For all that men do, for all that men dare,
That river still runs with its stateliest flow.
The sun and the moon I scarcely think care
A fig for the fallen, of friend or of foe.
But the moss-mantled cypress, the old soldiers say,
Still mantles in smoke of that battle day!

These men in the dust! These pitiful dead!
The gray and the blue, the blue and the gray,
The headless trunk and the trunkless head;
The image of God in the gory clay!

And who was the bravest? Say, can you tell
If Death throws dice with a loaded shell?

TWILIGHT AT THE HIGHTS.

The brave young city by the Balboa seas
Lies compassed about by the hosts of night—
Lies humming, low, like a hive of bees;
And the day lies dead. And its spirit's flight
Is far to the west; while the golden bars
That bound it are broken to a dust of stars.

Come under my oaks, oh, drowsy dusk!
The wolf and the dog; dear incense hour
When Mother Earth hath a smell of musk,
And things of the spirit assert their power—
When candles are set to burn in the west—
Set head and foot to the day at rest.

ARBOR DAY.

Against our golden orient dawns
We lift a living light to-day,
That shall outshine the splendid bronze
That lords and lights that lesser Bay.

Sweet Paradise was sown with trees;
Thy very name, lorn Nazareth,
Means woods, means sense of birds and bees,
And song of leaves with lisping breath.

God gave us Mother Earth, full blest
With robes of green in healthful fold;
We tore the green robes from her breast!
We sold our mother's robes for gold!

We sold her garments fair, and she
Lies shamed and naked at our feet!
In penitence we plant a tree;
We plant the cross and count it meet.

Lo, here, where Balboa's waters toss,
Here in this glorious Spanish bay,
We plant the cross, the Christian cross,
The Crusade Cross of Arbor Day.

PETER COOPER.

DIED 1883.

Give honor and love forevermore
To this great man gone to rest;
Peace on the dim Plutonian shore,
Rest in the land of the blest.

I reckon him greater than any man
That ever drew sword in war;
I reckon him nobler than king or khan,
Braver and better by far.

And wisest he in this whole wide land
Of hoarding till bent and gray;
For all you can hold in your cold dead hand
Is what you have given away.

So whether to wander the stars or to rest
Forever hushed and dumb,
He gave with a zest and he gave his best—
Give him the best to come.

THE DEAD MILLIONAIRE.

The gold that with the sunlight lies
In bursting heaps at dawn,
The silver spilling from the skies
At night to walk upon,

The diamonds gleaming in the dew
He never saw, he never knew.

He got some gold, dug from the mud,
Some silver, crushed from stones.
The gold was red with dead men's blood,
The silver black with groans;
And when he died he moaned aloud
"There'll be no pocket in my shroud."

THE LARGER COLLEGE.

ON LAYING THE COLLEGE CORNER-STONE.

Where San Diego seas are warm,
Where winter winds from warm Cathay
Sing sibilant, where blossoms swarm
With Hybla's bees, we come to lay
This tribute of the truest, best,
The warmest daughter of the West.

Here Progress plants her corner-stone
Against this warm, still, Cortez wave.
In ashes of the Aztec's throne,
In tummals of the Toltec's grave,
We plant this stone, and from the sod
Pick painted fragments of his god.

Here Progress lifts her torch to teach
God's pathway through the pass of care;
Her altar-stone Balboa's Beach,
Her incense warm, sweet, perfumed air;
Such incense! where white strophes reach
And lap and lave Balboa's Beach!

We plant this stone as some small seed
Is sown at springtime, warm with earth;
We sow this seed as some good deed
Is sown, to grow until its worth
Shall grow, through rugged steeps of time,
To touch the god-built stars sublime.

We lift this lighthouse by the sea,
The westmost sea, the westmost shore,
To guide man's ship of destiny
When Scylla and Charybdis roar;
To teach him strength, to proudly teach
God's grandeur, where His white palms reach:

To teach not Sybil books alone;
Man's books are but a climbing stair,
Lain step by step, like stairs of stone;
The stairway here, the temple there—
Man's lampad honor, and his trust,
The God who called him from the dust.

Man's books are but man's alphabet,
Beyond and on his lessons lie—
The lessons of the violet,
The large gold letters of the sky;
The love of beauty, blossomed soil,
The large content, the tranquil toil:

The toil that nature ever taught,
The patient toil, the constant stir,
The toil of seas where shores are wrought,
The toil of Christ, the carpenter;
The toil of God incessantly
By palm-set land or frozen sea.

Behold this sea, that sapphire sky!
Where nature does so much for man,
Shall man not set his standard high,
And hold some higher, holier plan?
Some loftier plan than ever planned
By outworn book of outworn land?

Where God has done so much for man!
Shall man for God do aught at all?
The soul that feeds on books alone—
I count that soul exceeding small
That lives alone by book and creed,—
A soul that has not learned to read.

The light is on us, and such light!
Such perfumed warmth of winter sea!

Such musky smell of maiden night!
Such bridal bough and orange tree!
Such wondrous stars! Yon lily moon
Seems like some long-lost afternoon!

More perfect than a string of pearls
We hold the full days of the year;
The days troop by like flower girls,
And all the days are ours here.
Here youth must learn; here age may live
Full tide each day the year can give.

No frosted wall, no frozen hasp,
Shuts Nature's book from us to-day;
Her palm leaves lift too high to clasp;
Her college walls the milky way.

The light is with us! Read and lead!
The larger book, the loftier deed!

THE POEM BY THE POTOMAC.*

Paine! The Prison of France! Lafayette!
The Bastile key to our Washington,
Whose feet on the neck of tyrants set
Shattered their prisons every one.
The key hangs here on his white walls high,
That all shall see, that none shall forget
What tyrants have been, what they may be yet;
And the Potomac rolling by.

---

* Two or three hundred steps to the right and up a general incline and you stand on the broad, high porch of Mount Vernon.

A great river creeps close underneath one hundred feet or two below. You might suppose you could throw a stone, standing on the porch, into the Potomac as seen through the trees that hug the hillside and the water's bank below. All was quiet, so quiet. Now and then a barnyard fowl, back in the rear, strained his glossy neck and called out loud and clear in the eternal Sabbath here; a fine shaggy dog wallowed and romped about the grassy dooryard, while far out over the vast river some black, wide-winged birds kept circling round and round. I went back and around into the barnyard to inquire what kind of birds they were. I met a very respectful but very stammery negro here. He took his cap in his hand, and twisting it all about and opening his mouth many times, he finally said:

"Do-do-dose burds was created by de Lord to p-p-pu-purify de yearth."

"But what do you call them, uncle?"

"Tur-tur-tur," and he twisted his cap, backed out, came forward, winked his eyes, but could not go on.

"Do you mean turkey buzzards?"

"Ya-ya-yas, sah, do-do-dose burds eats up de carrion ob de yearth, sah."

Down yonder is the tomb, the family vault. Back in the rear of the two marble coffins about thirty of the Washington family lie. The vault is locked up and closed forever. The key has been thrown into the trusty old Potomac to lie there until the last trump shall open all tombs.

Let no one hereafter complain of having to live in a garret alone and without a fire. For here, with all this spacious and noble house to select from, the widow of Washington chose a garret looking to the south and out upon his tomb. This is the old tomb where he was first laid to rest and where the fallen oak leaves are crowding in heaps now and almost filling up the low, dark doorway.

This garret has but one window, a small and narrow dormer window, and is otherwise quite dark. A bottom corner of the door is cut away so that her cat might come and go at will. And this is the saddest, tenderest sight at Mount Vernon. It seemed to me that I could see this noble lady sitting here, looking out upon the tomb of her mighty dead, the great river sweeping fast beyond, her heart full of the memory of a mighty Nation's birth, waiting, waiting, waiting.

The thing, however, of the most singular interest here is a key of the Bastile, presented by Thomas Paine to Lafayette, who brought it to America and presented it to Mount Vernon. It hangs here in a glass case, massive and monstrous. It is a hideous, horrible thing, and has, perhaps, more blood and misery on it than any other piece of iron or steel that was ever seen.

On Washington's walls let it rust and rust,
And tell its story of blood and of tears,
That Time still holds to the Poet's trust,
To people his pages for years and years.
The monstrous shape on the white walls high,
Like a thief in chains let it rot and rust—
Its kings and adorers crowned in dust:
And the Potomac rolling by.

A DEAD CARPENTER.

What shall be said of this soldier now dead?
This builder, this brother, now resting forever?
What shall be said of this soldier who bled
Through thirty-three years of silent endeavor?

Why, name him thy hero! Yea, write his name down
As something far nobler, as braver by far
Than purple-robed Cæsar of battle-torn town
When bringing home glittering trophies of war.

Oh, dark somber pines of my starlit Sierras,
Be silent of song, for the master is mute!
The Carpenter, master, is dead and lo! there is
Silence of song upon nature's draped lute!

Brother! Oh, manly dead brother of mine!
My brother by toil 'mid the toiling and lowly,
My brother by sign of this hard hand, by sign
Of toil, and hard toil, that the Christ has made holy:

Yea, brother of all the brave millions that toil;
Brave brother in patience and silent endeavor,
Rest on, as the harvester rich from his soil,
Rest you, and rest you for ever and ever.

OLD GIB AT CASTLE ROCKS.*

His eyes are dim, he gropes his way,
His step is doubtful, slow,
And now men pass him by to-day:
But forty years ago—
Why forty years ago I say
Old Gib was good to know.

For forty years ago to-day,
Where cars glide to and fro,
The Modoc held the world at bay,
And blood was on the snow.
Ay, forty years ago I say
Old Gib was good to know.

---

*Parties with Indian depredation claims against the Government desiring exact information touching the first trouble with the Modocs, now nearly forty years ago, the venerable leader of the volunteers in the first battle made out, with his own hand, the following quaint account of it, swore to it before a Notary, and sent it to Washington. The italics, capitals, and all are as he set them down in his crude but truthful way.—*Frank Leslie's Magazine*, 1893.

I Reuben P Gibson Was Born in Lowell Mass in 1826 of American Parents, shiped on board a whaler of New Bedford in 1846, Rounded Cape Horn, spent several years on the Paciffic Ocean, and in 1846 landed in California. Came to the Mines in Shasta County California, and have lived here in Shasta County more than 40 years, most of

Full forty years ago to-day
This valley lay in flame;
Up yonder pass and far away,
Red ruin swept the same:
Two women, with their babes at play,
Were butchered in black shame.

'T was then with gun and flashing eye
Old Gib loomed like a pine;
"Now will you fight, or will you fly ?
I'll take a fight in mine.
Come let us fight; come let us die!"
There came just twenty-nine.

Just twenty-nine who dared to die,
And, too, a motley crew
Of half-tamed red men; would they fly,
Or would they fight him too?
No time to question or reply,
This was a time to *do*.

---

which time I have been and am now a Magistrate. I have had much to do with Indians, and in 1855 they became Very Restless, and some of them took to the Castle Rocks, Called Castle del Diablo, at that time by the Mexicans, and they—the Hostiles began to destroy our Property, and Kill White people. Troops of the Regular Army tried to engage them, but found them inaccessible. I then raised a Company of Twenty-Nine White men and thirty Indian (friendly) Scouts and after hard Perilous Marches by Night, We engaged and *destroyed* the Hostiles, having taken Many Scalps. This battle was Fought in the Castle Rocks in this Shasta County and was in June 1855. The hostiles were Modocs and Other Renegades and this was the first Battle in a war that *Spread all over the Coast* I had Some Indians hurt, and one man mortally wounded, James Lane by name. Some Others were more or less hurt with Arrows. Joaquin Miller Received an Arrow in the face and Neck at my Side and we thought would die but at last got Well. He and Mountain Joe had a Post at Soda Springs below Castle Rocks, and their property had been destroyed and made untenable. In all My Experience I know of nothing in Indian warfare so effectual for good as this Campaign. The indians had Possession of the lines of travel *connecting* Middle and Northern California and it Was impossible for the Mails to get through until the Hostiles were destroyed.

(Signed) Reuben P Gibson

Subscribed and sworn to before me this 17th day of November, 1892, and I hereby certify that I am well acquainted with said affiant and know him to be a person of veracity and entitled to credit. He is a Justice of the Peace in this Shasta County

F. P. Primm,
Notary Public in and for Shasta County, Cal.

[SEAL.]

Let me here introduce a line of facts stranger than anything imagined in all these pages. I had not intended to insert these verses and had delivered to my publishers the completed collection without them. Against my objection that the lines were not only too personal, but unequal, it was urged that they would be missed by my readers; besides their preservation was due to my old commander, and as this was the first of my three terrible Indian campaigns, and I had served only as private instead of leader, I could hardly be held guilty of egotism. Deference to the dead made me consent to try and find the lines at once in some library. On my way I met a man whom I knew but slightly as U. S. Marshal under President Hayes. My weary eyes were unequal to the task before me, and I asked him to go with me. We found the magazine and he kindly offered to copy the lines and send them to me. This he did; and now let his letter tell the rest.

"Oakland, Dec. 20, 1896.

"Joaquin, my dear fellow, I enclose herewith the copies you expressed a wish for. I think they are exact. I was especially careful in making the affidavit of Old Gib; so where he differs with Webster orthographically, I follow Gib.

"Now my boy, I've a little story. I'll be considerate and make it brief. In the early part of the summer of 1855, I was one of a company of about twenty that left Auburn, Placer Co., on a prospecting expedition, intending, unless we found satisfactory prospects nearer, to go to the Trinity. We crossed the Yuba and Feather, camping a few days on Nelson Creek, then traveling in a northwesterly direction, we reached the headwaters of the Sacramento, where we found a party of white men and Indians who, a day or two previous to our meeting them, had had a desperate fight with Indians. They told us they had lost several men, killed and wounded, but had nearly

Up, up, straight up where thunders grow
And growl in Castle Rocks,
Straight up till Shasta gleamed in snow,
And shot red battle shocks;
Till clouds lay shepherded below,
A thousand ghostly flocks.

Yet up and up Old Gibson led,
No looking backward then;
His bare feet bled; the rocks were red
From torn, bare-footed men.
Yet up, up, up, till well nigh dead—
The Modoc in his den!

Then cried the red chief from his height,
"Now, white man, what would you ?
Behold my hundreds for the fight,
But yours so faint and few;
We are as rain, as hail at night
But you, you are as dew.

"White man, go back; I beg go back,
I will not fight so few;
Yet if I hear one rifle crack,
Be that the doom of you!
Back! down, I say, back down your track,
Back, down! What else to do?"

"What else to do? Avenge or die!
Brave men have died before;
And you shall fight, or you shall fly.
You find no women more,
No babes to butcher now; for I
Shall storm your Castle's door!"

Then bang! whiz bang! whiz bang and ping!
Six thousand feet below,
Sweet Sacramento ceased to sing,
But wept and wept, for oh!
These arrows sting as adders sting,
And they kept stinging so.

Then one man cried: "Brave men have died,
And we can die as they;
But ah! my babe, my one year's bride!
And they so far away.
Brave Captain lead us back—aside,
Must all here die to-day?"

His face, his hands, his body bled:
Yea, no man there that day—
No white man there but turned to red,
In that fierce fatal fray;
But Gib with set teeth only said:
"No; we came here to stay!"

They stayed and stayed, and Modocs stayed,
But when the night came on,
No white man there was now afraid,
The last Modoc had gone;
His ghost in Castle Rocks was laid
Till everlasting dawn.

---

exterminated the Indians. I saw one of their men, a boy in appearance, who had, as I understood, received two arrow wounds in the face and neck. He was in great pain, and no one believed he could recover.

"Twelve years later I, then Sheriff of Placer Co., had occasion to go to Shasta on official business. W. E. Hopping was then Sheriff of Shasta Co. In the course of conversation with him, I spoke of the incident narrated above. He interrupted me, and said: 'The Captain of the volunteers at the battle is in town.' He found him, and introduced me to the man who was doubtless Old Gib, though his name has gone from my memory. I asked about the young fellow who was so desperately wounded. 'Oh, he pulled through all right, the game little cuss,' said he, 'he's up in Oregon, I believe.' I don't think he mentioned his name, but in copying the affidavit of Old Gib, it dawned upon me who that 'game little cuss' was.

Yours,

A. W. Poole."

DON'T STOP AT THE STATION DESPAIR.

We must trust the Conductor, most surely;
Why, millions of millions before
Have made this same journey securely
And come to that ultimate shore.
And we, we will reach it in season;
And ah, what a welcome is there!
Reflect then, how out of all reason
To stop at the Station Despair.

Ay, midnights and many a potion
Of bitter black water have we
As we journey from ocean to ocean—
From sea unto ultimate sea—
To that deep sea of seas, and all silence
Of passion, concern and of care—
That vast sea of Eden-set Islands—
Don't stop at the Station Despair!

Go forward, whatever may follow,
Go forward, friend-led, or alone;
Ah me, to leap off in some hollow
Or fen, in the night and unknown—
Leap off like a thief; try to hide you
From angels, all waiting you there!
Go forward; whatever betide you
Don't stop at the Station Despair!

THE FORTUNATE ISLES.

You sail and you seek for the Fortunate Isles,
The old Greek Isles of the yellow bird's song?
Then steer straight on through the watery miles,
Straight on, straight on and you can't go wrong.
Nay not to the left, nay not to the right,
But on, straight on, and the Isles are in sight,
The Fortunate Isles where the yellow birds sing
And life lies girt with a golden ring.

These Fortunate Isles they are not so far,
They lie within reach of the lowliest door;
You can see them gleam by the twilight star;
You can hear them sing by the moon's white shore—
Nay, never look back! Those leveled grave stones
They were landing steps; they were steps unto thrones
Of glory for souls that have sailed before,
And have set white feet on the fortunate shore.

And what are the names of the Fortunate Isles?
Why, Duty and Love and a large content.
Lo! these are the Isles of the watery miles,
That God let down from the firmament.
Lo! Duty, and Love, and a true man's trust;
Your forehead to God though your feet in the dust;
Lo! Duty, and Love, and a sweet babe's smiles,
And these, O friend, are the Fortunate Isles.

BACK TO THE GOLDEN GATE.

Yea, we have tracked the hemispheres,
Have touched on fairest land that lies
This side the gates of Paradise,
Have ranged the universe for years;
Have read the book of Truth right on,
From title leaf to colophon.

DEAD IN THE LONG, STRONG GRASS.*

Dead! stark dead in the long, strong grass!
But he died with his sword in his hand.
Who says it? who saw it? God saw it!
And I knew him! St. George! he would draw it,
Though they swooped down in mass
Till they darkened the land!
Then the seventeen wounds in his breast!
Ah! these witness best.

Dead! stark dead in the long, strong grass!
Dead! and alone in the great dark land!
O mother! not Empress now, mother!
A nobler name, too, than all other,
The laurel leaf fades from thy hand!
O mother that waiteth, a mass!
Masses and chants must be said,
And cypress, instead.

GARFIELD. †

"*Bear me out of the battle, for lo, I am sorely wounded.*"

From out the vast, wide-bosomed West,
Where gnarled old maples make array,
Deep scarred from Redmen gone to rest,
Where unnamed heroes hew the way
For worlds to follow in their quest,

---

* Born to the saddle and bred by a chain of events to ride with the wind until I met the stolid riders of England, I can now see how it was that Anthony Trollope, Lord Houghton and others of the saddle and "meet" gave me ready place in their midst. Not that the English were less daring; but they were less fortunate; may I say less experienced. I recall the fact that I once found Lord Houghton's brother, Lord Crewe, and his son also, under the hands of the surgeon in New York—one with a broken thigh, and the other with a few broken ribs. But in all our hard riding I never had a scratch.

One morning Trollope hinted that my immunity was due to my big Spanish saddle, which I had brought from Mexico City. I threw my saddle on the grass and rode without so much as a blanket. And I rode neck to neck; and then left them all behind and nearly everyone unhorsed.

Prince Napoleon was of the party that morning; and as the gentlemen pulled themselves together on the return he kept by my side, and finally proposed a tour through Notts and Sherwood Forest on horseback. And so it fell out that we rode together much.

But he had already been persistently trained in the slow military methods, and it was in vain that I tried to teach him to cling to his horse and climb into the saddle as he ran, after the fashion of Indians and vaqueros. He admired it greatly, but seemed to think it unbecoming a soldier.

It was at the Literary Fund dinner, where Stanley and Prince Napoleon stood together when they made their speeches, that I saw this brave and brilliant young man for the last time. He was about to set out for Africa with the English troops to take part in the Zulu war.

He seemed very serious. When about to separate he took my hand, and, looking me all the time in the face, placed a large diamond on my finger, saying something about its being from the land to which he was going. I refused to take it, for I had heard that the Emperor died poor. But as he begged me to keep it, at least till he should come back, it has hardly left my hand since he placed it there.

Piteous that this heir to the throne of France should die alone in the yellow grass at the hand of savages in that same land where the great Emperor had said, "Soldiers, from yonder pyramids twenty centuries behold your deeds."

† Walt Whitman chanced to be in Boston when I last visited Mr. Longfellow, and I was delighted to hear the poet at his table in the midst of his perfect family speak of him most kindly; for at this time the press and all small people were abusing Whitman terribly. Soon after he looked me up at my hotel in Boston, and we two called on the good, gray poet together. I mention this merely to italicize the suggestion that Longfellow's was a large nature.

Many others, I know, stood nearer him, so much nearer and dearer, and maybe I ought not to claim the right to say much of a sacred nature; but somehow I always felt, when he reached out his right hand and drew me to

Where pipes the quail, where squirrels
play
Through tops of trees with nuts for
toy,
A boy stood forth clear-eyed and tall,
A timid boy, a bashful boy;
Yet comely as a son of Saul—
A boy all friendless, all unknown,
Yet heir apparent to a throne:

A throne the proudest yet on earth
For him who bears him noblest, best,
And this he won by simple worth,
That boy from out the wooded West.
And now to fall! Pale-browed and prone
He lies in everlasting rest.
The nations clasp the cold, dead hand;
The nations sob aloud at this;
The only dry eyes in the land
Now at the last we know are his;
While *she* who sends a wreath won
More conquest than her hosts had done.

Brave heart, farewell. The wheel has
run
Full circle, and behold a grave
Beneath thy loved old trees is done.
The druid oaks lift up and wave
A solemn beckon back. The brave
Old maples welcome, every one.
Receive him, earth. In center land,
As in the center of each heart,
As in the hollow of God's hand,
The coffin sinks. And we depart
Each on his way, as God deems best
To *do*, and so deserve to rest.

him, and looked me fairly and silently in the face with his earnest seer eyes, that he knew me, did not dislike me, and that he knew, soul to soul, we each sought the good and the beautiful and true, each after his fashion, and as best he knew.

He had a pretty way of always getting out of the house—that beautiful house of his, where Washington had dwelt—into the woods. He possessed a wonderful lot of books, but he knew the birds, the crickets, the flowers, woods and grasses were more in my way, and with rare delicacy he never talked on books at all, but led out at once, whenever possible, to our mutual friends in the rear of the old Headquarters of Washington.

It was on this occasion that a pall of black suddenly fell upon the Republic. Garfield lay dead at Elberon!

A publisher solicited from each of the several authors then in and about Boston some tribute of sorrow for the dead. The generous sum of $100 was checked as an earnest. I remember how John Boyle O'Reilly and I went to big-hearted Walt Whitman and wrestled with him in a vain effort to make him earn and accept his $100.

"Yes, I'm sorry as the sorriest; sympathize with the great broken heart of the world over this dead sovereign citizen. But I've nothing to say."

And so, persuade as we might, even till past midnight, Walt Whitman would not touch the money or try to write a line. He was poor; but bear it forever in testimony that he was honest, and would not promise to sell that which he felt that God had not at that moment given him to sell. And hereafter, whenever any of you are disposed to speak or even think unkindly of Walt Whitman, remember this refusal of his to touch a whole heap of money when he might have had it for ten lines, and maybe less than ten minutes' employment. I love him for it. There is not a butcher, nor a baker, nor a merchant, nor a banker in America, perhaps, who would have been, under the circumstances, so stubbornly, savagely honest with the world and himself.

Early next morning I went to Mr. Longfellow in great haste and read my lines. Kindly he listened as I read, and then carefully looked them all over and made some important improvements. He had also partly written, and read me, his poem on the sad theme. But it was too stately and fine for company with our less mature work, and at the last moment it was withheld on the plea that it was still incomplete. It soon after appeared in the New York *Independent*. As I was hastening away with my manuscript for the press, he said as he came with me down to the gate, that the Queen of England had done more to conquer America by sending the wreath for the funeral of the dead President than all the Georges had ever done with all their troops and cannon. And he said it in such a poetical way that I thought it an unfinished couplet of his poem. I never saw him any more.

TO THE CALIFORNIA PIONEERS.

READ IN SAN FRANCISCO, 1894.

How swift this sand, gold-laden, runs!
How slow these feet, once swift and firm!
Ye came as romping, rosy sons,
Come jocund up at College term;
Ye came so jolly, stormy, strong,
Ye drown'd the roll-call with your song.
But now ye lean a list'ning ear
And—"*Adsum! Adsum!* I am here!"

My brave world-bearers of a world
That tops the keystone, star of States,
All hail! Your battle flags are furled
In fruitful peace. The golden gates
Are won. The jasper walls be yours.
Your sun sinks down yon soundless shores.
Night falls. But lo! your lifted eyes
Greet gold outcroppings in the skies.

Companioned with Sierra's peaks
Our storm-born eagle shrieks his scorn
Of doubt or death, and upward seeks
Through unseen worlds the coming morn.
Or storm, or calm, or near, or far,
His eye fixed on the morning star,
He knows, as God knows, there is dawn;
And so keeps on, and on, and on!

So ye, brave men of bravest days,
Fought on and on with battered shield,
Up bastion, rampart, till the rays
Of full morn met ye on the field.
Ye knew not doubt; ye only knew
To do and dare, and dare and do!
Ye knew that time, that God's first-born,
Would turn the darkest night to morn.

Ye gave your glorious years of youth
And lived as heroes live—and die.
Ye loved the truth, ye lived the truth;
Ye knew that cowards only lie.
Then heed not now one serpent's hiss,
Or trait'rous, trading, Judas kiss.
Let slander wallow in his slime;
Still leave the truth to God and time.

Worn victors, few and true, such clouds
As track God's trailing garment's hem
Where Shasta keeps shall be your shrouds,
And ye shall pass the stars in them.
Your tombs shall be while time endures,
Such hearts as only truth secures;
Your everlasting monuments
Sierra's snow-topt battle tents.

JAVA.

"*And darkness was upon the face of the deep; and the Spirit of God moved upon the waters.*"

The oceans roar; the mountains reel;
The world stands still, with bated breath.
Now burst of flame! and woe and weal
All drowned in darkness and in death.
Wild beasts in herds, strange, beauteous birds—
God's rainbow birds,—gone in a breath!

O God! is earth, then, incomplete—
The six days' labor not yet done—
That she must melt beneath Thy feet
And her fair face forget the sun?
Must isles go down, and cities drown,
And good and evil be as one?

The great, warm heart of Mother Earth
Is broken o'er her Javan Isles.
Lo! ashes strew her ruined hearth
Along a thousand watery miles.
I hear her groan, I hear her moan,
All day above her drowning isles.

Tall ships are sailing silently
Above her buried isles to-day.
In marble halls beneath the sea

The sea-god's children shout and play;
They mock and shout in merry rout
Where mortals dwelt but yesterday.

MOTHER EGYPT.

Dark-browed, she broods with weary lids
Beside her Sphynx and Pyramids,
With low and never-lifted head.
If she be dead, respect the dead;
If she be weeping, let her weep;
If she be sleeping, let her sleep;
For lo, this woman named the stars!
She suckled at her tawny dugs
Your Moses while you reeked in wars
And prowled your woods, nude, painted thugs.

Then back, brave England; back in peace
To Christian isles of fat increase!
Go back! Else bid your high priests mold
Their meek bronze Christs to cannon bold;
Take down their cross from proud St. Paul's
And coin it into cannon-balls!
You tent not far from Nazareth.
Your camps trench where his child-feet strayed.
If Christ had seen this work of death!
If Christ had seen these ships invade!

I think the patient Christ had said,
"Go back, brave men! Take up your dead;
Draw down your great ships to the seas;
Repass the gates of Hercules.
Go back to wife with babe at breast,
And leave lorn Egypt to her rest."
Or is Christ dead, as Egypt is?
Ah, England, hear me yet again;
There's something grimly wrong in this—
So like some gray, sad woman slain.

What would you have your mother do?
Hath she not done enough for you?
Go back! And when you learn to read,
Come read this obelisk. Her deed
Like yonder awful forehead is
Disdainful silence. Like to this
What lessons have you writ in stone
To passing nations that shall stand?
Why, years as hers will leave you lone
And level as yon yellow sand.

Saint George? Your lions? Whence are they?
From awful, silent Africa.
This Egypt is the lion's lair;
Beware, brave Albion, beware!
I feel the very Nile should rise
To drive you from this sacrifice.
And if the seven plagues should come?
The red seas swallow sword and steed?
Lo! Christian lands stand mute and dumb
To see thy more than Moslem deed.

THE PASSING OF TENNYSON.

My kingly kinsmen, kings of thought,
I hear your gathered symphonies,
Such nights as when the world is not,
And great stars chorus through my trees.

We knew it, as God's prophets knew;
We knew it, as mute red men know,
When Mars leapt searching heaven through
With flaming torch, that he must go.
Then Browning, he who knew the stars,
Stood forth and faced insatiate Mars.

Then up from Cambridge rose and turned
Sweet Lowell from his Druid trees—
Turned where the great star blazed and burned,
As if his own soul might appease.

Yet on and on through all the stars
Still searched and searched insatiate Mars.

Then stanch Walt Whitman saw and knew;
Forgetful of his "Leaves of Grass,"
He heard his "Drum Taps," and God drew
His great soul through the shining pass,
Made light, made bright by burnished stars;
Made scintillant from flaming Mars.

Then soft-voiced Whittier was heard
To cease; was heard to sing no more.
As you have heard some sweetest bird
The more because its song is o'er.
Yet brighter up the street of stars
Still blazed and burned and beckoned Mars:

* * * * * *

And then the king came; king of thought,
King David with his harp and crown....
How wisely well the gods had wrought
That these had gone and sat them down
To wait and welcome mid the stars
All silent in the light of Mars.

All silent....So, he lies in state....
Our redwoods drip and drip with rain....
Against our rock-locked Golden Gate
We hear the great, sad, sobbing main.
But silent all....He passed the stars
That year the whole world turned to Mars.

IN CLASSIC SHADES.

Alone and sad I sat me down
To rest on Rousseau's narrow islè
Below Geneva. Mile on mile,
And set with many a shining town,
Tow'rd Dent du Midi danced the wave
Beneath the moon. Winds went and came
And fanned the stars into a flame.
I heard the far lake, dark and deep,
Rise up and talk as in its sleep ;
I heard the laughing waters lave
And lap against the further shore,
An idle oar, and nothing more
Save that the isle had voice, and save
That 'round about its base of stone
There plashed and flashed the foamy Rhone.

A stately man, as black as tan,
Kept up a stern and broken round
Among the strangers on the ground.
I named that awful African
A second Hannibal.

I gat
My elbows on the table ; sat
With chin in upturned palm to scan
His face, and contemplate the scene.
The moon rode by a crownéd queen.
I was alone. Lo! not a man
To speak my mother tongue. Ah me!
How more than all alone can be
A man in crowds! Across the isle
My Hannibal strode on. The while
Diminished Rousseau sat his throne
Of books, unnoticed and unknown.

This strange, strong man, with face austere,
At last drew near. He bowed; he spake
In unknown tongues. I could but shake

*The germ of song is, to my mind, a solemn gift. The prophet and the seer should rise above the levities of this life. And so it is that I make humble apology for now gathering up from recitation books these next half dozen pieces. The only excuse for doing it is their refusal to die; even under the mutilations of the compilers of "choice selections."

My head. Then half achill with fear,
Arose, and sought another place.
Again I mused. The kings of thought
Came by, and on that storied spot
I lifted up a tearful face.
The star-set Alps they sang a tune
Unheard by any soul save mine.
Mont Blanc, as lone and as divine
And white, seemed mated to the moon.
The past was mine; strong-voiced and
vast—
Stern Calvin, strange Voltaire, and Tell,
And two whose names are known too well
To name, in grand procession passed.

And yet again came Hannibal;
King-like he came, and drawing near,
I saw his brow was now severe
And resolute.

In tongue unknown
Again he spake. I was alone,
Was all unarmed, was worn and sad;
But now, at last, my spirit had
Its old assertion.

I arose,
As startled from a dull repose;
With gathered strength I raised a hand
And cried, "I do not understand.

His black face brightened as I spake;
He bowed; he wagged his woolly head;
He showed his shining teeth, and said,
"Sah, if you please, dose tables heah
Am consecrate to lager beer;
And, sah, what will you have to take?"

Not that I loved that colored cuss—
Nay! he had awed me all too much—
But I sprang forth, and with a clutch
I grasped his hand, and holding thus,
Cried, "Bring my country's drink for two!"
For oh! that speech of Saxon sound
To me was as a fountain found
In wastes, and thrilled me through and
through.

* * * * * *

On Rousseau's isle, in Rousseau's shade,
Two pink and spicy drinks were made,
In classic shades, on classic ground,
We stirred two cocktails round and round.

THAT GENTLE MAN FROM BOSTON.

AN IDYL OF OREGON.

Two noble brothers loved a fair
Young lady, rich and good to see;
And oh, her black abundant hair!
And oh, her wondrous witchery!
Her father kept a cattle farm,
These brothers kept her safe from harm:

From harm of cattle on the hill;
From thick-necked bulls loud bellowing
The livelong morning, long and shrill,
And lashing sides like anything!
From roaring bulls that tossed the sand
And pawed the lilies of the land.

There came a third young man. He
came
From far and famous Boston town.
He was not handsome, was not "game,"
But he could "cook a goose" as brown
As any man that set foot on
The mist kissed shores of Oregon.

This Boston man he taught the school,
Taught gentleness and love alway,
Said love and kindness, as a rule,
Would ultimately "make it pay."
He was so gentle, kind, that he
Could make a noun and verb agree.

So when one day these brothers grew
All jealous and did strip to fight,
He gently stood between the two
And meekly told them 'twas not right.
"I have a higher, better plan,"
Outspake this gentle Boston man.

"My plan is this: Forget this fray
About that lily hand of hers;
Go take your guns and hunt all day
High up yon lofty hill of firs,
And while you hunt, my ruffled doves,
Why, I will learn which one she loves."

The brothers sat the windy hill,
Their hair shone yellow, like spun gold,
Their rifles crossed their laps, but still
They sat and sighed and shook with cold.
Their hearts lay bleeding far below;
Above them gleamed white peaks of snow.

Their hounds lay crouching, slim and neat,
A spotted circle in the grass.
The valley lay beneath their feet;
They heard the wide-winged eagles pass.
Two eagles cleft the clouds above;
Yet what could they but sigh and love?

"If I could die," the elder sighed,
"My dear young brother here might wed."
"Oh, would to heaven I had died!"
The younger sighed with bended head.
Then each looked each full in the face
And each sprang up and stood in place.

"If I could die"—the elder spake,—
"Die by your hand, the world would say
'Twas accident—; and for her sake,
Dear brother, be it so, I pray."
"Not that!" the younger nobly said;
Then tossed his gun and turned his head.

And fifty paces back he paced!
And as he paced he drew the ball;
Then sudden stopped and wheeled and faced
His brother to the death and fall!
Two shots rang wild upon the air!
But lo! the two stood harmless there!

Two eagles poised high in the air;
Far, far below the bellowing
Of bullocks ceased, and everywhere
Vast silence sat all questioning.
The spotted hounds ran circling round,
Their red, wet noses to the ground.

And now each brother came to know
That each had drawn the deadly ball;
And for that fair girl far below
Had sought in vain to silent fall.
And then the two did gladly "shake,"
And thus the elder bravely spake:

"Now let us run right hastily
And tell the kind schoolmaster all!
Yea! yea! and if she choose not me,
But all on you her favors fall,
This valiant scene, till all life ends,
Dear brother, binds us best of friends.

The hounds sped down, a spotted line,
The bulls in tall abundant grass
Shook back their horns from bloom and vine,
And trumpeted to see them pass—
They loved so good, they loved so true,
These brothers scarce knew what to do.

They sought the kind schoolmaster out
As swift as sweeps the light of morn—
They could but love, they could not doubt
This man so gentle, "in a horn,"
They cried: "Now whose the lily hand—
That lady's of this emer'ld land?"

They bowed before that big-nosed man,
That long-nosed man from Boston town;
They talked as only lovers can,
They talked, but he would only frown;
And still they talked and still they plead;
It was as pleading with the dead.

At last this Boston man did speak—
"Her father has a thousand ceows,
An hundred bulls, all fat and sleek;
He also had this ample heouse."
The brothers' eyes stuck out thereat
So far you might have hung your hat.

"I liked the looks of this big heouse—
My lovely boys, won't you come in?
Her father had a thousand ceows—
He also had a heap o' tin.
The guirl? Oh yes, the guirl, you see—
The guirl, this morning married me."

WILLIAM BROWN OF OREGON.

They called him Bill, the hired man,
But she, her name was Mary Jane,
The squire's daughter; and to reign
The belle from Ber-she-be to Dan
Her little game. How lovers rash
Got mittens at the spelling school!
How many a mute, inglorious fool
Wrote rhymes and sighed and dyed—mustache?

This hired man had loved her long,
Had loved her best and first and last,
Her very garments as she passed
For him had symphony and song.
So when one day with flirt and frown
She called him "Bill," he raised his heart,
He caught her eye and faltering said,
"I love you; and my name is Brown,"

She fairly waltzed with rage; she wept;
You would have thought the house on fire.
She told her sire, the portly squire,
Then smelt her smelling-salts and slept.
Poor William did what could be done;
He swung a pistol on each hip,
He gathered up a great ox-whip
And drove right for the setting sun.

He crossed the big backbone of earth,
He saw the snowy mountains rolled
Like nasty billows; saw the gold
Of great big sunsets; felt the birth
Of sudden dawn upon the plain;
And every night did William Brown
Eat pork and beans and then lie down
And dream sweet dreams of Mary Jane.

Her lovers passed. Wolves hunt in packs,
They sought for bigger game; somehow
They seemed to see about her brow
The forky sign of turkey tracks.
The teter-board of life goes up,
The teter-board of life goes down,
The sweetest face must learn to frown;
The biggest dog has been a pup.

O maidens! pluck not at the air;
The sweetest flowers I have found
Grow rather close unto the ground
And highest places are most bare.
Why, you had better win the grace
Of one poor cussed Af-ri-can
Than win the eyes of every man
In love alone with his own face.

At last she nursed her true desire.
She sighed, she wept for William Brown.
She watched the splendid sun go down
Like some great sailing ship on fire,
Then rose and checked her trunks right on;
And in the cars she lunched and lunched,

And had her ticket punched and punched,
Until she came to Oregon.

She reached the limit of the lines,
She wore blue specs upon her nose,
Wore rather short and manly clothes,
And so set out to reach the mines.
Her right hand held a Testament,
Her pocket held a parasol,
And thus equipped right on she went,
Went water-proof and water-fall.

She saw a miner gazing down,
Slow stirring something with a spoon;
"O, tell me true and tell me soon,
What has become of William Brown?"
He looked askance beneath her specs,
Then stirred his cocktail round and round,
Then raised his head and sighed profound,
And said, "He's handed in his checks."

Then care fed on her damaged cheek,
And she grew faint, did Mary Jane,
And smelt her smelling salts in vain,
Yet wandered on, way-worn and weak.
At last upon a hill alone;
She came, and there she sat her down;
For on that hill there stood a stone,
And, lo! that stone read, "William Brown."

"O William Brown! O William Brown!
And here you rest at last," she said,
"With this lone stone above your head,
And forty miles from any town!
I will plant cypress trees, I will,
And I will build a fence around,
And I will fertilize the ground
With tears enough to turn a mill."

She went and got a hired man,
She brought him forty miles from town,
And in the tall grass squatted down
And bade him build as she should plan.
But cruel cowboys with their bands
They saw, and hurriedly they ran
And told a bearded cattle man
Somebody builded on his lands.

He took his rifle from the rack,
He girt himself in battle pelt,
He stuck two pistols in his belt,
And mounting on his horse's back,
He plunged ahead. But when they shewed
A woman fair, about his eyes
He pulled his hat, and he likewise
Pulled at his beard, and chewed and chewed.

At last he gat him down and spake:
"O lady, dear, what do you here?"
"I build a tomb unto my dear,
I plant sweet flowers for his sake."
The bearded man threw his two hands
Above his head, then brought them down
And cried, "O, I am William Brown,
And this the corner-stone of my lands!"

The preacher rode a spotted mare,
He galloped forty miles or more;
He swore he never had before
Seen bride or bridegroom half so fair.
And all the Injins they came down
And feasted as the night advanced,
And all the cowboys drank and danced,
And cried: Big Injin! William Brown.

HORACE GREELEY'S DRIVE.

The old stage-drivers of the brave old days!
The old stage-drivers with their dash and trust!
These old stage-drivers they have gone their ways
But their deeds live on, though their bones are dust;

And many brave tales are told and retold
Of these daring men in the days of old:

Of honest Hank Monk and his Tally-Ho,
When he took good Horace in his stage to climb
The high Sierras with their peaks of snow
And 'cross to Nevada, "and come in on time;"
But the canyon below was so deep—oh! so deep—
And the summit above was so steep—oh! so steep!

The horses were foaming. The summit ahead
Seemed as far as the stars on a still, clear night.
And steeper and steeper the narrow route led
Till up to the peaks of perpetual white;
But faithful Hank Monk, with his face to the snow,
Sat silent and stern on his Tally-Ho!

Sat steady and still, sat faithful and true
To the great, good man in his charge that day;
Sat vowing the man and the mail should "go through
On time" though he bursted both brace and stay;
Sat silently vowing, in face of the snow,
He'd "get in on time" with his Tally-Ho!

But the way was so steep and so slow—oh! so slow!
'T was silver below, and the bright silver peak
Was silver above in its beauty and glow.
An eagle swooped by, Hank saw its hooked beak;
When, sudden out-popping a head snowy white—
"Mr. Monk, I *must* lecture in Nevada to-night!"

With just one thought that the mail must go through;
With just one word to the great, good man—
But weary—so weary—the creaking stage drew
As only a weary old creaking stage can—
When again shot the head; came shrieking outright:
"Mr. Monk, I MUST lecture in Nevada to-night!"

Just then came the summit! And the far world below,
It was Hank Monk's world. But he no word spake;
He pushed back his hat to that fierce peak of snow!
He threw out his foot to the eagle and break!
He threw out his silk! He threw out his reins!
And the great wheels reeled as if reeling snow skeins!

The eagle was lost in his crag up above!
The horses flew swift as the swift light of morn!
The mail must go through with its message of love,
The miners were waiting his bright bugle horn.
The *man* must go through! And Monk made a vow
As he never had failed, why, he wouldn't fail now!

How his stage spun the pines like a far spider's web!
It was spider and fly in the heavens up there!
And the clanging of hoofs made the blood flow and ebb,
For 'twas death in the breadth of a wheel or a hair.
Once more popped the head, and the piping voice cried:
"Mr. Monk! Mr. Monk!" But no Monk replied!

Then the great stage it swung, as if swung from the sky;
Then it dipped like a ship in the deep jaws of death;
Then the good man he gasped as men gasping for breath,
When they deem it is coming their hour to die.
And again shot the head, like a battering ram,
And the face it was red, and the words they were hot:
"Mr. Monk! Mr. Monk! I don't care a (mill?) *dam*.
Whether I lecture in Nevada or not!"

THAT FAITHFUL WIFE OF IDAHO.

Huge silver snow-peaks, white as wool,
Huge, sleek, fat steers knee deep in grass,
And belly deep, and belly full,
Their flower beds one fragrant mass
Of flowers, grass tall-born and grand,
Where flowers chase the flying snow!
Oh, high held land in God's right hand,
Delicious, dreamful Idaho!

We rode the rolling cow-sown hills,
That bearded cattle man and I;
Below us laughed the blossomed rills,
Above the dappled clouds blew by.
We talked. The topic? Guess. Why, sir,
Three-fourths of all men's time they keep
To talk, to think, to *be* of HER;
The other fourth they give to sleep.

To learn what he might know, or how,
I laughed all constancy to scorn.
"Behold yon happy, changeful cow!
Behold this day, all storm at morn,
Yet now 'tis changed by cloud and sun,
Yea, all things change—the heart, the head,
Behold on earth there is not one
That changeth not in love," I said.

He drew a glass, as if to scan
The steeps for steers; raised it and sighed.
He craned his neck, this cattle man,
Then drove the cork home and replied:
"For twenty years (forgive these tears),
For twenty years no word of strife—
I have not known for twenty years
One folly from my faithful wife."

I looked that tarn man in the face—
That dark-browed, bearded cattle man.
He pulled his beard, then dropped in place
A broad right hand, all scarred and tan,
And toyed with something shining there
Above his holster, bright and small.
I was convinced. I did not care
To agitate his mind at all.

But rest I could not. Know I must
The story of my stalwart guide;
His dauntless love, enduring trust;
His blesséd and most wondrous bride.
I wondered, marveled, marveled much;
Was she of Western growth? Was she

Of Saxon blood, that wife with such
Eternal truth and constancy?

I could not rest until I knew—
"Now twenty years, my man," I said,
"Is a long time." He turned, he drew
A pistol forth, also a sigh.
"'Tis twenty years or more," sighed he.
"Nay, nay, my honest man, I vow
I do not doubt that this may be;
But tell, oh! tell me truly how?"

"'Twould make a poem, pure and grand;
All time should note it near and far;
And thy fair, virgin, gold-sown land
Should stand out like some winter star.
America should heed. And then
The doubtful French beyond the sea—
'Twould make them truer, nobler men
To know how this might truly be."

"'Tis twenty years or more, urged he;
"Nay, that I know, good guide of mine;
But lead me where this wife may be,
And I a pilgrim at a shrine,
And kneeling as a pilgrim true"—
He, leaning, shouted loud and clear:
"I cannot show my wife to you;
She's dead this more than twenty year."

SARATOGA AND THE PSALMIST.

These famous waters smell like—well,
Those Saratoga waters may
Taste just a little of the day
Of judgment; and the sulphur smell
Suggests, along with other things,
A climate rather warm for springs.

But restful as a twilight song,
The land where every lover hath
A spring, and every spring a path
To lead love pleasantly along.
Oh, there be waters, not of springs—
The waters wise King David sings.

Sweet is the bread that lovers eat
In secret, sang on harp of gold,
Jerusalem's high king of old.
"The stolen waters they are sweet!"
Oh, dear, delicious piracies
Of kisses upon love's high seas!

The old traditions of our race
Repeat for aye and still repeat;
The stolen waters still are sweet
As when King David sat in place,
All purple robed and crowned in gold,
And sang his holy psalms of old.

Oh, to escape the searching sun;
To seek these waters over sweet;
To see her dip her dimpled feet
Where these delicious waters run—
To dip her feet, nor slip nor fall,
Nor stain her garment's hem at all:

Nor soil the whiteness of her feet,
Nor stain her whitest garment's hem—
Oh, singer of Jerusalem,
You sang so sweet, so wisely sweet!
Shake hands! shake hands! I guess you knew
For all your psalms, a thing or two.

A TURKEY HUNT ON THE COLORADO

(AS TOLD AT DINNER.)

No, sir; no turkey for me, sir. But soft, place it there,
Lest friends may make question and strangers may stare.
Ah, the thought of that hunt in the cañon, the blood—

Nay, gently, please, gently! You open a flood
Of memories, memories melting me so
That I rise in my place and—excuse me—I go.
No? You must have the story? And you, lady fair?
And you, and you all? Why, it's blood and despair;
And 'twere not kind in me, not manly or wise
To bring tears at such time to such beautiful eyes.

I remember me now the last time I told
This story a Persian in diamonds and gold
Sat next to good Gladstone, there was Wales to the right,
Then a Duke, then an Earl, and such ladies in white!
But I stopped, sudden stopped, lest the story might start
The blood freezing back to each feminine heart.
But they all said, "The story!" just as you all have said,
And the great Persian monarch he nodded his head
Till his diamond-decked feathers fell, glittered and rose,
Then nodded almost to his Ishmaelite nose.

The story! Ah, pardon! 'Twas high Christmas tide
And just beef and beans; yet the land, far and wide,
Was alive with such turkeys of silver and gold
As men never born to the north may behold.
And Apaches? Aye, Apaches, and they took this game
In a pen, tolled it in. Might not we do the same?

So two of us started, strewing corn, Indian corn,
Tow'rd a great granite gorge with the first flush of morn;
Started gay, laughing back from the broad mesa's breast,
At the bravest of men, who but warned for the best.

We built a great pen from the sweet cedar wood
Tumbled down from a crown where the sentry stars stood.
Scarce done, when the turkeys in line—such a sight!
Picking corn from the sand, russet gold, silver white,
And so fat that they scarcely could waddle or hobble.
And 'twas "Queek, tukee, queek," and 'twas, "gobble and gobble!"
And their great, full crops they did wabble and wabble
As their bright, high heads they did bob, bow and bobble,
Down, up, through the trench, crowding up in the pen.
Now, quick, block the trench! Then the mules and the men!

Springing forth from our cove, guns leaned to a rock,
How we laughed! What a feast! We had got the whole flock.
How we worked till the trench was all blocked close and tight,
For we hungered, and, too, the near coming of night,
Then the thought of our welcome. The news? We could hear
Already, we fancied, the great hearty cheer
As we rushed into camp and exultingly told

Of the mule loads of turkeys in silver and gold.
Then we turned for our guns. Our guns? In their place
Ten Apaches stood there, and five guns in each face.

And we stood! we stood straight and stood strong, track solid to track.
What, turn, try to fly and be shot in the back?
No! We threw hats in the air. We should not need them more.
And yelled! Yelled as never yelled man or Comanche before.
We dared them, defied them, right there in their lair.
Why, we leaned to their guns in our splendid despair.
What! spared us for bravery, because we dared death?
You know the tale? Tell it, and spare me my breath.
No, sir. They killed us, killed us both, there and then,
And then nailed our scalps to that turkey pen.

THE CAPUCIN OF ROME.

Only a basket for fruits or bread
And the bits you divide with your dog, which you
Had left from your dinner. The round year through
He never once smiles. He bends his head
To the scorn of men. He gives the road
To the grave ass groaning beneath his load.
He is ever alone. Lo! never a hand
Is laid in his hand through the whole wide land,
Save when a man dies, and he shrives him home.
And that is the Capucin monk of Rome.

He coughs, he is hump'd, and he hobbles about
In sandals of wood. Then a hempen cord
Girdles his loathsome gown. Abhorr'd!
Ay, lonely, indeed, as a leper cast out.
One gown in three years! and—bah! how he smells!
He slept last night in his coffin of stone,
This monk that coughs, this skin and bone,
This living dead corpse from the damp, cold cells,—
Go ye where the Pincian, half-level'd down,
Slopes slow to the south. These men in brown
Have a monkery there, quaint, builded of stone;
And, living or dead, 'tis the brown men's home,—
These dead brown monks who are living in Rome!

You will hear wood sandals on the sanded floor;
A cough, then the lift of a latch, then the door
Groans open, and—horror! Four walls of stone
All gorgeous with flowers and frescoes of bone!
There are bones in the corners and bones on the wall;
And he barks like a dog that watches his bone,
This monk in brown from his bed of stone—
He barks, and he coughs, and that is all.
At last he will cough as if up from his cell;

Then strut with considerable pride about,
And lead through his blossoms of bone, and smell
Their odors; then talk, as he points them out,
Of the virtues and deeds of the gents who wore
The respective bones but the year before.

Then he thaws at last, ere the bones are through,
And talks right well as he turns them about
And stirs up a most unsavory smell;
Yea, talks of his brown dead brothers, till you
Wish them, as they are, no doubt, in—well,
A very deep well....And that may be why,
As he shows you the door and bows good-by,
That he bows so low for a franc or two,
To shrive their souls and to get them out—
These bony brown men who have their home,
Dead or alive, in their cells at Rome.

What good does he do in the world? Ah! well,
Now that is a puzzler....But, listen! He prays.
His life is the fast of the forty days.
He seeks the despised; he divides the bread
That he begg'd on his knees, does this old shavehead.
And then, when the thief and the beggar fell!
And then, when the terribie plague came down,
Christ! how we cried to these men in brown
When other men fled! Ah, who then was seen
Stand firm to the death like the Capucin?

SUNRISE IN VENICE.

Night seems troubled and scarce asleep;
Her brows are gather'd as in broken rest.
A star in the east starts up from the deep!
'Tis morn, new-born, with a star on her breast,
White as my lilies that grow in the West!
Hist! men are passing me hurriedly.
I see the yellow, wide wings of a bark,
Sail silently over my morning star.
I see men move in the moving dark,
Tall and silent as columns are;
Great, sinewy men that are good to see,
With hair push'd back, and with open breasts;
Barefooted fishermen, seeking their boats,
Brown as walnuts, and hairy as goats,—
Brave old water-dogs, wed to the sea,
First to their labors and last to their rests.

Ships are moving! I hear a horn,—
Answers back, and again it calls.
'Tis the sentinel boats that watch the town
All night, as mounting her watery walls,
And watching for pirate or smuggler. Down
Over the sea, and reaching away,
And against the east, a soft light falls,
Silvery soft as the mist of morn,
And I catch a breath like the breath of day.

The east is blossoming! Yea, a rose,
Vast as the heavens, soft as a kiss,
Sweet as the presence of woman is,
Rises and reaches, and widens and grows
Large and luminous up from the sea,
And out of the sea as a blossoming tree.
Richer and richer, so higher and higher,
Deeper and deeper it takes its hue;
Brighter and brighter it reaches through
The space of heaven to the place of stars.
Then beams reach upward as arms, from the sea;

Then lances and arrows are aimed at me.
Then lances and spangles and spars and bars
Are broken and shiver'd and strown on the sea;
And around and about me tower and spire
Start from the billows like tongues of fire.

COMO.

The lakes lay bright as bits of broken moon
Just newly set within the cloven earth;
The ripen'd fields drew round a golden girth
Far up the steeps, and glittered in the noon;
And when the sun fell down, from leafy shore
Fond lovers stole in pairs to ply the oar;
The stars, as large as lilies, fleck'd the blue;
From out the Alps the moon came wheeling through
The rocky pass the great Napoleon knew.

A gala night it was,—the season's prime.
We rode from castled lake to festal town,
To fair Milan—my friend and I; rode down
By night, where grasses waved in rippled rhyme:
And so, what theme but love at such a time?
His proud lip curl'd the while with silent scorn
At thought of love; and then, as one forlorn,
He sigh'd; then bared his temples, dash'd with gray;
Then mock'd, as one outworn and well *blase.*

A gorgeous tiger lily, flaming red,—
So full of battle, of the trumpets blare,
Of old-time passion, uprear'd its head.
I gallop'd past. I lean'd, I clutch'd it there
From out the stormy grass. I held it high,
And cried: "Lo! this to-night shall deck her hair
Through all the dance. And mark! the man shall die
Who dares assault, for good or ill design,
The citadel where I shall set this sign."

O, she shone fairer than the summer star,
Or curl'd sweet moon in middle destiny;
More fair than sun-morn climbing up the sea,
Where all the loves of Adriana are....
Who loves, who truly loves, will stand aloof:
The noisy tongue makes most unholy proof
Of shallow passion....All the while afar
From out the dance I stood and watched my star,
My tiger lily borne, an oriflamme of war.

Adown the dance she moved with matchless grace.
The world—my world—moved with her. Suddenly
I question'd whom her cavalier might be?
'Twas he! His face was leaning to her face!
I clutch'd my blade; I sprang, I caught my breath,—
And so, stood leaning cold and still as death.
And they stood still. She blushed, then reach'd and tore
The lily as she pass'd, and down the floor
She strew'd its heart like jets of gushing gore....

'Twas *he* said heads, not hearts, were made to break:
He taught this that night in splendid scorn.
I learn'd too well....The dance was done. ere morn
We mounted—he and I—but no more spake....
And this for woman's love! My lily worn
In her dark hair in pride, to then be torn
And trampled on, for this bold stranger's sake!....
Two men rode silent back toward the lake;
Two men rode silent down—but only one
Rode up at morn to meet the rising sun.

The red-clad fishers row and creep
Below the crags as half asleep,
Nor ever make a single sound.
The walls are steep,
The waves are deep;
And if a dead man should be found
By these same fishers in their round,
Why, who shall say but he was drown'd?

BURNS.

Eld Druid oaks of Ayr,
Precepts! Poems! Pages!
Lessons! Leaves, and Volumes!
Arches! Pillars! Columns
In corridors of ages!
Grand patriarchal sages
Lifting palms in prayer!

The Druid beards are drifting
And shifting to and fro,
In gentle breezes lifting,
That bat-like come and go.
The while the moon is sifting
A sheen of shining snow
On all these blossoms lifting
Their blue eyes from below.

No, 'tis not phantoms walking
That you hear rustling there,
But bearded Druids talking,
And turning leaves in prayer.
No, not a night-bird singing
Nor breeze the broad bough swinging,
But that bough holds a censer,
And swings it to and fro.
'Tis Sunday eve, remember,
That's why they chant so low.

I linger in the autumn noon,
I listen to the partridge call,
I watch the yellow leaflets fall
And drift adown the dimpled Doon.
I lean me o'er the ivy-grown
Auld brig, where Vandal tourists' tools
Have ribb'd out names that would be known,
Are known—known as a herd of fools.

Down Ailsa Craig the sun declines,
With lances level'd here and there—
The tinted thorns! the trailing vines!
O braes of Doon! so fond, so fair!
So passing fair, so more than fond!
The Poet's place of birth beyond,
Beyond the mellow bells of Ayr!

I hear the milk-maid's twilight song
Come bravely through the storm-bent oaks;
Beyond, the white surf's sullen strokes
Beat in a chorus deep and strong;
I hear the sounding forge afar,
And rush and rumble of the car,
The steady tinkle of the bell
Of lazy, laden, home-bound cows
That stop to bellow and to browse;
I breathe the soft sea-wind as well.

O Burns! where bid? where bide ye now?
Where rest you in this night's full noon,
Great master of the pen and plow?
Might you not on yon slanting beam
Of moonlight kneeling to the Doon,
Descend once to this hallow'd stream?
Sure yon stars yield enough of light
For heaven to spare your face one night.

O Burns! another name for song,
Another name for passion—pride;
For love and poesy allied;
For strangely blended right and wrong.

I picture you as one who kneel'd
A stranger at his own hearthstone;
One knowing all, yet all unknown,
One seeing all, yet all conceal'd;
The fitful years you linger'd here
A lease of peril and of pain;
And I am thankful yet again
The gods did love you, plowman! peer!

In all your own and other lands,
I hear your touching songs of cheer;
The lowly peasant, lordly peer.
Above your honor'd dust strike hands.

A touch of tenderness is shown
In this unselfish love of Ayr,
And it is well, you earn'd it fair;
For all unhelmeted, alone,
You proved a plowman's honest claim
To battle in the lists of fame;
You earn'd it as a warrior earns
His laurels fighting for his land,
And died—it was your right to go.
O eloquence of silent woe!
The Master leaning, reach'd a hand,
And whisper'd, "It is finish'd, Burns!"

O sad, sweet singer of a Spring!
Yours was a chill, uncheerful May,
And you knew no full days of June;
You ran too swiftly up the way,
And wearied soon, so over-soon!
You sang in weariness and woe;
You falter'd, and God heard you sing,
Then touch'd your hand and led you so,
You found life's hill-top low, so low,
You cross'd its summit long ere noon.
Thus sooner than one would suppose
Some weary feet will find repose.

BYRON.*

In men whom men condemn as ill
I find so much of goodness still,
In men whom men pronounce divine
I find so much of sin and blot,
I do not dare to draw a line
Between the two, where God has not.

O cold and cruel Nottingham!
In disappointment and in tears,
Sad, lost, and lonely, here I am
To question, "Is this Nottingham,
Of which I dream'd for years and years?"
I seek in vain for name or sign
Of him who made this mold a shrine,
A Mecca to the fair and fond
Beyond the seas, and still beyond.

Where white clouds crush their drooping wings

*The little old church where Byron, with all his kindred, are buried, at Hucknall Tokard, Nottes, has been twice torn down and rebuilt since the above was written, although it had stood for centuries little better than a ruin. A wreath of bay was laid above his dust, from Ina D. Coolbrith. The vicar there protested. The matter was appealed to the Bishop. The Bishop answered by sending another wreath. Then the King of Greece sent a wreath. Then the rebuilding began.

Against my snow-crown'd battlements,
And peaks that flash like silver tents;
Where Sacramento's fountain springs,
And proud Columbia frets his shore
Of somber, boundless wood and wold,
And lifts his yellow sands of gold
In plaintive murmurs evermore;
Where snowy dimpled Tahoe smiles,
And where white breakers from the sea,
In solid phalanx knee to knee,
Surround the calm Pacific Isles,
Then run and reach unto the land
And spread their thin palms on the sand,—
Is he supreme—there understood:
The free can understand the free;
The brave and good the brave and good.

Yea, he did sin; who hath reveal'd
That he was more than man, or less?
Yet sinn'd no more; but less conceal'd
Than they who cloak'd their follies o'er,
And then cast stones in his distress.
He scorn'd to make the good seem more,
Or make the bitter sin seem less.
And so his very manliness
The seeds of persecution bore.

When all his songs and fervid love
Brought back no olive branch or dove,
Or love or trust from any one,
Proud, all unpitied and alone
He lived to make himself unknown,
Disdaining love and yielding none.
Like some high-lifted sea-girt stone
That could not stoop, but all the days,
With proud brow fronted to the breeze,
Felt seas blown from the south, and seas
Blown from the north, and many ways,
He stood—a solitary light
In stormy seas and settled night—
Then fell, but stirr'd the seas as far
As winds and waves and waters are.

The meek-eyed stars are cold and white
And steady, fix'd for all the years;
The comet burns the wings of night,
And dazzles elements and spheres,
Then dies in beauty and a blaze
Of light, blown far through other days.

The poet's passion, sense of pride,
His boundless love, the wooing throng
Of sweet temptations that betide
The warm and wayward child of song,
The world knows not: I lift a hand
To ye who know, who understand.

*   *   *   *   *   *

The ancient Abbey's breast is broad,
And stout her massive walls of stone;
But let him lie, repose alone
Ungather'd with the great of God,
In dust, by his fierce fellow man.
Some one, some day, loud voiced will speak
And say the broad breast was not broad,
The walls of stone were all too weak
To hold the proud dust, in their plan;
The hollow of God's great right hand
Receives it; let it rest with God.

In sad but beautiful decay
Gray Hucknall kneels into the dust,
And, cherishing her sacred trust,
Does blend her clay with lordly clay.

No sign or cryptic stone or cross
Unto the passing world has said,
"He died, and we deplore his loss."
No sound of sandall'd pilgrims' tread
Disturbs the pilgrim's peaceful rest,
Or frets the proud, impatient breast.
The bat flits through the broken pane,
The black swift swallow gathers moss,
And builds in peace above his head,
Then goes, then comes, and builds again.

And it is well; not otherwise
Would he, the grand sad singer, will.

The serene peace of paradise
He sought—'tis his—the storm is still.
Secure in his eternal fame,
And blended pity and respect,
He does not feel the cold neglect,
And England does not fear the shame.

ABOVE THE CLOUDS.

'Mid white Sierras, that slope to the sea,
Lie turbulent lands. Go dwell in the skies,
And the thundering tongues of Yosemite
Shall persuade you to silence, and you shall be wise.

I but sing for the love of song and the few
Who loved me first and shall love me last;
And the storm shall pass as the storms have pass'd,
For never were clouds but the sun came through.

A CALIFORNIA CHRISTMAS.

Behold where Beauty walks with Peace!
Behold where Plenty pours her horn
Of fruits, of flowers, fat increase,
As generous as light of morn.

Green Shasta, San Diego, seas
Of bloom and green between them rolled.
Great herds in grasses to their knees,
And green earth garmented in gold.

White peaks that prop the sapphire blue
Look down on Edens, such as when
That fair, first spot perfection knew
And God walked perfect earth with men.

I say God's kingdom is at hand
Right here, if we but lift our eyes;
I say there lies no line or land
Between this land and Paradise.

THANKSGIVING, 1896.

Thank God for high, white holy Truth,
To feed the world instead of sham;
Lo, laden, patient, lowly Ruth!
Lo, Abram's sacrificial ram!
Thank God for Abram's faith of old;
Thank God for man's faith in God's plan.
But thank God most—and manifold
For man's great, growing faith in man.

We round up, up; round on and on,
As rounding eagles rise and rise!
The darkest hour ushers dawn,
And dawn is dashing up the skies!
Thank God for light, God's face is light;
The light of Truth, of faith in kind—
The light of Love, the light of Right,
The blind no more may lead the blind!

Just Truth and Faith and steady Light,
And mad sensation is no more;
The fakir folds his tent of night
And finds his dim Plutonian shore.
The people live, the people love,
The people are once more divine:
Put forth thy hand, receive the dove,
Descend and taste the corn and wine.

Thank God so much for laden Ruth,
For plenty poured from pole to pole;
But thank God most for Faith and Truth,
For meats that feed the famished soul:
For light wherewith to know to feed,
For Light, for God's face far and near;
For love that knows not lust nor greed,
For faith that calmly smiles at fear.

"49."*

We have worked our claims,
We have spent our gold,
Our barks are astrand on the bars;
We are battered and old,
Yet at night we behold,
Outcroppings of gold in the stars.

Chorus—Tho' battered and old,
Our hearts are bold,
Yet oft do we repine;
For the days of old,
For the days of gold,
For the days of forty-nine.

Where the rabbits play,
Where the quail all day
Pipe on the chaparral hill;
A few more days,
And the last of us lays
His pick aside and all is still.
Chorus—

We are wreck and stray,
We are cast away,
Poor battered old hulks and spars;
But we hope and pray,
On the judgment day,
We shall strike it up in the stars.
Chorus—

BATTLES.

Nay, not for fame, but for the Right;
To make this fair world fairer still.
Or lordly lily of a night,
Or sun-topped tower of a hill,
Or high or low, or near or far,
Or dull or keen, or bright or dim,
Or blade of glass, or brightest star,
All, all are but the same to Him.

O pity of the strife for place;
O pity of the strife for power;
How scarred, how marred a mountain's face;
How fair the fair face of a flower.
The blade of grass beneath your feet,
The bravest sword: ay, braver far,
To do and die in mute defeat,
Thou bravest Conqueror of war.

When I am dead say this, but this,
He grasped at no man's blade or shield,
Or banner bore, but helmetless,
Alone, unknown, he held the field;
He held the field with saber drawn,
Where God had set him in the fight;
He held the field, fought on and on,
And so fell fighting for the Right.

SAN DIEGO.

"O for a beaker of the warm South;
The true, the blushful hypocrine!"

What shall be said of the sun-born Pueblo?
This town sudden born in the path of the sun?
This town of St. James, of the calm San Diego,
As suddenly born as if shot from a gun?

Why, speak of her warmly; why, write her name down
As softer than sunlight, as warmer than wine!

*This poem is taken from "'49, or the Gold Seekers," by permission of Funk & Wagnalls, New York, publishers of the book. The words have been set to music and selected as the Song of the Native Sons of California. It was sung in Mining Camps long before it was in print. They are my first lines that have lived, but are much altered from the original.

Why speak of her bravely; this ultimate
town
With feet in the foam of the vast Argentine:

The vast argent seas of the Aztec, of
Cortez!
The boundless white border of battle-torn
lands—
The fall of Napoleon, the rise of red
Juarez—
The footfalls of nations are heard on her
sands.

PIONEERS TO THE GREAT EMERALD LAND.

READ AT PORTLAND, 1896.

Emerald, emerald, emerald Land;
Land of the sun mists, land of the sea,
Stately and stainless and storied and grand
As cloud-mantled Hood in white majesty—
Mother of States, we are worn, we are
gray—
Mother of men, we are going away.

Mother of States, tall mother of men,
Of cities, of churches, of homes, of sweet
rest,
We are going away, we must journey
again,
As of old we journeyed to the vast, far
West.
We tent by the river, our feet once more,
Please God, are set for the ultimate shore.

Mother, white mother, white Oregon
In emerald kilt, with star-set crown
Of sapphire, say is it night? Is it dawn?
Say what of the night? Is it well up
and down?
We are going away....From yon high
watch tower,
Young men, strong men, say, what of the
hour?

Young men, strong men, there is work
to be done;
Faith to be cherished, battles to fight,
Victories won were never well won
Save fearlessly won for God and the right.
These cities, these homes, sweet peace
and her spell
Be ashes, but ashes, with the infidel.

* * * * * *

Have Faith, such Faith as your fathers
knew,
All else must follow if you have but Faith.
Be true to their Faith, and you must be
true.
"Lo! I will be with you," the Master
saith.
Good by, dawn breaks; it is coming full
day
And one by one we strike tent and away.

Good by. Slow folding our snow-white tents,
Our dim eyes lift to the farther shore,
And never these riddled, gray regiments
Shall answer full roll-call any more.
Yet never a doubt, nay, never a fear
Of old, or now, knew the Pioneer.

ALASKA.

Ice built, ice bound and ice bounded,
Such cold seas of silence! such room!
Such snow-light, such sea light confounded
With thunders that smite like a doom!
Such grandeur! such glory! such gloom!
Hear that boom! Hear that deep distant
boom

Of an avalanche hurled
Down this unfinished world!

Ice seas! and ice summits! ice spaces
In splendor of white, as God's throne!
Ice worlds to the pole! and ice places
Untracked, and unnamed, and unknown!
Hear that boom! Hear the grinding, the
groan
Of the ice-gods in pain! Hear the moan
Of yon ice mountain hurled
Down this unfinished world.

"THE FOURTH" IN OREGON.*

Hail, Independence of old ways!
Old worlds! The West declares the West,
Her storied ways, her gloried days,
Because the West deserveth best.
This new, true land of noblest deeds
Has rights, has sacred rights and needs.

Sing, ye who may, this natal day;
Of dauntless thought, of men of might,
In lesser lands and far away.
But truth is truth and right is right.
And, oh, to sing like sounding flood,
These boundless boundaries writ in blood!

Three thousand miles of battle deeds,
Of burning Moscows, Cossacks, snows;
Then years and years of British greed,
Of grasping greed; of lurking foes.
I say no story ever writ
Or said, or sung, surpasses it!

And who has honored us, and who
Has bravely dared stand up and say;
"Give ye to Cæsar Cæsar's due?"
Unpaid, unpensioned, mute and gray,
Some few survivors of the brave,
Still hold enough land for a grave.

How much they dared, how much they
won—
Why, o'er your banner of bright stars,
Their star should be the blazing sun
Above the battle star of Mars.

* This poem was read, 1896, near the scene of the Whitman massacre at the old Mission. The story of Oregon—*Aure il Agua;* Hear the Waters—glowing with great deeds, drama, tragedy, surpassing anything in the history of any other State, east or west, old or new. When the paw of the British lion reached down from Canada and laid heavy hand on Oregon, these pioneers met under their great firs and proclaimed to the world that they were not British subjects, but American citizens. Marcus P. Whitman mounted horse in midwinter and set out alone and rode 3,000 miles to lay the facts before the President. Yet the Government never lifted a hand to help save Oregon to the Nation. So far from that, a Senator rose in his place and literally denounced all effort in that direction, saying "I would to God we had never heard of that country; we do not want a foot of ground on the Pacific Ocean." Webster was hardly less cruel. But undaunted, Whitman gathered up hundreds of wagons and led back to Oregon; the first that ever crossed the plains. He saved Oregon, but lost his life and all his house. Then the pioneers, to avenge the massacre, declared war on their own account, fought it to a finish without so much as a single man or gun from the Government, made peace on their own account, and then went to work and dug their own gold from their own ground, and with their own hands coined it and paid their war debts and from the first kept their paper with its face in virgin gold. The coins, virgin gold with a sheaf of wheat on one side, showing the richness of the soil, and a beaver on the reverse, typifying the industry of the people. Oregon is the only division of this republic that ever coined gold under authority of law. And even in later Indian wars Oregon was always treated meanly, most meanly. More than once every man and boy who could carry a gun or drive a team was in the field. My father and his three sons, aged ten, twelve, and fourteen, were all at one time teamsters in a supply train. And the Government paid for services and supplies but tardily, if at all. The meanness is incredible. There are millions still due Oregon. No, I am not angry, or selfish either; I never received or claimed one cent fo services, supplies or losses. But some of these old pioneers are in need now, and it makes a man blush for his country to see them so meanly treated even to the last.

Here, here beside brave Whitman's dust,
Let us be bravely, frankly just.

The mountains from the first were so.
The mountains from the first were free.
They ever laid the tyrant low,
And kept the boon of liberty.
The levels of the earth alone
Endured the tyrant, bore the throne.

The levels of the earth alone
Bore Sodoms, Babylons of crime,
And all sad cities overthrown
Along the surging surf of time.
The coward, slave, creeps in the fen:
God's mountains only cradle men.

Aye, wise and great was Washington,
And brave the men of Bunker Hill;
Most brave and worthy every one,
In work and faith and fearless will
And brave endeavor for the right,
Until yon stars burst through their night.

Aye, wise and good was Washington.
Yet when he laid his sword aside,
The bravest deed yet done was done.
And when in stately strength and pride
He took the plow and turned the mold
He wrote God's autograph in gold.

He wrought the fabled fleece of gold
In priceless victories of peace,
With plowshare set in mother mold;
Then gathering the golden fleece
About his manly, martial breast,
This farmer laid him down to rest.

O! this was godlike! And yet, who
Of all men gathered here to-day
Has not drawn sword as swift as true,
Then laid its reddened edge away,
And took the plow, and turned the mold
To sow yon sunny steeps with gold.

Aye, this true valor! Sing who will
Of battle charge, of banners borne
Triumphant up the blazing hill
On battle's front, of banners torn,
Of horse and rider torn and rent,
Red regiment on regiment.

Yet this were boy's play to that man
Who, far out yonder lone frontier,
With wife and babe fought in the van,
Fought on, fought on, year after year.
No brave, bright flag to cheer the brave,
No farewell gun above his grave.

I say such silent pioneers
Who here set plowshare to the sun,
And silent gave their sunless years,
Were kings of heroes every one.
No Brandywine, no Waterloo
E'er knew one hero half so true!

A nation's honor for our dead,
God's pity for the stifled pain;
And tears as ever woman shed,
Sweet woman's tears for maimed or slain.
But man's tears for the mute, unknown,
Who fights alone, who falls alone.

The very bravest of the brave,
The hero of all lands to me?
Far up yon yellow lifting wave
His brave ship cleaves the golden sea.
And gold or gain, or never gain,
No argosy sails there in vain.

And who the coward? Hessian he,
Who turns his back upon the field,
Who wears the slavish livery
Of town or city, sells his shield

Of honor, as his ilk of old
Sold body, soul, for British gold.

My heroes, comrades of the field,
Content ye here; here God to you,
Whatever fate or change may yield,
Has been most generous and true.
Yon everlasting snow-peaks stand
His sentinels about this land.

Yon bastions of God's house are white
As heaven's porch with heaven's peace.
Behold His portals bathed in light!
Behold at hand the golden fleece!
Behold the fatness of the land
On every hill, on every hand!

Yon bannered snow-peaks point and plead
God's upward path, God's upward plan
Of peace, God's everlasting creed
Of love and brotherhood of man.
Thou mantled magistrates in white,
Give us His light! Give us His light!

AN ANSWER.

Well! who shall lay hand on my harp but me,
Or shall chide my song from the sounding trees?
The passionate sun and the resolute sea,
These were my masters, and only these.

These were my masters, and only these,
And these from the first I obey'd, and they
Shall command me now, and I shall obey
As a dutiful child that is proud to please.

There never were measures as true as the sun,
The sea hath a song that is passingly sweet,
And yet they repeat,.and repeat, and repeat,
The same old runes though the new years run.

By unnamed rivers of the Oregon north,
That roll dark-heaved into turbulent hills,
I have made my home...... The wild heart thrills
With memories fierce, and a world storms forth.

On eminent peaks that are dark with pine,
And mantled in shadows and voiced in storms,
I have made my camps: majestic gray forms
Of the thunder-clouds, they were companions of mine;

And face set to face, like to lords austere,
Have we talk'd, red-tongued, of the mysteries
Of the circling sun, of the oracled seas,
While ye who judged me had mantled in fear.

Some fragment of thought in the unfinish'd words;
A cry of fierce freedom, and I claim no more.
What more would you have from the tender of herds
And of horse on an ultimate Oregon shore?

From men unto God go forth, as alone,
Where the dark pines talk in their tones of the sea
To the unseen God in a harmony
Of the under seas, and know the unknown.

'Mid white Sierras, that slope to the sea,
Lie turbulent lands. Go dwell in the skies,
And the thundering tongues of Yosemite
Shall persuade you to silence, and you shall be wise.

Yea, men may deride, and the thing it is well;
Turn well and aside from the one wild note
To the song of the bird with the tame, sweet throat;
But the sea sings on in his cave and shell.

Let the white moons ride, let the red stars fall,
O great, sweet sea! O fearful and sweet!
Thy songs they repeat, and repeat, and repeat:
And these, I say, shall survive us all.

YOSEMITE.

Sound! sound! sound!
O colossal walls and crown'd
In one eternal thunder!
Sound! sound! sound!
O ye oceans overhead,
While we walk, subdued in wonder,
In the ferns and grasses, under
And beside the swift Merced!

Fret! fret! fret!
Streaming, sounding banners, set
On the giant granite castles
In the clouds and in the snow!
But the foe he comes not yet,—
We are loyal, valiant vassals,
And we touch the trailing tassels
Of the banners far below.

Surge! surge! surge!
From the white Sierra's verge,
To the very valley blossom.
Surge! surge! surge!
Yet the song-bird builds a home,
And the mossy branches cross them,
And the tasselled tree-tops toss them,
In the clouds of falling foam.

Sweep! sweep! sweep!
O ye heaven-born and deep,
In one dread, unbroken chorus!
We may wonder or may weep,—
We may wait on God before us;
We may shout or lift a hand,—
We may bow down and deplore us,
But may never understand.

Beat! beat! beat!
We advance, but would retreat
From this restless, broken breast
Of the earth in a convulsion.
We would rest, but dare not rest,
For the angel of expulsion
From this Paradise below
Waves us onward and...... we go.

DEAD IN THE SIERRAS.

His footprints have failed us,
Where berries are red,
And madroños are rankest,
The hunter is dead!

The grizzly may pass
By his half-open door;
May pass and repass
On his path, as of yore;

The panther may crouch
In the leaves on his limb;
May scream and may scream,—
It is nothing to him.

Prone, bearded, and breasted
Like columns of stone;
And tall as a pine—
As a pine overthrown!

His camp-fires gone,
What else can be done
Than let him sleep on
Till the light of the sun?

Ay, tombless! what of it?
Marble is dust,
Cold and repellent;
And iron is rust.

IN PERE LA CHAISE.

I.

An avenue of tombs! I stand before
The tomb of Abelard and Eloise.
A long, a dark bent line of cypress trees
Leads past and on to other shrines; but o'er
This tomb the boughs hang darkest and most dense,
Like leaning mourners clad in black. The sense
Of awe oppresses you. This solitude
Means more than common sorrow. Down the wood
Still lovers pass, then pause, then turn again,
And weep like silent, unobtrusive rain.

II.

'Tis but a simple, antique tomb, that kneels
As one that weeps above the broken clay.
'Tis stained with storms; 'tis eaten well away,
Nor half the old—new story now reveals
Of heart that held beyond the tomb to heart.
But oh, it tells of love! And that true page
Is more in this cold, hard, commercial age,
When love is calmly counted some lost art,
Than all man's mighty monuments of war
Or archives vast of art and science are.

III.

Here poets pause and dream a listless hour;
Here silly pilgrims stoop and kiss the clay,
Here sweetest maidens leave a cross or flower,
While vandals bear the tomb in bits away.
The ancient stone is scarred with name and scrawl
Of many tender fools. But over all,
And high above all other scrawls, is writ
One simple thing; most touching and most fit.
Some pitying soul has tiptoed high above,
And with a nail has scrawled but this: "O Love!"

IV.

O Love!....I turn; I climb the hill of tombs
Where sleeps the "bravest of the brave," below,
His bed of scarlet blooms in zone of snow—
No cross, nor sign, save this red bed of blooms.
I see grand tombs to France's lesser dead,—
Colossal steeds, white pyramids, still red
At base with blood, still torn with shot and shell,
To testify that here the Commune fell;
And yet I turn once more from all of these,
And stand before the tomb of Eloise.

ROME.

I.

Some leveled hills, a wall, a dome
That lords its gilded arch and lies,
While at its base a beggar cries
For bread, and this—and that is Rome.

II.

Yet Rome is Rome, and Rome she must
And shall remain beside her gates,
And tribute take of Kings and States,
Until the stars have fallen to dust.

III.

Yea, Time on yon Campagnan plain
Has pitched in siege his battle-tents;
And round about her battlements
Has marched and trumpeted in vain.

IV.

These skies are Rome! The very loam
Lifts up and speaks in Roman pride;
And Time, outfaced and still defied,
Sits by and wags his beard at Rome.

"POVERIS! POVERIS!"

"Feed my sheep."

Come, let us ponder; it is fit—
Born of the poor, born to the poor.
The poor of purse, the poor of wit,
Were first to find God's opened door—
Were first to climb the ladder round by round
That fell from heaven's door unto the ground.

God's poor came first, the very first!
God's poor were first to see, to hear,
To feel the light of heaven burst
Full on their faces. Far or near,
His poor were first to follow, first to fall!
What if at last his poor stand forth the first of all?

AMERICA TO AMERICANS.

Behold America! my land,
Unarmed, unharmed, whilst Europe groans
With weight of arms on either hand,
And hears a starving woman's moans.

My land that feeds, that leads the world,
Where dwells more strength in one small star
Of her brave, beauteous flag unfurled
Than all their armaments of war.

My land, where man first knew his strength—
His strength of right, his fearful might;
His fearful, tawny, tiger-length
Of arm in battle for the right.

My land that shook from off her shores
A thousand British battle ships—
As when some lion wakes and roars
And walks the world and licks his lips!

My land that sows the world with gold,
That taught old worlds in lightning tongue,
That leads the old, that feeds the old,
And yet so young, so very young!

My land that reaches kindly, fair,
For cactus spear, for maple leaf,
As peaceful, loving harvester
Would gather sheaf to golden sheaf.

Come maple leaf, come stalwart man
Of stout and sterling Canada;

Come cactus spear, come Darien—
To-morrow, if not yet to-day.

One flag for all, or far or near,
One faith for all whate'er befall—
Or maple leaf, or cactus spear,
One star-built banner, built for all.

FATHER DAMIEN OF HAWAII.

The best of all heroes that ever may be,
The best and the bravest in peace or in war
Since that lorn sad night in Gethsemane—
Horns of the moon or the five-horned star?
Why, merely a Belgian monk, and the least,
The lowliest — merely a peasant-born priest.

And how did he fight? And where did he fall?
With what did he conquer in the name of God?
The cross! And he conquered more souls than all
Famed captains that ever fought fire-shod.
Now, lord of the sapphire-set sea and skies,
Far under his Southern gold Cross he lies.

Far under the fire-sown path of the sun
He sleeps with his lepers; but a world is his!
His great seas chorus and his warm tides run
To dulcet and liquid soft cadences.
And, glories to come or great deeds gone,
I'd rather be he than Napoleon.

He rests with his lepers, for whom he died;
The lorn outcasts in their cooped up isle,
While Slander purses her lips in pride
And proud men gather their robes and smile.
They mock at his deeds in their daily talk,
Deriding his work in their Christian(?) walk.

But the great wide, honest, the wise, big world;
Or sapphire splendors or midnight sun,
It is asking the while that proud lips are curled,
Why do not ye as that monk hath done?
Why do not ye, if so braver than he,
Some one brave deed that the world might see?

AT OUR GOLDEN GATE.

At our gate he groaneth, groaneth,
Chafes as chained, and chafes all day;
As leashed greyhound moaneth, moaneth,
When the master keeps away.
Men have seen him steal in lowly,
Lick the island's feet and face,
Lift a cold wet nose up slowly,
Then turn empty to his place:
Empty, idle, hungered, waiting
For some hero, dauntless-souled,
Glory-loving, pleasure-hating,
Minted in God's ancient mold.

What ship yonder stealing, stealing,
Pirate-like, as if ashamed?
Black men, brown men, red, revealing—
Not one white man to be named!
What flag yonder, proud, defiant,
Topmast, saucy, and sea blown?
Tall ships lordly and reliant—
All flags yonder save our own!
Surged atop yon half-world water

Once a tuneful tall ship ran;
Ran the storm king, too, and caught her,
Caught and laughed as laughs a man:

Laughed and held her, and so holden,
Holden high, foam-crest and free
As famed harper, hoar and olden,
Held his great harp on his knee.
Then his fingers wildly flinging
Through chords, ropes—such symphony
As if some wild Wagner singing—
Some wild Wagner of the sea!
Sang he of such poor cowed weaklings,
Cowed, weak landsmen such as we.
While ten thousand storied sea kings
Foam-white, storm-blown, sat the sea.

Oh, for England's old sea thunder!
Oh, for England's bold sea men,
When we banged her over, under
And she banged us back again!
Better old time strife and stresses,
Cloud top't towers, walls, distrust;
Better wars than lazinesses,
Better loot than wine and lust!
Give us seas? Why, we have oceans!
Give us manhood, sea men, men!
Give us deeds, loves, hates, emotions!
Else give back these seas again.

THE VOICE OF THE DOVE.*

Come, listen O Love to the voice of the dove,
Come, hearken and hear him say
There are many To-morrows, my Love, my Love,
There is only one To-day.
And all day long you can hear him say
This day in purple is rolled
And the baby stars of the milkyway
They are cradled in cradles of gold.

Now what is thy secret serene gray dove
Of singing so sweetly alway?
"There are many To-morrows, my Love, my Love,
There is only one To-day."

WASHINGTON BY THE DELAWARE.

The snow was red with patriot blood,
The proud foe tracked the blood-red snow.
The flying patriots crossed the flood
A tattered, shattered band of woe.
Forlorn each barefoot hero stood,
With bare head bended low.

"Let us cross back! Death waits us here:
Recross or die!" the chieftain said.
A famished soldier dropped a tear—
A tear that froze as it was shed:
For oh, his starving babes were dear—
They had but this for bread!

A captain spake: "It cannot be!
These bleeding men, why, what could they?
'Twould be as snowflakes in a sea!"
The worn chief did not heed or say.
He set his firm lips silently,
Then turned aside to pray.

And as he kneeled and prayed to God,
God's finger spun the stars in space;

*Taken from "The Building of the City Beautiful," by permission of the publishers, Stone and Kimball, Chicago and Cambridge. I can commend this little book to my lovers. It was first written in verse as The Life of Christ. But when Sir Edwin Arnold's "Light of the World" appeared I saw that he, by help of his knowledge of the Orient, had gone deeper than I could, so I destroyed all but about twenty fragments, heads of chapters, and wrote the rest of the book in prose. It is, in the main, the Story of the Hights.

He spread his banner blue and broad,
He dashed the dead sun's stripes in place,
Till war walked heaven fire shod
And lit the chieftain's face:

Till every soldier's heart was stirred,
Till every sword shook in its sheath—
"Up! up! Face back. But not one word!"
God's flag above; the ice beneath—
They crossed so still, they only heard
The icebergs grind their teeth!

Ho! Hessians, hirelings at meat
While praying patriots hunger so!
Then, bang! Boom! Bang! Death and defeat!
And blood? Ay, blood upon the snow!
Yet not the blood of patriotic feet,
But heart's blood of the foe!

O ye who hunger and despair!
O ye who perish for the sun,
Look up and dare, for God is there;
And man can do what man has done!
Think, think of darkling Delaware!
Think, think of Washington!

FOR THOSE WHO FAIL.*

"All honor to him who shall win the prize,"
The world has cried for a thousand years;
But to him who tries, and who fails and dies,
I give great honor and glory and tears:

Give glory and honor and pitiful tears
To all who fail in their deeds sublime;
Their ghosts are many in the van of years,
They were born with Time, in advance of Time.

Oh, great is the hero who wins a name,
But greater many and many a time
Some pale-faced fellow who dies in shame,
And lets God finish the thought sublime.

And great is the man with a sword undrawn,
And good is the man who refrains from wine;
But the man who fails and yet still fights on,
Lo, he is the twin-born brother of mine.

THE LIGHT OF CHRIST'S FACE.

Behold how glorious! Behold
The light of Christ's face; and such light!
The Moslem, Buddhist, as of old,
Gropes helpless on in hopeless night.
But lo! where Christ comes, crowned with flame,
Ten thousand triumphs in Christ's name,
Ten thousand triumphs in Christ's name.
But lo! where Christ comes crowned with flame,
Ten thousand triumphs in Christ's name,
Ten thousand triumphs in Christ's name.

Elijah's chariot of fire
Chained lightnings harnessed to his car!
Jove's thunders bridled by a wire—
Call unto nations "here we are!"
Lo! all the world one sea of light,
Save where the Paynim walks in night,
Lo, all the world one sea of light,
Lo, all the world one sea of light,

* From "Memorie and Rime," by permission of Funk & Wagnalls, publishers of the Standard Dictionary and the Standard Library, of which the above book is one.

Save where the Paynim walks in night,
Lo, all the world one sea of light.

What more? What sermons like to these;
This light of Christ's face, power, speed,
In these full rounded centuries,
To prove the Christ, the Christ in deed?
Yea, Christ is life, and Christ is light,
And anti-Christ is death and night,
Yea, Christ is life, and Christ is light.
Yea, Christ is life, and Christ is light,
And anti-Christ is death and night,
Yea Christ is life, and Christ is light.

COLUMBUS.

Behind him lay the gray Azores,
Behind the Gates of Hercules;
Before him not the ghost of shores;
Before him only shoreless seas.
The good mate said: "Now must we pray,
For lo! the very stars are gone.
Brave Adm'r'l, speak; what shall I say?"
"Why, say: 'Sail on! sail on! and on!'"

"My men grow mutinous day by day;
My men grow ghastly wan and weak."
The stout mate thought of home; a spray
Of salt wave washed his swarthy cheek.
"What shall I say, brave Adm'r'l, say,
If we sight naught but seas at dawn?"
"Why, you shall say at break of day:
'Sail on! sail on! sail on! and on!'"

They sailed and sailed, as winds might blow,
Until at last the blanched mate said:
"Why, now not even God would know
Should I and all my men fall dead.
These very winds forget their way,
For God from these dread seas is gone.
Now speak, brave Adm'r'l; speak and say——"
He said: "Sail on! sail on! and on!"

They sailed. They sailed. Then spake the mate:
"This mad sea shows his teeth to-night.
He curls his lip, he lies in wait,
With lifted teeth, as if to bite!
Brave Adm'r'l, say but one good word:
What shall we do when hope is gone?"
The words leapt like a leaping sword:
"Sail on! sail on! sail on! and on!"

Then, pale and worn, he kept his deck,
And peered through darkness. Ah, that night
Of all dark nights! And then a speck—
A light! A light! A light! A light!
It grew, a starlit flag unfurled!
It grew to be Time's burst of dawn.
He gained a world; he gave that world
Its grandest lesson: "On! sail on!"

CUBA LIBRE.

Comes a cry from Cuban water—
From the warm, dusk Antilles—
From the lost Atlanta's daughter,
Drowned in blood as drowned in seas;
Comes a cry of purpled anguish—
See her struggles, hear her cries!
Shall she live, or shall she languish?
Shall she sink, or shall she rise?

She shall rise, by all that's holy!
She shall live and she shall last;
Rise as we, when crushed and lowly
From the blackness of the past.
Bid her strike! Lo, it is written
Blood for blood and life for life.
Bid her smite, as she is smitten;
Stars and stripes were born of strife.

Once we flashed her lights of freedom,
Lights that dazzled her dark eyes
Till she could but yearning heed them,
Reach her hands and try to rise.
Then they stabbed her, choked her, drowned her,
Till we scarce could hear a note.
Ah! these rusting chains that bound her!
Oh! these robbers at her throat!

And the kind who forged these fetters?
Ask five hundred years for news.
Stake and thumbscrew for their betters?
Inquisitions! Banished Jews!
Chains and slavery! What reminder
Of one red man in that land?
Why, these very chains that bind her
Bound Columbus, foot and hand!

She shall rise as rose Columbus,
From his chains, from shame and wrong—
Rise as Morning, matchless, wondrous—
Rise as some rich morning song—
Rise a ringing song and story,
Valor, Love personified.
Stars and stripes espouse her glory,
Love and Liberty allied.

FINALE.

When ye have conned the hundredth time
My sins and sagely magnified
Your ofttold fictions into crimes
Dark planned, and so turned all aside,
Why then have done, I beg, I pray.
These shadows ye have fashioned lie
So heavily along my way.
And I would fain have light: And I
Would fain have love: Have love one little hour
Ere God has plucked my day, a tearful flower.

But when the cloud-draped day is done,
Now happily not long for me,
For lo! I see no more the sun,
Say this, if say ye must, and see
That ye mouth not the simple truth:
"From first to last this man had naught
Of us but insolence. From youth
Right on, alone he silent wrought
Nor answered us. And yet from us he knew
But thrust of lance that thrust him through and through."

Ah me! I mind me long agone,
Once on a savage snow-bound height
We pigmies pierced a king. Upon
His bare and upreared breast till night
We rained red arrows and we rained
Hot lead. Then up the steep and slow
He passed; yet ever still disdained
To strike, or even look below.
We found him, high above the clouds next morn
And dead, in all his silent, splendid scorn.

So leave me, as the edge of night
Comes on a little time to pass,
Or pray. For steep the stony height
And torn by storm, and bare of grass
Or blossom. And when I lie dead
Oh, do not drag me down once more.
For Jesus' sake let my poor head
Lie pillowed with these stones. My store
Of wealth is these. I earned them. Let me keep
Still on alone, on mine own star-lit steep.

My books were written largely for magazines and papers while I kept roaming about the world when and where I would, writing verse or prose as I pleased or could place it. And now let me note an error. A poet should not live by prose. Only a Scott can do that. Better be a day laborer, anything in reason, than write for mere money. Only of late, since I leaned on my hoe and plow for bread rather than on prose, have I felt my full strength in verse. Much of my prose was patched together, making the book and play of "The Danites," the book and play of "'49," and also the books, "Shadows of Shasta" and "The One Fair Woman," all unsatisfactory. I had early written a descriptive personal novel, the scenes laid in the region of Mount Shasta, and failing to dispose of it Prentice Mulford, who had joined me in London about the time of the Modoc war, proposed that we make it still more personal and publish it as "My Life Among the Modocs." He was led to this by the correspondents at the seat of war making the startling discovery that the poem, "The Tall Alcalde," was my own life. He had little more to do than take graphic accounts, conceived when war news was scarce, and sandwich them in through the novel and weld them fast. He did all the work, reading me now and then, for my eyes had almost quite failed me; and it proved to be popular both abroad and at home. Bently, publisher to the Queen, brought it out and it still refuses to die, although I have at times cut and slashed it terribly. It owes its long life to Mulford; and the lesson to me is that no poet can write ordinary prose without writing very ordinary verse.

Why have we so few true poets and fearless prophets to lead the people upward to-day? Because they gather money, and gather money, and gather money with the right hand, and at the same time try to write poetry with the left hand.

It is more important to the Nation, and quite as easy if rightly directed, to be a mental than a physical athlete. In the first place, then, be well rested and well fed; rested in mind as the athlete is rested in body for his work, fed in mind as the boxer is fed in body. Repose of mind is power. Yet has the foolish world ever stoned its prophets; therefore it is that the poets ever have, ever must, and ever will, if true poets go apart. For only with God, away from the marts, is that repose which of itself is power to be possessed. But, mark you, not as a hermit, not as a hater, but as a lover of all men, all things, must you go to mount your throne and rule your own beautiful world.

Having peace, repose of mind, rest the body, keeping in mind the careful training of the physical athlete continuously. As to the position of the body when at work, that is as you please. I generally found George Eliot doubled up on a sofa, her legs up under her, heaps of robes, and a pad on her lap. I read that Mrs. Browning always wrote in bed. I know that Mrs. Wagner—Madge Morris—does; while Miss Coolbrith writes, she tells me, on her feet, going along about her affairs till her poem is complete, and then writing it down exactly as she has framed it in her mind. Harriet Prescott Spofford writes on a pad in her lap in the parlor, under the trees with a party, takes part in the talk as she writes, and is generally the brightest of the company. Lady Hardy told me she could only write with her face to the blank wall, while Mrs. Braddon, the prolific, showed me her desk bowered in her Richmond Hill garden, where she wrote to the song of birds about forty popular novels. I find that men differ quite as widely in their preference of place and attitude. But it is to be noted that each person has a preference; and this preference must be respected to have your best results.

For instance, Anthony Trollope, a ponderous man, always wrote standing straight as a post to a high desk, his watch before him, beginning always at a certain minute and ending exactly the same. That watch would have landed me in a madhouse. Whittier and Longfellow wrote on their desks with everything at hand and in order, and had perfect quiet. I am told that the other great scribes of New England were all of the same discipline. Bret Harte is equally exacting and orderly. He once told me that his first line was always a cigar, and sometimes two cigars. I reckon Walt Whitman could write anywhere. I once was with him on top of a Fifth Avenue omnibus, above a sea of people, when he began writing on the edge of a newspaper, and he kept it up for half an hour, although his elbow was almost continuously tangled up with that of the driver.

As for myself, I can write but in one place and in one position, and but at one certain time. Yet this may be all a habit. At the same time I must respect this habit or preference to do my work as duty demands. In the first place, then, a good dinner at my mother's table, with all my house, and maybe some friends about me, no newspapers on the place, no mail maybe for a week if the work to be done is important—and all work should be—then to bed with the birds and a full night's rest, my door wide open; my coffee in bed at daylight, then a cigar, if I can find one, and as it burns to the end I begin and write till about twelve, when I dress, breakfast, and then I spend the rest of the day in the fields till dinner. Let me explain that, years ago, I went to the French Hospital, Pincean Hill, Rome, with the late Senator Miller of California, who had a bullet in an eye from Stone's River, and as I was limping badly from an old arrow hurt, a famous surgeon there kindly treated me. But he kept me lashed down so long that I had to work on my back; and have preferred that position ever since. This much for habit; yet I really believe with George Eliot, that "there is nothing like keeping the back and legs warm while at work." As for stimulants, don't think of such things, not even to start or conceive a thought. My own best stimulant or conception of work with life and action in it is a strong house, room, woods, the wild, rolling hills. In truth, were you to take all out that has come to me in this way, there would be little left worth reading. Yet to tie things down in black and white, as said before, take absolute repose.

These later poems, so far as written at that time, were compiled and revised during my first years at my mountain home overlooking San Francisco Bay, put in book form in Chicago, 1890, and dedicated to my daughter.

JUANITA.

You will come my bird, Bonita?
Come! For I by steep and stone
Have built such nest for you, Juanita,
As not eagle bird hath known.

Rugged! Rugged as Parnassus!
Rude, as all roads I have trod—
Yet are steeps and stone-strewn passes
Smooth o'er head, and nearest God.

Here black thunders of my cañon
Shake its walls in Titan wars!
Here white sea-born clouds companion
With such peaks as know the stars!

Here madrona, manzanita—
Here the snarling chaparral
House and hang o'er steeps, Juanita,
Where the gaunt wolf loved to dwell!

Dear, I took these trackless masses
Fresh from Him who fashioned them;
Wrought in rock, and hewed fair passes,
Flower set, as sets a gem.

Aye, I built in woe. God willed it;
Woe that passeth ghosts of guilt;
Yet I built as His birds builded—
Builded, singing as I built.

All is finished! Roads of flowers
Wait your loyal little feet.
All completed? Nay, the hours
Till you come are incomplete.

Steep below me lies the valley,
Deep below me lies the town,
Where great sea-ships ride and rally,
And the world walks up and down.

O, the sea of lights far streaming
When the thousand flags are furled—
When the gleaming bay lies dreaming
As it duplicates the world!

You will come my dearest, truest?
Come my sovereign queen of ten;
My blue skies will then be bluest;
My white rose be whitest then:

Then the song! Ah, then the saber
Flashing up the walls of night!
Hate of wrong and love of neighbor—
Rhymes of battle for the Right!

The Hights, Cal.

SONGS OF THE SOUL.

O thou To-morrow! Mystery!
O day that ever runs before!
What hast thine hidden hand in store
For mine, To-morrow, and for me?
O thou To-morrow! what hast thou
In store to make me bear the Now?

O day in which we shall forget
The tangled troubles of to-day!
O day that laughs at duns, at debt!
O day of promises to pay!
O shelter from all present storm!
O day in which we shall reform!

O days of all days to reform!
Convenient day of promises!
Hold back the shadow of the storm.
Let not thy mystery be less,
O bless'd To-morrow! chiefest friend,
But lead us blindfold to the end.

THE IDEAL AND THE REAL.

And full these truths eternal
O'er the yearning spirit steal,
That the real is the ideal,
And the ideal is the real.

She was damn'd with the dower of beauty, she
Had gold in shower by shoulder and brow.
Her feet!—why, her two blessed feet, were so small,
They could nest in this hand. How queenly, how tall,
How gracious, how grand! She was all to me,—
My present, my past, my eternity!

She but lives in my dreams. I behold her now
By shoreless white waters that flow'd like a sea
At her feet where I sat; her lips push'd out
In brave, warm welcome of dimple and pout!
'Twas æons agone. By that river that ran
All fathomless, echoless, limitless, on.

And shoreless, and peopled with never a man,
We met, soul to soul.... No land; yet I think
There were willows and lilies that lean'd to drink.
The stars they were seal'd and the moons were gone.
The wide shining circles that girdled that world,
They were distant and dim. And an incense curl'd
In vapory folds from that river that ran
All shoreless, with never the presence of man.

How sensuous the night; how soft was the sound
Of her voice on the night! How warm was her breath
In that world that had never yet tasted of death
Or forbidden sweet fruit!....In that far profound.

We were camped on the edges of god-land. We
Were the people of Saturn. The watery fields,
The wide-wing'd, dolorous birds of the sea,
They acknowledged but us. Our brave battle shields
Were my naked white palms; our food it was love.
Our roof was the fresco of gold belts above.

How turn'd she to me where that wide river ran,
With its lilies and willows and watery reeds,
And heeded as only your true love heeds!....
How tender she was, and how timid she was!
But a black, hoofed beast, with the head of a man,
Stole down where she sat at my side, and began
To puff his tan cheeks, then to play, then to pause,
With his double-reed pipe; then to play and to play
As never played man since the world began,
And never shall play till the judgment day.

How he puff'd! how he play'd! Then down the dim shore,
This half-devil man, all hairy and black,
Did dance with his hoofs in the sand, laughing back
As his song died away....She turned never more
Unto me after that. She rose, and she pass'd
Right on from my sight. Then I followed as fast
As true love can follow. But ever before
Like a spirit she fled. How vain and how far
Did I follow my beauty, red belt or white star!
Through foamy white sea, unto fruit laden shore!

How long I did follow! My pent soul of fire
It did feed on itself. I fasted, I cried;
Was tempted by many. Yet still I denied
The touch of all things, and kept my desire....
I stood by the lion of St. Mark in that hour
Of Venice when gold of the sunset is roll'd

From cloud to cathedral, from turret to tower,
In matchless, magnificent garments of gold;
Then I knew she was near; yet I had not known
Her form or her face since the stars were sown.

We two had been parted—God pity us!—when
This world was unnamed and all heaven was dim;
We two had been parted far back on the rim
And the outermost border of heaven's red bars;
We two had been parted ere the meeting of men,
Or God had set compass on spaces as yet;
We two had been parted ere God had once set
His finger to spinning the purple with stars,—
And now at the last in the sea and fret
Of the sun of Venice, we two had met.

Where the lion of Venice, with brows a-frown,
With tossed mane tumbled, and teeth in air,
Looks out in his watch o'er the watery town,
With paw half lifted, with claws half bare,
By the blue Adriatic, at her bath in the sea,—
I saw her. I knew her, but she knew not me.
I had found her at last! Why I, I had sail'd
The antipodes through, had sought, and had hail'd
All flags; I had climbed where the storm clouds curl'd,
And call'd o'er the awful arch'd dome of the world.

I saw her one moment, then fell back abash'd,
And fill'd to the throat....Then I turn'd me once more,
Thanking God in my soul, while the level sun flashed
Happy halos about her....Her breast!—why, her breast
Was white as twin pillows that lure you to rest.
Her sloping limbs moved like to melodies told,
As she rose from the sea, and threw back the gold
Of her glorious hair, and set face to the shore....
I knew her! I knew her, though we had not met
Since the red stars sang to the sun's first set!

How long I had sought her! I had hunger'd, nor ate
Of any sweet fruits. I had followed not one
Of all the fair glories grown under the sun.
I had sought only her, believing that she
Had come upon earth, and stood waiting for me
Somewhere by my way. But the pathways of Fate
They had led otherwhere; the round world round,
The far North seas and the near profound
Had fail'd me for aye. Now I stood by that sea
Where she bathed in her beauty,....God, I and she!

I spake not, but caught in my breath; I did raise
My face to fair heaven to give God praise
That at last, ere the ending of Time, we had met,
Had touch'd upon earth at the same sweet place....
Yea, we never had met since creation at all;
Never, since ages ere Adam's fall,
Had we two met in that hunger and fret
Where two should be one, but had wander'd through space;
Through space and through spheres, as some bird that hard fate
Gives a thousand glad Springs but never one mate.

Was it well with my love? Was she true? Was she brave
With virtue's own valor? Was she waiting for me?
Oh, how fared my love? Had she home? had she bread?
Had she known but the touch of the warm-temper'd wave?
Was she born to this world with a crown on her head,
Or born, like myself, but a dreamer instead?....
So long it had been! So long! Why, the sea—
That wrinkled and surly, old, time-temper'd slave—
Had been born, had his revels, grown wrinkled and hoar
Since I last saw my love on that uttermost shore.

Oh, how fared my love? Once I lifted my face,
And I shook back my hair and look'd out on the sea;
I press'd my hot palms as I stood in my place,
And I cried, "Oh, I come like a king to your side
Though all hell intervene!".... "Hist! she may be a bride,
A mother at peace, with sweet babes at her knee!
A babe at her breast and a spouse at her side!—
Had I wander'd too long, and had Destiny
Set mortal between us?" I buried my face
In my hands, and I moan'd as I stood in my place.

'Twas her year to be young. She was tall, she was fair—
Was she pure as the snow on the Alps over there?
'Twas her year to be young. She was queenly and tall;
And I felt she was true, as I lifted my face
And saw her press down her rich robe to its place,
With a hand white and small as a babe's with a doll.
And her feet!—why, her feet in the white shining sand
Were so small, 'twas a wonder the maiden could stand.
Then she push'd back her hair with a round hand that shone
And flash'd in the light with a white starry stone.

Then my love she is rich! My love she is fair!
Is she pure as the snow on the Alps over there?
She is gorgeous with wealth! "Thank God, she has bread,"
I said to myself. Then I humbled my head
In gratitude deep. Then I question'd me where

Was her palace, her parents? What name
did she bear?
What mortal on earth came nearest her
heart?
Who touch'd the small hand till it thrill'd
to a smart?
Twas her year to be young. She was
rich, she was fair—
Was she pure as the snow on the Alps
over there?

Then she loosed her rich robe that was
blue like the sea,
And silken and soft as a baby's new born.
And my heart it leap'd light as the sun-
light at morn
At the sight of my love in her proud
purity,
As she rose like a Naiad half-robed from
the sea.
Then careless and calm as an empress can
be
She loosed and let fall all the raiment of
blue,
As she drew a white robe in a melody
Of moving white limbs, while between
the two,
Like a rift in a cloud, shone her fair pres-
ence through.

Soon she turn'd, reach'd a hand; then
a tall gondolier
Who had lean'd on his oar, like a long
lifted spear,
Shot sudden and swift and all silently,
And drew to her side as she turn'd from
the tide.
It was odd, such a thing, and I counted
it queer
That a princess like this, whether virgin
or bride,
Should abide thus apart as she bathed in
the sea;
And I chafed and I chafed, and so unsat-
isfied,
That I flutter'd the doves that were perch'd
close about,
As I strode up and down in dismay and
in doubt.

Swift she stept in the boat on the bor-
ders of night
As an angel might step on that far won-
der land
Of eternal sweet life, which men mis-name
Death.
Quick I called me a craft, and I caught at
my breath
As she sat in the boat, and her white baby
hand
Held vestments of gold to her throat,
snowy white.
Then her gondola shot,—shot sharp for
the shore:
There was never the sound of a song or
of oar,
But the doves hurried home in white
clouds to Saint Mark,
Where the brass horses plunge their high
manes in the dark.

Then I cried: "Follow fast! Follow
fast! Follow fast!
Aye! thrice double fare, if you follow her
true
To her own palace door!" There was
plashing of oar
And rattle of rowlock....I sat peering
through,
Looking far in the dark, peering out as
we passed
With my soul all alert, bending down,
leaning low.
But only the oaths of the fisherman's
crew
When we jostled them sharp as we sud-
den shot through
The watery town. Then a deep, distant
roar—
The rattle of rowlock; the rush of the oar.

The rattle of rowlock, the rush of the sea....
Swift wind like a sword at the throat of us all!
I lifted my face, and, far, fitfully
The heavens breathed lightning; did lift and let fall
As if angels were parting God's curtains. Then deep
And indolent-like, and as if half asleep,
As if half made angry to move at all,
The thunder moved. It confronted me.
It stood like an avalanche poised on a hill,
I saw its black brows. I heard it stand still.

The troubled sea throbb'd as if rack'd with pain.
Then the black clouds rose and suddenly rode,
As a fiery, fierce stallion that knows no rein;
Right into the town. Then the thunder strode
As a giant striding from star to red star,
Then turn'd upon earth and frantically came,
Shaking the hollow heaven. And far
And near red lightning in ribbon and skin
Did seam and furrow the cloud with flame,
And write on black heaven Jehovah's name.

Then lightnings came weaving like shuttlecocks,
Weaving rent robes of black clouds for death.
And frightened doves fluttered them home in flocks,
And mantled men hied them with gather'd breath.
Black gondolas scattered as never before,
And drew like crocodiles up on the shore;
And vessels at sea stood further at sea,
And seamen haul'd with a bended knee,
And canvas came down to left and to right,
Till ships stood stripp'd as if stripp'd for fight!

Then an oath. Then a prayer. Then a gust, with rents
Through the yellow sail'd fishers. Then suddenly
Came sharp fork'd fire! Then again thunder fell
Like the great first gun! Ah, then there was rout
Of ships like the breaking of regiments,
And shouts as if hurled from an upper hell.

Then tempest! It lifted, it spun us about,
Then shot us ahead through the hills of the sea
As a great steel arrow shot shoreward in wars—
Then the storm split open till I saw the blown stars.

On! on! through the foam! through the storm! through the town!
She was gone! She was lost in that wilderness
Of leprous white palaces....Black distress!
I stood in my gondola. All up and all down
We pushed through the surge of the salt-flood street
Above and below....'Twas only the beat
Of the sea's sad heart....I leaned, listened; I sat....
'Twas only the water-rat; nothing but that;
Not even the sea-bird screaming distress,
As she lost her way in that wilderness.

I listen'd all night. I caught at each sound;

I clutch'd and I caught as a man that
drown'd—
Only the sullen, low growl of the sea
Far out the flood-street at the edge of the
ships;
Only the billow slow licking his lips,
A dog that lay crouching there watching
for me,—
Growling and showing white teeth all the
night;
Only a dog, and as ready to bite;
Only the waves with their salt-flood tears
Fretting white stones of a thousand years.

And then a white dome in the loftiness
Of cornice and cross and of glittering
spire
That thrust to heaven and held the fire
Of the thunder still; the bird's distress
As he struck his wings in that wilderness,
On marbles that speak, and thrill, and in-
spire,—
The night below and the night above;
The water-rat building, the sea-lost dove;
That one lost, dolorous, lone bird's call,
The water-rat building,—but that was all.

Silently, slowly, still up and still down,
We row'd and we row'd for many an hour,
By beetling palace and toppling tower,
In the darks and the deeps of the watery
town.
Only the water-rat building by stealth,
Only the lone bird astray in his flight
That struck white wings in the clouds of
night,
On spires that sprang from Queen Adria's
wealth;
Only one sea dove, one lost white dove:
The blackness below, the blackness above!

Then, pushing the darkness from pillar
to post,
The morning came sullen and gray like a
ghost
Slow up the canal. I lean'd from the
prow,
And listen'd. Not even that dove in dis-
tress
Crying its way through the wilderness;
Not even the stealthy old water-rat now,
Only the bell in the fisherman's tower,
Slow tolling at sea and telling the hour,
To kneel to their sweet Santa Barbara
For tawny fishers at sea, and to pray.

* * * * * * *

High over my head, carved cornice,
quaint spire.
And ancient built palaces knock'd their
gray brows
Together and frown'd. Then slow-creep-
ing scows
Scraped the walls on each side. Above
me the fire
Of sudden-born morning came flaming in
bars;
While up through the chasm I could count
the stars.
Oh, pity! Such ruin! The dank smell of
death
Crept up the canal: I could scarce take
my breath!
'Twas the fit place for pirates, for women
who keep
Contagion of body and soul where they
sleep....

God's pity! A white hand now beck'd
me
From an old mouldy door, almost in my
reach.
I sprang to the sill as one wrecked to a
beach;
I sprang with wide arms: it was she! it
was she!....
And in such a damn'd place! And what
was her trade?
To think I had follow'd so faithful, so far
From eternity's brink, from star to white
star,

To find her, to find her, nor wife nor sweet maid!
To find her a shameless poor creature of shame,
A nameless, lost body, men hardly dared name.

All alone in her shame, on that damp dismal floor
She stood to entice me....I bow'd me before
All-conquering beauty. I call'd her my Queen!
I told her my love as I proudly had told
My love had I found her as pure as pure gold.
I reach'd her my hands, as fearless, as clean,
As man fronting cannon. I cried, "Hasten forth
To the sun! There are lands to the south, to the north,
Anywhere where you will, Dash the shame from your brow;
Come with me, for ever; and come with me now!"

Why, I'd have turn'd pirate for her, would have seen
Ships burn'd from the seas, like to stubble from field.
Would I turn from her now? Why should I now yield,
When she needed me most? Had I found her a queen,
And beloved by the world,—why, what had I done?
I had woo'd, and had woo'd, and had woo'd till I won!
Then, if I had loved her with gold and fair fame,
Would not I now love her, and love her the same?
My soul hath a pride. I would tear out my heart
And cast it to dogs, could it play a dog's part!

"Don't you know me, my bride of the wide world of yore?
Why, don't you remember the white milky-way
Of stars, that we traversed the æons before?....
We were counting the colors, we were naming the seas
Of the vaster ones. You remember the trees
That sway'd in the cloudy white heavens, and bore
Bright crystals of sweets, and the sweet manna-dew?
Why, you smile as you weep, you remember, and you,
You know me! You know me! You know me! Yea,
You know me as if 'twere but yesterday!

I told her all things. Her brow took a frown;
Her grand Titan beauty, so tall, so serene,
The one perfect woman, mine own idol queen—
Her proud swelling bosom, it broke up and down
As she spake, and she shook in her soul as she said,
With her small hands held to her bent, aching head:
"Go back to the world! Go back, and alone
Till kind Death comes and makes white his own."
I said; "I will wait! I will wait in the pass
Of death, until Time he shall break his glass."

Then I cried, "Yea, here where the gods did love,
Where the white Europa was won,—she rode
Her milk-white bull through these same warm seas,—
Yea, here in the land where huge Hercules,
With the lion's heart and the heart of the dove,
Did walk in his naked great strength, and strode
In the sensuous air with his lion's skin
Flapping and fretting his knotted thews;
Where Theseus did wander, and Jason cruise,—
Yea, here let the life of all lives begin.

"Yea! Here where the Orient balms breathe life,
Where heaven is kindest, where all God's blue
Seems a great gate open'd to welcome you.
Come, rise and go forth, my empress, my wife."
Then spake her great soul, so grander far
Than I had believed on that outermost star;
And she put by her tears, and calmly she said,
With hands still held to her bended head:
"I will go through the doors of death and wait
For you on the innermost side death's gate.

"Thank God that this life is but a day's span,
But a wayside inn for weary, worn man—
A night and a day; and, to-morrow, the spell
O, darkness is broken. Now, darling, farewell!"

I caught at her robe as one ready to die—
"Nay, touch not the hem of my robe—it is red
With sins that your own sex heap'd on my head!
Now turn you, yes, turn! But remember how I
Wait weeping, in sackcloth, the while I wait
Inside death's door, and watch at the gate."

I cried yet again, how I cried, how I cried,
Reaching face, reaching hands as a drowning man might.
She drew herself back, put my two hands aside,
Half turned as she spoke, as one turned to the night:
Speaking low, speaking soft as a wind through the wall
Of a ruin where mold and night masters all;

"I shall live my day, live patient on through
The life that man hath compelled me to,
Then turn to my mother, sweet earth, and pray
She keep me pure to the Judgment Day!
I shall sit and wait as you used to do,
Will wait the next life, through the whole life through.
I shall sit all alone, I shall wait alway;
I shall wait inside of the gate for you,
Waiting, and counting the days as I wait;
Yea, wait as that beggar that sat by the gate
Of Jerusalem, waiting the Judgment Day."

A DOVE OF ST. MARK.

O terrible lion of tame Saint Mark!
Tamed old lion with the tumbled mane
Tossed to the clouds and lost in the dark,
With teeth in the air and tail-whipp'd back,
Foot on the Bible as if thy track
Led thee the lord of the desert again
Say, what of thy watch o'er the watery town?
Say, what of the worlds walking up and down?

O silent old monarch that tops Saint Mark,
That sat thy throne for a thousand years,
That lorded the deep that defied all men,—
Lo! I see visions at sea in the dark;
And I see something that shines like tears,
And I hear something that sounds like sighs,
And I hear something that seems as when
A great soul suffers and sinks and dies.

The high-born, beautiful snow came down,
Silent and soft as the terrible feet
Of time on the mosses of ruins. Sweet
Was the Christmas time in the watery town.
'Twas full flood carnival swell'd the sea
Of Venice that night, and canal and quay
Were alive with humanity. Man and maid,
Glad in mad revel and masquerade,
Moved through the feathery snow in the night,
And shook black locks as they laugh'd outright.

From Santa Maggiore, and to and fro,
And ugly and black as if devils cast out,
Black streaks through the night of such soft, white snow,
The steel-prow'd gondolas paddled about;
There was only the sound of the long oars' dip,
As the low moon sail'd up the sea like a ship
In a misty morn. High the low moon rose,
Rose veil'd and vast, through the feathery snows,
As a minstrel stept silent and sad from his boat,
His worn cloak clutched in his hand to his throat.

Low under the lion that guards St. Mark,
Down under wide wings on the edge of the sea
In the dim of the lamps, on the rim of the dark,
Alone and sad in the salt-flood town,

Silent and sad and all sullenly,
He sat by the column where the crocodile
Keeps watch o'er the wave, far mile upon mile....
Like a signal light through the storm let down,
Then a far star fell through the dim profound—
A jewel that slipp'd God's hand to the ground.

The storm had blown over! Now up and then down,
Alone and in couples, sweet women did pass,
Silent and dreamy, as if seen in a glass,
Half mask'd to the eyes, in their Adrian town.
Such women! It breaks one's heart to think.
Water! and never one drop to drink!
What types of Titian! What glory of hair!
How tall as the sisters of Saul! How fair!
Sweet flowers of flesh, and all blossoming,
As if 'twere in Eden, and in Eden's spring.

"They are talking aloud with all their eyes,
Yet passing me by with never one word.
O pouting sweet lips, do you know there are lies
That are told with the eyes, and never once heard
Above a heart's beat when the soul is stirr'd?
It is time to fly home, O doves of St. Mark!
Take boughs of the olive; bear these to your ark,
And rest and be glad, for the seas and the skies
Of Venice are fair....What! wouldn't go home?
What! drifting and drifting as the soil'd seafoam?

"And who then are you? You, masked, and so fair?
Your half seen face is a rose full blown,
Down under your black and abundant hair?....
A child of the street, and unloved and alone!
Unloved; and alone?....There is something then
Between us two that is not unlike!....
The strength and the purposes of men
Fall broken idols. We aim and strike
With high-born zeal and with proud intent.
Yet let life turn on some accident....

"Nay, I'll not preach. Time's lessons pass
Like twilight's swallows. They chirp in their flight,
And who takes heed of the wasting glass?
Night follows day, and day follows night,
And no thing rises on earth but to fall
Like leaves, with their lessons most sad and fit.
They are spread like a volume each year to all;
Yet men or women learn naught of it,
Or after it all, but a weariness
Of soul and body and untold distress.

"Yea, sit, lorn child, by my side, and we,
We will talk of the world. Nay, let my hand
Fall kindly to yours, and so, let your face
Fall fair to my shoulder, and you shall be
My dream of sweet Italy. Here in this place,

Alone in the crowds of this old careless land,
I shall shelter your form till the morn and then—
Why, I shall return to the world and to men,
And you, not stain'd for one strange, kind word
And my three last francs, for a lorn night bird.

"Fear nothing from me, nay, never once fear.
The day, my darling, comes after the night.
The nights they were made to show the light
Of the stars in heaven, though the storms be near....
Do you see that figure of Fortune up there,
That tops the Dogana with toe a-tip
Of the great gold ball? Her scroll is a-trip
To the turning winds. She is light as the air.
Her foot is set upon plenty's horn,
Her fair face set to the coming morn.

"Well, trust we to Fortune....Bread on the wave
Turns ever ashore to the hand that gave.
What am I? A poet—a lover of all
That is lovely to see. Nay, naught shall befall....
Yes, I am a failure. I plot and I plan,
Give splendid advice to my fellow-man,
Yet ever fall short of achievement....Ah me!
In my lorn life's early, sad afternoon,
Say, what have I left but a rhyme or a rune?
An empty hand for some soul at sea,
Some fair, forbidden, sweet fruit to choose,
That 'twere sin to touch, and—sin to refuse?

"What! I go drifting with you, girl, to-night?
To sit at your side and to call you love?
Well, that were a fancy! To feed a dove,
A poor soil'd dove of this dear Saint Mark,
Too frighten'd to rest and too weary for flight....
Aye, just three francs, my fortune. There! He
Who feeds the sparrows for this will feed me.
Now, here 'neath the lion, alone in the dark,
And side by side let us sit, poor dear,
Breathing the beauty as an atmosphere..,

"We will talk of your loves, I write tales of love....
What! Cannot read? Why, you never heard then
Of your Desdemona, nor the daring men
Who died for her love? My poor white dove,
There's a story of Shylock would drive you wild.
What! Never have heard of these stories, my child?
Of Tasso, of Petrarch? Not the Bridge of Sighs?
Not the tale of Ferrara? Not the thousand whys
That your Venice was ever adored above
All other fair lands for her stories of love?

"What then about Shylock? 'Twas gold. Yes—dead.
The lady? 'Twas love....Why, yes; she too
Is dead. And Byron? 'Twas fame. Ah, true....

Tasso and Petrarch? All died, just the same....
Yea, so endeth all, as you truly have said,
And you, poor girl, are too wise; and you,
Too sudden and swift in your hard, ugly youth,
Have stumbled face fronting an obstinate truth.
For whether for love, for gold, or for fame,
They but lived their day, and they died, the same.

But let's talk not of death? Of death or the life
That comes after death? 'Tis beyond your reach,
And this too much thought has a sense of strife....
Ah, true; I promised you not to preach...
My maid of Venice, or maid unmade,
Hold close your few francs and be not afraid.
What! Say you are hungry? Well, let us dine
Till the near morn comes on the silver shine
Of the lamp-lit sea. At the dawn of day,
My sad child-woman, you can go your way.

"What! You have a palace? I know your town;
Know every nook of it, left and right,
As well as yourself. Why, far up and down
Your salt flood streets, lo, many a night
I have row'd and have roved in my lorn despair
Of love upon earth, and I know well there
Is no such palace. What! and you dare
To look in my face and to lie outright,
To lift your face, and to frown me down?
There is no such palace in that part of the town!

"You would woo me away to your rickety boat!
You would pick my pockets! You would cut my throat,
With help of your pirates! Then throw me out
Loaded with stones to sink me down,
Down into the filth and the dregs of your town!
Why, that is your damnable aim, no doubt!
And, my plaintive voiced child, you seem too fair,
Too fair, for even a thought like that;
Too fair for ever such sin to dare—
Ay, even the tempter to whisper at.

"Now, there is such a thing as being true,
True, even in villiany. Listen to me:
Black-skinn'd women and low-brow'd men,
And desperate robbers and thieves; and then,
Why, there are the pirates!....Ay, pirates reform'd—
Pirates reform'd and unreform'd;
Pirates for me girl, friends for you,—
And these are your neighbors. And so you see
That I know your town, your neighbors; and I—
Well, pardon me, dear—but I know you lie.

"Tut, tut, my beauty! What trickery now?
Why, tears through your hair on my hand like rain!
Come! look in my face: laugh, lie again
With your wonderful eyes. Lift up your brow,

Laugh in the face of the world, and lie!
Now, come! This lying is no new thing.
The wearers of laces know well how to lie,
As well, ay, better, than you or I....
But they lie for fortune, for fame: instead,
You, child of the street, only lie for your bread.

...."Some sounds blow in from the distant land.
The bells strike sharp, and as out of tune,
Some sudden, short notes. To the east and afar,
And up from the sea, there is lifting a star
As large, my beautiful child, and as white
And as lovely to see as some lady's white hand.
The people have melted away with the night,
And not one gondola frets the lagoon.
See! Away to the mountain, the face of morn.
Hear! Away to the sea—'tis the fisherman's horn.

"'Tis morn in Venice! My child, adieu!
Arise, sad sister, and go your way;
And as for myself, why, much like you,
I shall sell this story to who will pay
And dares to reckon it truthful and meet.
Yea, each of us traders, poor child of pain;
For each must barter for bread to eat
In a world of trade and an age of gain;
With just this difference, waif of the street,
You sell your body, I sell my brain.

"Poor lost little vessel, with never a keel.
Saint Marks, what a wreck! Lo, here you reel,
With never a soul to advise or to care;
All cover'd with sin to the brows and hair,
You lie like a seaweed, well a-strand;
Blown like the sea-kelp hard on the shale,
A half-drown'd body, with never a hand
Reach'd out to help where you falter and fail:
Left stranded alone to starve and to die,
Or to sell your body to who may buy.

"My sister of sin, I will kiss you! Yea,
I will fold you, hold you close to my breast;
And here as you rest in your first fair rest,
As night is push'd back from the face of day,
I will push your heavy, dark heaven of hair
Well back from your brow, and kiss you where
Your ruffian, bearded, black men of crime
Have stung you and stain'd you a thousand time;
I will call you my sister, sweet child, and keep
You close to my heart, lest you wake but to weep.

"I will tenderly kiss you, and I shall not be
Ashamed, nor yet stain'd in the least, sweet dove,—
I will tenderly kiss, with the kiss of Love,
And of Faith, and of Hope, and of Charity.
Nay, I shall be purer and be better then;
For, child of the street, you, living or dead,

Stain'd to the brows, are purer to me
Ten thousand times than the world of men,
Who reach you a hand but to lead you astray,—
But the dawn is upon us. There! go your way.

"And take great courage. Take courage and say,
Of this one Christmas when I am away,
Roving the world and forgetful of you,
That I found you as white as the snow and knew
You but needed a word to keep you true.
When you fall weary and so need rest,
Then find kind words hidden down in your breast;
And if rough men question you,—why, then say
That Madonna sent them. Then kneel and pray,
And pray for me, the worst of the two:
Then God will bless you, sweet child, and I
Shall be the better when I come to die.

"Yea, take great courage, it will be as bread;
Have faith, have faith while this day wears through.
Then rising refresh'd, try virtue instead;
Be stronger and better, poor, pitiful dear,
So prompt with a lie, so prompt with a tear,
For the hand grows stronger as the heart grows true....
Take courage, my child, for I promise you
We are judged by our chances of life and lot;
And your poor little soul may yet pass through
The eye of the needle, where laces shall not.

"Sad dove of the dust, with tear-wet wings,
Homeless and lone as the dove from its ark,—
Do you reckon yon angel that tops St. Mark,
That tops the tower, that tops the town,
If he knew us two, if he knew all things,
Would say, or think, you are worse than I?
Do you reckon yon angel, now looking down,
Far down like a star, he hangs so high,
Could tell which one were the worse of us two?
Child of the street—it is not you!

"If we two were dead, and laid side by side
Right here on the pavement, this very day,
Here under the sun-flushed maiden sky,
Where the morn flows in like a rosy tide,
And the sweet Madonna that stands in the moon,
With her crown of stars, just across the lagoon,
Should come and should look upon you and I,—
Do you reckon, my child, that she would decide
As men do decide and as women do say,
That you are so dreadful, and turn away?

"If angels were sent to choose this day
Between us two as we stand here,
Here side by side in this storied place,—

If God's angels were sent to choose, I say,
This very moment the best of the two,
You, white with a hunger and stain'd with a tear,
Or I, the rover the wide world through,
Restless and stormy as any sea,—
Looking us two right straight in the face,
Child of the street, he would not choose me.

"The fresh sun is falling on turret and tower,
The far sun is flashing on spire and dome,
The marbles of Venice are bursting to flower,
The marbles of Venice are flower and foam:
Good night and good morn; I must leave you now.
There! bear my kiss on your pale, soft brow
Through earth to heaven: and when we shall meet
Beyond the darkness, poor waif of the street,
Why, then I shall know you, my sad, sweet dove;
Shall claim you, and kiss you, with the kiss of love."

SUNSET AND DAWN IN SAN DIEGO.

My city sits amid her palms;
The perfume of her twilight breath
Is something as the sacred balms
That bound sweet Jesus after death,
Such soft, warm twilight sense as lies
Against the gates of Paradise.

Such prayerful palms, wide palms upreached!
This sea mist is as incense smoke,
Yon ancient walls a sermon preached,
White lily with a heart of oak.
And O, this twilight! O the grace
Of twilight on my lifted face!

I love you, twilight,—love with love
So loyal, loving, fond that I
When folding these worn hands to die,
Shall pray God lead me not above,
But leave me, twilight, sad and true,
To walk this lonesome world with you.

Yea, God knows I have walked with night;
I have not seen, I have not known
Such light as beats upon His throne.
I know I could not bear such light;
Therefore, I beg, sad sister true,
To share your shadow-world with you.

I love you, love you, maid of night,
Your perfumed breath, your dreamful eyes,
Your holy silences, your sighs
Of mateless longing; your delight
When night says, Hang on yon moon's horn
Your russet gown, and rest till morn.

The sun is dying; space and room,
Serenity, vast sense of rest,
Lie bosomed in the orange west
Of orient waters. Hear the boom
Of long, strong billows; wave on wave,
Like funeral guns above a grave.

Now night folds all; no sign or word;
But still that rocking of the deep—
Sweet mother, rock the world to sleep:
Still rock and rock; as I have heard
Sweet mother gently rock and rock
The while she folds the little frock.

* * * * * *

Broad mesa, brown, bare mountains, brown,
Bowed sky of brown, that erst was blue;
Dark, earth-brown curtains coming down—
Earth-brown, that all hues melt into;
Brown twilight, born of light and shade;
Of night that came, of light that passed...
How like some lorn, majestic maid
That wares not whither way at last!

Now perfumed Night, sad-faced and far,
Walks up the world in somber brown.
Now suddenly a loosened star
Lets all her golden hair fall down—
And Night is dead Day's coffin-lid,
With stars of gold shot through his pall....
I hear the chorus, katydid;
A katydid, and that is all.

Some star-tipt candles foot and head;
Some perfumes of the perfumed sea;
And now above the coffined dead
Dusk draws great curtains lovingly;
While far o'er all, so dreamful far,
God's Southern Cross by faith is seen
Tipt by one single blazing star,
With spaces infinite between.

* * * * *

Come, love His twilight, the perfume
Of God's great trailing garment's hem;
The sense of rest, the sense of room,
The garnered goodness of the day,
The twelve plucked hours of His tree,
When all the world has gone its way
And left perfection quite to me
And Him who, loving, fashioned them.

I know not why that wealth and pride
Win not my heart or woo my tale.
I only know I know them not;
I only know to cast my lot
Where love walks noiselessly with night
And patient nature; my delight
The wild rose of the mountain side,
The lowly lily of the vale;

To live not asking, just to live;
To live not begging, just to be;
To breathe God's presence in the dusk
That drives out loud, assertive light—
To never ask, but ever give;
To love my noiseless mother, Night;
Her vast hair moist with smell of musk,
Her breath sweet with eternity.

* * * * *

I.

A hermit's path, a mountain's perch,
A sandaled monk, a dying man—
A far-off, low, adobe church,
Below the hermit's orange-trees
That cap the clouds above the seas,
So far, its spire seems but a span.

* * * * *

A low-voiced dove! The dying Don
Put back the cross and sat dark-browed
And sullen, as a dove flew out
The bough, and circling round about,
Was bathed and gathered in a cloud,
That, like some ship, sailed on and on.

But let the gray monk tell the tale;
And tell it just as told to me.
This Don was chiefest of the vale
That banks by San Diego's sea,
And who so just, so generous,
As he who now lay dying thus?

But wrong, such shameless Saxon wrong,
Had crushed his heart, had made him hate
The sight, the very sound, of man.
He loved the lonely wood-dove's song;
He loved it as his living mate.
And lo! the good monk laid a ban
And penance of continual prayer—
But list, the living, dying there!

For now the end was, and he lay
As day lies banked against the night—
As lies some bark at close of day
To wait the dew-born breath of night;
To wait the ebb of tide, to wait
The swift plunge through the Golden Gate:

The plunge from bay to boundless sea—
From life through narrow straits of night,
From time to bright eternity—
To everlasting walks of light.
Some like as when you sudden blow
Your candle out and turn you so
To sleep unto the open day:
And thus the priest did pleading say:

"You fled my flock, and sought this steep
And stony, star-lit, lonely height,
Where weird and unnamed creatures keep
To hold strange thought with things of night
Long, long ago. But now at last
Your life sinks surely to the past.
Lay hold, lay hold, the cross I bring,
Where all God's goodly creatures cling.

"Yea! You are good. Dark-browed and low
Beneath your shaggy brows you look
On me, as you would read a book:
And darker still your dark brows grow
As I lift up the cross to pray,
And plead with you to walk its way.

"Yea, you are good! There is not one,
From Tia Juana to the reach
And bound of gray Pacific Beach,
From Coronado's palm-set isle
And palm-hung pathways, mile on mile,
But speaks you, Señor, good and true.
But oh, my silent, dying son!
The cross alone can speak for you
When all is said and all is done.

"Come! Turn your dim old eyes to me,
Have faith and help me plant this cross
Beyond where blackest billows toss,
As you would plant some pleasant tree:
Some fruitful orange-tree, and know
That it shall surely grow and grow,
As your own orange-trees have grown,
And be, as they, your very own.

"You smile at last, and pleasantly:
You love your laden orange-trees
Set high above your silver seas
With your own honest hand; each tree
A date, a day, a part, indeed,
Of your own life, and walk, and creed.

"You love your steeps, your star-set blue:
You watch yon billows flash, and toss,
And leap, and curve, in merry rout,
You love to hear them laugh and shout—
Men say you hear them talk to you;
Men say you sit and look and look,
As one who reads some holy book—
My son, come, look upon the cross?

"Come, see me plant amid your trees
My cross, that you may see and know
'T will surely grow, and grow, and grow,
As grows some trusted little seed;
As grows some secret, small good deed;
The while you gaze upon your seas......
Sweet Christ, now let it grow, and bear
Fair fruit, as your own fruit is fair.

"Aye! ever from the first I knew,
And marked its flavor, freshness, hue,
The gold of sunset and the gold
Of morn, in each rich orange rolled.

"I mind me now, 't was long since, friend,
When first I climbed your path alone,
A savage path of brush and stone,
And rattling serpents without end.

"Yea, years ago, when blood and life
Ran swift, and your sweet, faithful wife—
What! tears at last; hot, piteous tears
That through your bony fingers creep
The while you bend your face, and weep
As if your heart of hearts would break—
As if these tears were your heart's blood,
A pent-up, sudden, bursting flood—
Look on the cross, for Jesus' sake."

II.

'T was night, and still it seemed not night.
Yet, far down in the cañon deep,
Where night had housed all day, to keep
Companion with the wolf, you might
Have hewn a statue out of night.

The shrill coyote loosed his tongue
Deep in the dark arroyo's bed;
And bat and owl above his head
From out their gloomy caverns swung:
A swoop of wings, a cat-like call,
A crackle of sharp chaparral!

Then sudden, fitful winds sprang out,
And swept the mesa like a broom;
Wild, saucy winds, that sang of room!
That leapt the cañon with a shout
From dusty throats, audaciously
And headlong tore into the sea,
As tore the swine with lifted snout.

Some birds came, went, then came again
From out the hermit's wood-hung hill;
Came swift, and arrow-like, and still,
As you have seen birds, when the rain—
The great, big, high-born rain, leapt white
And sudden from a cloud like night.

And then a dove, dear, nun-like dove,
With eyes all tenderness, with eyes
So loving, longing; full of love,
That when she reached her slender throat
And sang one low, soft, sweetest note,
Just one, so faint, so far, so near,
You could have wept with joy to hear.

The old man, as if he had slept,
Raised quick his head, then bowed and wept
For joy, to hear once more her voice.
With childish joy he did rejoice;
As one will joy to surely learn
His dear, dead love is living still;
As one will joy to know, in turn,
He, too, is loved with love to kill.

He put a hand forth, let it fall
And feebly close; and that was all.
And then he turned his tearful eyes
To meet the priest's, and spake this wise:—

Now mind, I say, not one more word
That livelong night of nights was heard

By monk or man, from dusk till dawn;
And yet that man spake on and on.

Why, know you not, soul speaks to soul?
I say the use of words shall pass.
Words are but fragments of the glass;
But silence is the perfect whole.

And thus the old man, bowed and wan,
And broken in his body, spake—
Spake youthful, ardent, on and on,
As dear love speaks for dear love's sake.

"You spake of her, my wife; behold!
Behold my faithful, constant love!
Nay, nay, you shall not doubt my dove,
Perched there above your cross of gold!

"Yea, you have books, I know, to tell
Of far, fair heaven; but no hell
To her had been so terrible
As all sweet heaven, with its gold
And jasper gates, and great white throne,
Had she been banished hence alone.

"I say, not God himself could keep,
Beyond the stars, beneath the deep,
Or 'mid the stars, or 'mid the sea,
Her soul from my soul one brief day,
But she would find some pretty way
To come and still companion me.

"And say, where bide your souls, good priest?
Lies heaven west, lies heaven east?
Let us be frank, let us be fair;
Where is your heaven, good priest, where?

"Is there not room, is there not place
In all those boundless realms of space?
Is there not room in this sweet air,
Room 'mid my trees, room anywhere,
For souls that love us thus so well,
And love so well this beauteous world,
But that they must be headlong hurled
Down, down, to undiscovered hell?

"Good priest, we questioned not one word
Of all the holy things we heard
Down in your pleasant town of palms
Long, long ago—sweet chants, sweet psalms,
Sweet incense, and the solemn rite
Above the dear, believing dead.
Nor do I question here to-night
One gentle word you may have said.
I would not doubt, for one brief hour,
Your word, your creed, your priestly power,
Your purity, unselfish zeal,
But there be fears I scorn to feel!

"Let those who will, seek realms above,
Remote from all that heart can love,
In their ignoble dread of hell.
Give all, good priest, in charity;
Give heaven to all, if this may be,
And count it well, and very well.

"But I—I could not leave this spot
Where she is waiting by my side.
Forgive me, priest; it is not pride;
There is no God where she is not!

"You did not know her well. Her creed
Was yours; my faith it was the same.
My faith was fair, my lands were broad.
Far down where yonder palm-trees rise
We two together worshiped God
From childhood. And we grew in deed,
Devout in heart as well as name,
And loved our palm-set paradise.

"We loved, we loved all things on earth,
However mean or miserable.
We knew no thing that had not worth,
And learned to know no need of hell.

"Indeed, good priest, so much, indeed,
We found to do, we saw to love,
We did not always look above
As is commanded in your creed,
But kept in heart one chiefest care,
To make this fair world still more fair.

"'T was then that meek, pale Saxon came;
With soulless gray and greedy eyes,
A snake's eyes, cunning, cold, and wise,
And I—I could not fight, or fly
His crafty wiles, at all; and I—
Enough, enough! I signed my name.

"It was not loss of pleasure, place,
Broad lands, or the serene delight
Of doing good, that made long night
O'er all the sunlight of her face.
But there be little things that feed
A woman's sweetness, day by day,
That strong men miss not, do not need,
But, shorn of all can go their way
To battle, and but stronger grow,
As grow great waves that gather so.

"She missed the music, missed the song,
The pleasant speech of courteous men,
Who came and went, a comely throng,
Before her open window, when
The sea sang with us, and we two
Had heartfelt homage, warm and true.

"She missed the restfulness, the rest
Of dulcet silence, the delight
Of singing silence, when the town
Put on its twilight robes of brown;
When twilight wrapped herself in night
And couched against the curtained west.

"But not one murmur, not one word
From her sweet baby lips was heard.
She only knew I could not bear
To see sweet San Diego town,
Her palm-set lanes, her pleasant square,
Her people passing up and down,
Without black hate, and deadly hate
For him who housed within our gate,
And so, she gently led my feet
Aside to this high, wild retreat.

"How pale she grew, how piteous pale
The while I wrought, and ceaseless wrought
To keep my soul from bitter thought,
And build me here above the vale.
Ah me! my selfish, Spanish pride!
Enough of pride, enough of hate,
Enough of her sad, piteous fate:
She died: right here she sank and died.

"She died, and with her latest breath
Did promise to return to me,
As turns a dove unto her tree
To find her mate at night and rest;
Died, clinging close against my breast;
Died, saying she would surely rise
So soon as God had loosed her eyes
From the strange wonderment of death.

"How beautiful is death! and how
Surpassing good, and true, and fair!
How just is death, how gently just,
To lay his sword against the thread
Of life when life is surely dead
And loose the sweet soul from the dust!
I laid her in my lorn despair
Beneath that dove, that orange-bough—
How strange your cross should stand just there!

"And then I waited hours and days:
Those bitter days, they were as years.
My soul groped through the darkest ways;
I scarce could see God's face for tears.

* * * * *

"I clutched my knife, and I crept down,
A wolf, to San Diego town.
On, on, 'mid mine own palms once more,
Keen knife in hand, I crept that night.
I passed the gate, then fled in fright;
Black crape hung fluttered from the door!

"I climbed back here, with heart of stone:
I heard next morn one sweetest tone;
Looked up, and lo! there on that bough
She perched, as she sits perching now.

* * * * *

"I heard the bells peal from my height,
Peal pompously, peal piously;
Saw sable hearse, in plumes of night
With not one thought of hate in me.

"I watched the long train winding by,
A mournful, melancholy lie—
A sable, solemn, mourning mile—
And only pitied him the while.
For she, she sang that whole day through:
Sad-voiced, as if she pitied, too.

"They said, 'His work is done, and well.'
They laid his body in a tomb
Of massive splendor. It lies there
In all its stolen pomp and gloom—
But list! his soul—his soul is where?
In hell! In hell! But where is hell?

"Hear me but this. Year after year
She trained my eye, she trained my ear;
No book to blind my eyes, or ought
To prate of hell, where hell is not,
I came to know at last, and well,
Such things as never book can tell.

"And where was that poor, dismal soul
Ye priests had sent to Paradise?
I heard the long years roll and roll,
As rolls the sea. My once dimmed eyes
Grew keen as long, sharp shafts of light.
With eager eyes and reaching face
I searched the stars night after night:
That dismal soul was not in space!

"Meanwhile my green trees grew and grew;
And sad or glad, this much I knew,
It were no sin to make more fair
One spot on earth, to toil and share
With man, or beast, or bird; while she
Still sang her soft, sweet melody.

"One day, a perfumed day in white—
Such restful, fresh, and friendlike day,—
Fair Mexico a mirage lay
Far-lifted in a sea of light—
Soft, purple light, so far away.
I turned yon pleasant pathway down,
And sauntered leisurely tow'rd town.

"I heard my dear love call and coo,
And knew that she was happy, too,
In her sad, sweet, and patient pain
Of waiting till I came again.

"Aye, I was glad, quite glad at last;
Not glad as I had been when she
Walked with me by yon palm-set sea,
But sadly and serenely glad:
As though 't were twilight like, as though
You knew, and yet you did not know,
That sadness, most supremely sad
Should lay upon you like a pall,
And would not, could not pass away
Till you should pass; till perfect day

Dawns sudden on you, and the call
Of birds awakens you to morn—
A babe new-born; a soul new-born.

"Good priest, what are the birds for? Priest,
Build ye your heaven west or east?
Above, below, or anywhere?
I only ask, I only say
She sits there, waiting for the day,
The fair, full day to guide me there.

* * * * *

"What, he? That creature? Ah, quite true!
I wander much, I weary you:
I beg your pardon, gentle priest.
Returning up the stone-strewn steep,
Down in yon jungle, dank and deep,
Where toads and venomed reptiles creep,
There, there, I saw that hideous beast!

"Aye, there! coiled there beside my road,
Close coiled behind a monstrous toad,
A huge flat-bellied reptile hid!
His tongue leapt red as flame; his eyes,
His eyes were burning hells of lies—
His head was like a coffin's lid:

'Saint George! Saint George! I gasped for breath.
The beast, tight coiled, swift, sudden sprang
High in the air, and, rattling, sang
His hateful, hissing song of death!

"My eyes met his. He shrank, he fell,
Fell sullenly and slow. The swell
Of braided, brassy neck forgot
Its poise, and every venomed spot
Lost luster, and the coffin head
Cowed level with the toad, and lay
Low, quivering with hate and dread:
The while I kept my upward way.

"What! Should have killed him? Nay, good priest,
I know not what or where 's your hell.
But be it west or be it east,
His hell is there! and that is well!

"Nay, do not, do not question me;
I could not tell you why I know;
I only know that this is so,
As sure as God is equity.

"Good priest, forgive me, and good-by,
The stars slow gather to their fold;
I see God's garment's hem of gold
Against the far, faint morning sky.

"Good, holy priest, your God is where?
You come to me with book and creed;
I cannot read your book; I read
Yon boundless, open book of air.
What time, or way, or place I look,
I see God in His garden walk;
I hear Him through the thunders talk,
As once He talked, with burning tongue,
To Moses, when the world was young;
And, priest, what more is in your book?

"Behold! the Holy Grail is found,
Found in each poppy's cup of gold;
And God walks with us as of old.
Behold! the burning bush still burns
For man, whichever way he turns;
And all God's earth is holy ground.

"And—and—good priest, bend low your head,
The sands are crumbling where I tread,
Beside the shoreless, soundless sea.
Good priest, you came to pray, you said;
And now, what would you have of me?"

The good priest gently raised his head,
Then bowed it low and softly said:
"Your blessing, son, despite the ban."
He fell before the dying man;
And when he raised his face from prayer,
Sweet Dawn, and two sweet doves were there.

SAPPHO AND PHAON.

SONG FIRST.

"In the beginning God ——"

When God's Spirit moved upon
The waters' face, and vapors curled
Like incense o'er deep-cradled dawn
That dared not yet the mobile world,—

When deep-cradled dawn uprose,
Ere the baby stars were born,
When the end of all repose
Came with that first wondrous morn,—

In the morning of the world
When light leapt,—a giant born:
O that morning of the world,
That vast, first tumultuous morn!

PART FIRST.

I.

What is there in a dear dove's eyes,
Or voice of mated melodies,
That tells us ever of blue skies
And cease of deluge on Love's seas?
The dove looked down on Jordan's tide
Well pleased with Christ the Crucified;
The dove was hewn in Karnak stone
Before fair Jordan's banks were known.
The dove has such a patient look,
I read rest in her pretty eyes
As in the Holy Book.

I think if I should love some day—
And may I die when dear Love dies—
Why, I would sail Francisco's Bay
And seek to see some sea-dove's eyes:
To see her in her air-built nest,
Her wide, warm, restful wings at rest;
To see her rounded neck reach out,
Her eyes lean lovingly about;
And seeing this as love can see,
I then should know, and surely know,
That love sailed on with me.

II.

See once this boundless bay and live,
See once this beauteous bay and love,
See once this warm, bright bay and give
God thanks for olive branch and dove.
Then plunge headlong yon sapphire sea
And sail and sail the world with me.
Some isles, drowned in the drowning sun,
Ten thousand sea-doves voiced as one;
Lo! love's wings furled and wings unfurled;

Who sees not this warm, half-world sea,
Sees not, knows not the world.

How knocks he at the Golden Gate,
This lord of waters, strong and bold,
And fearful-voiced and fierce as fate,
And hoar and old, as Time is old;
Yet young as when God's finger lay
Against Night's forehead that first day,
And drove vast Darkness forth, and rent
The waters from the firmament.
Hear how he knocks and raves and loves!
He wooes us through the Golden Gate
With all his soft sea-doves.

Now on and on, up, down, and on,
The sea is oily grooves; the air
Is as your bride's sweet breath at dawn
When all your ardent youth is there.
And oh, the rest! and oh, the room!
And oh, the sensuous sea perfume!
Yon new moon peering as we passed
Has scarce escaped our topmost mast.
A porpoise, wheeling restlessly,
Quick draws a bright, black, dripping blade,
Then sheathes it in the sea.

* * * * * * * *

Vast, half-world, wondrous sea of ours!
Dread, unknown deep of all sea deeps!
What fragrance from thy strange sea-flowers
Deep-gardened where God's silence keeps!
Thy song is silence, and thy face
Is God's face in His holy place.
Thy billows swing sweet censer foam,
Where stars hang His cathedral's dome.
Such blue above, below such blue!
These burly winds so tall, they can
Scarce walk between the two.

Such room of sea! Such room of sky!
Such room to draw a soul-full breath!
Such room to live! Such room to die!
Such room to roam in after death!
White room, with sapphire room set 'round,
And still beyond His room profound;
Such room-bound boundlessness o'erhead
As never has been writ or said
Or seen, save by the favored few,
Where kings of thought play chess with stars
Across their board of blue.

* * * * * * * *

III.

The proud ship wrapped her in the red
That hung from heaven, then the gray,
The soft dove-gray that shrouds the dead
And prostrate form of perfumed day:
Some noisy, pigmy creatures kept
The deck a spell, then, leaning, crept
Apart in silence and distrust,
Then down below in deep disgust.
An albatross,—a shadow cross
Hung at the head of buried day,—
At foot the albatross.

Then came a warm, soft, sultry breath—
A weary wind that wanted rest;
A breath as from some house of death
With flowers heaped; as from the breast
Of such sweet princess as had slept
Some thousand years embalmed, and kept,
In fearful Karnak's tomb-hewn hill,
Her perfume and spiced sweetness still,—
Such breath as bees droop down to meet,
And creep along lest it may melt
Their honey-laden feet.

The captain's trumpet smote the air!
Swift men, like spiders up a thread,
Swept suddenly. Then masts were bare
As when tall poplars' leaves are shed,
And ropes were clamped and stays were clewed.
'T was as when wrestlers, iron-thewed,

Gird tight their loins, take full breath,
And set firm face, as fronting death.
Three small brown birds, or gray, so small,
So ghostly still and swift they passed,
They scarce seemed birds at all.

Then quick, keen saber-cuts, like ice;
Then sudden hail, like battle-shot,
Then two last men crept down like mice,
And man, poor pigmy man, was not.
The great ship shivered, as with cold—
An instant staggered back, then bold
As Theodosia, to her waist
In waters, stood erect and faced
Black thunder; and she kept her way
And laughed red lightning from her face
As on some gala day.

The black sea-horses rode in row;
Their white manes tossing to the night
But made the blackness blacker grow
From flashing, phosphorescent light.
And how like hurdle steeds they leapt!
The low moon burst; the black troop swept
Right through her hollow, on and on.
A wave-wet simitar was drawn,
Flashed twice, flashed thrice triumphantly,
But still the steeds dashed on, dashed on,
And drowned her in the sea.

What headlong winds that lost their way
At sea, and wailed out for the shore!
How shook the orient doors of day
With all this mad, tumultuous roar!
Black clouds, shot through with stars of red;
Strange stars, storm-born and fire fed;
Lost stars that came, and went, and came;
Such stars as never yet had name.
The far sea-lions on their isles
Upheaved their huge heads terrified,
And moaned a thousand miles.

What fearful battle-field! What space
For light and darkness, flame and flood!
Lo! Light and Darkness, face to face,
In battle harness battling stood!
And how the surged sea burst upon
The granite gates of Oregon! *
It tore, it tossed the seething spume,
And wailed for room! and room! and room!
It shook the crag-built eaglets' nest
Until they screamed from out their clouds,
Then rocked them back to rest.

How fiercely reckless raged the war!
Then suddenly no ghost of light,
Or even glint of storm-born star.
Just night, and black, torn bits of night;
Just night, and midnight's middle noon,
With all mad elements in tune;
Just night, and that continuous roar
Of wind, wind, night, and nothing more.
Then all the hollows of the main
Sank down so deep, it almost seemed
The seas were hewn in twain.

How deep the hollows of this deep!
How high, how trembling high the crest!
Ten thousand miles of surge and sweep
And length and breadth of billow's breast!
Up! up, as if against the skies!
Down! down, as if no more to rise!
The creaking wallow in the trough,
As if the world was breaking off.
The pigmies in their trough down there!
Deep in their trough they tried to pray—
To hide from God in prayer.

Then boomed Alaska's great, first gun
In battling ice and rattling hail;

* There is a small granite island, or great rock standing on pillars, eight miles off Cape Blanco. Fishermen may row their boats between these columns and they call the rock The Gates.

Then Indus came, four winds in one!
Then came Japan in counter mail
Of mad cross winds; and Waterloo
Was but as some babe's tale unto.
The typhoon spun his toy in play
And whistled as a glad boy may
To see his top spin at his feet:
The captain on his bridge in ice,
His sailors mailed in sleet.

What unchained, unnamed noises, space!
What shoreless, boundless, rounded reach
Of room was here! Fit field, fit place
For three fierce emperors, where each
Came armed with elements that make
Or unmake seas and lands, that shake
The heavens' roof, that freeze or burn
The seas as they may please to turn.
And such black silence! Not a sound
Save whistling of that mad, glad boy
To see his top spin round.

Then swift, like some sulked Ajax, burst
Thewed Thunder from his battle-tent;
As if in pent-up, vengeful thirst
For blood, the elements of Earth were rent,
And sheeted crimson lay a wedge
Of blood below black Thunder's edge.
A pause. The typhoon turned, upwheeled,
And wrestled Death till heaven reeled.
Then Lightning reached a fiery red,
And on Death's fearful forehead wrote
The autograph of God.

IV.

God's name and face—what need of more?
Morn came: calm came; and holy light,
And warm, sweet weather, leaning o'er,
Laid perfumes on the tomb of night.
The three wee birds came dimly back
And housed about the mast in black,
And all the tranquil sense of morn
Seemed as Dakota's fields of corn,
Save that some great soul-breaking sigh
Now sank the proud ship out of sight
Now sent her to the sky.

V.

One strong, strange man had kept the deck—
One silent, seeing man, who knew
The pulse of Nature, and could reck
Her deepest heart-beats through and through.
He knew the night, he loved the night.
When elements went forth to fight
His soul went with them without fear
To hear God's voice, so few will hear
The swine had plunged them in the sea,
The swine down there, but up on deck
The captain, God and he.

VI.

And oh, such sea-shell tints of light
High o'er those wide sea-doors of dawn!
Sail, sail the world for that one sight,
Then satisfied, let time begone.
The ship rose up to meet that light,
Bright candles, tipped like tasseled corn,
The holy virgin, maiden morn,
Arrayed in woven gold and white.
Put by the harp—hush minstrelsy;
Nor bard or bird has yet been heard
To sing this scene, this sea.

VII.

Such light! such liquid, molten light!
Such mantling, healthful, heartful morn!
Such morning born of such mad night!
Such night as never had been born!
The man caught in his breath, his face
Was lifted up to light and space;
His hand dashed o'er his brow, as when
Deep thoughts submerge the souls of men;

And then he bowed, bowed mute, appalled
At memory of scenes, such scenes
As this swift morn recalled.

He sought the ship's prow, as men seek
The utmost limit for their feet,
To lean, look forth, to list nor speak,
Nor turn aside, nor yet retreat
One inch from this far vantage-ground,
Till he had pierced the dread profound
And proved it false. And yet he knew
Deep in his earth that all was true;
So like it was to that first dawn
When God had said, "Let there be light,"
And thus he spake right on:

"My soul was born ere light was born,
When blackness was, as this black night.
And then that morn, as this sweet morn!
That sudden light, as this swift light!
I had forgotten. Now, I know
The travail of the world, the low,
Dull creatures in the sea of slime
That time committed unto time,
As great men plant oaks patiently,
Then turn in silence unto dust
And wait the coming tree.

"That long, lorn blackness, seams of flame,
Volcanoes bursting from the slime,
Huge, shapeless monsters without name
Slow shaping in the loom of time;
Slow weaving as a weaver weaves;
So like as when some good man leaves
His acorns to the centuries
And waits the stout ancestral trees.
But ah, so piteous, memory
Reels back, as sickened, from that scene—
It breaks the heart of me!

"Volcanoes crying out for light!
The very slime found tongues of fire! *
Huge monsters climbing in their might
O'er submerged monsters in the mire
That heaved their slimy mouths, and cried
And cried for light, and crying, died.
How all that wailing through the air
But seems as some unbroken prayer.
One ceaseless prayer that long night
The world lay in the loom of time
And waited so for light!

"And I, amid those monsters there,
A grade above, or still below?
Nay, Time has never time to care;
And I can scarcely dare to know.
I but remember that one prayer;
Ten thousand wide mouths in the air,
Ten thousand monsters in their might,
All eyeless, looking up for light.
We prayed, we prayed as never man,
By sea or land, by deed or word,
Has prayed since light began.

"Great sea-cows laid their fins upon
Low-floating isles, as good priests lay
Two holy hands, at early dawn,
Upon the altar cloth to pray.
Aye, ever so, with lifted head,
Poor, slime-born creatures and slime-bred,
We prayed. Our sealed-up eyes of night
All lifting, lifting up for light.
And I have paused to wonder, when
This world will pray as we then prayed,
What God may not give men!

"Hist! Once I saw,—What was I then?
Ah, dim and devious the light
Comes back, but I was not of men.
And it is only such black night

* I saw this when with Capt. Eads at the mouth of our great river. The débris of more than a dozen States pouring into the warm waters of the Mexican seas creates fermentation which finds expression in volcanoes that spring flaming up out of the sea almost nightly. I know nothing so terrible as certain nights in the Mississippi delta.

As this, that was of war and strife
Of elements, can wake that life,
That life in death, that black and cold
And blind and loveless life of old.
But hear! I saw—heed this and learn
How old, how holy old is Love,
However Time may turn:

"I saw, I saw, or somehow felt,
A sea-cow mother nurse her young.
I saw, and with thanksgiving knelt,
To see her head, low, loving, hung
Above her nursling. Then the light,
The lovelight from those eyes of night!
I say to you 't was lovelight then
That first lit up the eyes of men.
I say to you lovelight was born
Ere God laid hand to clay of man,
Or ever that first morn.

"What though a monster slew her so,
The while she bowed and nursed her young?
She leaned her head to take the blow,
And dying, still the closer clung—
And dying gave her life to save
The helpless life she erstwhile gave,
And so sank back below the slime,
A torn shred in the loom of time.
The one thing more I needs must say,
That monster slew her and her young;
But Love he could not slay."

SONG SECOND.

"And God said, Let there be light."

Rise up! How brief this little day?
We can but kindle some dim light
Here in the darkened, wooded way
Before the gathering of night.
Come, let us kindle it. The dawn
Shall find us tenting farther on.
Come, let us kindle ere we go—
We know not where; but this we know.
Night cometh on, and man needs light.
Come! camp-fire embers, ere we grope
Yon gray archway of night.

Life is so brief, so very brief,
So rounded in, we scarce can see
The fruitage grown about the leaf
And foliage of a single tree
In all God's garden; yet we know
That goodly fruits must grow and grow
Beyond our vision. We but stand
In some deep hollow of God's hand,
Hear some sweet bird its little day,
See cloud and sun a season pass,
And then, sweet friend, away!

Clouds pass, they come again; and we,
Are we, then, less than these to God?
Oh, for the stout faith of a tree
That drops its small seeds to the sod,
Safe in the hollow of God's hand,
And knows that perish from the land
It shall not! Yea, this much we know,
That each, as best it can, shall grow
As God has fashioned, fair or plain,
To do its best, or cloud or sun,
Or in His still, small rain.

Oh, good to see is faith in God!
But better far is faith in good:
The one seems but a sign, a nod,
The one seems God's own flesh and blood.
How many names of God are sung!
But good is good in every tongue.
And this the light, the Holy Light
That leads thro' night and night and night;
Thro' nights named Death, that lie between
The days named Life, the ladder round
Unto the Infinite Unseen.

PART SECOND.

I.

The man stood silent, peering past
His utmost verge of memory.
What lay beyond, beyond that vast
Bewildering darkness and dead sea
Of noisome vapors and dread night?
No light! not any sense of light
Beyond that life when Love was born
On that first, far, dim rim of morn:
No light beyond that beast that clung
In darkness by the light of love
And died to save her young.

And yet we know life must have been
Before that dark, dread life of pain;
Life germs, love germs of gentle men,
So small, so still; as still, small rain.
But whence this life, this living soul,
This germ that grows a godlike whole?
I can but think of that sixth day
When God first set His hand to clay,
And did in His own image plan
A perfect form, a manly form,
A comely, godlike man.

II.

Did soul germs grow down in the deeps,
The while God's Spirit moved upon
The waters? High-set Lima keeps
A rose-path, like a ray of dawn;
And simple, pious peons say
Sweet Santa Rosa passed that way;
And so, because of her fair fame
And saintly face, these roses came.
Shall we not say, ere that first morn,
Where God moved, garmented in mists,
Some sweet soul germs were born?

III.

The strange, strong man still kept the prow;
He saw, still saw before light was,
The dawn of love, the huge sea-cow,
The living slime, love's deathless laws.
He knew love lived, lived ere a blade
Of grass, or ever light was made;
And love was in him, of him, as
The light was on the sea of glass.
It made his heart great, and he grew
To look on God all unabashed;
To look lost eons through.

IV.

Illuming love! what talisman!
That Word which makes the world go 'round!
That Word which bore worlds in its plan!
That Word which was the Word profound!
That Word which was the great First Cause,

Before light was, before sight was!
I would not barter love for gold
Enough to fill a tall ship's hold;
Nay, not for great Victoria's worth-
So great the sun sets not upon
In all his round of earth.

I would not barter love for all
The silver spilling from the moon;
I would not barter love at all
Though you should coin each afternoon
Of gold for centuries to be,
And count the coin all down as free
As conqueror fresh home from wars,—
Coin sunset bars, coin heaven-born stars,
Coin all below, coin all above,
Count all down at my feet, yet I—
I would not barter love.

V.

The lone man started, stood as when
A strong man hears, yet does not hear.
He raised his hand, let fall, and then
Quick arched his hand above his ear
And leaned a little; yet no sound
Broke through the vast, serene profound.
Man's soul first knew some telephone
In sense and language all its own.
The tall man heard, yet did not hear;
He saw, and yet he did not see
A fair face near and dear.

For there, half hiding, crouching there
Against the capstan, coils on coils
Of rope, some snow still in her hair,
Like Time, too eager for his spoils,
Was such fair face raised to his face
As only dream of dreams give place;
Such shyness, boldness, sea-shell tint,
Such book as only God may print,
Such tender, timid, holy look
Of startled love and trust and hope,—
A gold-bound story-book.

And while the great ship rose and fell,
Or rocked or rounded with the sea,
He saw,—a little thing to tell,
An idle, silly thing, maybe,—
Where her right arm was bent to clasp
Her robe's fold in some closer clasp,
A little isle of melting snow
That round about and to and fro
And up and down kept eddying.
It told so much, that idle isle,
Yet such a little thing.

It told she, too, was of a race
Born ere the baby stars were born;
She, too, familiar with God's face,
Knew folly but to shun and scorn;
She, too, all night had sat to read
By heaven's light, to hear, to heed
The awful voice of God, to grow
In thought, to see, to feel, to know
The harmony of elements
That tear and toss the sea of seas
To foam-built battle-tents.

He saw that drifting isle of snow,
As some lorn miner sees bright gold
Seamed deep in quartz, and joys to know
That here lies hidden wealth untold.
And now his head was lifted strong,
As glad men lift the head in song.
He knew she, too, had spent the night
As he, in all that wild delight
Of tuneful elements; she, too,
He knew, was of that olden time
Ere oldest stars were new.

VI.

Her soul's ancestral book bore date
Beyond the peopling of the moon,
Beyond the day when Saturn sate
In royal cincture, and the boon
Of light and life bestowed on stars
And satellites; ere martial Mars

Waxed red with battle rage, and shook
The porch of heaven with a look;
Ere polar ice-shafts propt gaunt earth,
And slime was but the womb of time,
That knew not yet of birth.

VII.

To be what thou wouldst truly be,
Be bravely, truly, what thou art.
The acorn houses the huge tree,
And patient, silent bears its part,
And bides the miracle of time.
For miracle, and more sublime
It is than all that has been writ,
To see the great oak grow from it.
But thus the soul grows, grows the heart,—
To be what thou wouldst truly be,
Be truly what thou art.

To be what thou wouldst truly be,
Be true. God's finger sets each seed,
Or when or where we may not see;
But God shall nourish to its need
Each one, if but it dares be true;
To do what it is set to do.
Thy proud soul's heraldry? 'T is writ
In every gentle action; it
Can never be contested. Time
Dates thy brave soul's ancestral book
From thy first deed sublime.

VIII.

Wouldst learn to know one little flower,
Its perfume, perfect form and hue?
Yea, wouldst thou have one perfect hour
Of all the years that come to you?
Then grow as God hath planted, grow
A lordly oak or daisy low,
As He hath set His garden; be
Just what thou art, or grass or tree.
Thy treasures up in heaven laid
Await thy sure ascending soul,
Life after life,—be not afraid!

IX.

Wouldst know the secrets of the soil?
Wouldst have Earth bare her breast to you?
Wouldst know the sweet rest of hard toil?
Be true, be true, be ever true!
Ah me, these self-made cuts of wrong
That hew men down! Behold the strong
And comely Adam bound with lies
And banished from his paradise!
The serpent on his belly still
Eats dirt through all his piteous days,
Do penance as he will.

Poor, heel-bruised, prostrate, tortuous snake!
What soul crawls here upon the ground?
God willed this soul at birth to take
The round of beauteous things, the round
Of earth, the round of boundless skies.
It lied, and lo! how low it lies!
What quick, sleek tongue to lie with here!
Wast thou a broker but last year?
Wast known to fame, wast rich and proud?
Didst live a lie that thou mightst die
With pockets in thy shroud?

X.

Be still, be pitiful! that soul
May yet be rich in peace as thine.
Yea, as the shining ages roll
That rich man's soul may rise and shine
Beyond Orion; yet may reel
The Pleiades with belts of steel
That compass commerce in their reach;
May learn and learn, and learning, teach,
The while his soul grows grandly old,
How nobler far to share a crust
Than hoard car-loads of gold!

XI.

Oh, but to know; to surely know
How strangely beautiful is light!
How just one gleam of light will glow

And grow more beautifully bright
Than all the gold that ever lay
Below the wide-arched Milky Way!
"Let there be light!" and lo! the burst
Of light in answer to the first
Command of high Jehovah's voice!
Let there be light for man to-night,
That all men may rejoice.

XII.

The little isle of ice and snow
That in her gathered garment lay,
And dashed and drifted to and fro
Unhindered of her, went its way.
The while the warm winds of Japan
Were with them, and the silent man
Stood by her, saying, hearing naught,
Yet seeing, noting all; as one
Sees not, yet all day sees the sun.
He knew her silence, heeded well
Her dignity of idle hands
In this deep, tranquil spell.

XIII.

The true soul surely knows its own,
Deep down in this man's heart he knew,
Somehow, somewhere along the zone
Of time, his soul should come unto
Its safe seaport, some pleasant land
Of rest where she should reach a hand.
He had not questioned God. His care
Was to be worthy, fit to share
The glory, peace, and perfect rest,
Come how or when or where it comes,
As God in time sees best.

Her face reached forward, not to him,
But forward, upward, as for light;
For light that lay a silver rim
Of sea-lit whiteness more than white.
The vast full morning poured and spilled
Its splendor down, and filled and filled
And overfilled the heaped-up sea
With silver molten suddenly.
The night lay trenched in her meshed hair;
The tint of sea-shells left the sea
To make her more than fair.

What massed, what matchless midnight hair!
Her wide, sweet, sultry, drooping mouth,
As droops some flower when the air
Blows odors from the ardent South—
That Sapphic, sensate, bended bow
Of deadly archery; as though
Love's legions fortressed there and sent
Red arrows from his bow fell bent.
Such apples! such sweet fruit concealed
Of perfect womanhood make more
Sweet pain than if revealed.

XIV.

How good a thing it is to house
Thy full heart treasures to that day
When thou shalt take her, and carouse
Thenceforth with her for aye and aye;
How good a thing to give the store
That thus the thousand years or more,
Poor, hungered, holy worshiper,
You kept for her, and only her!
How well with all thy wealth to wait
Or year, or thousand thousand years,
Her coming at love's gate!

XV.

The winds pressed warm from warm Japan
Upon her pulsing womanhood.
They fanned such fires in the man
His face shone glory where he stood.
In Persia's rose-fields, I have heard,
There sings a sad, sweet, one-winged bird;
Sings ever sad in lonely round
Until his one-winged mate is found;
And then, side laid to side, they rise
So swift, so strong, they even dare
The doorway of the skies.

XVI.

How rich was he! how richer she!
Such treasures up in heaven laid,
Where moth and rust may never be,
Nor thieves break in, or make afraid.
Such treasures, where the tranquil soul
Walks space, nor limit nor control
Can know, but journeys on and on
Beyond the golden gates of dawn;
Beyond the outmost round of Mars;
Where God's foot rocks the cradle of
His new-born baby stars.

XVII.

As one who comes upon a street,
Or sudden turn in pleasant path,
As one who suddenly may meet
Some scene, some sound, some sense that hath
A memory of olden days,
Of days that long have gone their ways,
She caught her breath, caught quick and fast
Her breath, as if her whole life passed
Before, and pendant to and fro
Swung in the air before her eyes;
And oh, her heart beat so!

How her heart beat! Three thousand years
Of weary, waiting womanhood,
Of folded hands, of falling tears,
Of lone soul-wending through dark wood;
But now at last to meet once more
Upon the bright, all-shining shore
Of earth, in life's resplendent dawn,
And he so fair to look upon!
Tall Phaon and the world aglow!
Tall Phaon, favored of the gods,
And oh, her heart beat so!

Her heart beat so, no word she spake;
She pressed her palms, she leaned her face,—
Her heart beat so, its beating brake
The cord that held her robe in place
About her wondrous, rounded throat,
And in the warm winds let it float
And fall upon her soft, round arm,
So warm it made the morning warm.
Then pink and pearl forsook her cheek,
And, "Phaon, I am Sappho, I—"
Nay, nay, she did not speak.

And was this Sappho, she who sang
When mournful Jeremiah wept?
When harps, where weeping willows hang,
Hung mute and all their music kept?
Aye, this was Sappho, she who knew
Such witchery of song as drew
The war-like world to hear her sing,
As moons draw mad seas following.
Aye, this was Sappho; Lesbos hill
Had all been hers, and Tempos vale,
And song sweet as to kill.

Her dark Greek eyes turned to the sea:
Lo, Phaon's ferry as of old!
He kept his boat's prow still, and he
Was stately, comely, strong, and bold
As when he ferried gods, and drew
Immortal youth from one who knew
His scorn of gold. The Lesbian shore
Lay yonder, and the rocky roar
Against the promontory told,
Told and retold her tale of love
That never can grow old.

Three thousand years! yet love was young
And fair as when Æolis knew
Her glory, and her great soul strung
The harp that still sweeps ages through.
Ionic dance or Doric war,
Or purpled dove or dulcet car,
Or unyoked dove or close-yoked dove,
What meant it all but love and love?
And at the naming of Love's name
She raised her eyes, and lo! her doves!
Just as of old they came.

SONG THIRD.

"And God saw the light that it was good."

I heard a tale long, long ago,
Where I had gone apart to pray
By Shasta's pyramid of snow,
That touches me unto this day.
I know the fashion is to say
An Arab tale, an Orient lay;
But when the grocer rings my gold
On counter, flung from greasy hold,
He cares not from Acadian vale
It comes, or savage mountain chine;—
But this the Shastan tale:

Once in the olden, golden days,
When men and beasts companioned, when
All went in peace about their ways
Nor God had hid His face from men
Because man slew his brother beast
To make his most unholy feast,
A gray coyote, monkish cowled,
Upraised his face and wailed and howled
The while he made his patient round;
For lo! the red men all lay dead,
Stark, frozen on the ground.

The very dogs had fled the storm,
A mother with her long, meshed hair
Bound tight about her baby's form,
Lay frozen, all her body bare.
Her last shred held her babe in place;
Her last breath warmed her baby's face.
Then, as the good monk brushed the snow
Aside from mother loving so,
He heard God from the mount above
Speak through the clouds and loving say:
"Yea, all is dead but Love."

"Now take up Love and cherish her,
And seek the white man with all speed,
And keep Love warm within thy fur;
For oh, he needeth love indeed.
Take all and give him freely, all
Of love you find, or great or small;
For he is very poor in this,
So poor he scarce knows what love is."
The gray monk raised Love in his paws
And sped, a ghostly streak of gray,
To where the white man was.

But man uprose, enraged to see
A gaunt wolf track his new-hewn town.
He called his dogs, and angrily
He brought his flashing rifle down.
Then God said: "On his hearthstone lay
The seed of Love, and come away;.
The seed of Love, 't is needed so,
And pray that it may grow and grow."
And so the gray monk crept at night
And laid Love down, as God had said,
A faint and feeble light.

So faint, indeed, the cold hearthstone
It seemed would chill starved Love to death;
And so the monk gave all his own
And crouched and fanned it with his breath
Until a red cock crowed for day.
Then God said: "Rise up, come away."
The beast obeyed, but yet looked back
All morn along his lonely track;
For he had left his all in all,
His own Love, for that famished Love
Seemed so exceeding small.

And God said: "Look not back again."
But ever, where a campfire burned,
And he beheld strong, burly men
At meat, he sat him down and turned
His face to wail and wail and mourn
The Love laid on that cold hearthstone.

Then God was angered, and God said:
"Be thou a beggar then; thy head
Hath been a fool, but thy swift feet,
Because they bore sweet Love, shall be
The fleetest of all fleet."

And ever still about the camp,
By chine or plain, in heat or hail,
A homeless, hungry, hounded tramp,
The gaunt coyote keeps his wail.
And ever as he wails he turns
His head, looks back and yearns and yearns
For lost Love, laid that wintry day
To warm a hearthstone far away.
Poor loveless, homeless beast, I keep
Your lost Love warm for you, and, too,
A cañon cool and deep.

PART THIRD.

I.

And they sailed on; the sea-doves sailed,
And Love sailed with them. And there lay
Such peace as never had prevailed
On earth since dear Love's natal day.
Great black-backed whales blew bows in
clouds,
Wee sea-birds flitted through the shrouds.
A wide-winged, amber albatross
Blew by, and bore his shadow cross,
And seemed to hang it on the mast,
The while he followed far behind,
The great ship flew so fast.

She questioned her if Phaon knew,
If he could dream, or halfway guess
How she had tracked the ages through
And trained her soul to gentleness
Through many lives, through every part
To make her worthy his great heart.
Would Phaon turn and fly her still,
With that fierce, proud, imperious will,
And scorn her still, and still despise?
She shuddered, turned aside her face,
And lo, her sea-dove's eyes!

II.

Then days of rest and restful nights;
And love kept tryst as true love will,
The prow their trysting-place. Delights
Of silence, simply sitting still,—
Of asking nothing, saying naught;
For all that they had ever sought
Sailed with them; words or deeds had been
Impertinence, a selfish sin.
And oh, to know how sweet a thing
Is silence on those restful seas
When Love's dove folds her wing!

The great sea slept. In vast repose
His pillowed head half-hidden lay,
Half-drowned in dread Alaskan snows
That stretch to where no man can say.
His huge arms tossed to left, to right,
Where black woods, banked like bits of
night,
As sleeping giants toss their arms

At night about their fearful forms.
A slim canoe, a night-bird's call,
Some gray sea-doves, just these and Love,
And Love indeed was all!

III.

Far, far away such cradled Isles
As Jason dreamed and Argos sought
Surge up from endless watery miles!
And thou, the pale high priest of thought,
The everlasting thronèd king
Of fair Samoa! Shall I bring
Sweet sandal-wood? Or shall I lay
Rich wreaths of California's bay
From sobbing maidens? Stevenson,
Sleep well. Thy work is done; well done!
So bravely, bravely done!

And Molokia's lord of love
And tenderness, and piteous tears
For stricken man! Go forth, O dove!
With olive branch, and still the fears
Of those he meekly died to save.
They shall not perish. From that grave
Shall grow such healing! such as He
Gave stricken men by Galilee.
Great ocean cradle, cradle, keep
These two, the chosen of thy heart,
Rocked in sweet, baby sleep.

IV.

Fair land of flowers, land of flame,
Of sun-born seas, of sea-born clime,
Of clouds low shepherded and tame
As white pet sheep at shearing time,
Of great, white, generous high-born rain,
Of rainbows builded not in vain—
Of rainbows builded for the feet
Of love to pass dry-shod and fleet
From isle to isle, when smell of musk
'Mid twilight is, and one lone star
Sits in the brow of dusk.

Oh, dying, sad-voiced, sea-born maid!
And plundered, dying, still sing on.
Thy breast against the thorn is laid—
Sing on, sing on, sweet dying swan.
How pitiful! And so despoiled
By those you fed, for whom you toiled!
Aloha! Hail you, and farewell,
Far echo of some lost sea-shell!
Some song that lost its way at sea,
Some sea-lost notes of nature, lost,
That crying, came to me.

Dusk maid, adieu! One sea-shell less!
Sad sea-shell silenced and forgot.
O Rachel in the wilderness,
Wail on! Your children they are not.
And they who took them, they who laid
Hard hand, shall they not feel afraid?
Shall they who in the name of God
Robbed and enslaved, escape His rod?
Give me some after-world afar
From these hard men, for well I know
Hell must be where they are.

V.

Lo! suddenly the lone ship burst
Upon an uncompleted world,
A world so dazzling white, man durst
Not face the flashing search-light hurled
From heaven's snow-built battlements
And high-heaved camp of cloud-wreathed tents.
And boom! boom! boom! from sea or shore
Came one long, deep, continuous roar,
As if God wrought; as if the days,
The first six pregnant mother morns,
Had not quite gone their way.

What word is fitting but the Word
Here in this vast world-fashioning?
What tongue here name the nameless Lord?
What hand lay hand on anything?

Come, let us coin new words of might
And massiveness to name this light,
This largeness, largeness everywhere!
White rivers hanging in the air,
Ice-tied through all eternity!
Nay, peace! It were profane to say:
We dare but hear and see.

Be silent! Hear the strokes resound!
'T is God's hand rounding down the earth
Take off thy shoes, 't is holy ground,—
Behold! a continent has birth!
The skies bow down, Madonna's blue
Enfolds the sea in sapphire. You
May lift, a little spell, your eyes
And feast them on the ice-propped skies,
And feast but for a little space:
Then let thy face fall grateful down
And let thy soul say grace.

VI.

At anchor so, and all night through,
The two before God's temple kept.
He spake: "I know yon peak; I knew
A deep ice-cavern there. I slept
With hairy men, or monsters slew,
Or led down misty seas my crew
Of cruel savages and slaves,
And slew who dared the distant waves,
And once a strange, strong ship—and *she*,
I bore her to yon cave of ice,—
And Love companioned me.

VII.

"Two scenes of all scenes from the first
Have come to me on this great sea:
The one when light from heaven burst,
The one when sweet Love came to me.
And of the two, or best or worst,
I ever hold this second first,
Bear with me. Yonder citadel
Of ice tells all my tongue can tell:
My thirst for love, my pain, my pride,
My soul's warm youth the while she lived,
Its old age when she died.

"I know not if she loved or no.
I only asked to serve and love;
To love and serve, and ever so
My love grew as grows light above,—
Grew from gray dawn to gold midday,
And swept the wide world in its sway.
The stars came down, so close they came,
I called them, named them with her name,
The kind moon came,—came once so near,
That in the hollow of her arm
I leaned my lifted spear.

"And yet, somehow, for all the stars,
And all the silver of the moon,
She looked from out her icy bars
As longing for some sultry noon;
As longing for some warmer kind,
Some far south sunland left behind.
Then I went down to sea. I sailed
Thro' seas where monstrous beasts prevailed,
Such slimy, shapeless, hungered things!
Red griffins, wide-winged, bat-like wings,
Black griffins, black or fire-fed,
That ate my fever-stricken men
Ere yet they were quite dead.

"I could not find her love for her,
Or land, or fit thing for her touch,
And I came back, sad worshiper,
And watched and longed and loved so much!
I watched huge monsters climb and pass
Reflected in great walls, like glass;
Dark, draggled, hairy, fearful forms
Upblown by ever-battling storms,
And streaming still with slime and spray;
So huge from out their sultry seas,
Like storm-torn islands they.

"Then even these she ceased to note,
She ceased at last to look on me,
But, baring to the sun her throat,
She looked and looked incessantly
Away against the south, away
Against the sun the livelong day.
At last I saw her watch the swan
Surge tow'rd the north, surge on and on.
I saw her smile, her first, faint smile;
Then burst a new-born thought, and I,
I nursed that all the while.

VIII.

"I somehow dreamed, or guessed, or knew,
That somewhere in the dear earth's heart
Was warmth and tenderness and true
Delight, and all love's nobler part.
I tried to think, aye, thought and thought;
In all the strange fruits that I brought
For her delight I could but find
The sweetness deep within the rind.
All beasts, all birds, some better part
Of central being deepest housed;
And earth must have a heart.

"I watched the wide-winged birds that blew
Continually against the bleak
And ice-built north, and surely knew
The long, lorn croak, the reaching beak,
Led not to ruin evermore;
For they came back, came swooping o'er
Each spring, with clouds of younger ones,
So dense, they dimmed the summer suns.
And thus I knew somehow, somewhere,
Beyond earth's ice-built, star-tipt peaks
They found a softer air.

"And too, I heard strange stories, held
In mem'ries of my hairy men,
Vague, dim traditions, dim with eld,
Of other lands and ages when
Nor ices were, nor anything;
But ever one warm, restful spring
Of radiant sunlight: stories told
By dauntless men of giant mold,
Who kept their cavern's icy mouth
Ice-locked, and hungered where they sat,
With sad eyes tow'rd the south:

"Tales of a time ere hate began,
Of herds of reindeer, wild beasts tamed,
When man walked forth in love with man,
Walked naked, and was not ashamed;
Of how a brother beast he slew,
Then night, and all sad sorrows knew;
How tame beasts were no longer tame;
How God drew His great sword of flame
And drove man naked to the snow,
Till, pitying, He made of skins
A coat, and clothed him so.

"And, true or not true, still the same,
I saw continually at night
That far, bright, flashing sword of flame,
Misnamed the Borealis light;
I saw my men, in coats of skin
As God had clothed them, felt the sin
And suffering of that first death
Each day in every icy breath.
Then why should I still disbelieve
These tales of fairer lands than mine,
And let my lady grieve?

IX.

"Yea, I would find that land for her!
Then dogs, and sleds, and swift reindeer;
Huge, hairy men, all mailed in fur,
Who knew not yet the name of fear,
Nor knew fatigue, nor aughf that ever
To this day has balked endeavor.
And we swept forth, while wide, swift wings
Still sought the Pole in endless strings.
I left her sitting looking south,
Still leaning, looking to the sun,—
My kisses on her mouth!

X.

"Far toward the north, so tall, so far,
One tallest ice shaft starward stood—
Stood as it were itself a star,
Scarce fallen from its sisterhood.
Tip-top the glowing apex there
Upreared a huge white polar bear;
He pushed his swart nose up and out,
Then walked the North Star round about,
Below the Great Bear of the main,
The upper main, and as if chained,
Chained with a star-linked chain.

XI.

"And we pushed on, up, on, and on,
Until, as in the world of dreams,
We found the very doors of dawn
With warm sun bursting through the seams.
We brake them through, then down, far down,
Until, as in some park-set town,
We found lost Eden. Very rare
The fruit, and all the perfumed air
So sweet, we sat us down to feed
And rest, without a thought or care,
Or ever other need.

"For all earth's pretty birds were here;
And women fair, and very fair;
Sweet song was in the atmosphere,
Nor effort was, nor noise, nor care.
As cocoons from their silken house
Wing forth and in the sun carouse,
My men let fall their housings and
Passed on and on, far down the land
Of purple grapes and poppy bloom.
Such warm, sweet land, such peaceful land!
Sweet peace and sweet perfume!

"And I pushed down ere I returned
To climb the cold world's walls of snow,
And saw where earth's heart beat and burned,
An hundred sultry leagues below;
Saw deep seas set with deep-sea isles
Of waving verdure; miles on miles
Of rising sea-birds with their broods,
In all their noisy, happy moods!
Aye, then I knew earth has a heart,
That Nature wastes nor space or place,
But husbands every part.

XII.

"My reindeer fretted: I turned back
For her, the heart of me, my soul!
Ah, then, how swift, how white my track!
All Paradise beneath the Pole
Were but a mockery till she
Should share its dreamful sweets with me....
I know not well what next befell,
Save that white heaven grew black hell.
She sat with sad face to the south,
Still sat, sat still; but she was dead—
My kisses on her mouth.

XIII.

"What else to do but droop and die?
But dying, how my poor soul yearned
To fly as swift south birds may fly—
To pass that way her eyes had turned,
The dear days she had sat with me,
And search and search eternity!
And, do you know, I surely know
That God has given us to go
The way we will in life or death—
To go, to grow, or good or ill,
As one may draw a breath?"

SONG FOURTH.

"And God saw everything that He had made, and, behold, it was very good."

Says Plato, "Once in Greece the gods
Plucked grapes, pressed wine, and reveled deep
And drowsed below their poppy-pods,
And lay full length the hills asleep.
Then, waking, one said, 'Overmuch
We toil: come, let us rise and touch
Red clay, and shape it into man,
That he may build as we shall plan!'
And so they shaped man, all complete,
Self-procreative, satisfied;
Two heads, four hands, four feet.

"And then the gods slept, heedless, long;
But waking suddenly one day,
They heard their valley ring with song
And saw man reveling as they.
Enraged, they drew their swords and said,
'Bow down! bend down!'—but man replied
Defiant, fearless, everywhere
His four fists shaking in the air.
The gods descending cleft in twain
Each man; then wiped their swords on grapes;
And let confusion reign.

"And such confusion! each half ran,
Ran here, ran there; or weep or laugh
Or what he would, each helpless man
Ran hunting for his other half.
And from that day, thenceforth the grapes
Bore blood and flame, and restless shapes
Of hewn-down, helpless halves of men,
Ran searching ever; crazed, as when
First hewn in twain, they grasped, let go,
Then grasped again; but rarely found
That lost half once loved so."

Now, right or wrong, or false or true,
'Tis Plato's tale of bitter sweet;
But I know well and well know you
The quest keeps on at fever heat.
Let Love, then, wisely sit and wait!
The world is round; sit by the gate,
Like blind Belisarius: being blind,
Love should not search; Love shall not find
By searching. Brass is so like gold,
How shall this blind Love know new brass
From pure soft gold of old?

PART FOURTH.

I.

Nay, turn not to the past for light;
Nay, teach not Pagan tale forsooth!
Behind lie heathen gods and night,
Before lift high, white light and truth.
Sweet Orpheus looked back, and lo,
Hell met his eyes and endless woe!
Lot's wife looked back, and for this fell
To something even worse than hell.
Let us have faith, sail, seek and find
The new world and the new world's ways:
Blind Homer led the blind!

II.

Come, let us kindle Faith in light!
Yon eagle climbing to the sun
Keeps not the straightest course in sight,
But room and reach of wing and run
Of rounding circle all are his,
Till he at last bathes in the light
Of worlds that look far down on this
Arena's battle for the right.
The stoutest sail that braves the breeze,
The bravest battle ship that rides,
Rides rounding up the seas.

Come, let us kindle faith in man!
What though yon eagle, where he swings,
May moult a feather in God's plan
Of broader, stronger, better wings!
Why, let the moulted feathers lie
As thick as leaves upon the lawn:
These be but proof we cleave the sky
And still round on and on and on.
Fear not for moulting feathers; nay,
But rather fear when all seems fair,
And care is far away.

Come, let us kindle faith in God!
He made, He kept, He still can keep.
The storm obeys His burning rod,
The storm brought Christ to walk the deep.
Trust God to round His own at will;
Trust God to keep His own for aye—
Or strife or strike, or well or ill;
An eagle climbing up the sky—
A meteor down from heaven hurled—
Trust God to round, reform, or rock
His new-born baby world.

III.

How full the great, full-hearted seas
That lave high, white Alaska's feet!
How densely green the dense green trees!
How sweet the smell of wood! how sweet!
What sense of high, white newness where
This new world breathes the new, blue air
That never breath of man or breath
Of mortal thing considereth!

And O, that Borealis light!
The angel with his flaming sword
And never sense of night!

IV.

Are these the walls of Paradise—
Yon peaks the gates man may not pass?
Lo, everlasting silencé lies
Along their gleaming ways of glass!
Just silence and that sword of flame;
Just silence and Jehovah's name,
Where all is new, unnamed, and white!
Come, let us read where angels write—
"In the beginning God"—aye, these
The waters where God's Spirit moved;
These, these, the very seas!

Just one deep, wave-washed chariot wheel:
Such sunset as that far first day!
An unsheathed sword of flame and steel;
Then battle flashes; then dismay,
And mad confusion of all hues
That earth and heaven could infuse,
Till all hues softly fused and blent
In orange worlds of wonderment:
Then dying day, in kingly ire,
Struck back with one last blow, and smote
The world with molten fire.

So fell Alaska, proudly, dead
In battle harness where he fought.
But falling, still high o'er his head
Far flashed his sword in crimson wrought,
Till came his kingly foeman, Dusk,
In garments moist with smell of musk.
The bent moon moved down heaven's steeps
Low-bowed, as when a woman weeps;
Bowed low, half-veiled in widowhood;
Then stars tiptoed the peaks in gold
And burned brown sandal-wood.

Fit death of Day; fit burial rite
Of white Alaska! Let us lay
This leaflet 'mid the musky night
Upon his tomb. Come, come away;
For Phaon talks and Sappho turns
To where the light of heaven burns
To love light, and she leans to hear
With something more than mortal ear.
The while the ship has pushed her prow
So close against the fir-set shore
You breathe the spicy bough.

V.

Some red men by the low, white beach;
Camp fires, belts of dense, black fir:
She leans as if she still would reach
To him the very soul of her.
The red flames cast a silhouette
Against the snow, above the jet
Black, narrow night of fragrant fir,
Behold, what ardent worshiper!
Lim'd out against a glacier peak,
With strong arms crossed upon his breast;
The while she feels him speak:

"How glad was I to walk with Death
Far down his dim, still, trackless lands,
Where wind nor wave nor any breath
Broke ripples o'er the somber sands.
I walked with Death as eagerly
As ever I had sailed this sea.
Then on and on I searched, I sought,
Yet all my seeking came to naught.
I sailed by pleasant, peopled isles
Of song and summer time; I sailed
Ten thousand weary miles!

"I heard a song! She had been sad,
So sad and ever drooping she;
How could she, then, in song be glad
The while I searched? It could not be.
And yet that voice! so like it seemed,
I questioned if I heard or dreamed.

She smiled on me. This made me scorn
My very self; for I was born
To loyalty. I would be true
Unto my love, my soul, my self,
Whatever death might do.

"I fled her face, her proud, fair face,
Her songs that won a world to her.
Had she sat songless in her place,
Sat with no single worshiper,
Sat with bowed head, sad-voiced, alone,
I might have known! I might have known!
But how could I, the savage, know
This sun, contrasting with that snow,
Would waken her great soul to song
That still thrills all the ages through?
I blindly did such wrong!

"Again I fled. I ferried gods;
Yet, pining still, I came to pine
Where drowsy Lesbos Bacchus nods
And drowned my soul in Cyprian wine.
Drowned! drowned my poor, sad soul so deep,
I sank to where damned serpents creep!
Then slowly upward; round by round
I toiled, regained this vantage-ground.
And now, at last, I claim mine own,
As some long-banished king comes back
To battle for his throne."

VI.

I do not say that thus he spake
By word of mouth, by human speech;
The sun in one swift flash will take
A photograph of space and reach
The realm of stars. A soul like his
Is like unto the sun in this:
Her soul the plate placed to receive
The swift impressions, to believe,
To doubt no more than you might doubt
The wondrous midnight world of stars
That dawn has blotted out.

VII.

And Phaon loved her; he who knew
The North Pole and the South, who named
The stars for her, strode forth and slew
Black, hairy monsters no man tamed;
And all before fair Greece was born,
Or Lesbos yet knew night or morn.
No marvel that she knew him when
He came, the chiefest of all men.
No marvel that she loved and died,
And left such marbled bits of song—
Of broken Phidian pride.

VIII.

Oh, but for that one further sense
For man that man shall yet possess!
That sense that puts aside pretense
And sees the truth, that scorns to guess
Or grope, or play at blindman's buff,
But knows rough diamonds in the rough!
Oh, well for man when man shall see,
As see he must man's destiny!
Oh, well when man shall know his mate,
One-winged and desolate, lives on
And bravely dares to wait!

IX.

Full morning found them, and the land
Received them, and the chapel gray;
Some Indian huts on either hand,
A smell of pine, a flash of spray,—
White, frozen rivers of the sky
Far up the glacial steeps hard by.
Far ice-peaks flashed with sudden light,
As if they would illume the rite,
As if they knew his story well,
As if they knew that form, that face,
And all that Time could tell.

X.

They passed dusk chieftains two by two,
With totem gods and stroud and shell

They slowly passed, and passing through,
He bought of all—he knew them well.
And one, a bent old man and blind,
He put his hands about, and kind
And strange words whispered in his ear,
So soft, his dull soul could but hear.
And hear he surely did, for he,
With full hands, lifted up his face
And smiled right pleasantly.

How near, how far, how fierce, how tame!
The polar bear, the olive branch;
The dying exile, Christ's sweet name—
Vast silence! then the avalanche!
How much this little church to them—
Alaska and Jerusalem!
The pair passed in, the silent pair
Fell down before the altar there,
The Greek before the gray Greek cross,
And Phaon at her side at last,
For all her weary loss.

The bearded priest came, and he laid
His two hands forth and slowly spake
Strange, solemn words, and slowly prayed,
And blessed them there, for Jesus' sake.
Then slowly they arose and passed,
Still silent, voiceless to the last.
They passed: her eyes were to his eyes,
But his were lifted to the skies,
As looking, looking, that lorn night,
Before the birth of God's first-born
As praying still for Light.

XI.

So Phaon knew and Sappho knew
Nor night nor sadness any more....
How new the old world, ever new,
When white Love walks the shining shore!
They found their long-lost Eden, found
Her old, sweet songs; such dulcet sound
Of harmonies as soothe the ear
When Love and only Love can hear.
They found lost Eden; lilies lay
Along their path, whichever land
They journeyed from that day.

XII.

They never died. Great loves live on.
You need not die and dare the skies
In forms that poor creeds hinge upon
To pass the gates of Paradise.
I know not if that sword of flame
Still lights the North, and leads the same
As when he passed the gates of old.
I know not if they braved the bold,
Defiant walls that fronted them
Where awful Saint Elias broods,
Wrapped in God's garment-hem.

I only know they found the lost,
The long-lost Eden, found all fair
Where naught had been but hail and frost;
As Love finds Eden anywhere.
And wouldst thou, too, live on and on?
Then walk with Nature till the dawn.
Aye, make thy soul worth saving—save
Thy soul from darkness and the grave.
Love God not overmuch, but love
God's world which He called very good;
Then lo, Love's white sea-dove!

XIII.

I know not where lies Eden-land;
I only know 't is like unto
God's kingdom, ever right at hand—
Ever right here in reach of you.
Put forth thy hand, or great or small,
In storm or sun, by sea or wood,
And say, as God hath said of all,
Behold, it all is very good.
I know not where lies Eden-land;
I only say receive the dove:
I say put forth thy hand.

* * * * * *

Grateful for my first good health, like this last, and it is the only thing of mine, except "The City Beautiful" that quite pleases me. For here is not only the largeness and glory of the great sea which I have been trying to lay hand on these twenty-five years, but here is also the lesson of immortality — this — these, however vaguely and inadequately uttered, have a high purpose and I hope are in the right line of inquiry. For oh, how the great soulful world is crying out at heart for something other than creeds and creeds and creeds and locks on the doors of God's House! And yet, how well I know I have only set up a little light here on the bank of these unwritten seas, a little house that is on a hill of sand. My hope is in, and my heart is with, the wiser and better prophets to come after.

How painfully sensitive I always was in both body and mind till of late years! I seem to have been born with the malaria, aggravated by life in Naples, Washington City and Mexico City, in each of which places I bought land and tried to settle down. But at last I dug health and strength and new life to complete and make my old work new right out of the earth here on my mountain side in the hot sun—ten years in doing it, and now am stronger and really younger than since I first came here. Let this lesson of hard contact with our common mother not be thrown away. In the sweat of thy face — not in the sweat of another's face — shalt thou eat bread. It was God's first command at the expulsion, and really includes all others.

One final word to the coming poets of the Sierras and the great Sea and the Universal Heart. For I would have them, not like the very many cedars but like the very few sequoias. I would have them not fear the elements, or seek station or office from any one; to owe no man; only God. Yes, I know — who should better know?—how long and lonely and terribly dark the night is when not well nourished and encouraged by earnest friends; but I have seen some, better, abler than I, halt, falter, fall, from very excess of kindly praise and patronage. My coming poets, there are offices, favors, high honors within the gift of good men, and good men are many; but the gift of song is from God only. Choose, and adhere to the end; for we cannot serve two masters. A good citizen you may be, have love, peace, plenty to the end, but you shall not even so much as ascend the mountain that looks down upon the Promised Land, however much you may be made to believe you have attained it if you follow mammon. On the other hand, plain, simple, apart, alone, God only at your side, you must toil by day and meditate by night, remembering always that the only true dignity is true humility; remembering always that the only true humility is true dignity. Poverty, pain, persecution, ingratitude, scorn, and may be obscurity at the end. But always and through all, and over and above all, Faith and Hope and Charity. The greatest and the humblest that has been, your one exemplor. And so, following Him, shall you never answer back except and only by some white banner set on your own splendid and inaccessible summits: the flag of forgiveness and good will.

If then, thus informed by one whose feet are worn, the starry steeps of song be still your aspiration, don your Capuchin garb and with staff and sandal shoon go forth alone to find your lofty acre, to plant and water your tree, to take your eternal lessons from Him, through the toil of bee and the song of bird. Nor shall you in your lofty seclusion and security from the friction and roar of trade for one day escape or seek to escape your duties to man. The poets are God's sentries set on the high watch-towers of the world. You must see with the true foresight of the seer of old the coming invasions, the internal evils, the follies of your age, and not only give warning but bravely lead to triumph or perish, as the prophets of old, if need be.

For example, by what right shall a man continue to devote his life to getting and getting and getting from those about him, and, fostered by the State in his continual getting, cut the State off without even the traditional shilling when he has done with his gatherings? All great men have to leave all their gettings to the State when they go. Why shall not a rich man? If all the Rothschilds should die to-morrow and leave all their riches to England they would not all together leave her as much as Shakespeare left. And you, too, shall break the horns of strange gods, coming from over this ocean or that. It is only a snake that has two heads or a double tongue.

Take another example, one of the monstrous evils of this hour: none the less monstrous, only the harder to destroy because encouraged and under the protection of every church in the land. To-day we are wasting enough to buy a house and provide a pension for every widow. Poor old women are made slaves, down on their knees scrubbing to pay monstrous ghouls for tawdry funerals, while the wishes of Dickens, Hugo and the like great men are ignored. And largely, too, because our own, sentimental weaklings choose to please and be made popular by catering to the dead in the grave instead of the living God over all; doleful night birds singing of God's Acre, as if all acres were not God's. When the great poet comes he will lead his people to put all this in the hands of the State, so that we may all be resolved, earth to earth, ashes to ashes, simply and alike, rich and poor, having choice only as to the kind, not the price of funerals.

Perhaps the greatest source of sorrow, sin, in this, our commercial age, is the periodical "hard times." There should be nothing of that sort. True, this age of gold and of getting will pass as the age of stone and man eating passed, but our work is with our own age. Then, can the seer, the prophet, priest, poet sing, and so teach a way to avert this tidal wave of calamity that every few years submerges the entire christian world? Let us look about us. In the first place why does China in all her thousands of prosperous years, notwithstanding her millions of poor, never have "hard times?" Simply because her people pay their debts. That is the secret of it. At the end of each year each man pays his debts; then there is a feast, and not till then. The Jews were not foolish in their generation; they are not foolish now you will agree. And why had they never such periods of depression? For the same reason; they paid their debts, paid their debts every seven years instead of every single year. And when we shall have a law like that, and live by it, the very name "hard times" in this land and age of boundless abundance can be turned over to the historian forever. The Jews let business go at loose ends nearly seven years, quite as long, perhaps, as it is best to let weak human nature run without adjustment. Then they compelled an absolute settlement; then they, too had the great feast, and all began business anew. Even the Romans, and more than once—but only when compelled—burned their books of mortgage, debt, and taxes.

As for our own laws of limitations, said to be fashioned after those of the Bible, they are simply a delusion and a blank falsehood. The money lender sits down with you, counts up the interest, compounds it, summons you to a new mortgage, and you get up and go forth tied just one knot tighter than before. And this is our "Statute of Limitations!"

What, this is not the poet's work! Sir, truth is the poet's sword, and his battle is for mankind. I like the story of that Orpheus piping on a hillside till people sat at his feet to hear him play; and so built a city there. Beautiful, divinely beautiful, the poet's story of the old shepherd king who had his strength restored each time the giant threw him down to earth, The people came crowding to the cities then as now. Ah! never was a great poet needed as now. These themes, or such themes are crying out continuously. The deaf do not hear; the blind cannot see. The seer only can see. "Let me sing the songs and I care not who make the laws."

Clearly then, you are not to go apart in consecration for your own ease, least of all for your own glory. The only glory that can long attend you or at all survive you is the glory of doing good; defending the weak, guiding the strong, making the blind to see; finding your reward entirely in the fact that you loyally love the true, the good and beautiful, this trinity in one.

The best thing any town, county, state or nation can do for itself, seen in the coldest and most commercial sense, is to encourage home, heart literature; the worst thing the reverse. There should be a system of pensions from all, or at least of scholarships, from centers of learning. For literature, the flower of civilization and the mother and nurse of men, should not be forever left to chance in a great age and land like this. Meantime, let some gentleman of fortune who reads and is thrilled by "The New Liberty Bell," or like thing, quietly set aside a bit of his income for its author. Truly it will be "twice blessed." This was nothing new in the Old World, from Augustus down, and was never so fit as in this New World, where new work is to be done. For new work is so hard to do, and so hardly received when done.

ADIOS.

And here, sweet friend, I go my way
Alone, as I have lived, alone
A little way, a brief half day,
And then, the restful, white milestone.
I know not surely where or when,
But surely know we meet again,
As surely know we love anew
In grander life the good and true;
Shall breathe together there as here
Some clearer, sweeter atmosphere,
Shall walk high, wider ways above
Our petty selves, shall lean to lead
Man up and up in thought and deed....
Dear soul, sweet friend, I love you, love
The love that led you patient through
This wilderness of words in quest
Of strange wild flowers from my West;
But here, dear heart, Adieu.

I.

Yon great chained sea-ship chafes to be
Once more unleashed without the Gate
On proud Balboa's boundless sea,
And I chafe with her, for I hate
The rust of rest, the dull repose,
The fawning breath of changeful foes,
Whose blame through all my bitter days
I have endured; spare me their praise!
I go, full hearted, grateful, glad
Of strength from dear good mother earth;
And yet am I full sad.

II.

Could I but teach man to believe—
Could I but make small men to grow,
To break frail spider-webs that weave
About their thews and bind them low;
Could I but sing one song and slay
Grim Doubt; I then could go my way
In tranquil silence, glad, serene,
And satisfied, from off the scene.
But ah, this disbelief, this doubt,
This doubt of God, this doubt of good,—
The damned spot will not out!

III.

Grew once a rose within my room
Of perfect hue, of perfect health;
Of such perfection and perfume,
It filled my poor house with its wealth.
Then came the pessimist who knew
Not good or grace, but overthrew
My rose, and in the broken pot
Nosed fast for slugs within the rot.
He found, found with exulting pride,
Deep in the loam, a worm, a slug;
The while my rose-tree died.

* * * * * *

IV.

Yea, ye did hurt me. Joy in this.
Receive great joy at last to know,
Since pain is all your world of bliss,
That ye did, hounding, hurt me so!
But mute as bayed stag on his steeps,
Who keeps his haunts, and, bleeding, keeps
His breast turned, watching where they come,
Kept I, defiant, and as dumb.
But comfort ye; your work was done
With devils' cunning, like the mole
That lets the life-sap run.

And my revenge? My vengeance is
That I have made one rugged spot
The fairer; that I fashioned this
While envy, hate, and falsehood shot
Rank poison; that I leave to those
Who shot, for arrows, each a rose;
Aye, labyrinths of rose and wold,
Acacias garmented in gold,
Bright fountains, where birds come to drink;
Such clouds of cunning, pretty birds,
And tame as you can think.

V.

Come here when I am far away,
Fond lovers of this lovely land,
And sit quite still and do not say,
Turn right or left, or lift a hand,
But sit beneath my kindly trees
And gaze far out yon sea of seas:—
These trees, these very stones, could tell
How long I loved them, and how well—
And maybe I shall come and sit
Beside you; sit so silently
You will not reck of it.

VI.

The old desire of far, new lands,
The thirst to learn, to still front storms,
To bend my knees, to lift my hands
To God in all His thousand forms—
These lure and lead as pleasantly
As old songs sung anew at sea.
But, storied lands or stormy deeps,
I will my ashes to my steeps—
I will my steeps, green cross, red rose,
To those who love the beautiful—
Come, learn to be of those.

* * * * * *

VII.

The sun has draped his couch in red;
Night takes the warm world in his arms
And turns to their espousal bed
To breathe the perfume of her charms:
The great sea calls, and I descend
As to the call of some strong friend.
I go, not hating any man,
But loving Earth as only can
A lover suckled at her breast
Of beauty from his babyhood,
And roam to truly rest.

VIII.

God is not far; man is not far
From Heaven's porch, where pæans roll.
Man yet shall speak from star to star.
In silent language of the soul;
Yon star-strewn skies be but a town,
With angels passing up and down.
"I leave my peace with you." Lo! these
His seven wounds, the Pleiades
Pierce Heaven's porch. But, resting there,
The new moon rocks the Child Christ in
Her silver rocking-chair.

These poems, "Songs of the Soul," although long in the weaver's loom, and given to the world now and then in shreds through the magazines, were, the most of them, not gathered into book form until 1896, when they were published by my present San Francisco publishers.

The book was dedicated with the following lines "TO MOTHER:"

And oh, the voices I have heard!
Such visions where the morning grows—
A brother's soul in some sweet bird,
A sister's spirit in a rose.

And oh, the beauty I have found!
Such beauty, beauty everywhere;
The beauty creeping on the ground,
The beauty singing through the air.

The love in all, the good, the worth,
The God in all, or dusk or dawn;
Good will to man and peace on earth;
The morning stars sing on and on.

* * *

NOTE.—It may be a bold thing to sing by one's own great sea-bank instead of abroad, as before; but I have faith in my own people, and believe the time has come to keep one's work at home. I hope to follow this soon with "Songs of the Sierras" and "Songs of the Sunlands," revised and complete.

The London and Boston plates of these books having been worn out, publication was suspended till such time as the revised works, with some additions, might be ready for the press. Meantime, while I was in Mexico, irresponsible parties in Chicago issued mutilated and unauthorized editions. It is due to all concerned to state that it is not only unlawful to handle all these Chicago poems, as well as the editions published in Canada by some of the same parties, but they are an imposition on the reader, as many lines are left out, and also many lines inserted that are new to the author.

JOAQUIN MILLER.

The Hights, Oakland, Cal., 1896.

* * *

And, here at the end be not impatient that you have found much of self in these foot-notes from title leaf to colophon, nor count it at all selfish. I had my lessons to teach to those whose desire to learn is above cheap curiosity, and with such souls there can be no sacrifice of true dignity, for here familiarity is not vulgarity. The best guide book to me, through a strange land, is the story of another's journey there. Let me say to the pilgrims of song, in conclusion, be not afraid. Sing from the heart, to the heart. Sing as the birds sing. Let the alleged lion roar. Let the dog bark. These beasts are of the earth. The birds are of the air. The dog must bay the moon, and the brighter the moon the louder the dog.

And now, maybe, you who have kindly gone through these leaves, listened to song of mine and fragmentary story, been with me face to face, soul to soul in savage scenes or tame, by land and by sea—maybe you will care to sit a minute with me here at the end under mine own vine and fig-tree. First then the story of my little mountain home that looks down upon many cities and away out through the Golden Gate. I owe the finding of it, or rather the love and large appreciation of it to Fremont. He had pitched tent here, taken his observations here, named the Golden Gate from this very spot when it was glorious with all its primal wood and grasses and waterfall. It was, even in his old age when I last saw him, such a memory that his voice trembled with emotion as he relived his early life here. But when misfortune—and how good is misfortune—led my feet from Mexico city in search of health to this spot it was devastations self. Not the vestige of tree, flower or waterfall; only a few holes of mud, where poor, starving cattle gathered and hogs wallowed or baked in the burning sun. The destruction of wood and grass had dried up the *water* springs. The steeps were laid bare to storms and landslides and washouts, and left but a skeleton—lone and stark—of the once glorious Hights. But now, ten, a dozen years of toil! I would that Fremont could see it now! It had been my dream to have him here when the place was once more restored; but he passed as my work was not yet half done. And now I can only thank him for having guided me here.

And who is here with me? Why mother, looking younger than I, and then students, lovers of the good and beautiful. And then a brother comes and goes, a native of Oregon, not one of those you saw when baby sister was born. The only one living is in Oregon, married to the daughter of a little orphan adopted by that greatest man that ever came west, Marcus P. Whitman. When he was tomahawked and all his house was being butchered this little girl got under the bed and finding a plank loose in the floor crept down; and as the mission was not burned till later, she got away. And now nine noble grandchildren of hers gather at my brother's hearthstone. And my old partner of the saddle in Idaho is here too. You remember we got all the gold-dust we wanted? I took mine to the mint, then, after my travels in Mexico and South America, took it home and mother let it down in the well with a stout rope. When anybody in the country, or passing California friends, wanted gold, papa and mother would pull up the lasso. After a few months they got tired of that and mother talked of burying it, but she finally stacked the gold up in the dining room, It melted fast now, for we were making investments and doing about what any folk will do who only have plenty of gold once in a lifetime. One morning mother looked up from the breakfast table and then gave a startled cry. The stacks of gold were gone! No one ever knew when it was taken or by whom. No one was accused or suspected. Nothing was ever heard of it nor was there any great bother about it. I never suspected it was stolen, but I always believed and still believe that mother must have gotten up in her sleep some night and buried it, as she had been talking of. As for my lone and honest old partner who has come to me with his face leaning to the earth, as if ready and willing to rest, he made even as little use of his hoard of gold as I did, and laments its loss even less than I.

Mrs. Fremont, writing me from Los Angeles, May, 1896, in connection with the spot from which General Fremont took his observations and gave the gate its name, says, quoting first from Fremont's reports to Congress, and then adding a paragraph of her own:

"The bay of San Francisco is separated from the sea by low mountains. Looking from the peaks of the Sierra Nevada the coast mountains present an apparently continuous line, with only a single gap, resembling a mountain pass. This is the entrance to the great bay and is the only water communication from the coast to the interior country. Approaching from the sea the coast presents a bold outline. On the south the bordering mountains come down in a narrow ridge of broken hills, terminating in a precipitous point, against which the sea breaks heavily. On the northern side the mountain presents a bold promontory, rising in a few miles to a height of two or three thousand feet. Between these points is the strait—about one mile broad in the narrowest part and five miles long from the sea to the bay.

"Passing through this gate (called Chrysopolæ on the map on the same principle that the harbor of Byzantium (Constantinople afterward) was called Chryoceras (Golden Horn). The form of the harbor and its advantages for commerce, and that before it became an entrepot of Eastern commerce, suggested the name to the Greek founders of Byzantium. The form of the entrance into the bay of San Francisco, and its advantages for commerce, Asiatic inclusive, suggests the name which is given to this entrance. The bay opens to the right and left, extending in each direction about thirty-five miles, having a total length of more than seventy and a coast of about 275 miles. Within the view presented is of a mountainous country, the bay resembling an interior lake of deep water lying between parallel ranges of mountains. * * * Directly fronting the entrance, mountains, a few miles from the shore, rise about 2,000 feet above the water, crowned by a forest of the lofty cypress, which is visible from the sea, and makes a conspicuous landmark for vessels entering the bay. Behind, the rugged peak of Mount Diablo, nearly 4,000 feet high (3770), overlooks the surrounding country of the bay and San Joaquin.

"[From a geographical memoir and map of explorations by J. C. Fremont, prepared as ordered by the United States Senate in 1847, and printed in Washington, D. C., in June, 1848. On this map is given, for the first time, the name of Golden Gate, and by J. C. Fremont.] J. B. FREMONT."

The Fremont road, that bends above Oakland from Berkeley to Mills Seminary, after being closed for half a century, is once more open, and it passes through our door yard; a stream of people, crowds of students, faces of many children dispel the foolish story that a hermit houses here.

You want to see San Francisco? Well, you must come to Oakland to see San Francisco. And do you want to see Oakland and San Francisco and the bay of all bays on the globe and the Golden Gate at a glance and all together? Then you must go two miles to the northeast and one mile perpendicular. In short, you must come to the Hights, to the camp where Fremont tented half a century ago and from which spot he named the now famous Golden Gate years before gold was found. And now please let me tell you how to get there. Mrs. Fremont, as before noted, confirms and locates beyond doubt the spot from which California's first Senator looked upon this marvel of nature in all its gorgeous magnificence and gave this opulent and color-crowned name to our doorway.

It is a bit remarkable that the bay of San Francisco was discovered by land. It is none the less noticeable that the Golden Gate was named, not by any navigator or voyager by sea, but from the solid land, by a man who bore the dust of 3,000 miles of wilderness and desert on his leathern garments. The first question asked by the novice in roadcraft and camp life is, "Why did Fremont and Kit Carson keep along these rugged Contra Costa steeps instead of the level valley?" Water. The one and only answer is, water. In all the broad levels from San Pablo Bay to the pleasant brooks of old San Jose Mission, there was not a drop of fresh water at certain seasons of the year. True, there were vast herds of cattle here when Fremont came, but these cattle had to take to the foothills for water in the arid months of August and September. General Beale, afterward our Minister to Austria, but "Midshipman Beale" at the time, as Fremont calls him in his early reports of his explorations, speaks of killing "Spanish elk" for supplies from his boat on San Pablo Bay, but these cattle watered from the hills. Of course, boats plied, at long periods, up and down the Sacramento from New Helvetia (Sacramento) to Yerba Buena (San Francisco), but no travel passed up and down the river bank; that way was not only perilous by water, but perilous from savages and lawless Mexicans. One of the most pathetic chapters in our naval history is the loss of a ship's boat and its entire crew in passing between these two points. Fremont had, as an army officer, procured from a man-of-war a large sum of money with which to pay his men at Sutter's Fort. The naval commander dispatched his boat with the money in charge of two of his officers and a picked crew to Fremont by way of the Sacramento River. Neither boat, men nor money was ever heard of any more. The names of the officers and marines were carried forward on the pay-roll for ten years, but no tidings of any sort ever came, and at the end of that time they were given up as lost. Probably a sudden squall—and the boatload of silver and the brave men are still together at the bottom of San Pablo or the Carquinez Straits; for it is not recorded in all our naval or military history that any officer ever betrayed such a trust. But such dalliance as this with every dramatic story of olden days and there will be no end.

I first passed over this spot in the fall of 1854, as bellboy and cook along with Mountain Jo, one of Fremont's former men, who was driving a band of half-wild horses from southern to northern California. The road was not in his line of travel, but there were two things almost indispensable to Mountain Jo and his horses, whisky and water. My duties were to ride an old bell mule in the lead of his band of wild horses and wilder Mexicans and look out for "wood, water and grass," and there pitch camp. My recollection of the road, after breaking camp at the "Embarcadero," is mainly of the beautiful wooded and watered cañon. I think it was then called Temescal. Now and then there were peeps through the pines and redwoods as the dusty trail rose and fell up and down the billowy but ever ascending foothills. The trail was knee-deep in dust; and wild oats, rusty, dusty and golden green, rose on either side to my shoulders as I climbed and climbed. Great long ox teams now and then crossed the trail, plodding sleepily down toward what is now Oakland.

I next saw the site of my mountain home nine years later, when I went to look on a great painter at work there. Mrs. Fremont writes me:

"When Bierstadt went to California to study its scenery (and the Rocky Mountains *en route*) we gave him letters to Starr King and other friends. It was about April of 1863. In giving him a commission to paint for us the Golden Gate, with the setting sun lighting the pathway into it, both of us, Mr. Fremont and myself, gave him fully our feeling. I clearly remember Mr. Fremont saying he must see the sunset from the Contra Costa, as he had to realize the force and splendid appropriateness of the name in its scenic sense, apart from the other idea of the gateway of commerce. Bierstadt made a grand picture. When we had to sell what would bring needed money Commodore Garrison bought this for $4,000, just what we had given Bierstadt.

"My daughter, who was from her seventh year a constant companion of her father on long horseback rides and days of working explorations on the Mariposas, as well as many a long ride around San Francisco—as often in quieter times on the Hudson—remembers many and many a talk on views, on physical geography, on beautiful camps, for she has her father's silent delight in nature and is his true child in loving to read of, study and inform herself of geographical travel. She says she is sure you are right. * * *

"The great rock stamps it. He loved a mass of detached rock. * * * When I was written to by a New York friend of an intended monument to the general I asked that they would spare him the commonplaces that make such sadly mourning-stones usurp our finer ideas. If they must, then put up a great rock, a rough mass of granite, such as he had carved the emblem of the cross upon 'according to the custom of early travelers'—for he felt the strong, invisible power that grasped the heavens and the earth—and on it put only his name."

Here at dawn we are above the clouds! What would the world do without clouds? And at no two hours of the day, no two minutes, indeed, are the views along here alike. You see the higher streets of San Francisco above the rolling, surging sea mist. The great cross of the Lone Mountain Cemetery lifting in grand and solemn loneliness above all things and looking strangely tall and vast. The clouds roll above Oakland, lift, rift a little, and church spires are pointing up and through the sea of snow that undulates, lifts, pulses at your feet. The whole bay is a mobile floor of silver. Not a suggestion of the sea! Tamalpais, with its winding track and trains above the clouds that conceal San Pablo Bay, a white lighthouse on the headlands below, Black Point, Sutro Heights, Fort Alcatraz, the tips and topmasts of sail, that is all—

Where phantom ships unchallenged pass
The gloomy guns of Alcatraz.

Twelve o'clock and not a cloud—not a cloud above or about the peaceful fair visage of beautiful Alameda below you. And yet do not despise the clouds, God's garments' hem. Truly, all that is good or great is veiled, garmented in mist, clouds, mystery. The priest has his sacred place, the house of God has its holy of holies. All things in nature have their mantled mysteries. The little seeds take life in the dark mold; all life begins in secret, silence, majestic mystery, the large solemnity of night.

At morning, noon or night, especially night, when the heavens and the earth are on fire—for you cannot tell where the lights leave off and the stars begin—the scene is the most gorgeously magnificent on all the globe.

Deep below us lies the valley,
  Steep below us lies the town,
Where great seaships ride and rally
  And the world walks up and down.

Oh, the sea of lights far streaming,
  When the thousand flags are furled
And the gleaming bay lies dreaming
  As it duplicates the world!

Let us conclude with a paragraph descriptive of the all-glorious outlook of my mountain home here from the pen of Mr. Harr Wagner, editor of *The Western Journal of Education*, San Francisco:

"The finest days here are the stormy or winter days, when there are no forest fires to make a haze and the clouds are at work below in all their mobile and ever-changing glory. Early spring is quite as effective. At that time the clouds are being driven out from the Oregon Edens by the flaming swords of approaching summer, and they surge down the coast as if terrified and pour in at the Golden Gate like flying fugitives, the California sun spilling all its golden opulence on this surging, inflowing sea; a ship's masts piercing through, a church spire, the green hills of San Francisco beyond—but how idle are all words here!

"It is noticeable that at each equinox the sun, from this—Fremont's—point of view, falls down exactly into the Golden Gate, and it is always at such times incredibly vast, blocking for a few moments the whole gate with its disk of gold.

"I once saw a black cloud—black as midnight and as boundless—hang above this ball of gold as it rolled down into the golden chasm of the Golden Gate. But the sun did not heed the cloud. The cloud was only blacker from the brightness of the golden globe, and the gate and the walls of the gate, and the bay, and the city, and all the cities up and down, and the islands, and the ships, and, indeed, all the world, the heavens and the earth, all things, save that awful nightmare of black cloud above the golden sun, were for a moment nothing but molten gold. Then the sun sank, sank suddenly into the sea, as if it had, indeed, been a mighty ball of gold, and the blackness fell down as suddenly in his place, and blackness was, only blackness, as if God Himself had closed the gate with a bang, and forever."

Yours.
Joaquin Miller.
July! 1897

APPENDIX.

My attention is called to the fact that I, who ever companioned with the eagles of my mountain peaks, have turned to the dove with a devotion that is monotonous in this book. I am amazed to find this the case. I can only say candidly that while it may be a fault, which I should have avoided had it been detected in time, yet this sweet symbol of peace is honestly in these pages and must now remain. And if ever I have a crest or coat-of-arms it will be a dove and olive leaf.

There are many to-morrows, my Love, my
Love!
There is only one to-day.

*　　*　　*　　*　　*　　*

It is further observed that my descriptions of deserts and desolate lands hardly invite the old world to share the fortunes of the new. I can only answer by pointing to Utah, a desert of wild beasts and wild men when I began my work, but now the garden of the globe. The following little story will tell how the desert is being made to blossom as the rose from Canada to Mexico in this western world:

ARTESIA OF TULARE.

An old Scotch shepherd with a tale
Of crofter strife, heartbroken wife;
A barefoot girl, sad-eyed and pale;
A dog, a gun, a buckhorn knife;
With garments torn, with face unshorn
And all his better life outworn;
But then his fond white flock of sheep
Where still Tulare's waters creep:

Fair, level water, willow-lined,
The one loved stream in all that land!
You should have seen it wind and wind
Through unfenced seas of loam and sand
Long years ago, with here and there
A pack of wolves, a waiting bear,
When this stout-hearted, lorn old man
Kept flock as only Scotchmen can!

And how he loved Tulare's bank,
And planned to buy, and build, and rest,
The while his white flock fed and drank.
Aye he had thrift and of the best.
And back, where no rich man laid hands,
Had bought and bought wide desert lands.
But sudden came the rich and strong—
The old, old tale of cruel wrong.

"I'll have his lands," the rich man cried,
"His lands are broad as his Scotch
brogue—
That's saying they are broad and wide.
I'll have his lands! He calls me rogue.
Out, out!—away! I will not spare
One drop from that deep river there."

And, banished so, they sadly turned,
The barefoot lass, the bent old man,
To where the barren desert burned—
His dog, his gun, a water-can;
His white flock bleating on before
All loath to leave the watered shore;
His dog with drooping tail and ears;
His barefoot, tattered child in tears.

They found a rounded mound not far,
That rose above the sage and sand,
Where one green willow, like a star
In some dark night, stood lone and grand.
And here the can and gun were swung
In grief, as when lorn Israel hung

Her harp on willow tree and kept
Sad silence where she sat and wept.

The dog crouched fretful at their feet;
The woolly fold crept close with fear,
And one meek lamb did bleat and bleat,
So pitiful, so sadly drear,
The girl crept from the bowed old man,
Reached up and took the water-can,
And gave it water while he slept,
The while she silent wept and wept.

Then came gaunt wolves—all sudden came—
And sat in circle close below!
The dog sprang up, his eyes aflame,
And all his frame did quiver so!
Then like a shot right forth he sped, ...
Crept back all blood, then fell down dead.
She snatched the gun. No more she wept,
But watched, the while the shepherd slept.

Then came the moon. Vast peaks of snow
Flashed silver from Sierra's height,
And lit the lonely scene below
As if with some unearthly light—
A light that only made a gloom
'Mid silence, space, and shoreless room.
Why, all that moonlit scene but seemed
Such as half-maddened men have dreamed.

At last the sun burst like a flame,
And shaggy wolves fled from the light.
Then wide-eyed, wondering rabbits came
And stood in circle left and right.
They stood so graceful, trim, and tall,
You might have guessed this was a ball
Where dainty dancers, slim and neat,
Stood waiting with impatient feet.

The old man wakened. Why, his fold
Had crept so close ere break of morn
That he reached out and there laid hold
Of his huge ram by one curled horn!
But then the dog! Ah, there were tears!
He scarce had wept for years and years,
But now it seemed his heart would break
In sorrow for that dead brute's sake.

He said no word, but silent took
In his broad, heavy, honest hand
His long, strong, steel-shod shepherd's crook,
And digged a deep grave in the sand.
But why so eager now? So wild?
He turns, he catches up his child:
"My bairn, my bairn, my eyes are dim;
But bide ye, bide, and trust to Him!"

Away he sped; and soon he brought
From some old camp a long black rod
On his bent back. Then, as he wrought,
She thought of Moses; prayed to God
That water for the thirsting flock
Might flow as from the smitten rock,
And save her father—save him sane
There in that fearful desert plain.

He forced the black tube through the sod
Beneath the waving willow tree
With giant's strength. Then, as if God
Had heard, it sank, sank swift and free—
Sank sudden through the slime and sand,
Sank deep, slid swift, slid from his hand!
Then he sprang up, aghast and dazed
And piteous, as if sudden crazed.

He caught his gun; he madly wrenched
The barrels out and thrust this down;
And then he fell, fell drenched, fell drenched
With floods that leapt as if to drown!
And all Tulare came to drink,
As happy-faced as you can think.

* * *

Would you hear a little more about my home and trees? I promise you that if ever you shall go apart and bend your face to the soil for ten years in planting trees, I will gladly give you twice the ten minutes required to read the story of it. Here it is, with a paragraph of my own at the end:

THE FIRST ARBOR DAY IN CALIFORNIA.

[Alister Grant, in the Golden Era Magazine, Jan., 1887.]

An account of the first Arbor Day in California, and the cause that led to it, may not be much in the way of light reading; but some account is at least necessary in complete form, so that those desirous of referring to its origin in the future may find a proper record of it. The movement has been well treated by the more important of the dailies of San Francisco, but for matters of future reference files of daily papers being unindexed are out of the question.

The movement that was so successfully carried out on the 27th of November, 1886, was by no means the beginning of the agitation for an Arbor Day; but the first decided step was taken by Mr. Joaquin Miller in addressing a letter to General O. O. Howard, Commander of the Department of the Pacific. The action was one, at least, worthy of a poet who, after a long absence has come back to his own country. The bare brown hills and sweltering valleys of his native land seem to have impressed him with these beautiful lines:

"God gave us mother earth, full blest
With robes of green in healthful fold;
We tore the green robes from her breast!
We sold our mother's robes for gold!"

This is very nice and very pretty; but the planting of trees has even a more important benefit than mere beautification. Groves of trees break up fogs and winds; forests bind the soil upon the hills, and even induce rainfall. Verdure tempers the wind to the shorn lamb.

To make any action effective, it was necessary to choose a conspicuous point, noted for its barrenness, where the first work would be in full view of the people. Such a point was found in Yerba Buena Island (Goat Island), and for that reason it was decided to ask the permission of General Howard.

A courteous reply having been received, in which the General heartily endorsed the work, in a letter to the *Call*, Mr. Miller suggested the 30th of October as an appropriate day. He says:

"We have agreed that the 30th of October is a good day to begin with. And on that day, at 12 M., if others do not come forward to take the work off our hands, the Greek cross will be laid on the apex of Yerba Buena Island by myself and some others writing for the press, and left to grow and do good like 'the still small rain.'"

* * * * * *

The spot on the Island selected for the tree-planting was at the top of the hill. The ascent was circuitous, a pathway having been made for most of the way up. Most of the visitors were ladies and girls, and the picture they presented as they followed each other by hundreds up the rather steep incline, was very striking. Those who wandered from the prepared path and sought an avenue of their own to the summit found the dry thick grass very slippery, and they went sliding down frequently.

On leaving the boats at the wharf the passengers were given souvenir programmes which were neatly gotten up. On the front page was a picture of Goat Island, with the ferry-boat passing by. Beneath it in attractive letters was the following:

"The gods, who mortal beauty chase,
Still in a tree did end their race."

On the other side was a poem dedicated to Joaquin Miller and written by John Vance Cheney.

The beginning of the exercises had been

set for 11 o'clock. When that hour arrived there were at least one thousand people at the top of the hill. Most of them were pretty school girls of various ages. From the time the United States First Infantry Band arrived it played popular airs at the summit.

The place chosen for the planting was arranged in the shape of a Greek cross, the longer part 300 feet long by 30 feet wide, and the transverse part 150 long by 30 feet wide. The Arbor Day poem was then read by Joaquin Miller, after which Mr. Fred M. Campbell of Oakland, read an address written by General Vallejo for the occasion.

Ex-Governor Perkins paid a tribute to General Howard, and spoke of the encouragement and assistance he had given to the celebration. He proposed three cheers for General Howard, which were given with a will.

General Howard spoke briefly. He alluded to the cross and to the catholic character of the occasion.

John P. Irish made a short address. He said he believed tree-planting originated in Nebraska, twenty-six years ago, where the wide plains had been made to yield rich harvests through this custom, the arable land steadily moving westward at the rate of three miles every year, as the trees were planted. In that State, and in others that had followed Nebraska's example, Arbor Day was a legal holiday, and he hoped to see the occasion entrenched as a legal holiday in the laws of this State. He was glad that this movement was due to the inspiration of Joaquin Miller, because he is to live in the world's immortal literature as the poet of the Sierras, along whose slopes man's hand is wasting God's prodigal gifts. It was eminently appropriate that to this poet's inspiration these mountains should be reclothed with their emerald robes and made majestic in their forests and groves. He hoped that the time would come when these trees would be planted in groups, by schools and churches—yes, by churches, for the groves were God's first temples, and would endure in solemn grandeur when the temples of stone and mortar shall molder to decay. Every tree is a tree of life, for it contains that which sustains life and gives to us a knowledge that leads us to a higher contemplation of the works of God. To-day we plant the tree of life and the tree of knowledge.

All this was done and recorded more than ten years ago. Permit me to add my own brief account of it, and also the story of the Arbor Day cross up to date:

Having helped to plant the eucalyptus on the fever-stricken campagna, and planted a little while at my cabin in Washington, it was proposed on returning to California, by some ladies, the Board of Forestry, and such men as Adolph Sutro, Gen. Howard, and Gen. Vallejo, that we should found an Arbor Day, and celebrate the event by planting an Arbor Day Cross on some conspicuous spot where it would be always seen, and perpetually plead the sanctity of the tree and the cause of our common mother. The Government gave Yerba Buena Island for the purpose and the use of a ship; Gen. Howard sent soldiers to prepare the ground, and Sutro sent 50,000 trees to the school children of Oakland and San Francisco. And so, on the 27th of November, 1886, the greatest day these cities have yet seen, the school children, amid the booming of guns and the floating of flags from every ship in the bay, planted their Arbor Day Cross on the island. But fire swept the island again and again, leaving it more barren even than before.

Then I bought the Hights, east of Oakland, overlooking both cities and the great bay; Sutro again sent trees, and again the school children's cross was planted; for the idea and their enthusiasm could not perish. Now, to the end that they, and the thousand inquiring friends might know what has become of their Arbor Day Cross after all these years, let me say briefly that it is one of the loveliest bits of forest in California. Some of the trees are higher than a horseman's head now, and the cross can be seen from all up and down the land, and the higher streets of San Francisco. It will be left to the school children of the two cities who planted it, forever; the probable nucleus of a park, which ought to include Redwood Peak.

* *
*

ART AND HEART ON THE HIGHTS.

In line with the continued story of my trees and home, let me tell more of the Hights and the life there. It really is required of me, even at the risk of repetition.

Pardon me if I must here still answer letters in this public way. But so much has been said about my "School of Poetry" here that I cannot very well end this work without a further note of warning, advice, explanation to my following:

The sweetest flowers grow closest to the ground. There is no art without heart. The art of all art is really to know nature—yourself. Better to know of your own knowledge, the color, the perfume, the nature, the twining, of a single little creeping vine in the cañon than to know all the rocky mountains through a book. Man reads too much and reasons too little. Great artists are not great readers but great observers. They see with the heart. The world seems to think the artist should be constantly busy with book, brush, or pen. His heart like a field, must lie fallow long to bring forth greatly. And do you know there are poets, great poets, perhaps the very greatest, who never read a line, and great painters who never knew a brush. A certain man comes here now and then who has a picture gallery in the cañon, which he says is worth a million. Few if any of us have the capacity to see all the pictures of this millionaire.

It is high time that the art world and the lesser half of the world should be on terms of better understanding. We of the art world are too apt to think that the rest of the world is heartless. The rest of the world is too apt to think that the art world is headless. The truth is, as said before, a man in trade may be at heart a great artist; while a great artist could in many cases make money as well as any other man; only he might be too ready to give it away to some less fortunate than himself.

Another thing let us note by way of finale. Poets, painters, composers, fashioners of beautiful forms, are the gentlest and purest and most temperate of all human beings. Take the poets, especially those of America, turn on the high white light that beats upon the throne. You will not find a fairer galaxy of names in all history. Even poor Poe, it is now seen, was the victim of envy and malice,—the forty failures assaulting the one success. You also find fifty would-be musicians defaming their betters; and so on all along the line.

It is best that we should get at the truth. A truly great poet can be great in almost anything, as witness King David, Michael Angelo, Milton, and so on.

We are a sort of hillside Bohemia up here, only we have no tape; not even a tow string or "strings" of any sort on any man or any woman. We don't want to know what anyone has been or aspires to be, nor are we curious to know what he is. These are matters of his own account with his Maker. We are never numerous, we are never very good, never very bad. We have some rules, or rather some ideas, that we have formulated, melted together, and rounded down, as the years rolled by, but we do not intrude them on anybody, nor are you to believe that we all live up to the best of them; at least, I know one who does not. He sees that man is still heaving a great stone up hill by day to find it rolling back on him at night. Yet he hopes and believes as his years pass that he grows a little better; as the human race grows better and better, while the centuries surge past.

Very reluctantly I here write down some of the ideas, rules, lessons. The sudden renown of a little brown-faced student here, a mere lad of twenty, famous in a day as a poet, almost compels some sort of statement; for people are coming here, some from far away, to ask idle questions, wasting their time and mine. One poor woman grimly demanded the terms for teaching how to "write poetry in paying quantities."

But mind you, I cannot write of this young man. Merit is always shy of mention, and it would hurt him and help no one to tell of him, or how he came to fame even while yet a boy. I can only give the general rules, tenets, lessons, by which we try to live.

In the first place, then, this Robin Hood's Bohemia on the hillside is rather an accident than a design. The first plan was to catch, coop up, or cage, the wasted energies of the State that had become a nuisance under the general name of "Tramp." A house was built on a large slice of land with the idea of gradually sobering these nomads with the thought that an acre with an orchard, cow, and so on, would be better than a bed in the hayfield or jail.

Well, read three volumes between the lines along here. Anyhow, I learned a lot. In the first place, these poor creatures are nearly all if not quite all crazy, and the marvel is that with their irregular food and regular drink they are not still more insane. Such experiences! And such emphasized types. Lots of them literary. Yet I still think that if I had been far away from any town, so that they could not have left the "Rest" any time of day to get drink and come back at any time of night to sleep, the idea would really have been of service to the State.

Our last experience was with a hairy and wild French cook, who had written a play,—for Mrs. Langtry, he said,—and he summoned mother and I late at night to the Rest to hear him read it. What a sight. He had cut holes in a white bolster case, and with hairy head and arms thrust through, a yellow window curtain about his waist, and an old pistol in his belt, he strode up and down, reading, gesturing, roaring, lamp in one hand and papers in the other for hours. At last the lamp was out and the other tramps fled to the barn, but mother could not get away and we had to stay till dawn, when he fell exhausted on the lounge; and that day the Tramps' Rest was forever "closed for repairs."

Then we kept on planting and planting and making roads and fountains for another year or so very quietly. I would work with the men for about half the day and work with my pen the rest, for I had put all my small fortune in the land, so must write to keep things going. One day a young man who had studied to be a preacher came. He put off his coat and worked hard all day. This was the first "student." He stayed and stayed, and to this day comes at intervals and toils and meditates, and then goes his way, as years ago. He has now some fame with his pen, although it is doubtful if he is yet writing poetry in "paying quantities."

Gradually others gathered about, young

men and women from colleges and universities. No one was ever asked to come. No one was ever asked to go. Not a dollar was ever passed between us. The young men were ready to work when anything wanted to be done. The women were useful as companions to my venerable mother.

Some students, not attached to schools, stayed a long time. One woman with her son stayed five years. Another stayed three years. They were a benediction for mother. Some men stayed one, two, and three years. The stranger always found a cot, oftentimes a cottage all to himself. He always found a storehouse with simple supplies, and even after the place was planted to trees and built up, there was always wood to get, cows to look after, horses, hens, and so on,—and a gentle foreman, who has had the management of the place from the first, to tell what should be done. His effort always has been to keep students from doing too much work rather than too little. It is doubtful if the place has ever lost a dime or if I have lost a day by any one after that first grim and terrible experience with the poor tramps.

And now what is taught, and how, and when? Frankly and truly, nothing, or almost nothing, is taught, and almost no time is given to the students. It is all in the atmosphere or sense of peace. There simply are three or four tenets or principles of life insisted upon. The first of these is that man is good. This admits of no debate. Sit down a little time as you stumble headlong in the dust up and down the steeps of life,—steeps of your own making or imagining as a rule,—and wait for the stars or the moon or the morning. You will then see that all the world is beautiful, beautiful,—magnificently beautiful. And meantime get a little acquainted with your own soul. You will find that you are better, a great deal better, than you believed as you stumbled so hurriedly and so blindly along in the dust, looking all the time down in the dirt for money. You will also find that those about you are better, vastly better than you believed.

No debating of any sort is allowed. See what a saving of time! If I could divert the time that is wasted in idle dispute for ten years into a right direction, I could make an Eden in any country. I simply say to my students, "There is not a man or woman with the breath of God in his or her nostrils who is not good or trying to be good according to the strength and light. It is your privilege and duty with your better culture and opportunities to give light and light continually, and not so much by word as by deed; not by the letter which killeth, but by the spirit which maketh alive."

The truth is, there is a great deal more good in the world than it has credit for. I doubt if there is a home, never so poor, but has some little unseen altar on which is daily, almost hourly, laid some little sweet sacrifice, some little touch of pity and tenderness for the poor pale mother, the weary worn father, the little sick baby. It is our place to give them more and more love to lay on the unseen altar, more light, more light; so that they may have more heart, hope, strength.

The second lesson after the love of man is the love of nature. As there is no entirely bad man in his right mind, on earth, so is there no entirely ugly thing in nature. My daughter's pony died one night, and as she dearly loved the poor beast, I had it buried under a little willow in the ditch. But the coyotes disturbed the earth and bad odors drew a circle of vultures.

"That seems to disprove the second tenet," said a student.

"Wait and see. Nature is too majestic to make haste. Perhaps even now she is building better than you know."

This was six years ago. Last month a

party of campers came by and asked consent to spend a week under the little willow. For it was now as broad as the barn. I was told in Jerusalem that Jesus passing down the valley of Jehosaphat with his disciples came upon the remains of a dog. They gathered their garments and with lifted faces hurried by. But Jesus, pausing a moment and reaching his face a little, said softly, "What beautiful teeth!"

The third and undebated lesson after the goodness of man and the beauty of the world is the immortality of man. Yes, there may be those who do not live again. You may sow your field as carefully as you can, yet there are many worthless grains that will not come up, but will rot and resolve again into earth. And may it not be that this fearful disease of unbelief is a sort of crucial test? May it not be that if you be so weak as to say you shall be blown out as a candle and so drop into everlasting darkness, that it shall be so?

We begin the next life where we leave off in this. I see this in the little seeds that sift down from the trees and lie under the shroud of snow in the hollow of His hand, the winter through, waiting the roaring March winds to trumpet through the pines and proclaim the resurrection. I read it in every blade of grass that carpets God's footstool; every spear is a spear to battle for this truth. Every blade of grass is a bent saber waving us forward with living evidence of immortality, for it has seen the resurrection, and each and all began where they left off in the life before.

A fourth and very practical lesson is on economy. Nature wastes nothing, nothing; least of all does nature waste time. Yet nature is never in haste, and this practical lesson broadens and broadens as we go forward. Ah me, the waste that is in this world at the hands of man! Looking away down yonder, I can count more than forty church spires. More than forty great big churches; and not one single place, except a library or two and a station or two, where a stranger can wash his hands or observe the simplest decencies of life without going into some saloon. Forty great empty churches, with soft cushions, some of them, yet not one place, outside of the jail, where a man without money can lay his head.

The other day one of my women students dropped quite a handful of beans where she was washing them at a fountain. When I saw those beans there in the grass and mud, I got down and picked most of them up and took them to her. Nothing was said. After a time, chancing to look that way, I saw she was down on her hands and knees hunting for beans where I had left off. I am sure she will never waste anything any more.

You say this is not poetry, that I teach only plain common sense? I assure you that the only true poetry is plain common sense. The only true poetry is *truth:* the RIGHT: HEART.

If we could only save the time and money that is wasted in barber shops. The barber is not a bad man, but we make him a slave, and then we will hardly speak to him on the street. I am sure he is often disgusted with some dirty customer. We make his place an unclean place of unclean stories. We Americans make more than one hundred thousand fairly good men most abject slaves. What a waste of their manhood! What a waste of our time and money; and all to flatter our own vanity, to conceal our honorable years, to fly in the face of nature, and to appear what we are not.

And the funerals! Poor Dickens crying out with Victor Hugo, "Please, please, no funeral when I am gone!" And yet see what we do! My students, and you may be many ere I leave my ashes on yon pine-set peak, do not depart from this lesson. Yes, we have our own little "God's acre;" for death is here, as elsewhere, gentle, dark-browed mother Death, and we lay our dead there with our own hands, all repeating the Lord's prayer. No waste of words or money or time. And we pass that way in our walks to the cañon and the redwoods and we are not sad. The cows rest there by the graves. There is no waste there. No poor man must water and weed them for hire. Earth to earth, dust to dust, and ashes to ashes; and all who care to come without noise or display and lay their dead with ours can do so.

Finally, in this the dark age of getting and getting,—and if getting and getting is not a crime, it is the parent of crime,—one word as to the question about "producing poetry in paying quantities." Does poetry pay? Aye, poetry pays as nothing on this earth ever paid. Where would Rome be to-day but for her poetry? She would be in the dust and despised with Nineveh and Babylon. But her poets preserved her, and to this day we are paying Italy millions and millions only to look upon the scenes they saw.

No, this is not a "School of Poetry." It is not even a fit place for it. But all along the Sierras, from Tacoma to San Diego, there are thousands of fit places, remote from the roar of trade and the intrusion of the foolish.

And these few simple lessons not from books, toil, faith in man, love of nature, certainty of immortality, the simple but severe teachings of economy in all nature, these are at hand for all, and anywhere that the morning sun of this land of song shall find you.

As for methods or detail of teaching the divine art of song, I have none. I never read, nor allow anyone to read to me a manuscript. The reasons are too many to mention, but mainly, it would destroy individuality. We are born alone, we must die alone; and so should meditate, work, live, alone.

Some general rules of course prevail. The first is some concession to the fact that the world is going at a swifter pace than of old. Even Homer could not find either publisher or readers to-day. Therefore, cut, cut, cut. Then work it over and cut again. Then, in most cases,—burn. Don't be afraid to rub out the sum. You are only at school, as a rule. And above all don't write for either fame or money. Write for your own soul, the good, the beautiful. First, the kingdom of Heaven, then all the rest.

Nor shall the true artist fear hunger. No one who is willing to work can go hungry in this fruitful land, and no one who is not willing to work, and live simply and apart from the tumult of trade, should aspire to be a poet, painter, composer, or fashioner of beautiful forms. For on all triumph in this life is laid a mighty tribute. You must render unto Cæsar the things that are Cæsar's. Take counsel of nature. Look at the trees casting down their golden leaves generously at the end of the year's fruitage, fearing nothing. They lift their arms in attitude of prayer to God, certain that they shall be garmented again and glorified and made even more beautiful than before, all in due season. Look at the rose,—the generous rose,

That tears the silken tassel of her purse
And all her perfume o'er the garden throws.

In brief, to be a poet, artist of any sort, you must not only feel your art, but live your art; humbly, patiently, continually live it. And do not disdain others in other walks of life. I repeat, the greatest poets never penned a line. Let us concede the same in other walks of art, for it is true.

In the line of economy I urge that artists, if not all men, should rest and rise with the birds. There is a deal of nonsense about "midnight oil," and little or no good. God made the day for man; but the night for beasts; and beasts have rights.

In the same line it is foolishness to fight back. See what a saving of time, temper, energy, by refusing to answer the low and envious who make a target of your fame. Equip yourself as best you can and then descend into the arena to fight, and to fight forward, not back. The man who stops and faces about to hit back at those who stab in the dark and when he is disadvantaged, as is always the way, is a weak man and ready to run. No truly great man will ever hit back.

We hold, with Socrates, that a man's first duty is to the State, and that however delightful it might be to house in Arcadia and forget all care, we are all born to responsibilities and must each account for the talent given him.

Among other mild reforms, we hold that when a man has done with a great fortune, it should go to the State, proportionately with the widow and orphan, when he leaves it. This crowding the law courts and compelling good citizens from their work to listen to the perjuries of heirs and the hard lives of depraved and miserly old men certainly is demoralizing.

But, as said before, we intrude nothing. We simply plow and plant and sow. When the State gets ready to reap it will reap.

* * *

NOTES ON A NEGLECTED BOOK.

And now, with this final appeal to the young sentinels on the watch towers of the world, I conclude this book; and much in the same strain with which it began.

I was once asked to join some earnest thinkers of the time in the review of important books—such as seemed to the writer to receive less attention than their merits challenged. I answered, as nearly as I can recall, about as follows: Remoteness from book centers, out here on the sunset rim of civilization, is my excuse, to say nothing of the merits of the matter, for calling attention to some pages that are not at all new. Behind this is the desire to answer, in some sort, the very many inquiries that continually pursue the writer as to what is the best book for young authors to read and follow in the formation of style.

The remarkable work to which I invite a few moments' attention, rare as all other books of special merit are and were, from the first, in California, was never missing in our midst here from the earliest days. But it was rarely read, Nobody would borrow it. This book refused to get lost. All other books were "dog-eared," worn at the corners, despoiled of cover and fly-leaf; but this special one would work its way down to the bottom of the trunk—although the fond mother or sister may have placed it tenderly at the top and ready at hand—and there it would lie for years and years, the neatest and the cleanest thing to be found. And yet for stateliness of style, simplicity of diction, directness of thought, and majesty of utterance, it is unmatched in all the array of books, old or new, to be found on the shelves of the British Museum.

Let the young authors whom I hope to profit in this answer take the very first line in this neglected work, take the very first words, "In the beginning." Lay down your book now. Pause right here and contemplate, comprehend if you can, even though it be never so little, the awful force and directness and simplicity of this. "In the beginning." Where? When? What? Above all, when? How fearfully and incomprehensibly far away!

But let us go on with the line: "In the

beginning God—" Pause here long, my young author. Now add the next words, and read: "In the beginning God created the heaven—" Now take the next sentence: "And the earth was without form, and void; and darkness was upon the face of the deep. And the Spirit of God moved upon the face of the waters. And God said, Let there be light: and there was light."

How many paragraphs, pages, books would a modern author devote to telling this?

Mark you, I am looking at this in quite a worldly way. It is the boast of too many of us that these words are, to our thinking, entirely the work of a man. As for myself, I can only say, "If so, oh for another such man!"

The present writer was required to address the Jews in their synagogue here recently on the subject of poetry. He searched for poetry in many pages; waded through modern books, and kept going back, back, back, till the very fountain-head was reached. And here, and here only, in his humble opinion, did he find poetry in all its largeness and splendor of thought and utterance. Take the picture of Jacob blessing his sons. "And when Jacob had made an end of commanding his sons, he gathered up his feet into the bed, and yielded up the ghost." To a man who has seen little of life, less of death, this last quotation may mean nothing. But I have stood by the death-bed of too many of the old gold-hunters to miss the realistic truth and simplicity of this sentence. Ah! those weary, weary feet. They had wandered as Jacob wandered. Their feet were weary as his feet were weary. And I know, as surely as I know I live, that he died just as it is written in this grand and neglected record: "he gathered up his feet into the bed, and yielded up the ghost."

I appeal to all young writers, let not priest, or preacher, or any early distastes stand between you and these pages in the sincerity and simplicity of utterance. Give the severe and naked truth. Leave imaginings to the reader, for this same reader is rarely the fool we conceive him to be. The fact is, the world is so flooded with our work that it has not nearly time to get through with it, and right soon we must return to simplicity if we hope to be read.

And not only simplicity of motive, but majesty of utterance must be ours. To find this largeness, brevity, and majesty in its most real and perfect form we must go back to the very heart of this great, neglected book. You will hardly find this perfect combination of great qualities in poetry this side of the book of Job.

"Where is the way where light dwelleth?
And as for darkness, where is the place of it?
Hast thou entered into the treasures of the snow, or hast thou seen the treasures of the hail?....
Hath the rain a father? Who hath begotten the drops of dew?....
The hoary frost of heaven, who hath gendered it?"

These lines, with their eternal inquiry, their knowledge of nature, their faith in a being above man, glorious and stately figures, are taken at random from a half page of the oldest written poem extant—so old that it is new. It was written when man was nearer to God than now. It was written when the page of nature was new; when the whole world was poetry.

"Where is the way where light dwelleth?" The golden doors of dawn, where are they? And as for darkness, with all its majesty, its mystery, its large solemnity, its somber and silent dominion of the universal world, where is the place of it?

Yes, I concede that science has located the source of light; and science has also sagely announced that darkness is the absence of light. But for all that, light and the ways of light are not the less new and wonderful and glorious and Godlike every day and hour to all who will heed—this first creation, this very first work of the Creator. And darkness is, to a sensate soul, none the less awful, mysterious—the mother of death.

"Hath the rain a father? And the hoary frost of heaven, who hath gendered it?"

These awful elements of nature are the same as when they first fell from the finger of God. The great white, beautiful, high-born rain is still the same as when the majestic poet of old sat and sang so close to Nature that he heard the beating of her heart. The fierce and fervid way of the lightning up the walls of heaven; the awful autograph of God, written audibly on the porch of His eternal house, is the same as of old. All, all are precisely the same; but our poets see these things no more now. Nature, God, has not forgotten us, but our poets have forgotten Nature, God!

The pursuit of happiness is a constitutional right; it is strengthening, refining, and, within certain limits, it is every way laudable. Well, it seems to me that I have found the path which leads to happiness, to wealth of soul, and to rest and health of body. There is no tax nor toll; no tribute-taker sits by this open way; and not only the treasures of the snow and the stormy glories of the hail, but the treasures of all the earth, the treasures and glories of the heavens and the earth; are his who cares to have them. But these treasures may not be taken up suddenly and then tossed aside as a child tosses aside its toys. Nor are they to be had by any foolish soul simply for the asking. These treasures, like all other treasures, must either be clearly inherited or honestly earned.

How long does it take to grow a rose-tree in a garden? How long are we willing to sit by and watch the growth of an olive grove? One, two, five, ten years? And yet how long is it since you planted in your soul, in the richest center of your heart, the love of nature, the love of beauty—beauty of form; beauty of light; beauty of color; beauty of life?

"And the Lord God planted a garden eastward in Eden, . . . and out of the ground made the Lord God to grow every tree *that is pleasant* to the sight, and good for food."

Please observe "that every tree that was pleasant to the sight" came first. That which was "good for food" came last. The soul was to be fed first, here in this garden which the Lord God planted eastward in Eden; the body last. Ah! far, very far, have we wandered away, like lost children, from the place where "the Lord God planted every tree that is pleasant to the sight;" and no prophets sit by the wayside, as of old, and cry aloud to the people, "Where is the way where light dwelleth?"

Were I to undertake to write down the alphabet—the very first lesson in the appreciation—of poetry, I should begin with the first lesson of God, the very first: "And God said, Let there be light: and there was light." The next lesson, the next letter of the alphabet, would be given in the garden. I would plant a tree "pleasant to the sight." I would mark the miracle of its development, its purity, its perfume, its perfect form and continual comeliness, its steady and upright stand against storms that sometimes seem almost to uproot it, and yet all for its own good; I would catch the airy colors of that tree, mark all its moods, the light and shade; would read its leaves through and through each day; I would listen to the song of the wind in its branches, for this is poetry—God's poetry.

But who of us cares now for "the way where light dwelleth?" Who cares now for the poetry written on the lisping leaves of a tree? Who cares now for "every tree that is pleasant to the sight?" Man has built for himself huge walls to shut *out* the light. The flowers that blossom continually along the pages of the prophets of old he never sees any more. The parables of that divinely beautiful young Jew, Christ, in the language of flowers all over the land, are to him as a book that is sealed. Yet the world keeps continually crying out: "Where are the prophets? Where are the poets?" I answer: Can a prophet prophecy without faith? Can a poet sing without hope? Hope is joyous, jubilant, immortal. Doubt is despair, desperation, death—death of body and soul.

I say you might as well send a man out in the darkness to gather flowers on yon sunny hillside as to ask poetry of an age when faith and hope and charity are rudely thrust aside by the hard, mailed hand of doubt. Yea, the blind man may gather some few flowers as the night goes by, but he will gather weeds and thistles and poisonous plants as well. We have gathered some few sweet flowers of song by the long, long road that reaches back to humble Bethlehem, but we have gathered weeds; much that is worse than weeds.

On the glowing, olive-set hills of Syria, the burning sands of Arabia, by the blazing shores of the Red Sea where Moses saw the face of God in the burning bush, *where* men believed, and *when* men believed, when they had faith in God and hope in the Promised Land, *there* and *then* was poetry conceived. The forty years in the wilderness, the full fervor of heat and light in the open fields, the communion, heart to heart, with nature—there in the wilderness and by the wayside was planted the germ of songs that have outlived the thousand thousand books written within the walls of luxurious Europe; books that, strangely enough, are often fashioned from story and incident stolen from the glowing Orient lands and the waters of the Levant.

Do you recall the time in our history when the sermon and the song were heard from Maine to the banks of the Mississippi?—when the Peter Cartwrights and the Lorenzo Dows blazed the way through the wilderness, for civilization to follow? Ah! there was faith then; there was hope then. By the light of their cabin fires these simple Methodists prayed and sang and believed. They and they alone, after the praying Puritans, set deep in the soil of freedom the foundation-stones of this nation. By the light of their cabin fires they married their daughters in Faith; by the light of their cabin fires they buried their dead in Hope. They, in that grand pilgrimage pointing to this westmost shore, planted seed that surely should have flowered long ere this by this great sea. But what followed? What followed over the graves of those grand and simple-minded old Methodists? those prophets in buckskin? What followed but the golden calf, with his cloven foot? The seed they planted was trampled into dust, so that to-day we not only have no poet, but we have not even the hope of a poet. For we have no faith; we have no charity; we have little or no real religion at all.

Not long ago a worthy friend, a rich San Francisco preacher, came to see me where I was at work among my olive-trees.

"Pretty rough piece of ground you have here."

"Yes, sir; rough under foot, but as smooth overhead as any man's land."

"Ahem! Will olives pay here?"

This was his first and last concern. The clink of the golden chain which bound that man's neck to the golden calf with the cloven foot was heard to rattle on my stony steeps as he spoke. Will olives pay here?

Pay? Pay? In every breath of the sweet sea-wind that lifts their silvery leaves in the sun I am paid; paid in imperishable silver every day. I see in their every leaf the olive branch of the dove of old. The olive branch and the breast of the dove are of the same subdued silver hue to-day as in the days of Noah—as if the olive branch and the dove had in some sort kept companionship ever since the days of the deluge.

If there is a poem, written or unwritten; a song, sung or unsung, sweeter or more plaintive than that of the dove singing in the silver-gray olive tree on the mountain steeps, singing in that sad, far-off way, as if the waste of waters still encompassed her, and "she found no rest for the sole of her foot,"—if there is anything at all in my humble path of life that is higher or holier with messages to man, I have not found it.

And yet, still must we ask, when will our great interpreter come? When will the true prophet, priest, poet, preacher come to us? For we are continually reminded that it is by the voice of the poet only that a nation is allowed to survive. Jerusalem has been permitted to come down to us forever glorified; she cherished the poets; but where is Babylon who cast the prophets in the lions' den? Nineveh was a city of three days' journey; Nineveh would not hear; and where is Nineveh now? But Jerusalem, city of poetry and song! And this is simply because she had Faith and Hope; and so had her poets, and did not despise them; and her poets made her immortal; and so of Athens.

The cloven foot of the golden calf is stamping out every page of this great, neglected book. So great is the wealth of the leading families of our cities that almost every hearthstone might be paved with gold. Yet Socrates died for want of money enough to pay a fine. True or false, the Greeks had gods, even the unknown God of which Paul spoke; and they BELIEVED. They had Faith and Hope. And so their poets sang, sang in marble. They sang in music, sang in the eternal melody of beauty; and their country lives forever.

No, the poet cannot prove to you the immortality of the soul. There are things that rise above the ordinary rules of police court evidence, and this is of them. He cannot prove to you, under the strict rules of legal evidence even that the sun will rise to-morrow. But it will surely rise. And just as surely shall the soul of man be saved; if it be worth saving, make your soul worth saving, that is all.

Let me invoke your adoration of the light—God's first born. Love the light, and every beautiful blade of grass, and all the myriad beauties that only light can bring. By this light read continually the pages of God's poetry; breathe the perfume, hear the melodies, love all the glorious things by the path of God through this beautiful, beautiful world, where, on every side, the heavens and the earth seem opening wide, as a book that is to be read. Then will come this new poet, this true prophet, toiling, maybe, in the fields, toiling certainly somewhere, as God toils continually, as Christ, the carpenter, toiled. He will come, and he will stay where he can hear the heart-beats of nature, and the birds can take him into their confidence. He will not come from marble halls or massive walls, but he will come lovingly, humbly, as divine in his humility as the men of old, as Christ, with lilies and the olive leaf.

Let me even at the risk of repetition once more call attention to the very few words in this marvelous and majestic book of poetry. I freely confess I owe more to this book than all others put together, and make no apology for continually referring to its beautiful lines. Only about seven thousand words! Yet Noah Webster died with the boast on his lips that he had made a dictionary of nearly two hundred thousand words! Then came the Century Dictionary of two hundred and fifty thousand words. The Standard comes next with three hundred thousand words! Why at this rate we will soon have as many words as a Chinaman, and perhaps as few ideas. My young followers, learn all the words you can, but use as few as possible. Have a whole standing army of words at your back; buy and read and learn these great big books, every one, if you can, but I repeat and repeat, and end this book where I began by begging you, if you have a victory to win, to remember the magic of the single short Roman sword in reaching the heart. Keep the truthful beauty, the brevity of the bible before you always. Look for good in all things and you will find good in all things. Look for the tree that is "pleasant to the sight," and you will see no other kind.

In line with this "Garden eastward in Eden," and of "every tree that is pleasant to the sight," what are we to do in the next world who see nothing "pleasant to the sight" in this? By what system of hydraulics are we to lift ourselves up to waters of life in the next world when we ignore them in this? It is out of nature that I shall enjoy the jasper walls, the melodies, the glory of the great white throne, the companionship of angels, the love of the great Jehovah, when I know nothing of these things here. I repeat and repeat that it is written in every breath, on every leaf, that we begin the next life exactly where we leave off in this. The honest man here must begin the honest man there; the thief here, must begin life the thief there; even though the penitent thief. And the beautiful story of the thief on the cross? Literally true. "This day thou shalt be with me in paradise." Aye, literally so. But paradise must be a vast place to receive all the endless generations of men. And I should say that when that poor honest thief, never so good, never so penitent, came to the shining presence of the angels, why he put up his hands pleadingly to his hurt eyes and cried, "Take me away, away to the green and wooded wilderness on the remotest outer edge of Paradise, and there leave me till I can learn to bear this light, till I by keeping my face to the light may be permitted to come this way slowly, surely, as I should have done in the beginning of my years. Trust me, I am penitent, so truly penitent that I know I cannot endure this light till I have learned a little of truth, harmony, melody, color, and love of all things that 'are pleasant to the sight.'"

I like the story of that honest old negro woman who, on telling her "experience" at camp meeting, said that she hoped to get to heaven, where she could "put on a white apron an' jis' sit down an' rest an' rest an' rest." Poor pent up and starved old soul, that was her idea of heaven, her highest idea, but she is of those who will be asked to "come up higher."

A quarter of a century ago, before they pulled down the cross and stations from the arena of the Coloseum and buried many pretty traditions under the ruins, there lay, half way from the Arch of Titus, a great shapeless block of marble, half buried in the weeds and grass by the dusty path. And here the renowned Michael Angelo, in the zenith of his might, was found in the twilight, leaning on this marble and mourning bitterly.

"And what means this? Michael Angelo alone and in tears, and yet all the world his to be had for the asking! Pray why is this, Michael Angelo?"

"Oh, my sweet friends, as I was passing by, I saw such a vision—such a divinely beautiful form, hidden in this dusty and shapeless block of marble—that I needs must weep because I am no longer young and strong to take my mallet and chisel and reveal that matchless beauty to man!"

Whose fault is it that we, too, do not see the beautiful form in the shapeless block? Who is to blame that we, too, do not at least see "every tree that is pleasant to the sight?" But, behold that is the source, the secret of light. There is not a block or a rock by the roadside but holds the image of an angel-God.

The happiest and the best people, at least of my class, are the humble woodcarvers high up in the northern Alps. They carve images of Jesus and the Virgin for the poorer churches of South America; and, like Michael Angelo, they see forms of beauty in every block at hand. And how many great men have descended from these bleak passes to take part in the story of the world! They love all beauty; all. When the first born, or the elder son, comes of age and goes forth, as is the custom, to battle with the world and better the fortunes of loved ones left behind, the mother pulls a flower, a leaf, a blade of grass, as she goes with the others down the rough field to the gate, and she places this between the lids of the little Book of books quietly, tenderly. Not a word is said as she hands him his holy equipments for the fight of life before him; but he understands. Another time, under other skies, he will open the Book, will read some sweet meaning, long and tender lesson from the flower, leaf or grass blade therein. And he the better, braver, for this simple bit from the book of nature. It is mother's flower, leaf or blade of grass, and wherever that meets his vision as he travels the wilds of Australia or the cornfields of America, his heart will beat high, and he will not be lonely then. He will hear the birds, as at home; he will smell the sweet, moist mosses of his mountain home; he will see goodness, glory, beauty, in "every tree that is pleasant to the sight." His heart is good. He has learned to love the beautiful, to look for the beautiful in all things, and so will he find the beautiful in all things to the end.

Let us remember always that man is not wicked, but weak, ignorant—piteously weak in his ignorance. The best of us have blemishes, weak spots here and there, now and then. There are spots even in the sun. There is also an infinity of light. God made the spots, and He will look to the spots. Let us concern ourselves with the light.

And ever and ever His boundless blue,
And ever and ever His green, green sod.
And ever and ever between the two
Walk the wonderful winds of God.

The Romantic Tradition in American Literature

An Arno Press Collection

Alcott, A. Bronson, editor. **Conversations with Children on the Gospels.** Boston, 1836/1837. Two volumes in one.

Bartol, C[yrus] A. **Discourses on the Christian Spirit and Life.** 2nd edition. Boston, 1850.

Boker, George H[enry]. **Poems of the War.** Boston, 1864.

Brooks, Charles T. **Poems, Original and Translated.** Selected and edited by W. P. Andrews. Boston, 1885.

Brownell, Henry Howard. **War-Lyrics** and Other Poems. Boston, 1866.

Brownson, O[restes] A. **Essays and Reviews Chiefly on Theology, Politics, and Socialism.** New York, 1852.

Channing, [William] Ellery (The Younger). **Poems.** Boston, 1843.

Channing, [William] Ellery (The Younger). **Poems of Sixty-Five Years.** Edited by F. B. Sanborn. Philadelphia and Concord, 1902.

Chivers, Thomas Holley. **Eonchs of Ruby**: A Gift of Love. New York, 1851.

Chivers, Thomas Holley. **Virginalia;** or, Songs of My Summer Nights. (Reprinted from *Research Classics,* No. 2, 1942). Philadelphia, 1853.

Cooke, Philip Pendleton. **Froissart Ballads,** and Other Poems. Philadelphia, 1847.

Cranch, Christopher Pearse. **The Bird and the Bell,** with Other Poems. Boston, 1875.

[Dall], Caroline W. Healey, editor. **Margaret and Her Friends.** Boston, 1895.

[D'Arusmont], Frances Wright. **A Few Days in Athens.** Boston, 1850.

Everett, Edward. **Orations and Speeches,** on Various Occasions. Boston, 1836.

Holland, J[osiah] G[ilbert]. **The Marble Prophecy,** and Other Poems. New York, 1872.

Huntington, William Reed. **Sonnets and a Dream.** Jamaica, N. Y., 1899.

Jackson, Helen [Hunt]. **Poems.** Boston, 1892.

Miller, Joaquin (Cincinnatus Hiner Miller). **The Complete Poetical Works of Joaquin Miller.** San Francisco, 1897.

Parker, Theodore. **A Discourse of Matters Pertaining to Religion.** Boston, 1842.

Pinkney, Edward C. **Poems.** Baltimore, 1838.

Reed, Sampson. **Observations on the Growth of the Mind.** *Including,* **Genius** (Reprinted from *Aesthetic Papers,* Boston, 1849). 5th edition. Boston, 1859.

Sill, Edward Rowland. **The Poetical Works of Edward Rowland Sill.** Boston and New York, 1906.

Simms, William Gilmore. **Poems:** Descriptive, Dramatic, Legendary and Contemplative. New York, 1853. Two volumes in one.

Simms, William Gilmore, editor. **War Poetry of the South.** New York, 1866.

Stickney, Trumbull. **The Poems of Trumbull Stickney.** Boston and New York, 1905.

Timrod, Henry. **The Poems of Henry Timrod.** Edited by Paul H. Hayne. New York, 1873.

Trowbridge, John Townsend. **The Poetical Works of John Townsend Trowbridge.** Boston and New York, 1903.

Very, Jones. **Essays and Poems.** [Edited by R. W. Emerson]. Boston, 1839.

Very, Jones. **Poems and Essays.** Boston and New York, 1886.

White, Richard Grant, editor. **Poetry:** Lyrical, Narrative, and Satirical of the Civil War. New York, 1866.

Wilde, Richard Henry. **Hesperia:** A Poem. Edited by His Son (William Wilde). Boston, 1867.

Willis, Nathaniel Parker. **The Poems, Sacred, Passionate, and Humorous, of Nathaniel Parker Willis.** New York, 1868.